THE NATURE COMPANIONS

ROCKS, FOSSILS
AND DINOSAURS

THE NATURE COMPANIONS
ROCKS, FOSSILS
AND DINOSAURS

ROCKS AND FOSSILS
ARTHUR B. BUSBEY III, ROBERT R. COENRAADS,
DAVID ROOTS, PAUL WILLIS

DINOSAURS
CHRISTOPHER A. BROCHU, JOHN LONG,
COLIN MCHENRY, JOHN D. SCANLON, PAUL WILLIS

CONSULTANT EDITORS
DAVID ROOTS AND PAUL WILLIS (ROCKS AND FOSSILS),
MICHAEL K. BRETT-SURMAN (DINOSAURS)

FOG CITY PRESS

Published by Fog City Press
814 Montgomery Street
San Francisco, CA 94133 USA

Copyright © 2002 Weldon Owen Pty Ltd

CHIEF EXECUTIVE OFFICER: John Owen
PRESIDENT: Terry Newell
PUBLISHER: Lynn Humphries
MANAGING EDITOR: Janine Flew
ART DIRECTOR: Kylie Mulquin
EDITORIAL COORDINATOR: Tracey Gibson
EDITORIAL ASSISTANT: Kiren Thandi
PRODUCTION MANAGER: Caroline Webber
PRODUCTION COORDINATOR: James Blackman
SALES MANAGER: Emily Jahn
VICE PRESIDENT INTERNATIONAL SALES: Stuart Laurence
EUROPEAN SALES DIRECTOR: Vanessa Mori

PROJECT EDITORS: Robert Coupe, Fiona Doig
ASSISTANT EDITOR: Greg Hassall
COPY EDITOR: Lynn Cole
EDITORIAL ASSITANTS: Louise Bloxham, Edan Corkill, Vesna Radojcic
PROJECT ART DIRECTORS: Sue Burk, Hilda Mendham
PROJECT DESIGNERS: Stephanie Cannon, Clive Collins,
Lena Lowe, Mark Nichols
PICTURE RESEARCH: Joanna Collard, Annette Crueger

ISBN 1 877019 02-X

Color reproduction by Colourscan Co Pte Ltd
Printed by Kyodo Printing Co (S'pore) Pte Ltd
Printed in Singapore

10 9 8 7 6 5 4 3 2

A Weldon Owen Production

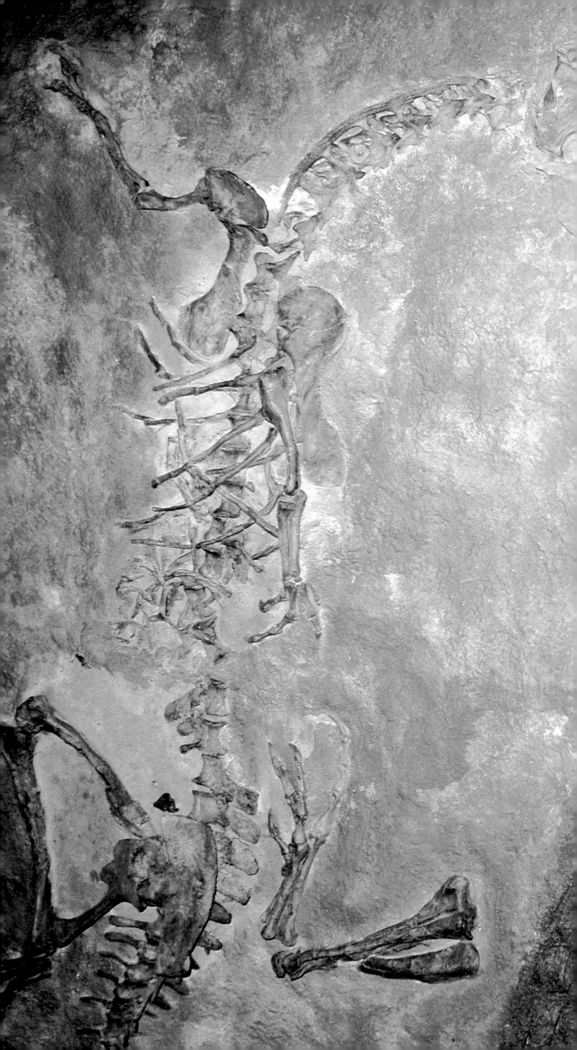

When people call this beast to mind
They marvel more and more.

The Bad Child's Book of Beasts,
HILAIRE BELLOC
(1870–1953),
French-born English writer

CONTENTS

DINOSAURS 252

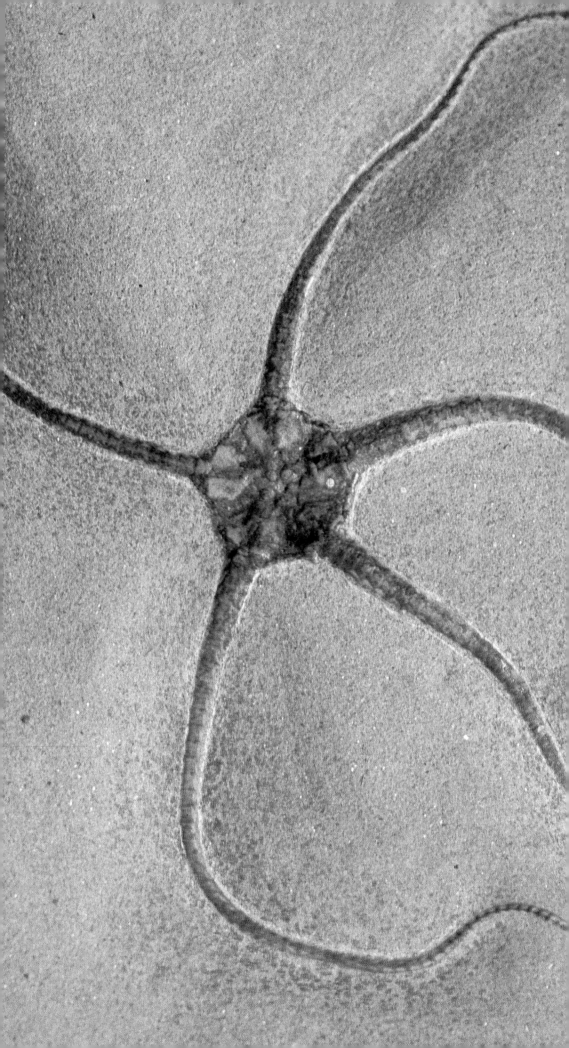

INTRODUCTION

The study of rocks and minerals enables us to uncover many extraordinary events that have taken place in the Earth's 4,600-million-year history, a story that continues to unfold as continents collide and pull apart, and as new fossil finds are made.

Some of the most famous fossils ever discovered are those of dinosaurs. A diverse and successful group of animals, dinosaurs occupied all the lands of the world for 160 million years in the Mesozoic era. The fame of these creatures—giants in popular culture—is as enduring as the rocks beneath our feet.

Rocks, Fossils and Dinosaurs is a fascinating, detailed reference source that draws on the knowledge, experience, and enthusiasm of many experts in the field. The Rocks and Fossils section of this book explains how, by studying fossils embedded in rocks, we can discover what organisms were alive at various times and establish which fossil families have survived to the present day and in what form. Also, this section opens our eyes to the critical role Earth's resources play in our daily lives and the importance of conserving them.

The key to understanding why dinosaurs are so popular is that they are real, and so was the lost world they inhabited. The Dinosaurs section brings to life many types of dinosaurs, from plant-eaters the size of a small sheep to the meat-eating giants such as *Tyrannosaurus rex*.

As you turn the pages of this book, you will be taken on a journey to the most significant geological and paleontological sites in the world. *Rocks, Fossils and Dinosaurs* provides a compelling look into our planet's past and the creatures that inhabited it.

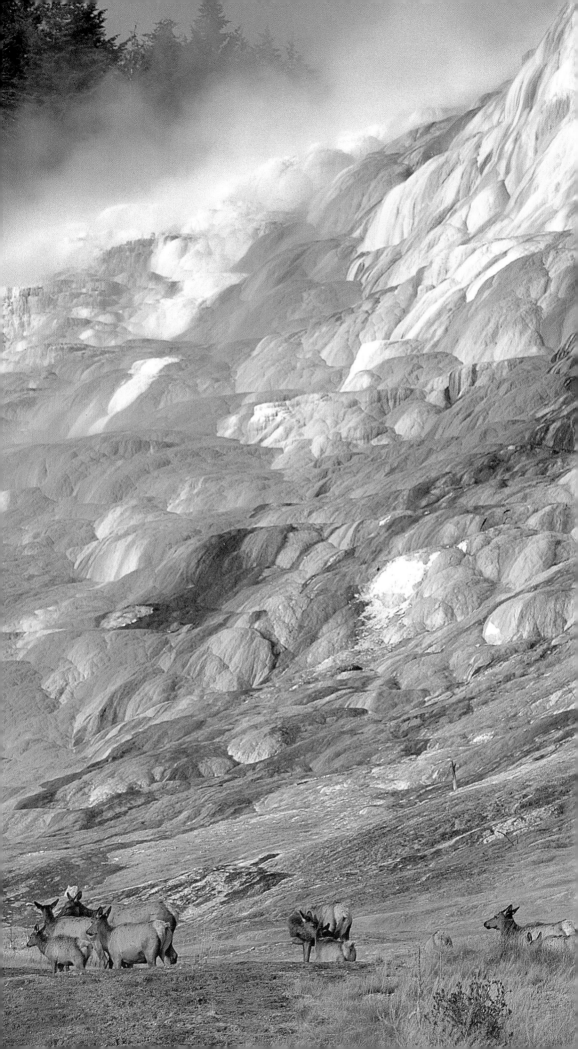

ROCKS and FOSSILS

Observe always that everything is the result of change, and get used to thinking that there is nothing Nature loves so well as to change existing forms and to make new ones like them.

Meditations,
MARCUS AURELIUS (121–180), Roman emperor devoted to stoic philosophy

CHAPTER ONE
OUR FASCINATION
with the PAST

Man is constantly adding to his knowledge of the world,
but to do any good it must be shared—by the people.

ALISTAIR COOKE
(b. 1908), British-born American radio and television commentator

UNRAVELING *the* PAST

Rocks are the pages of Earth's diary, and fossils are the words on the pages, recounting surprising details of the history of life.

The Earth and the rocks from which it is made have always been a benchmark for stability: we use such expressions as "solid as a rock", and "firm as the Earth beneath our feet". Rocks are the foundation upon which civilizations are built. Earth is a quarry from which we extract the minerals we need, but science views Earth and its rocks in a very different light. To a geologist, rocks are the chronicle of Earth's history. The Earth is far from stable: it is a dynamic place, constantly changing, moving, and being dramatically rearranged.

Geology not only reveals the immense history of the Earth and explains its myriad geological formations, it also gives us a new perspective on our place in Nature. From a geological viewpoint, the whole of humanity is little more than an extremely recent flash in the pan.

While geology is the science of rocks, its sister discipline, paleontology, deals

with fossils, the remains of ancient organisms that have been turned to stone. While geology has demonstrated our insignificance with respect to the history of the Earth, paleontology has spelled out our peripheral importance in the history of life. Not only is humanity a recent arrival, it is only one species among many millions that share a common heritage. Humans are of the Earth and are only a small part of life.

ANCIENT GIANTS *have left their mark. This dinosaur footprint (left) was found near Broome in Western Australia.*

EXQUISITE CRYSTALS *in a cave (left) delight all who see them. Beautifully worked pieces (far top left) can have great artistic value.*

AMATEUR ACTIVITIES

With an understanding of geology, one can reconstruct an ancient shoreline or delve into the heart of an extinct volcano. With an appreciation of paleontology, and armed with little more than a hammer and chisel, the amateur can confront the largest animals of all time. For those with minimal equipment, paleontology and geology remain the most accessible of the sciences. Indeed, many breakthrough discoveries in both disciplines are made by interested amateurs.

The great thrill of finding a rare and beautiful mineral or fossil specimen is combined with a profoundly humbling respect that comes from understanding how the material came to be formed. There is immense satisfaction in being able to read a multi-million-year-old rock formation as easily as you would read a newspaper.

There are many levels at which the hobbyist can enjoy geology and paleontology. Some people are satisfied

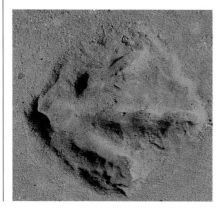

THE DELIGHT *of an amateur collector is to marvel at amazing landscapes, such as Mesa Arch, Utah, USA, seen above at dawn. Some hobbyists specialize in particular groups of fossils, such as the intriguing pearlescent ammonites (top right).*

THE AMATEUR'S CONTRIBUTION

The participation of hobbyists has brought rewards to both paleontology and geology. A classic instance is the find of William Walker, an English plumber and amateur collector. In 1983, while looking for fossils in a quarry in the south of England, he unearthed a fearsome-looking claw more than 12 inches (30 cm) long. When Walker showed it to staff of The British Museum (Natural History), they were rather excited—nothing like this claw had ever been seen before.

Some two tons of rock was collected from the site by staff of the museum. From it, they recovered a relatively complete skeleton of a totally new type of meat-eating dinosaur. It was named *Baryonyx walkeri* in honor and recognition of the keen hobbyist (shown below with his prize) who had found it.

simply with knowledge of the geological processes that have shaped the world we inhabit. Others collect specimens, perhaps of a particular type of mineral or group of fossils. Some people enjoy fieldwork and organize complex collecting expeditions to exotic places. Others prefer to clean specimens at home, or to cut and facet minerals into items of jewelry and other ornaments. A few are so enthused by their hobby that they become "professional amateurs" and make a career of it. The sciences of geology and paleontology are filled with practitioners who started as keen amateur collectors and later dedicated their lives to the science of their hobby.

Both geology and paleontology can be environmentally beneficial activities. Scouring geological formations in search of specimens is a most enjoyable form of exercise. The conscientious collector disturbs each area as little as possible and removes only the minimum of specimens. A deepening understanding of the history of the Earth and of life upon it comes with the pursuit of geology and paleontology as a hobby—it broadens the individual's perspective on human values and our place in Nature. If we recognize our position within the natural scheme, concern for and appreciation of the environment will follow.

DAWNING *of* CURIOSITY

Belief in Creation concepts preceded the development of inquiry into the nature of rocks and the formation of the Earth.

Early understandings of the Earth and its history were usually rooted in and intertwined with prevailing religious concepts that a god or gods had created the world in the form we know some time in the past. Variations on this theme were the ancestor myths of particular cultures. These held that certain features in the landscape had been created by specific actions of mythical ancestral beings. Native Americans, for example, hold many such creation myths, and Australian Aborigines believe that all landscape features, as well as animals and plants, were created in a "Dreamtime" by the activities of an array of totemic ancestral spirits. Beliefs such as these preceded the development of inquiry into the

ACTS OF NATURE, *such as volcanoes (above), were seen as punishment from a deity. Ammonites (right) were named after the Egyptian god Ammon. The Rainbow Serpent (top left) appears in the creation myths of Australian Aborigines.*

essential nature of rocks and the formation of Earth. The landscape was as God or the ancestors had created it and there the matter ended.

Such religious ideas of Creation persisted for a very long time. In 1731, Johann Scheuchzer (1672–1733), a Swiss philosopher, published an engraving of a fossil he had found in 1726. He called it *Homo diluvii testis* (man who witnessed the biblical flood), and described it as "the bony skeleton of one of those infamous men whose sins had brought

upon the world the dire misfortune of the deluge". This specimen was later shown to be an eight-million-year-old salamander.

Even today, many groups believe in religious creation myths at the expense of accepting the scientific understanding of the origin and history of Earth. In such cases, the adherence to a creation myth is usually associated with restricted religious values rather than a rejection of the science-based world view.

SUPERSTITIONS

Associated with religious understandings of Earth were a number of superstitions of varying origins. Mineral deposits were not located by

DOWSING, *being demonstrated (left) in Paris in 1913, was used to locate mineral deposits.*

To be surprised,

to wonder, is to begin

to understand.

The Revolt of the Masses,
JOSE ORTEGA Y GASSET
(1883–1955), Spanish
philosopher

SEA URCHINS (left) were thought to be magical snake eggs.
The philosopher Pliny noted that they were greatly prized by the Druids.

their geological settings but by dowsing, a pseudoscientific method by which an experienced practitioner located hidden materials by holding a divining rod that apparently responded to the attraction of the deposit. Some people still use dowsing as a way of locating underground water, but in the past, it was used for detecting an array of mineral deposits, including copper, lead, and gold. There is no scientific support for this method—any success in locating materials by dowsing is usually related to a known abundance of the material in that particular area.

Fossils also provided a long and contentious history as to their origin, significance, and use. While some of the philosophers of ancient Greece held amazingly accurate insights into the origin and formation of fossils, they were very much in the minority. For most of the past 2,500 years, fossils were shrouded in mystery. A few philosophers of medieval times thought that fossils were the remains of ancient animals and plants that had been turned to stone.

A more widespread theory was that fossils grew inside the Earth as a result of certain mystical forces flowing through rocks. Some fossils were thought to have magical powers, and others attracted names such as "devil's toenails" and "serpent stones", betraying the associations that these objects had for prescientific peoples.

DEVIL'S TOENAILS AND SERPENT STONES

A minority of prescientific philosophers believed that fossils were the remains of ancient organisms. A more popular philosophy was that fossils had grown within the Earth and were organisms that had not had a chance to "germinate" properly on the surface where they belonged.

Lay people needed to identify fossils with living or mythical creatures familiar to them. The large, curled shells of the bivalve *Gryphaea* were common fossils in many parts of Europe. These robust shells were often found on the surface, having eroded out of the rocks. At a loss to explain what they were, people called them devil's toenails because they resembled the horny cuticle from the hoof of a goat. In Yorkshire, England, the beautifully coiled shells of Jurassic ammonites were thought to be snakes that St Hilda had turned to stone. Heads were sometimes carved on the ends of them by local craftsmen.

A SCIENTIFIC VIEWPOINT

It is only during the past 200 years or so that there has been scientific consideration of the Earth and its rocks and fossils.

The work of surveyor and geologist William Smith (1769–1839) marked the start of a period of enlightenment in England. He mapped coal mines and worked on the construction of an expanding national network of canals, needed to support the industrial revolution in the late eighteenth century. In the process, Smith noticed that the same layers of sedimentary rocks were revealed in cuttings over large areas. He also discovered that the order in which rock units were laid down never varied across their geographic extent.

These observations signaled a level of organization in the formation of rocks that had not previously been recognized, and logic decreed that the rock units at the bottom of these stacks or columns were older than those above. Smith was able to test his theories by accurately predicting the geology of places he had never been.

LAVA FLOWS *(above) and erosion (right) are ways the Earth recycles rocks. James Hutton (top left) devised his theory of recycling after observing geological processes.*

Another breakthrough in the development of geology as a modern science came with the work of a Scottish geologist, James Hutton (1726–97). Hutton contributed the theory that the history of rocks occurs in cycles. Rocks are broken down to sediment by the process of weathering. The sediment is moved by the forces of erosion and mass transportation to accumulate in a new place. The sediment consolidates to

COAL MINES *were mapped in England by William Smith, who noticed the similarity in the order of the rock layers.*

a new type of rock, which could be buried under more rock until, heated to its melting point, it flows back to the surface as lava. Lava cools into rock that can be broken down by weathering, and the whole cycle starts over again.

Combined with Smith's observations, the implications of Hutton's theory were profound. Prior to this, the Earth was thought to have had a definite beginning, being created in the form we know at a comparatively recent time. The work of Hutton and Smith raised the possibility that the Earth was far older and was continually changing and recycling itself.

The father of modern geology is the English scientist Sir Charles Lyell (1797–1875). His main contribution to the young science of geology was the introduction of the concept of "uniformitarianism".

This proposed that past events occurred at the same rate as they do today. The accumulations of deep units of sedimentary rock were formed by the same processes of sediment deposition, and at the same rate, as those that can be observed in the modern world. Since most geological processes were shown to be very slow, and the rock units that were formed by these processes were often very large, Lyell concluded that the Earth was extremely old. He was the first person to talk of its age in millions of years.

TODAY'S THINKING

The application and refinement of these basic principles have generated most of the science of geology during the past 200 years. The other major theory that has so dramatically reshaped our understanding of Earth's history is the theory of Plate Tectonics. In 1912, German meteorologist Alfred Wegener

ACCORDING TO *Charles Lyell (below), geological processes proceed at the rate they always have. Alfred Wegener (left) devised the complex theory of Continental Drift.*

(1880–1930) published *The Origin of Continents and Oceans*, in which he proposed his theory of continental drift. This held that the continents were not fixed in position but that they slowly moved across the surface of the Earth. His main evidence for this was the apparent fit of some continental margins—for example, the east coast of South America and the west

coast of Africa seemed an almost perfect match. Wegener could not, however, propose a suitable mechanism by which the continents moved, so his ideas were largely ridiculed and ignored.

During the early part of the Cold War in the '50s, both the USA and Russia set up sensitive vibration detectors to monitor atomic tests conducted by the opposing side. They also logged thousands of earthquakes, and nearly all occurred in distinct lines across the Earth. It was soon clear that these lines were the edges of enormous plates that covered the Earth's surface and that earthquakes were the result of friction between the plates. Continents on the plates were slowly moving on the surface of the Earth. This is the concept of plate tectonics, which is related, but not identical, to continental drift. Wegener was vindicated, but he had died before plate tectonics was accepted as a theory. Today, most geological phenomena can be explained by these two concepts.

UNDERSTANDING GEOLOGICAL TIME

The immensity of geological time is staggering: it is measured in thousands of millions of years.

There are two ways of looking at geological time: as relative time, or as absolute time. The work of early geologists William Smith, James Hutton, and Charles Lyell resulted in an understanding that rocks accumulate in layers with the oldest at the bottom, and that this process occurred in the past at the same slow rate as it does today (Lyell's principle of uniformitarianism). After careful mapping of all the world's known rock units, a theoretical continuous stack, called the stratigraphic column, was constructed. From this, it is easy to determine the age of a particular rock unit relative to others.

RELATIVE TIME

To facilitate working with this cumbersome intellectual structure, the column was divided into a number of subsequences called Eras, Periods, and Epochs. These equate to the period when the subsequences were laid down and often take the name of the area where they occur. For example, the chalk deposits that form the White Cliffs of Dover were laid down in the "Cretaceous" Period, from the Greek word for chalk. So when we talk about a fossil being from the Cretaceous Period, we are assigning it a relative age.

It was apparent from Lyell's principle of uniformitarianism that the many thick deposits of the stratigraphic column must have taken a long time to accumulate. This was based on his discovery that many types of rock accumulated at imperceptibly slow rates. The Earth clearly was ancient, but no one knew just how old.

THE DEVONIAN PERIOD *was named after the rocks of Devon in southern England (below). An early rendering of a geological time chart (above), and an early depiction of a Jurassic scene (right).*

CHALK DEPOSITS, *such as those in southern England (left), gave the Creta-ceous its name. This painting,* Strata at Cape Misena, Bay of Naples *(below), was done before the significance of the strata was understood.*

Such vast periods

of time baffle

the imagination.

Life on Earth,
DAVID ATTENBOROUGH
(b. 1926), British naturalist

ABSOLUTE TIME

To establish the absolute age of a rock (in millions of years), we must find and read some form of clock within the rock itself. Today, we recognize several "rock-clocks" that operate in different ways. One is the decay of particular types of isotopes (forms of an element) to other isotopes. In cases where the rate of decay from one to another is known, reading the ratio of the first (parent) isotope to the second (daughter) isotope tells how long that particular process of decay has been going on.

There are a few restrictions on this technique. The rock-clock must be set to zero when the rock is laid down, as occurs in molten rocks where the product isotope is a gas that can bubble off. After the rock solidifies, new gases formed by isotope decay are trapped inside the rock. Ideally, there should be no contamination of the rock by either parent or daughter isotope from other sources.

Another rock-clock uses a technique called fission-track dating. The common mineral zircon contains a small number of uranium atoms. Being unstable, these atoms eventually emit particles that leave minute tracks inside the crystal. The longer the zircon crystal has been around, the more tracks will be visible inside the crystal. By counting the number of tracks, we can work out how long it has been since the crystal formed.

Not all rock types can be dated, but enough datable rocks occur throughout the stratigraphic column to allow most to be closely dated.

A well-known dating technique is called C14, or carbon dating. This measures the decay of one isotope of carbon to another. In this case, the original C14 accumulates only while an organism lives, and decay begins at the death of the organism. Unfortunately, carbon dating is useful for only the past 50,000 years or so. While this range is of use to archeologists (who study ancient human cultures), the periods geologists and paleontologists are interested in are far too great to be determined by this method.

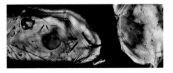

TINY TRACKS *in zircon crystals (left) in a rock date it at 3,600 million years.*

THE TIMELINE

The whole of human history is no more than the blink

of an eye compared to the history of the Earth.

Dating techniques and the stratigraphic column have provided us with a history of the Earth. By looking at rocks, we can date many events that took place at particular points in that history. By looking at fossils within those rocks, we can see what organisms were alive at different times. So by putting rock units in their correct sequence within the stratigraphic column, we can read the history of Earth and of life upon it.

A popular abstraction of the stratigraphic column is the geological timeline. This is a summary of time-related information from the stratigraphic column. It shows the geological periods in their correct succession, but rarely refers back to the rocks from which this information was originally derived. Other events are often superimposed on the timeline in their true, relative positions. These may include the movements of the continents, major glaciations, the first appearances of particular forms of life, and the formation of the "red beds", 2,500-million-year-old iron-rich rocks that indicate the presence of a well-oxygenated atmosphere.

Although the division of the stratigraphic column into Eras, Periods (and also Epochs, which are not shown), is standard around the world, there are some regional variations. The best known of these is the practice in North America of dividing the Carboniferous Period into sub-periods, the Mississippian and Pennsylvanian. These sub-periods refer to the lower

SPECTACULAR EPISODES *of intense vulcanism (left) are recorded in Earth's rocks. Fossils, such as the palm (above), tell the story of ancient life forms.*

MAKING A TIMELINE

The average toilet roll contains 500 sheets. Imagine a roll with 40 sheets removed. Each of the 460 remaining sheets represents 10 million of Earth's 4,600-million-year history, a basic scale model for a timeline. The length along the roll represents time, one end being the beginning of the Earth and the other representing the present. Unicellular life started on the 350th sheet back from the present end. Multicellular life appeared almost 300 sheets later (60 sheets from the present end). Dinosaurs emerged 22 sheets from the present end and disappeared 15½ sheets later. Our human species first appeared just 1/20 of a sheet from the present end. On this scale, our current calendar (less than 2,000 years old) would be represented by the last 1/5,000 of a sheet from the present end. Plot these points on your timeline as well as other events indicated on the timeline shown here.

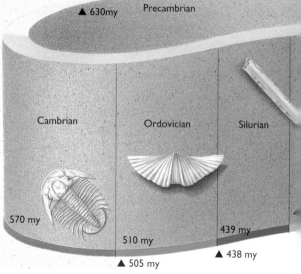

▲ 630my   Precambrian

Cambrian   Ordovician   Silurian

570 my

510 my

439 my

▲ 505 my

▲ 438 my

Zircon crystals 4,200 my

Stromatolite 3,500 my

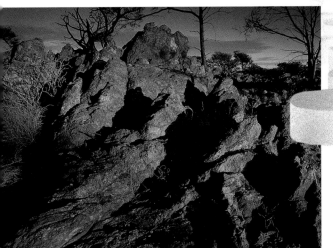

and upper Carboniferous, respectively. For consistency, this book refers only to the Carboniferous.

In the representation of a geological timeline shown here, the sequence of geological periods from the present back to the beginning of the Earth, 4,600 million years ago. It is very difficult to show the timeline in its correct proportions because so many well-documented and interesting developments have occurred in just the past 600 million years.

EARTH'S OLDEST ROCKS
(above) are the granitic foundations of the Western Gneiss Terrane in Western Australia.

TIMELINE
This diagram of the geological timeline shows the sequence of geological periods from the present back to the beginning of the Earth. Numbers are in millions of years (my).

▲ = mass extinction

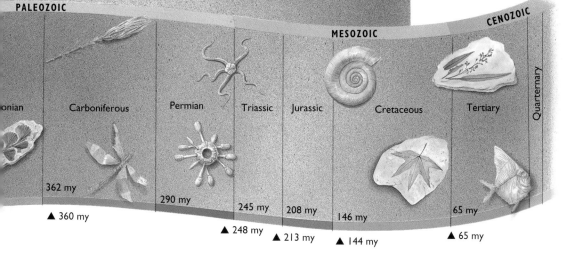

PALEOZOIC

MESOZOIC

CENOZOIC

...onian

Carboniferous

Permian

Triassic

Jurassic

Cretaceous

Tertiary

Quarternary

362 my

290 my

245 my

208 my

146 my

65 my

▲ 360 my

▲ 248 my

▲ 213 my

▲ 144 my

▲ 65 my

SEPARATING FACT
from FICTION

Rocks and fossils have always been a source of wonder, but sometimes imagination rather than reason takes over in their interpretation.

"DRAGONS' TEETH" *sold by Chinese apothecaries were credited with curing a multitude of ailments.*

The systematic methods of the sciences of geology and paleontology ensure that hoaxes, superstitions, suppositions, and even outright fraud will eventually be explained. A number of naturally occurring phenomena are erroneously thought to be fossils. One of the most common of these false fossils, or pseudofossils, are the thin deposits of manganese oxides that form fern-like patterns, called dendrites, on rock surfaces.

More insidious are deliberate hoaxes that have been planted in the field. Although highly unusual, such an episode occurred in the 1720s in Würzburg, Germany. Johann Beringer found a huge variety of carved "fossils" representing many different types of animal and plant, as well as depictions of comets and stars. Today, we know that these were fabrications, but the maker of them is even now a matter of debate.

Some suspect it was a student prank, but a more sinister scenario

EXCAVATING PILTDOWN MAN *(right). The bones and tooth (inset) of this missing link were "found" in 1912 but were later shown to be fraudulent. Dendrites (top left and bottom right) resemble fossil ferns.*

suggests that Beringer's professional rivals deliberately made and planted the specimens for Beringer to unearth. It is not entirely clear if Beringer was taken in, and study of his work indicates that he was uncertain of the origin of his finds. Legend has it that Beringer finally realized the extent of the fraud when he found his own name reproduced on one of the pseudofossils. Unfortunately, he made this crucial discovery the day after his huge manuscript on the specimens had been published, and spent a considerable amount of his

time and money buying up as many copies of the manuscript as he could.

FRAUDS

Cases such as this are, thankfully, rather rare in geology and paleontology. One of the most infamous cases was the Piltdown Man. In the early 1900s, the fossilized remains of a half-human, half-ape were discovered in a quarry in southern England. This specimen received the name Piltdown Man and was heralded as the missing link between apes and humans.

THE HIMALAYAS
(right), said to be one source of rock and fossil specimens "found" by Dr Gupta, an eminent Indian paleontologist.

It was not until during the 1950s that the fossils were shown to be fakes consisting of a mixture of chemically treated human and orangutan bones. The person behind this fraud is still unknown.

More recently, there was the saga surrounding Dr Gupta in India. For most of the 1960s through the late 1980s, Gupta was considered the pre-eminent authority on the geology and fossils of the Himalayas and northern India. He produced specimens of fossils and rocks, supposedly found at particular localities in the mountains, and published his results. By the mid 1980s, it had become obvious that work associated with him did not tally with that of other workers in the same region. Slowly, a vast and systematic fraud was revealed—Gupta had been buying specimens from around the world and pretending to have found them in the Himalayas. His motives are unclear and he still protests his innocence, despite all the evidence.

MISTAKEN SUPPOSITIONS

With hindsight, many mistaken identifications made before rocks and fossils were understood are rather humorous. At one time it was thought that all fossils were the remains of animals and plants that had perished in the biblical flood and that, before this, giants roamed the Earth. Given this background, it is

A reasonable probability is the only certainty.

Country Town Sayings,
EDGAR WATSON HOWE
(1853–1937), American journalist

not surprising that a fossil measuring two feet (60 cm) in diameter and weighing 20 pounds (9 kg) should be identified as the scrotum of a giant human. English scientist Robert Plot had described the find in 1677, but it was identified by others. We now know that *Scrotum humanum* is actually the bottom part of the thigh bone of the meat-eating dinosaur *Megalosaurus*.

In China, fossilized teeth of dinosaurs and other animals, thought to be dragons' teeth, were ground down for use in traditional medicines. In fact, the cave deposits that contained the fossils of Peking Man (*Homo erectus*) were located after an amateur fossil collector noticed teeth from the deposit on sale in a Chinese apothecary's shop.

SCROTUM HUMANUM *(above) was really the base of a dinosaur thigh bone.*

CRYSTALS AND THE NEW AGE

The perfect geometrical shapes of crystals have fascinated people for a long time. Before the processes of their formation were understood, crystals were thought to have magical powers and were sometimes used in religious and sacred ceremonies.

By and large, these misunderstandings have disappeared in favor of more rational explanations of their structure, but during the past decade or so, the New Age movement has revitalized interest in the supposed power of crystals. Certain types of crystal are claimed by various practitioners to have healing properties for some ailments. There is no scientific evidence to support such claims. It is no coincidence that, since the advent of this New Age of mysticism, the price of crystal specimens has increased dramatically.

Rocks do not recommend the land to the tiller of the soil, but they recommend it to those who reap a harvest of another sort—the artist, the poet, the walker, the student, the lover of all primitive open-air things.

The Friendly Rocks,
JOHN BURROUGHS (1837–1921), American naturalist and poet

CHAPTER TWO
FORCES SHAPING
the EARTH

IN SEARCH *of a* THEORY

During the twentieth century, a revolution occurred in the Earth sciences that has resulted in the textbooks being rewritten.

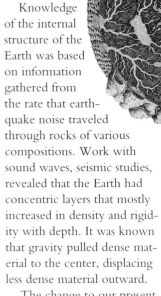

Until the 1950s, almost nothing was known of the ocean basins, comprising some 70 percent of the Earth's surface. Some thought that the continents progressively collapsed inwards, creating oceans, and that the Earth was shrinking like a drying orange, with mountains forming as the surface wrinkled. Deep ocean trenches were known from the Pacific Ocean, but ocean floors were thought to be mostly flat and evenly covered with sediment.

The differences between types of volcanoes were puzzling, but there were simple models to explain them. Steep volcanoes were located next to trenches, but the reason for this was a great mystery, and it was not understood how or why they formed. The occurrences of granite and other igneous rocks were mapped, but why they occurred where they did was another puzzle.

Knowledge of the internal structure of the Earth was based on information gathered from the rate that earthquake noise traveled through rocks of various compositions. Work with sound waves, seismic studies, revealed that the Earth had concentric layers that mostly increased in density and rigidity with depth. It was known that gravity pulled dense material to the center, displacing less dense material outward.

The change to our present understanding of the Earth really began in 1912, when climatologist Alfred Wegener drew maps showing how the scratches left by the Permian glaciation would form a clear radial pattern out from the South Pole if the several continents on which they occurred had been joined in a tight polar cluster during the glaciation. Although now widely dispersed, and with the patterns pointing in odd directions, when reassembled as they once were, the scratch marks fit together perfectly. Such an alignment brought Africa and South America together into a close fit, closing the Atlantic Ocean. Wegener argued that

DEEP GOUGES *(above) and scratches (left) made during the Permian glaciation provide evidence that continents were once joined.*

CHANGES IN UNDERSTANDING *An early depiction of subterranean lakes and rivers (left). Later theories tried to explain volcanoes (above), but Wegener's theory (right) introduced the concept of plate tectonics.*

the Atlantic coasts of Africa and South America were too similar in shape to have been produced independently, and showed how closing the Atlantic Ocean would make sense of many such puzzling biological, geological, and climatological observations.

Wegener's theory was hotly debated, but foundered on the arguments of the most notable physicists of the day. They wanted him to propose a mechanism that caused the drifting, something he could not do. They were also sure that the Earth was younger than Wegener's theory implied, believing that had it been older, it would have cooled to a solid long before.

BREAKTHROUGH
In 1913, geologist–physicist Arthur Holmes (1890–1965) argued that the slowly released energy from newly discovered radioactive elements could have kept the Earth hot. Holmes also explained how the breakdown

of the small quantities of these naturally occurring radioactive isotopes in igneous rocks could be used to determine when the rocks had solidified. He also suggested that Earth's hot mantle convected sluggishly like soup in a pot, setting up a motion that made continents collide and rift.

Although the theory of continental drift was unpopular for several decades, a dramatic about-face occurred in the 1960s, when our knowledge of the ocean floors exploded with new technology. Echo sounders

recorded ocean depths and mapped the huge mid-ocean ridges. Oceanic magnetic patterns were found to be symmetrical about mid-ocean ridges. This simple pattern, absent from continents, suggested that the ocean floor, actively forming at mid-ocean ridges, was younger than the continents.

With this flood of information, scientists have built a model of Earth, continuously convecting, covered by thin, rigid surface plates driven by convection to rift, overlap, and fold. The plates grow at mid-ocean ridges, sink at trenches, and fold at mountain ranges, creating oceans and moving continents.

HYDROTHERMAL VENTS *deep in the ocean (right) mark the mid-ocean ridge. The symmetry and young age of the oceans are quite recent discoveries.*

When you have eliminated the impossible, whatever remains, however improbable, must be the truth.

The Sign of Four,
SIR ARTHUR CONAN DOYLE
(1859–1930), English writer

31

ANCIENT LANDS

All of the continents in the world today are fragments of the supercontinent Pangea, which began to break up some 200 million years ago.

The surface of the Earth appears to us to be stable but it is actually moving continually. We now know that the Earth has had a long and complicated history. With sufficient time, the slow movements of its surface plates are enough to rip apart old continents and put together new ones.

By 250 million years ago, all of the landmasses on Earth had collided to form one supercontinent, Pangea. It was a long, narrow continent stretching from Pole to Pole. The single ocean that lapped both its shores was a larger version of the Pacific, and covered more than 75 percent of the Earth's surface. Modern mountains, such as the Andes, Himalayas, and Rockies, did not yet exist.

BEECH LEAVES *(left). Ancient relatives of these trees once forested Gondwana. Mount Washington, (right) in the North American Appalachians, which were once connected to the Caledonian Mountains in Europe.*

The present Appalachian Mountains, in eastern USA, are the remnants of a giant mountain range that formed when earlier continents collided during the formation of Pangea.

If we could reassemble the continents as they were before the Atlantic Ocean opened more than 150 million years ago, the continental shelves of North and South America would fit precisely together with those of Africa and Europe. The Appalachian Mountains of North America and the Caledonian Mountains of Europe would fit together to form a single, continuous mountain range. That is why today these two separate mountain ranges contain the same rock layers in the same sequence,

with the same fold patterns, and with identical fossils of the same age.

Fossils provide further strong evidence of continental connections. For example, fossils of the small, amphibious, freshwater reptile *Mesosaurus*, are found in both Africa and South America. Reassembling the continents brings these areas together, and the 270-million-year-old rocks in which the fossils are found match precisely. The only way that the living *Mesosaurus*

EVIDENCE *of Gondwana's final split (below) at Cape Raoul, in Tasmania, Australia. Rocks on the northern tip of Antarctica match these rocks exactly.*

THE SHIFTING CONTINENTS

*About 200 million years ago, the supercontinent
Pangea began to split into Gondwana and Laurasia.
By 65 million years ago, these continents had begun to split apart.*

FUTURE EARTH?

*How the Earth's
continents might
appear in 65
million years.*

could have occurred on both continents would be if they were once joined.

THE BREAKUP BEGINS

Pangea began to break up about 200 million years ago. The evolution of life had begun long before, so as the supercontinent cracked and the continental fragments rifted apart, they carried with them a common basic stock of the species living at the time. Isolated on separate continental fragments, these life forms evolved in different ways to produce flora and fauna unique to each fragment.

The rifting process first split Pangea into two smaller supercontinents. The southern part (Gondwana) contained all the modern Southern Hemisphere continents as well as India. The northern sector (Laurasia) was composed of the present Northern Hemisphere continents. These two super-continents then began the ongoing breakup that has resulted in the continents of today. The rifting of Gondwana and Laurasia into smaller continents formed the Atlantic, Indian, and Southern oceans. These ocean basins have increased in size at the expense of the Pacific Ocean, which has shrunk steadily since Pangea's breakup.

DETECTIVE WORK

Scientists have deduced this story from Alfred Wegener's mappings of glacial scrapings, the fossil record, the present-day distribution of species, and from marine, continental, and satellite geophysics. Further evidence lies in the identical matching of bedrock geology of continental shelf areas that were once joined. The most precise evidence currently available, however, comes from marine geophysics and from the precision of the modern satellite-dependent Global Positioning System (GPS). The GPS can track the exact position of all continents on a daily basis. We can measure their movements so precisely that we know the exact distances and directions they are traveling. In general, the continents are separating at a rate of up to 3 inches (7.5 cm) per year—about the same rate that your finger-nails grow.

THE FUTURE

With this knowledge, we can speculate how the Earth may look in the distant future. One likely scenario is that the Atlantic Ocean will keep opening, and the Pacific Ocean closing. Australia will continue moving north until it collides with South East Asia and Japan, squeezing all of these into a mountain range. At about this time, the Asian continent will rift in two through China, spreading east-west. As a result, the western half of the Atlantic Ocean will begin to close. The rifting of China will speed the collision between North America and the Australia–East Asia mass. As a result, Alaska and Siberia will overlap to become the highest mountains in the world.

DISTANT RELATIVES

Mesosaurus *(above
left) occurred on
two separate
continents.
Australian
waratahs (left)
and South African
proteas (right) share
a Gondwanan ancestry.*

THE DYNAMIC EARTH

Inside the "solid" Earth, huge amounts of energy, in the form of heat,

continuously move the continents and reshape the oceans.

Although the Earth appears to be solid, it has evolved, during the 4,600 million years of its life, from a totally molten planet to one with a rigid skin. Today, we know the outer skin, or crust, as either continents or ocean floor.

Originally, the whole Earth was composed of magma without a surface crust. Gravity separated the magma, bringing the lighter elements (mostly silica) to the surface where, being too buoyant to sink, they collected and cooled into a floating rock scum. With further cooling, this surface material solidified to form the early continents and the exposed molten magma between the continents also solidified into a thin skin of basalt (the most common rock to solidify from

CONVECTION CURRENTS *crack the surface of molten lava, mimicking the action beneath the Earth's crust.*

magma). This situation is still apparent today: the light continents ride higher than the more dense basalt.

Gases also rose to the surface and formed the early atmosphere. Among these gaseous elements were oxygen and hydrogen, combined as water. The water remained in a gaseous state, however, until the surface of the Earth was cool enough for water to condense and stabilize as a liquid. The water pooled in the lowest points to form the first

oceans. Invariably, the oceans formed on the basalt, while the higher continents shed water and became dry land.

EARTH'S ENGINES

The semi-molten interior has always circulated in what are known as convection cells, where the hottest magma rises, spreads out, releases heat at the surface, cools, and descends again. The heat is slow to escape through continents, which results in convection cells rising and rifting, cracking the continents, opening oceans, and creating mountains and trenches elsewhere.

To picture a single convection cell at work, think of a pot of soup on a burner. Heated from below, a hot plume rises in the center, and the hottest soup spreads out across the top, then subsides around the edges. Many such convection cells interact inside the Earth.

Where hot rising fluid at the center of each cell (an "up plume"), reaches the surface and spreads out, it pushes the surface scum outwards, so the area is called a divergent zone.

CONVECTION CELLS *form beneath both oceanic and continental crust (left). The rising and falling heat they generate causes continents to crack, oceans to spread, and mountains to form.*

Up plume

Divergent zone: upwelling under continents causes uplift and crustal thinning, initiating vulcanism and rifting

Passive margin: continent and ocean on the same plate

Convergent zone: downwelling subducts dense oceanic crust into the mantle

Down plume

Mid-ocean ridge

Divergent zone: upwelling under ocean creates an active, spreading ridge

THE ANDES *formed at a convergent zone where an oceanic plate was subducted under a continental plate.*

THE HIMALAYAS *formed at a convergent zone where two continental plates collided and squeezed together.*

SHIFTING GROUND *The movement of the Earth's plates shapes the land. The Andes (above) rise over a subduction zone. The San Andreas Fault (left) is responsible for many major earthquakes.*

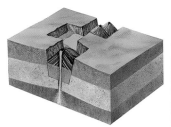

THE SAN ANDREAS FAULT *marks the transform boundary between the Pacific and North American plates.*

THE EAST AFRICAN RIFT VALLEY *represents a continental divergent zone. Africa will split and a new ocean will form.*

Where two convection cells meet, the cooler material sinks back (a "down plume"), leaving a collection of buoyant material on the surface. Where two cells touch in this way, the line of contact is called a convergent zone.

Large rigid areas of the Earth's crust are called plates, and these are separated from each other by distinct boundaries. Where two plates meet, they actively collide, separate, or just pass by. These activities generate vibrations that we feel as earthquakes. Earthquakes are easy to locate and plotting them identifies all plate boundaries.

The location of plate boundaries is largely controlled by the convergent and divergent flows in the mantle beneath. Divergent flows pull continents apart (a phenomenon known as rifting), and basalt fills such continental rifts. As they open further, more basalt forms along the rift, creating new ocean floor.

At convergent zones, plates come together and different phenomena can happen, depending on the type of plate involved. The dense basaltic oceanic plates are sucked down into the convergent zone (subduction) but the lighter, silica-rich continental plates are too buoyant to be subducted. Instead, they fold and thicken with the force of the collision. These differences produce either oceanic trenches or mountain ranges.

A region where two plates slide by each other is known as a transform boundary. While such boundaries are prone to earthquakes, continental crust is neither created nor destroyed there. A major transform boundary is the San Andreas Fault, which cuts through the west coast of the USA and represents the boundary between the Pacific and North American plates.

THE MID-ATLANTIC RIDGE *is a mid-ocean divergent zone where oceanic crust is formed continually.*

PLATE TECTONICS
in ACTION

*All geological and geographical phenomena can
be explained with respect to plate tectonics.*

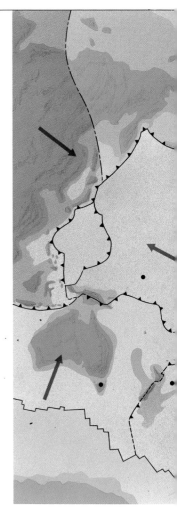

The formation and movement of the Earth's plates is a continuous process. Cooling, convecting mantle pulls down oceanic plates and causes continents to collide, forming supercontinents. These land masses prevent heat escaping from below and the underlying magma begins to heat up and expand. Eventually, the underlying magma begins to rise, reversing its previous direction. When this happens, the supercontinent rifts apart, sending smaller continents in opposite directions. They eventually collide with other continents

ROWS OF VOLCANOES *mark plate edges like dot-to-dot puzzles. A series (above) of volcanoes in Iceland. Snow-covered volcanoes (below) in Chile.*

to form new supercontinents where oceans once existed, starting a new cycle.

ACTIVE AND PASSIVE MARGINS

All geological and geographical features have a tectonic "address", a certain environment within the tectonic

cycle where they occur. The basic nature of coastlines is a good example. Those on the side of a continent that face a new mid-ocean ridge are "passive margins". They tend to be flat and have wide continental shelves. These coasts usually have deltas from large rivers flowing into them and

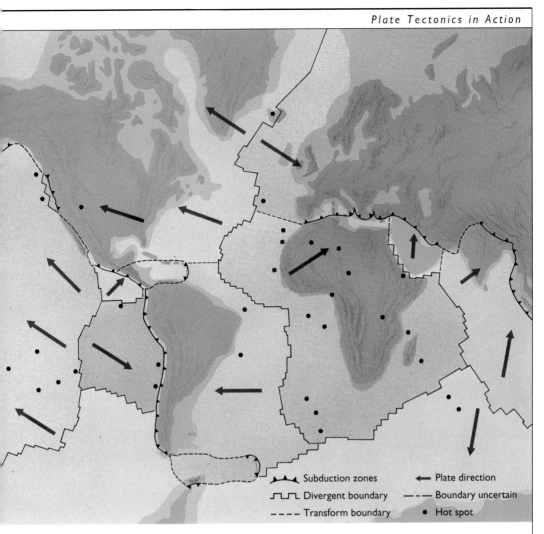

▲▲▲ Subduction zones	← Plate direction
ᒣᒣᒐ Divergent boundary	--- Boundary uncertain
- - - - Transform boundary	• Hot spot

THE WORLD AS WE KNOW IT *(above), showing the tectonic plates, continental shelves, and hot spots.*

so they have extensive sedimentary deposits that are not folded. Metamorphic and igneous rocks are rare. Mineral deposits, such as salt, coal, and iron, are usually associated with these flat-lying sedimentary beds. There is no vulcanism associated with passive margins and earthquakes are rare. The coasts surrounding the Atlantic Ocean are all typical passive margins.

Continental margins that face subduction zones are completely different, and are referred to as "active margins". These are mountainous, with thin or non-existent continental shelves. Rivers on these

PASSIVE MARGIN *(right) in Argentina, showing the typically flat topography.*

active coastlines tend to be short and turbulent and carry little sediment. As a result, most of the sedimentary rocks that occur here are from sediments that have been scrapped from the downgoing ocean plate at the subduction zone. These rocks are folded, faulted, and fractured into convoluted beds.

Metamorphic rocks are common on active margins, brought up from deep within the crust and exposed at the surface as a result of mountain

building. The extensive vulcanism in the mountains produced by the rising magma means that igneous rocks are also common. Minerals associated with metamorphic or igneous rocks, such as gold, silver, lead, and copper, are most likely to be found on active margins.

Volcanoes are common in mountains along active margins and earthquakes are frequent and often violent. The west coast of North and South America is typical.

BIRTH *of* OCEANS

Oceans are born when, pulled by the moving magma beneath, continents crack. A new basalt ocean floor forms progressively, filling the rift.

Major oceans begin their lives in the middle of continents. Breakup (rifting) occurs when a heat-generated divergent zone develops under a continent creating a bulge in the crust. The greatest stress on the crust is directly above the upwelling magma, and eventually, the bulge will crack three ways—the three splits being at 120 degrees to each other and growing from the central point outward. The East African Rift Valley, the Red Sea, and the Gulf of Aden provide a classic example of a three-split rifting system.

THE NORTHERN TIP *of the Red Sea (above), part of the great African rift. Now widening, this embyonic ocean is separating Africa from the Saudi Peninsula. The Galapagos Vent (far left) warms surrounding water, creating an isolated ecosystem.*

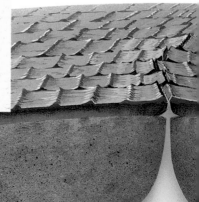

The first feature to form during a rifting episode is a rift valley, such as the rift valley of eastern Africa.

Rift valleys are typically long and steep-sided with active volcanoes along their length. Both surface erosion and erosion by the upwelling magma beneath thins the crust at a rift valley by as much as 80 percent. This thin crust very slowly pulls apart, splitting the old continent.

Each of the three rift arms extends outward and, eventually, one arm will reach an ocean. Since the rift floor is below sea level, ocean water enters and floods the rift. The hot, spreading basalt floor of the rift causes rapid evaporation of the sea water, which

PERFECT SYMMETRY

Ocean floors are built from vertical basalt dykes, or rather half-dykes. These form when hot rock enters the vertical cracks that develop across rifting plates, and later mid-ocean ridges. Basalt lava rises to fill the cracks. As these dykes chill to the crack sides, the center holds heat longer and this weaker core is pulled apart by continuing plate separation, leaving half the dyke on each side. The next intrusion enters between the halves. Continued spreading pulls every following dyke in half. This produces the perfect symmetry of mid-ocean ridges between their flanking continents.

OLDUVAI GORGE *(above left) in the East African Rift Valley. Volcanoes often occur in this rift, as seen here in Virunga National Park, Zaire (left). A mid-ocean ridge runs through Iceland (above).*

concentrates the salt. With rising salinity, the salt is precipitated. This, in turn, stimulates rapid breeding of microorganisms that produce carbon-rich muds. These muds accumulate in the rift, creating an excellent environment for the later production of oil and gas. Rifting continues until a second rift arm reaches an ocean and creates a through passage for water, preventing more salt from being deposited.

Spreading continues at what has now become a mid-ocean ridge, and the continents move progressively farther apart as the new ocean opens. As the new continental margins cool, they sink a little

into the underlying magma. Cool continental edges float lower in the mantle, sinking below the ocean surface and creating continental shelves. This explains the presence of salt deposits and oil fields on such continental shelves—originally, they were all rift valley deposits.

MARKS ON THE OCEAN FLOOR

Across the ocean floor, beneath the sediment, are long marks that show the paths that plates have taken as they separated. These marks run between opposed continental shelf edges and are called fracture zones. Fracture zones restrict the possible movements of

plates and can be used to unravel plate movement and reassemble past supercontinents.

Once a plate begins to move, it rarely changes direction, unless its movement is interrupted by continents colliding. When pulled apart, basalt breaks at right angles to the direction of pull, as does a toffee bar.

So mid-ocean ridges are composed of many short, straight segments at 90 degrees to the opening direction of the separating plates. These segments are connected by short "transform faults", which record the opening shape of the rift and are the cause of the fracture zones on the ocean floor.

MID-OCEAN RIDGES *are offset by many fractures that mimic the line of the original rift, which began to form in the center of a continent.*

COLLISIONS
and SUBDUCTIONS

For millions of years, the continents have moved slowly about the surface of the Earth, their progress producing and altering complex geographic features.

The Earth has been about the same size for most of its life and its surface area has remained relatively constant. This being so, crust being consumed in some areas must be balanced by what is being formed at about the same rate elsewhere. Convergent zones where plates collide are consumers of crust.

In convergent zones, plates come together. These plate collisions produce different features, depending on the type of crust involved. The basaltic crust of oceanic plates is dense enough to be sucked down into the convergent zone, a process called subduction. Eventually, the sinking oceanic crust will melt into the magma again. Subduction zones create oceanic trenches,

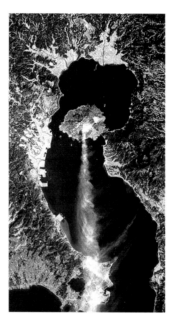

SATELLITE VIEW *of the eruption of Sakura-jima, Japan, taken in 1984. This volcano has erupted often since AD 708.*

the deepest parts of the ocean, which can extend to a depth of seven miles (11 km).

The silica-rich continental crust is too light to be sucked into a convergent zone, so continents above convergent zones tend to buckle up into mountain ranges—think of a rug being pushed against a wall, where it buckles and folds up into mini-mountain ranges. This is precisely the way the world's major mountain ranges were formed.

When an oceanic plate collides with a continental plate, the oceanic plate is sucked under. At the convergent zone, magma that contains both quartz and basalt collects. The resultant liquid rock rises through the overlying continental crust to erupt volcanically. This type of volcano is always present on the continent side of the subduction zone, and the resulting active volcanoes can line the plate edge.

RIM OF FIRE
An almost complete ring of such volcanoes exists parallel to the subduction zones around the Pacific margin, from the southern tip of South America, up the west coasts of both South and North America, across the Aleutian Islands, through Japan and the western Pacific to New Zealand. The Rim of Fire is a name often used for the active circum-Pacific

island of stacked ocean floor sediment

continental plate

trench

ocean

convecting mantle

convecting mantle

SUBDUCTION *occurs when dense oceanic plates are sucked under buoyant continental plates. Molten rock is thrust volcanically upwards.*

oceanic plate

VAST MOUNTAIN RANGES, *such as the Andes (above), and active volcanoes, such as Mt Bromo (right), Indonesia, mark the edges of subduction zones.*

volcanoes that mark where subduction now occurs. The earliest volcanoes are still at the continental edges, while younger ones have moved out into the Pacific, forming island arcs.

In the western Pacific, it appears that the underlying convergent zone is moving into the Pacific, creating new subduction zones as it goes. Island arcs form above these new subduction zones and, to compensate for the consumption of crust, rifts appear to the west that eventually form small ocean basins.

Japan is a classic case of this moving subduction zone. Japan is composed mostly of a rifted fragment of continental eastern Asia, and Japanese volcanoes mark the location of an underlying subduction zone. The rift is now the Sea of Japan. Similar rifting phenomena have occurred around the western margins of the Pacific Ocean creating island arcs such as the Marianas.

A similar process of island arc formation probably took place in the eastern Pacific. The opening of the Atlantic Ocean pushed the Americas over island arcs that formed off their Pacific coasts, push-ing the islands into the Andes Mountains to the south, and adding a complex set of terrains to the Pacific coast of Canada and the USA. Olympic National Park, Washington, for example, is composed of very rough, stacked ocean floor sediments that include a marine volcano. These all attest to North America having been pushed over the Pacific Ocean floor as the Atlantic Ocean expanded.

VOLCANOES

Molten rock erupting through Earth's crust forms three types of volcano, varying in shape and the chemistry of their lavas.

I n 1943, Mr Mimatsu, a postmaster on the island of Hokkaido, Japan, found a volcano starting to form in a local potato field. Steam, then plumes of ash and lava, burst forth and a volcano was born. In 1995, it was 1,320 feet (403 m) and still growing.

Mimatsu, who had once been a geologist's assistant, knew he was seeing a momentous event. With all the geologists away at war, he wanted to record proceedings, but how? Watching through the mesh on the office window, he noticed that it was squared like a sheet of graph paper, so month by month, he graphed the volcano's growth from his desk. When the geologists eventually read his reports, they were staggered by their precision. Mimatsu was an amateur, but his method is now famous.

His volcano, Showa Shinsan (meaning "New Volcano"), is above a long-active subduction zone and the lava that rises there is andesite, which can be considered a basalt with a high silica content.

FIERY ERUPTIONS
At subducting plate boundaries, volcanoes puncture the overriding plate in very narrow, continuous lines. For example, the Banda Island arc of Indonesia and the Antilles Island arc in the Caribbean, have many active volcanic

ASTRIDE *the mid-ocean ridge, Icelanders live with the threat of constant eruptions (left). Showa Shinsan volcano (above), observed by Mimatsu.*

RED-HOT LAVA *flows from Kilauea (left), in Hawaii. The 1883 eruption of Krakatau (top left), Indonesia, resulted in a tsunami that killed nearly 40,000.*

islands, each in a band stretching for thousands of miles.

Above subduction zones, earthquakes abound, and very steep andesite volcanoes repeatedly form, explode, and rebuild. They are closely spaced in bands that precisely parallel the trench, yet are uniformly offset to one side. Rising majestically above their surroundings, they steepen upward in a conical shape that has great beauty—until the next eruption.

Volcanoes near trenches occur where wet sediment sitting on the descending plate mixes with molten rock. This releases gases and fluids into the molten rock above the subducting plate making it more fluid. The fluids and gases escape through the overlying plate, and are followed by molten rock, which reaches the surface to form volcanoes.

The eruptions that occur above subduction zones are spectacular, violent, and noisy. For example, the Krakatau eruption in Indonesia in 1883 blew away a 2,620-foot (798-m) volcano, leaving an under-sea caldera 985 feet (300 m) deep.

Seawater flooding into this hole and dropping onto red-hot rock, caused repeated violent, noisy explosions.

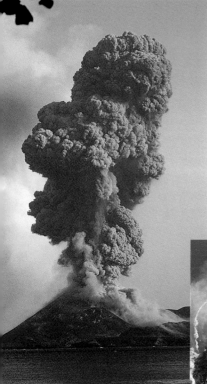

THREE TYPES
of volcano: Anak Krakatau, Indonesia, (far left) and Mt Redoubt, Alaska, (below) both sit above subduction zones; Kilauea (top), Hawaii, is a hot-spot volcano; and Surtsey Island (left), near Iceland, is a mid-ocean ridge volcano.

The terrifying din was heard 2,250 miles (3,650 km) away, a tenth of the way around the world. The volcano is now rebuilding, as Anak Krakatau (Child of Krakatau), toward another spectacular eruption.

HOT-SPOT VOLCANOES

Straight lines of hot-spot volcanoes can occur mid plate. They are the exception to the tectonic rule that nothing much happens in the middle of plates. Being easy-flowing, low-silica basalt, these volcanoes form wide and very low-angled cones. In contrast to island arcs, where all the volcanoes may be active, only the few youngest in the hot-spot chains are active.

The Hawaiian Islands are at the active end of the Hawaiian–Emperor sea mount hot-spot chain. This is a chain of hot-spot volcanoes, mostly submerged, that stretches in an unbroken line for 3,000 miles (5,000 km) from Hawaii to Kamchatka, north of Japan (where the oldest of them

subduct at the Kurile Trench). The magma sources for hot-spot volcanoes lie so deep in the mantle that they are not affected by mantle convection and plate movement. Deep hot spots keep producing magma at the same site, while the plate moves steadily past overhead. Repeated eruptions puncture the plate over the hot spot, leaving a closely spaced chain of volcanoes. The age of rocks in each volcano can be determined, so a volcanic track across the plate allows the speed and direction of the plate to be calculated.

MID-OCEAN RIDGE

The third type of volcano is part of the world-encircling mid-ocean ridge (MOR), visible in Iceland. The MOR is really a single, extremely long, active, linear volcano, connecting all spreading plate boundaries through all oceans. Along its length, small, separate volcanoes occur.

The MOR exudes low-silica, highly fluid basalt and, having produced the entire ocean floor, must rate as the largest volcano of all and the largest single structure on the face of the Earth.

EARTHQUAKES

More than a million earthquakes, ranging from tiny tremors to cataclysmic disasters, are recorded on Earth every year.

Earthquakes are very common events. They occur inevitably when stress that has built up in the Earth's crust is released suddenly as the crust breaks. Evidence of such crustal fractures can sometimes be seen after earthquakes as vertical- or sideways-thrown surface faults.

EARTHQUAKE ZONES

Virtually all the world's major earthquakes occur at tectonic plate boundaries, particularly those that are converging or sliding past one another. The San Andreas Fault, along the west coast of the USA, is a famous example of two sliding plates, and it can be traced for miles, offsetting roads and river channels. At such a fault, the two plates may move at a slow, steady rate and the resulting movement of the Earth will be imperceptible. However, if the plates lock fast, stresses build up and when the plates finally shift, the massive release of energy can have devastating effects.

The shock waves, known as seismic waves, from such a release can be highly destructive in built-up, populated areas. Initial damage, such as collapsed buildings and dams, is sometimes surpassed by subsequent fires and explosions resulting from broken electricity and gas lines.

Even earthquakes that occur on the sea floor can be destructive. Movement of the sea floor causes waves in the

PAST AND PRESENT *San Francisco in 1906 (top) after being struck by an earthquake measuring 8.3 on the Richter scale. A cartoon (top left) from that year. Kobe, in Japan (above), following the 1995 quake, which registered 7.2 on the Richter scale.*

ocean, known as tsunamis, that move out concentrically from the source. Barely perceptible in the deep ocean, these waves rise in shallow coastal waters, flooding shores and causing major damage.

VALUABLE LESSONS

As terrible as they are, earthquakes have given us a greater understanding of the Earth's interior, and of the workings of plate tectonics. Scientists are now able to calculate the Earth's structure and composition from the velocity of seismic waves. These waves are reflected and refracted as they pass through layers of different densities. The absence of seismic reverberations on the opposite side of the planet from an earthquake is known as a "shadow zone", and from this, scientists have been able to deduce the existence of a liquid outer core.

DEVASTATION in California, USA, following powerful quakes in 1989 (left) and 1994 (far left).

SHAKY GROUND *A railway line in Kobe (above) after the 1995 quake. An ancient Chinese seismometer (below): a tremor would cause a ball to fall into a frog's mouth.*

The concentration of earthquakes and volcanoes in narrow belts around the globe lends great support to the theory of plate tectonics. Such a belt, known as the "Rim of Fire", runs around the perimeter of the Pacific Ocean, marking the region where the Pacific plate is being dragged beneath adjacent plates. Exact plotting of the earthquake foci define the precise plane of the plate as it dips away from the surface near the oceanic trenches.

Earthquakes do not generally occur beyond a depth of about 430 miles (700 km), because at this point, the subducting slab becomes hot and plastic and all stress is relaxed.

What happens to us is irrelevant to the world's geology, but what happens to the world's geology is not irrelevant to us.

HUGH MACDIARMID
(1892–1978),
Scottish poet

MEASURING EARTHQUAKES

The energy released by earthquakes is recorded on seismometers. Consisting of a freely suspended mass in a frame that is firmly attached to the bedrock, a seismometer measures the relative movement of the frame, which shakes with the Earth, with respect to the inertial mass, which remains relatively still.

The size of an earthquake at its source is known as its Richter magnitude. On this scale, a magnitude of one can be detected only by instruments, while a magnitude of eight is recorded only during major quakes (the San Francisco earthquake of 1906 had a magnitude of 8.3). Each increase of one on the scale represents a sixtyfold increase in energy released.

ROCKS *and* MINERALS

Rocks, composed of one or more minerals, are the thin, cool skin of the Earth, keeping us insulated from the inferno within.

Rocks are the solid materials of the outer Earth. Minerals are naturally occurring inorganic crystalline solids, natural assemblies of one or more known chemical elements. Although there are thousands of different minerals, just a handful of these make up virtually all of the Earth's rocks. The most common rock-forming minerals include quartz, olivine, feldspar, amphibole (hornblende), pyroxene (augite), and mica (muscovite and biotite). Feldspar alone makes up more than 50 percent of rocks. If you can recognize these common rock-forming minerals, you will be able to identify almost any rocks you might find (see pp. 70–75).

There is a geological history inherent in each rock. Basalt is the most abundant rock, covering more than 70 percent of the Earth's surface, most of this under the ocean. By comparison, all other rocks are rare. We name rocks to define their aggregate minerals, appearance, mode of formation, and particular plate tectonic address. One scheme for naming rocks separates them into three classes, each indicating a physical mode of formation. Igneous rocks form when magma, molten earth material, cools and crystallizes. Sedimentary rocks are cemented fragments of rocks, minerals, or biological material. Metamorphic rocks were once one of the former two, but have been changed by heat and/or pressure.

Rocks can form in less obvious ways. Some precipitate from water, for example, chert, phosphorite, and some limestones. Some settle in water from volcanic dust clouds, for example, bedded tuff, an igneous–sedimentary rock. Some form when coral reefs, built by microorganisms, consolidate to limestone.

SPREADING PLATE MARGINS

There is a direct relationship between specific rock locations and plate tectonics.

LIMESTONE CAVES

(left), cut by ground-water, are later decorated as lime-rich water evaporates to create intricate calcite formations. White veins form as quartz fills cracks in sandstone (below).

IGNEOUS ROCKS *Ignimbrite tuff (left) from the 1912 eruption of Katmai, Valley of 10,000 Smokes, Alaska, USA. Granite (far left) showing feldspar (pink), quartz (white), and mica (black).*

miles distant. So this sediment characterizes the collision, but not the site of the collision.

Metamorphic rocks also characterize subduction zones. The subduction process folds, squeezes, and heats both igneous and sedimentary rocks as they plunge to hot depths. This produces twin bands of metamorphic rocks, paralleling the subduction zone.

AWAY FROM MARGINS

Many rocks are formed far from all the activity at plate margins. Mid-plate processes are slower, extending for longer periods than is possible at plate margins, so the end products are fully weathered. Plate margins, in contrast, usually produce incompletely weathered rocks.

Most mid-plate volcanic rocks form from hot-spot basaltic volcanoes, both in ocean basins and on continents. Mid-plate sedimentary rocks, mostly marine, are formed from particles from a variety of sources. Ocean-floor sediments are carried far from the continental margin, where they originated as eroding rocks, or the debris of living organisms. Recognizing the indicator rocks of past tectonic locations allows the ancient history of most locations to be unravelled.

Before the theory of plate tectonics evolved, every rock seemed of equal importance. We now see greater significance in the few rocks that characterize certain locations.

Basalt is the primary melt from the upper mantle, and the only rock produced at spreading ridges. A rift valley opens across a rifting continent, fills with basalt then, later, the sea enters to flood the widening gulf.

The basalt basement of oceans is uniform in composition but the plate thickens with time to about 50 miles (80 km). Olivine, a magnesium iron silicate, and similar minerals increase in proportion with depth, until the basalt changes to peridotite. When found with chert and marine sediment, this rock indicates past ocean floor, whereas basalt is too common to be diagnostic.

CONVERGENT PLATE MARGINS

The igneous rocks andesite, ignimbrite, and granite, all high in quartz, characterize subduction zones, where all three collect as magmas. Andesite outpourings above subduction zones can cause collapse depressions, or calderas, that might fill with hot, foaming clouds of andesite-composition ash, consolidating to welded tuff, or ignimbrite. Granite collects at depth until it is buoyant enough to rise, sometimes up the feeder pipes of volcanoes to reach the surface.

When continents collide, rivers are born that strip sediments from the uplifted areas and deposit them at continental edges, possibly thousands of

SPECTACULAR MINERALS *include aragonite (above), and amazonite embedded with smoky quartz crystal (right).*

ROCKS *from* MELTS

Igneous rocks solidify from molten magmas, and their composition depends on where they collected and how quickly they surfaced.

THE FLUID *nature of magma is apparent when it surfaces as lava (left). Cooling basaltic lava forms columns (above) as it shrinks. Andesite (top left).*

Watching white-hot molten basalt pour slowly from a lava tube directly into the ocean engenders an almost primeval feeling. Seeing a cloud of ash particles surging violently from the base of an explosive volcanic eruption makes a very different and terrifying impression. In contrast, the slow rise of crystalline granite plutons 60 miles (100 km) through the Earth's crust seems pretty tame, but when magma cools in any of these ways, igneous rocks form.

Of the hundreds of named igneous rocks, we shall look at only three—granite, andesite, and basalt. Each has a different composition, according to where its magma collected. The type of igneous rock, determined by its mineral composition, can be gauged from its relative darkness. Being mostly quartz and feldspar, granites are light in color. They form from magma high in silica. Andesite, containing

feldspar, hornblende, quartz, and micas, is darker and forms from magma of moderate silica content. Basalts, which rarely have any quartz, contain feldspar, micas, and hornblende, and are darker still.

Most igneous rocks have well-developed crystal structures, although a microscope may be needed to see them. The grain size of any igneous rock is increased by slow cooling and low viscosity, which allow elements to migrate through a melt and reach sites where crystals are growing. When basalt magma cools rapidly on the Earth's surface, it is fine-grained; when it cools at depth, its crystals will be larger—this form is called dolerite (or diabase). Even deeper cooling, taking millions of years, produces a coarser form called gabbro, still with the same chemistry.

FORMATION

Magma is a fluid, or rather a mixture of fluids. Earth's upper mantle is partly molten, with minerals floating in the melt. Many minerals join this magma soup from rocks that have been pushed deep and partly melted. Within a melt, minerals have great mobility, so buoyant minerals rise and dense minerals sink. Think of adding marbles and marshmallows to boiling water. The marbles roll to the center of the pot, but do not rise. The marshmallows float to the outside of the pot but do not sink. We now have a marshmallow magma, and a marble magma, each in distinctly located reservoirs, held in position by convection. Similar mechanisms operate in the Earth's mantle.

Silica-rich melts, such as granite and andesite, form above subducting slabs, but rarely elsewhere. The silica content of over-slab volcanoes is higher near continents than farther out to sea. Silica is melted from beneath the

GRANITE *Although the Devil's Marbles, Australia (left) are in the center of the continent, it is likely that they indicate the site of a former subduction zone.*

WHEN ANDESITIC *volcanoes, such as Ruapehu, New Zealand (background above) erupt, they are sudden and violent, flinging out clouds of ash (left).*

Andesite forms in this way during active subduction, reaching the surface to build explosive volcanoes. Later, after subduction has ceased or moved on, slower-collecting, slower-rising, and slower-cooling granite will follow, at much the same locations.

Basalt, on the other hand, forms from partial melting of the mantle. A rise in the temperature triggers the melting, and the heated basalt rises to the surface. A localized area of hot magma, a "hot spot", deep under a plate will release hot basaltic magma upwards, producing isolated basaltic volcanoes. Hot-spot volcanoes occur in a series with other extinct volcanoes produced as the plate moves over the hot spot (see p. 175).

Andesite indicates past subduction, as does granite. Granite takes longer to rise and typically arrives well after the start of andesitic vulcanism. All other igneous rocks form from melts when magmas mix, or lose some components, or when gravity separates minerals in a melt by density, allowing different compositions to be present in a single magma chamber. Some volcanoes change composition through time, and such changes are evidence that, deep within the mantle, geological processes are at work.

continent and carried to the top of the slab by convection. In this way, some silica, water, and carbon dioxide may be added to magma at the subduction zone. Water and carbon dioxide flux the semi-solid mantle, producing a very mobile, silica-rich magma. Being buoyant, this magma does not convect down with the convection flow, but collects above the slab and sometimes rises through the overlying crust.

EXFOLIATING GRANITE *(right), a common weathering pattern caused by expansion and erosion of surface layers.*

ROCKS *from* PARTICLES

Sedimentary rocks hold information about past environments, telling of the origin, travels, and final deposition of their particles.

The Grand Canyon, Arizona, USA, provides geologists with a nearly continuous sedimentary record of Earth's history. Those 5,000 feet (1,500 m) of bedded horizontal layers, all stacked in sequence with the oldest at the bottom, rest upon even older folded rocks at river level.

Many layers of these sedimentary rocks contain fossil life forms, and these increase in complexity from the floor of the canyon to its rim, revealing the progression of life through time. The layers of conglomerate, shale, sandstone, limestone, ash, and lava indicate past environmental changes as deserts were replaced by rivers, then lakes and inland seas. Erosional breaks interrupt the sequence, but even so, this canyon shows an unusually detailed slice of Earth's story.

CEMENTS

Sedimentary rocks are formed by the cementing of loose particles produced by the breakdown of other rocks. Most sediments settle in water in horizontal layers with flat upper and lower surfaces. Cementing them are the

THE LAYERING of this lakeshore sandstone (right) has formed intricate patterns. Conglomerate (above) is comprised of particles of various sizes.

SEDIMENTS are deposited at river deltas, such as the Mississippi River Delta (below), Louisiana, USA. Calcite (right) cements particles.

common materials, quartz, calcite, and iron oxide. These lock in the record of the past.

The cements that hold sedimentary rocks together are precipitated among the grains. Quartz cements most sediments; particles of limey composition are usually cemented by calcite; while iron oxide, because of its small particle size, finds its way into many rocks with the groundwater and is easily identified by its dark red-brown color.

Sediments collect in slow-moving streams, or in swamps and lakes. The sediment may have traveled vast distances, along the Mississippi, for example, or have fallen from a nearby volcano. Where stream gradients are gentle, river channels meander and floods cover the land with mud and sand. Some sedimentary deposits collect in steep alluvial fans when infrequent flash floods discharge from rocky gorges into desert lake beds, such as in Death Valley, California, USA.

Most sediments, however, collect in oceans. They are

THE GRAND CANYON, *Arizona, USA, (left) reveals a nearly complete sedimentary record of 360 million years of Earth's history. The chalk cliffs (below), typical of south-eastern England, were formed from organic debris.*

The direct...evidence for this history lies in the archives of the Earth, the sedimentary rocks.

Life on Earth,
DAVID ATTENBOROUGH
(b. 1926), British naturalist

deposited on continental shelves, then flood down submarine canyons, slump into the deep ocean, and travel for hundreds of miles as turbid flows. Turbid flows are a mix of water and muddy sand with twice the density of water and great gravitational power. They hug the ocean floor, spreading out in low-angle alluvial fans and depositing muddy sand over large areas. Turbid flows first drop coarse sand, then finer grades, in order of reducing size.

One slump produces a number of cascading flows, so the deposits are rhythmically layered. The resulting sedimentary rocks, turbidites, are a major component of all rocks deposited in ocean basins. These are squeezed when plates collide, becoming the predominant continental sedimentary rock.

PARTICLE SIZE
A simple approach to the study of sedimentary rocks is to consider three grades: mudstone, sandstone, and conglomerate. Mudstone has no visible grains, and such fine sediments settle gradually on quiet flood plains, in lakes, or deep ocean environments. Sandstone has visible grains like coarse sugar, up to almost $\frac{1}{10}$ inch (2 mm). To move particles of this size, the water must have some force, such as in a river. For larger particles, which form conglomerate

pebbles, greater force, such as a high flood, is needed.

Descriptive words can be added to grain size to indicate grain composition, color, cement, and other visible features, for example, "black fossil-bearing mudstone with pyrite grains". Sediments may have internal patterns that reveal their depositional environments, such as the desert sand dune cross-beds that typify the Navajo Sandstone of Zion National Park in the USA.

Many sediments are carried by wind. For example, volcanic ash blows into nearby lakes and the ocean. Some falls into rivers and travels to the sea as mud. Airborne ash drops over vast areas, and will become a broadly recognizable future sediment layer.

Some sedimentary rocks are formed from organic debris, for example, coal. Such matter, collected by flood waters, is dumped in basins and covered by massive river-borne sand waves that squeeze out air and prevent rotting.

CHANGED ROCKS

*Heat and pressure can change rocks and begin a new episode
in their life story—the variety of metamorphic rocks is exceptional.*

Rocks that are exposed to heat and pressure, can change in character, a process known as metamorphism. There are two different types of metamorphic rocks, formed in different environments.

When continents collide, rocks can be metamorphosed over an entire region, which is known as regional metamorphism. Localized, or contact, metamorphism occurs when hot igneous rock rises to the surface and heats surrounding rocks, causing them to be recrystallized. These changes alter the physical environment in which the original minerals formed, forcing new minerals to form. The effects of metamorphism range from simple compaction to a total remake of the rock.

Marble is perhaps the best known metamorphic rock, and the most famous marble is the Carrara marble from Italy. This lustrous white stone has

THIS TIGHTLY FOLDED *metamorphic structure features visible quartz veins.*

GLACIAL EROSION *has sculpted this exquisitely foliated schist (above). Strong regional squeezing crystallizes minerals such as pyrite (top left) and garnet (red, far right).*

been quarried for 2,000 years, and was the choice of Bernini and Michelangelo for sculpting. Marble is limestone that has been recrystallized, a process that pushes impurities outside the growing new crystals. This results in large, clean grains surrounded by dark shadings of impurities, which creates the beautiful marbled effect. When large grains grow, they often obliterate earlier textures, such as fossil shapes, from the limestone.

REGIONAL METAMORPHISM

When plates collide, the squeezing and burial of rocks produces high-pressure minerals, whereas heating rocks forms minerals stable at high temperatures. Subducting crust is subjected first to high pressure, then to high temperature. This produces a gradation from high-pressure to high-temperature minerals, which can be recognized in the field. Colliding plates cause folds that are regionally aligned, and squeeze all the minerals in the same

is similar, but from a parent rock of basaltic composition rather than from a more quartz-rich origin. Schist is distinguished by the growth of the mineral garnet in a body of micas. Garnet shows how strong, round crystals can grow as temperature rises. Gneiss forms after schist and is a strongly foliated, coarse, metamorphic rock that resembles granite in its minerals. Beyond gneiss, rocks become molten and igneous.

direction. There is no such alignment where contact metamorphism occurs.

A regional squeeze generates many mica minerals, all precisely aligned. Regional pressure assists such thin, flat, disc-shaped minerals to grow. They do so with the flat sides perpendicular to the squeeze. Mica splits very easily into flat sheets, and with all mica crystals identically aligned, the whole rock splits into sheets or slabs. Slate, formed from fine-grained rocks that have been mildly heated and strongly squeezed over geological time, is a good example.

If the squeezing continues, slate changes to phyllite, a rock with more strongly developed micas, but with some higher-pressure minerals, such as garnet and pyrite, starting to crystallize. The minerals in metamorphic rocks can either be randomly spread throughout the rock, or foliated, meaning that the minerals are arranged in rough

planes, producing a striped appearance. Foliation occurs at temperatures approaching melting point, when elements have greater mobility.

Even higher pressures and temperatures produce schist, a coarse-grained, much more foliated rock than phyllite, with larger minerals forming and segregating. Amphibolite

CONTACT METAMORPHISM

Where rock is metamorphosed by contact with igneous bodies, chemical changes are possible. Elements may be added or subtracted by fluids escaping from granite plutons (rising bodies or "blobs" of hot molten rock).

Temperature decreases outward from the granite pluton, so the degree of contact metamorphism lessens with distance from the intrusion. Some of the minerals that characterize metamorphic grades are (in order of increasing temperature): chlorite, biotite/andalusite, garnet, kyanite, and sillimanite. The high-pressure minerals are (in order of increasing pressure): mica, garnet, kyanite, and sillimanite.

QUARTZITE *in this gorge in the MacDonnell Ranges, Australia, is 1,000 million years old.*

THE RECYCLING *of* ROCKS

The Earth recycles rocks by natural processes that, even as they are finishing in one place, are starting again elsewhere.

Ａll of Earth's minerals and rocks follow a cycle of continuous breakdown and rebirth, a process driven by plate tectonics. On the one hand, minerals are being crystallized from magma, sediments are being cemented into rocks, and rocks are being reformed by high heat and pressure. On the other hand, as physical changes occur, particles are being eroded from rocks, dissolving in water, and being moved by rivers, ice, wind, and gravity. As continents collide, plates sweep sediment into fold belts and bury them so deeply that they melt, to begin the cycle again. All minerals are driven toward a stable form, but they alter as their environments change.

Standing on the edge of Half Dome in Yosemite,

HALF DOME *(above), Yosemite, California, USA, a vertical cliff of granite. When the skeletons of diatoms (above left) are cemented with dissolved quartz, they form chert.*

California, USA, looking all the way down the vertical, granite cliff to the valley, the deep gorge appears to have been cut by the small Merced River and Tenaya Creek, but how? The answer lies in the changing environments affecting the valley. The Yosemite granite began as deep, hot magma under high pressure, and crystallized progressively as it rose and cooled. Part-way up, it became solid, with all minerals stable at that level and tightly interlocked. As the rise continued, both temperature and pressure fell, upsetting stability and starting the process of breakdown.

Falling temperature shrinks minerals, while falling pressure expands them, so the dimensions of each mineral alter as the granite rises. Cooling produces a network

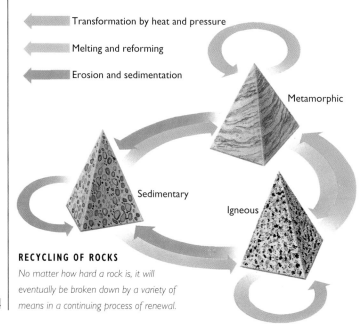

Transformation by heat and pressure

Melting and reforming

Erosion and sedimentation

Metamorphic

Sedimentary

Igneous

RECYCLING OF ROCKS
No matter how hard a rock is, it will eventually be broken down by a variety of means in a continuing process of renewal.

CLEARLY DEFINED *layers (left) of sandstone and diabase, Antarctica. Clay particles collect on flood plains (below).*

Nothing is wasted,

nothing is in vain:

The seas roll over

but the rocks remain.

Tough at the Top,
A. P. HERBERT (1890–1971),
English writer and poet

of shrinkage cracks through-out the granite. Cracks develop among adjacent grains as the minerals adjust to changing stresses, and this allows water and oxygen to penetrate deep into the granite. Stresses fracture feldspar grains along internal cleavage planes, speeding the removal of soluble elements.

The once-solid granite gradually changes to a collection of loosely attached grains, ready to be eroded by water, wind, and ice. With the breakdown of the easily soluble components of feldspar, particles of clay are formed. Rivers move clay and quartz to the sea, where it collects in deep marginal basins, waiting to be folded and melted, continuing the cycle. About 40,000 years ago, the onset of glaciation carved out a U-shaped valley at Yosemite,

truncating ridges, moving debris, and creating Half Dome's vertical cliffs. As the glacier melted, the valley floor filled with debris, leaving the river little to do but rework and sift clay from quartz sand.

WEAK POINTS

Easily soluble minerals are the weak points of rocks. As soon as one mineral is penetrated by groundwater, others come under attack. Every crack speeds rock breakdown—faces erode slowly, edges faster, and corners fastest, leading to the roughly spherical blocks that characterize all granite areas.

Many other processes speed breakdown. Limestone is directly dissolved by rainwater, assisted by soluble gases and plant acids, which greatly accelerate the process. All minerals are soluble eventually, even quartz. In the swamps of brackish Macquarie Harbour, Tasmania, Australia, brown water, rich in organic acids from button grass, dissolves glass bottles by about $\frac{1}{50}$ inch (0.5 mm) every 50 years. In geological terms,

this is a phenomenal rate for dissolving the most common sedimentary sand grain, quartz, from which glass is made.

As a result of the vast total volume of dissolved quartz that rivers bring to the ocean, quartz is spontaneously precipitated as light showers of super-fine crystals that settle as an ooze on the deep ocean floor. This acts to cement the decaying silica skeletons of ocean-dwelling diatoms (microorganisms that extract dissolved quartz from sea water) to form the rock chert.

Soluble minerals may remain in solution as part of the saltiness of the ocean, or form salt lakes in areas of restricted drainage. Clay mineral particles are very small and are easily transported in suspension. They settle only in quiet conditions, so collect in lakes, oceans, and on flood plains—until the next plate collision, when the cycle continues.

SOLITARY PINNACLE *left by erosion at Hells Half Acre, Wyoming, USA.*

55

How Soils Form

We take soil very much for granted, but we must heed the lessons of the past so that we do not waste its precious nutrients.

GLACIERS *are the mechanism by which new soil is created (left). Pitcher plants (top left) supplement poor soil by consuming insects.*

Soil is a mixture of weathered fragments of rocks and biological material. It mostly forms from the local bedrock and debris moved in from elsewhere, sometimes from quite distant areas. The value of soil depends on the nutrients it contains, and this includes both the breakdown products of plants, and elements contained in rocks that plants extract. Primary rocks, such as basalt and granite, bring a variety of nutritious elements up from the Earth's mantle. If sandstone contains little but quartz, it is of no value to most plants. Being a recycled rock, made from weathered grains of other rocks, the nutrients once present have been removed by chemical and mechanical means and by plants. When crops are grown in quartz-rich soils, they must usually be supported by the addition of fertilizer.

Glaciers bulldoze all past soils and mix them with newly ground till, the debris of glacial scraping. They then cover the scraped land with thick deposits of new till. This is, perhaps, the best of all soils, because plants have direct access to the nutrients in the finely milled rock "flour". Glaciers continuously deposit large quantities of till as they melt. Extending glaciers push up large mounds of till, while retreating glaciers dump hummocky sheets of it over the land. The till is then reworked by the strong winds that are a feature of glacial areas, and the more consistent winds of the open plains.

North v. South

There is a fundamental difference between the soils of the northern and southern hemispheres, arising from their different geographic locations during the most recent ice age. Between 40,000 and 10,000 years ago, atmospheric cooling created major Arctic and Antarctic ice caps. The massive sheet glaciers that formed at the poles spread away from these centers, gouging and scratching the rocks beneath, grinding some to dust, and moving the debris across the land.

All the northern continents, connected as Laurasia around the North Pole, were

HAYSTACK ROCKS

As one travels across the endless northern prairies and through New England, North America, large "haystacks" appear in the distance. These are solitary monolithic rocks. No other rocks may be visible in any direction. Close inspection shows that they sit on soil, but no amount of digging reveals any bedrock. They are glacier-transported haystack rocks, or erratics, the source of which may be 1,000 miles (1,600 km) closer to the North Pole than where they stand. Most haystack rocks bear no resemblance to local bedrock, but if you follow the direction of past glacial travel back toward its source, the origin can be found. They were carried and dumped amid the debris of glacial scraping by a melting glacier in the most recent glaciation. Prairie winds then totally exposed them.

RICH SOILS *are the heritage of northern continents (above), while those of the south are poor, except in volcanic areas, such as the Andes foothills (right).*

covered in ice in the most recent glaciation. The glaciers moved south over Europe, Asia, and North America, spreading till as they melted and retreated. Antipodean glaciers ran into the ocean around the perimeter of Antarctica and no other southern continents were affected. The result is now reflected in the agricultural wealth northern hemisphere countries enjoy, all top-dressed with freshly milled rock flour. Southern hemisphere continents (Australia, Africa, and South America), largely unaffected by that glaciation, have to rely on older, poorer soils.

The real difference lies in the available nutrients. Northern-hemisphere soils consist of a deep layer of rock flour. Southern-hemisphere soils, often very shallow, have little crystalline rock mineral nutrient and each crop of plants waits on the death and decay of the previous generation. When crops are harvested from southern hemisphere soils, nutrients for subsequent plant generations are totally removed, and cannot be replaced from the local barren soils. For example, wheat crops from Australia and trees used for wood chips in the Amazon Basin of South America both grow in quartz-sand soils. Harvesting from these areas guarantees future deserts in both locations. Although clear division is made here between northern and southern hemispheres, the real division lies between areas that have and have not undergone a recent glaciation.

In southern hemisphere countries, the soil that was present at the time of the assembly of Gondwana is still in use. Rain during 250 million years has leached soluble minerals from this soil, leaving only the most insoluble residues: quartz, iron oxide, and aluminum oxide. These are the typical components of desert sands, and a long, slow succession of plants is needed to return such areas to forest.

DEFORESTATION *in Madagascar has caused severe soil erosion (right).*

Happy the man whose lot is to know
The secrets of the Earth.

EURIPIDES (480–405)
Greek tragic playwright

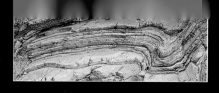

CHAPTER THREE

UNLOCKING *the*
SECRETS *of* ROCKS

How Geology Affects Us

All plants and animals, including ourselves,

are composed of the Earth's elements, and

have evolved to survive the conditions that exist here.

The Earth and all its elements are stardust, produced in a cosmic process that began between 10,000 and 20,000 million years ago. We are dependent upon the Sun's rays for energy, with Earth's atmosphere providing a protective blanket against harmful solar radiation. Energy from the Sun is also stored on the Earth's surface and in its upper layers, in the form of wood, coal, petroleum, and natural gas.

Life forms have evolved to survive the specific conditions that exist on Earth. Any changes to these conditions, such as atmospheric composition, barometric pressure, the temperature on the surface, or the strength of the gravitational field, would produce devastating results. Even relatively slight changes can be detrimental, as demonstrated by the difficulties that

we face when exposed to depths, high altitudes, or extreme temperatures.

In the same way as our bodies have evolved in response to naturally occurring conditions, so too have our cultures and customs. The length of a day and a year, and our seasonal schedule of planting and harvesting crops, are determined by the Earth's rotation around both its own axis and the Sun.

The Earth's Elements

Elements are made up of atoms, which are in turn made up of protons, neutrons, and electrons. The elements occurring on Earth are listed in the Periodic Table. There are 109 elements, listed in order of the number of protons contained in their nuclei (their atomic weight), although only 94 of them actually occur naturally. Eight of these

elements make up virtually all matter, with the others occurring only in tiny amounts.

The first and lightest element on the table is hydrogen, whose atom contains only one proton and one electron. It is so light that it cannot exist as a free gas in

ELEMENTS are arranged on the Periodic Table, a portion of which is shown above with the native element gold. Humans and the Earth itself consist mainly of only a few elements (below). Hydrogen, the lightest element, was used in airships, but its flammability led to disasters such as the loss of the Hindenburg (left) in 1937.

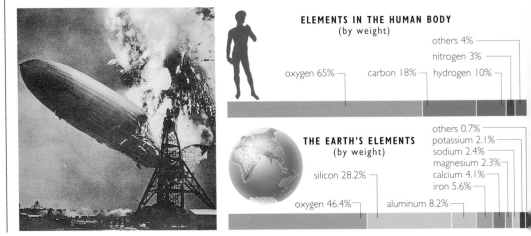

ELEMENTS IN THE HUMAN BODY
(by weight)

oxygen 65% carbon 18% hydrogen 10% nitrogen 3% others 4%

THE EARTH'S ELEMENTS
(by weight)

oxygen 46.4% silicon 28.2% aluminum 8.2% iron 5.6% calcium 4.1% magnesium 2.3% sodium 2.4% potassium 2.1% others 0.7%

our atmosphere, escaping from the Earth's gravitational pull into space. At the bottom end of the table, the atoms are so large and complex that they are likely to break down into lighter, more stable "daughter products", releasing vast quantities of nuclear energy in doing so. Unstable elements, such as uranium, comprise about a third of the table but are very rare.

Minerals are naturally occurring elements or chemical compounds, and have distinct, measurable physical and chemical properties. A few elements, such as sulfur, carbon, silver, gold, and copper, can occur alone in their natural state, and are known as native elements or elemental minerals. Others exist only in various combinations. For example, sodium chloride, or common salt, is made up of sodium and chlorine and occurs naturally as the mineral halite. On the basis of chemical composition,

THE PERIODIC TABLE

The Periodic Table was formulated in the mid nineteenth century by a Russian chemist, Dimitry Ivanovich Mendeleyev (1834–1907), who grouped the 62 elements known at the time in order of increasing atomic weight. Element 101, a recent addition to the Periodic Table, is known as mendelevium, in recognition of his contribution.

The most common element in the universe is hydrogen, accounting for 90 percent of all known matter. The rarest of the naturally occurring elements is astatine, with only 0.0056 of an ounce (0.16 gram) present in the Earth's crust. The lightest solid element is lithium and the heaviest is osmium.

New elements are being added to the table all the time. In addition to the 94 naturally occurring elements, a further 15 heavier elements have been artificially developed. In 1982, physicists working in Darmstadt, Germany, announced that they had created an isotope of element number 109, unnilenium, from the decay of a single atom.

the main mineral groups are the silicates, carbonates, oxides, sulfides, halides, sulfates, and phosphates.

There are now more than 3,600 mineral species known to science and the number is steadily increasing. Rocks, in turn, are composed of minerals in various combinations.

A DAY IN OUR LIVES

From the natural world to the world of modern technology, we are constantly interacting with the Earth's elements.

THE HUMAN ELEMENT
Surprisingly, human beings are made up of very few of the simplest elements: carbon, hydrogen, oxygen, and nitrogen, with some others present in tiny amounts. We also rely on a steady intake of elements, such as calcium, iron, sodium, potassium, and phosphorus, with our food to maintain our physiological well-being.

A single morning in our busy lives will see us encountering about a fifth of the elements on the Periodic Table. The house in which we live, the food, utensils, and power we use to make our food, and the clothes and jewelry we wear, are all derived from the same building blocks. By the time we've entered the world of modern technology, virtually all of the table's stable elements will have been encountered.

STARTING *a* ROCK COLLECTION

To observe, study, and collect rocks allows one to marvel at the natural beauty and complexity of our planet.

Rocks and minerals are found all around us, whether we live in a crowded city or the remote countryside. They are used to build almost everything we use, and are always present beneath our feet.

Get to know the rocks around you. If you live in a city, a wealth of rocks can be found making up the buildings themselves. Note any information you can find about them. How are the rocks being used? Are they igneous, metamorphic, or sedimentary? Note their colors and textures and, of course, their location.

For rocks in natural formations, note any characteristic structures such as columns, spires, or stacked boulders. These usually typify particular rock types. How far do you have to go before the rocks around you change? If there is a cover of soil on the rocks, note its thickness, color, and texture, and whether the vegetation it supports changes as the rocks do. Try to identify the minerals that make up the rocks

START BY IDENTIFYING *the rocks around you. These boulders in Australia (above) are granite, an igneous rock. Your collection might include carved stones, such as this turquoise medallion (top left), or cheaper ornamental stones, such as agate (top right).*

using the simple tests described on pages 70–75, and note what elements make up these minerals. Persevere, bearing in mind that identification skills will come with practice.

THE ROCK COLLECTION

One of the best ways to learn about geology is to start a collection. You could begin with simple carved and polished items, such as statues, book ends, or slabs, and get to know the rocks and minerals used. Inexpensive ornamental stones, such as agate, onyx, limestone, marble, obsidian,

and hematite, make a good starting point. If you begin by gathering rocks in the field, don't worry about trying to find the "perfect" specimen at first. Any sample of a particular rock or mineral is all that is necessary for you to become familiar with its natural features.

Eventually, most collectors are forced by the overwhelming variety of material to specialize in one particular

ORNAMENTAL STONES *in unworked forms, such as malachite (left) and chalcedony (right), make interesting collection pieces.*

TINY CRYSTAL CLUSTERS, *such as these naturolite crystals (left), are beautiful and a convenient size to collect. To get the most out of your collection, give each specimen a label (below) and then add a description.*

branch, for example, crystal specimens, gem minerals, ore minerals, building stones, or even particular mineral groups. You may wish to display each in a variety of forms: a fine worked piece, a cut stone, the rough material, and, if possible, a natural crystal.

Growing in popularity are miniature rock and mineral collections known as micro mounts. Tiny specimens, such as crystal clusters, are fixed in small transparent boxes that can be stored in larger trays. Ideal for apartment dwellers, such collections are enjoyed with the aid of a hand lens or microscope and are generally more beautiful and complete than collections of conventional-sized specimens for two main reasons. First,

crystal clusters in cavities tend to be closer to perfect the smaller they are, and second, the rarity of some of the material in large sizes means that they are prohibitively expensive.

Any cabinet or set of drawers can be used to house a collection. Those with glass sides or tops are preferable as the exhibits can be enjoyed from all angles and less dust will settle on them.

LABELING THE COLLECTION

Labeling your collection can be just as much fun as acquiring it. Assign each specimen a catalog number by numbering the box in which it sits. If the specimens are handled frequently, you may wish to number them directly, using an inconspicuous dot of white enamel paint, and writing a

number in India ink. Elsewhere, on a card, in a book, or on a computer file, give a detailed description of the specimen.

If it is a rock, list its name and constituent minerals, as well as where and when it was found or bought. If it is a mineral, list its name; chemical formula; physical properties such as hardness, specific gravity, luster, streak, and crystal system; and uses of the mineral or any elements that may be extracted from it. Labels summarizing each specimen's information can be placed in the cabinet, giving the collection a professional appearance and allowing visitors to enjoy it fully.

FINE SPECIMENS, *such as these topaz crystals growing on white quartz (left), are impressive, but may be expensive. Instead, you might collect examples of the same mineral in a variety of forms, such as turquoise (above). You can use any cabinet to house a collection (right).*

GETTING PREPARED

Knowing which equipment is required in the field and being well prepared will increase the safety and enjoyment of your collecting trips.

The basic gear you need for mineral and rock collecting is simple, although you can add to it over time. For a start, a geological map and a compass will help point you in the right direction, while a notebook and pencil are essential for recording details of locality, geology, and sample descriptions. You should also carry old newspaper and tape to wrap and protect each specimen, an indelible marking pen to number each package, and a backpack or a cardboard box in which to carry your specimens once wrapped.

For breaking rocks to see unweathered surfaces, or to trim up samples, a standard geological hammer is most suitable. The flat end is used for breaking rocks, while the pointed end is used for digging or gouging in soft material. Some collectors prefer a short-handled mallet with a heavier head to make breaking safer and easier. Sturdy gloves and eye protection should be worn at all times, as there will invariably be sharp chips of rock flying about.

Chisels are handy to trim down heavy specimens in the field and are relatively light to

carry. A flat chisel allows you to break selectively along bedding planes or cracks and fractures. Remember, only trim a good sample if you are sure that you will not damage it. Otherwise, have it cut up later with a rock saw.

For serious rock breaking, such as when searching for

mineral-filled cavities in hard basalt, a sledge hammer is recommended, along with overalls, hard hat, goggles, face protection, leggings, and gloves, to protect yourself against rock chips. When working below cliffs or quarry faces, always wear a hard hat.

Other useful items include a hand lens with ten times magnification to see finer detail, a magnet for detecting magnetic minerals, a porcelain streak plate, a Mohs' hardness set or equivalent standards (see p. 71), and a well-sealed plastic bottle with very dilute hydrochloric acid for testing carbonates, chalk, and limestones. (See pp. 70–75 for details on mineral testing.)

Metal detectors can be useful when looking for gold nuggets, as well as antiquities, such as coins, medals, rings, or bullets. Based on the principle that metals conduct electricity, they will, unfortunately, also detect cans, bottle caps, wire, and nails, but experienced operators with modern

THE RIGHT EQUIPMENT *for a field trip includes a geological map (right) and clothing to protect you from flying chips of rock (top and above right).*

GOLD COLLECTING *with a "cradle" (left). Gravels and sediments are washed across an old carpet, which will trap any fine gold particles.*

sunburn. Be aware of the dangers particular to your area, whether they be tropical diseases, dangerous wildlife, unstable ground, or extreme weather conditions. Always carry maps, let others know where you are going, and get permission before collecting on private or public land. Never take unnecessary risks and be particularly careful near abandoned mine sites and quarries. Underground mine shafts are often unstable and should never be entered.

machines can discriminate among these. Other equipment, generally beyond the scope of the amateur collector, includes ultraviolet lamps for detecting luminescent minerals and scintillometers for radioactive minerals.

COLLECTING IN CREEKS AND RIVERS

Creeks and rivers are good places to look for heavy minerals, such as gold, sapphire, ruby, zircon, spinel, topaz, tourmaline, chrysoberyl, and cassiterite. In order to reach the bedrock, you will need a pick, a spade, and a trowel to move small rocks and sediment. A crowbar may also come in handy for moving larger rocks, and hand-held suction pumps will help you reach material in narrow crevices, where such minerals tend to concentrate.

For fossicking on a larger scale, more sophisticated motorized equipment can be used to process more material, more efficiently. Dredges or suction pumps draw gravels from the river bed into a hand-operated pipe, and discharge them over gravity-separation machinery, known

as riffle boxes or jigs. These operate like huge sieves, separating and concentrating the heavy minerals. They are generally emptied only at the end of the day, making for an exciting culmination to a day's collecting.

PRECAUTIONS

Whenever you are rock collecting, dress sensibly—good, sturdy footwear and clothes that will protect you against cold, heat, rain, or

PANNING FOR GOLD AND GEMS

To isolate heavy minerals, first sieve the gravels into various sizes. Stack a coarse sieve, with holes of about ⅕ inch (5 mm), on a fine sieve, with holes of about ¹⁄₁₀ inch (2.5 mm), and place a gold pan underneath. Heap all of the sample material into the top sieve and work both sieves and the pan in a circular motion in water. This will concentrate the heavy minerals toward the center of the sieves and throw the lighter material toward the edges, while allowing the finest material to pass into the pan. After several minutes of sieving, flip the contents of each sieve onto a hessian bag and pick out any gemstones with tweezers. If gold or small gems are present, they will be concentrated in the bottom of the pan.

IN *the* FIELD

The shapes of mountains, the patterns of rivers,

and the types of soil and vegetation on the ground,

all hold clues to the geology beneath.

Before setting out to collect rocks and minerals, do a little research about the area you are exploring, and the rocks and minerals you might find there. Your collecting will be more productive and enjoyable.

READING THE SIGNS *The color of the Red Mountains (right), in Colorado, USA, indicates the presence of iron. Rivers flowing from volcanoes, such as in the Andes (below), are often a good source of gemstones. On this geological map (left), an old volcanic neck (pink) is shown surrounded by its lavas (yellow).*

GEOLOGICAL MAPS

Your rock collecting will be assisted by basic navigation skills and an understanding of geological maps. These are the same as any other maps, except they also show where different rock types occur. With such a map, you can take yourself to the most likely areas to find particular rocks, minerals, or fossils.

For every rock type, a geological map has a corresponding color and/or symbol. The key gives pertinent details about the rock, such as its appearance, age, and, often, its fossil or mineral content.

Learn to recognize the different rock types on the map and collect samples of each to compare. You will soon come to associate certain minerals and gemstones with particular rock types. This is the basis of geological exploration.

WHERE TO LOOK

Landform types, soils, and vegetation are like beacons guiding you to particular rock types. Streams and rivers often mimic the patterns in the underlying geological strata, so look at the pattern of the rivers on a standard map. Do any of the rivers head radially out from an area, or converge into a depression? This arrangement may reveal the presence of old volcanoes, often a source of gemstones. Look at the soils for further evidence. They may be a different color from other soils in the area, perhaps rich red or brown, indicating the presence of iron-rich volcanic rocks. These soils will, in turn, support a different type of vegetation or landuse pattern. The more familiar you become with these features, the easier rock collecting will be.

COASTAL CLIFFS, *such as this one (above) in Dorset, England, provide plenty of broken rocks. Panning for gold in a river in northern Madagascar (below).*

In the field, creek beds, road cuttings, and quarries are some of the best locations to see fresh rock exposures, but always ask permission before entering quarries and keep clear of unstable areas and falling rocks. Mine dumps are a good source of fresh material and often contain minerals that miners have left behind. In Australia, collectors walking over opal mine dumps are often surprised by a good find, especially after a fall of rain, when the opal pieces, washed clean of dirt and dust, glint in the sunlight.

Coastal cliffs provide excellent opportunities for

collecting as there are always piles of fallen, broken rocks at their base. Mountainous areas are also good, with large sections of rockface often free from soil cover. In areas of natural beauty, do not damage the cliff faces. Collect only from those rocks that are already broken.

Searching in creeks and rivers is a good way to find durable, heavy minerals. Check areas where they are likely to have accumulated, known as trap sites. When water slows down, its carrying capacity decreases and heavy minerals are likely to collect there, so be on the lookout for features that might slow the water, such as potholes, crevices, large boulders, rock bars running across the direction of flow, or even a sudden widening of the creek or river.

For good results, persevere with trap sites. Always excavate right back to bedrock and process the material found there, as it is against this surface that heavy material, especially gold, will accumulate. Constantly check fine material in the pan for traces of gemstones. If fine gemstones are present, you are certain to come across larger material sooner or later. Heavy storms will recharge good trap sites so there should always be something to find.

The World is the geologist's great puzzle box.

LOUIS AGASSIZ
(1807–73), Swiss naturalist

HOW TO USE A COMPASS

Take a compass, hold it in front of you, and turn a full circle. There are 360 degrees in a full turn. The magnetic needle will always point north (take your magnet and other metal objects out of your pockets for this exercise or it might point to those instead).

To follow a particular direction (for example, 40 degrees north east), turn the rotating ring on the compass until 40 degrees lines up with the center line. Holding the compass before you, turn your body until the north end of the magnetic needle lines up with the north direction (N) on the dial. You can now walk in the selected direction by keeping the north needle on the N mark as you walk. This simple exercise is the basis of navigation.

HOW *to* READ *the* LANDSCAPE

*An understanding of the forces that shape the Earth makes
geological exploration easier and more rewarding.*

Minerals and gemstones are not distributed evenly throughout the Earth's crust. Rather, they tend to be concentrated within particular rock types related to specific geological events that have occurred deep beneath the ground. Often, the surface features of the landscape offer clues as to what lies beneath. However, in other cases, the geological signs are hidden far below the surface and may be glimpsed only by drilling and through the use of advanced geophysical techniques.

TECTONIC FORCES

The massive tectonic forces that move the continents and shape the ground beneath our feet transform and redistribute the Earth's rocks and minerals. A basic understanding of these processes and the effects they have on the local geology provides the key to successful geological exploration.

Mountain ranges form when continental plates collide, squeezing, buckling, and lifting the once-horizontal sedimentary strata. If the squeezing is intense enough, the sedimentary rocks will change under pressure into metamorphic rocks. These often contain a host of interesting and precious minerals, such as garnet, ruby, mica, sapphire, kyanite, andalusite, and staurolite.

The zones where ancient continents once collided are often marked by long serpentine belts and highly deformed marine rocks, such as chert, jasper, and limestone. These rocks are remnants of the once-great oceans that were crushed between the continental plates. A range of interesting minerals is associated with such rocks, including chrysotile and antigorite, chromite (the ore of chromium), pyrolusite (the ore of manganese), nephrite jade, asbestos, talc, rhodonite, and cryptocrystalline quartz.

MINERALS AND GEMSTONES *are associated with particular geological features, many of which are shown in this illustration (right). Active volcanoes, such as Kilauea Iki, in Hawaii (left), may carry interesting minerals, such as peridot (top) to the Earth's surface.*

RISING MAGMA

Beneath the Earth's thin crust, lies a hot, plastic interior. As crustal plates shift and collide, magma is generated and works its way toward the surface, sometimes erupting violently to form volcanoes. Often, however, it cools before reaching the surface, forming granite intrusions through the underlying strata. Element-rich fluids, known as pegmatites, penetrate cracks in the rocks

pegmatite
vein —————

metamorphic rock
formed by pressure

THE PATTERN *of drainage of the Green River, in Utah, USA, is starkly illustrated in this aerial view (right).*

surrounding the intrusion and produce large and beautiful crystals of minerals such as topaz, beryl (emerald), tourmaline, cassiterite (the ore of tin), quartz, feldspar, gold, and mica.

Around the edges of these intrusions, heat from the granite transforms the surrounding rocks to produce new minerals such as calcite, garnet, wollastonite, and lapis lazuli. Erosion will eventually expose these granitic bodies as circular outcrops that can be located using a geological map

When magma reaches the surface, it may form conical shields of basalt. The rising magma cuts through and covers up all earlier geological structures and often carries minerals, such as sapphire, ruby, zircon, spinel, and peridot, to the surface from deep within the Earth. After weathering, these minerals will be released from the basalts and end up in the rivers that drain from the volcano, from where they can be collected with sieves and pans.

Small, but explosive, volcanoes are formed when silica-poor lavas erupt from deep within the mantle. These eruptions, sometimes reaching the surface in a matter of days, can carry with them one of the most sought after of all gems—the diamond.

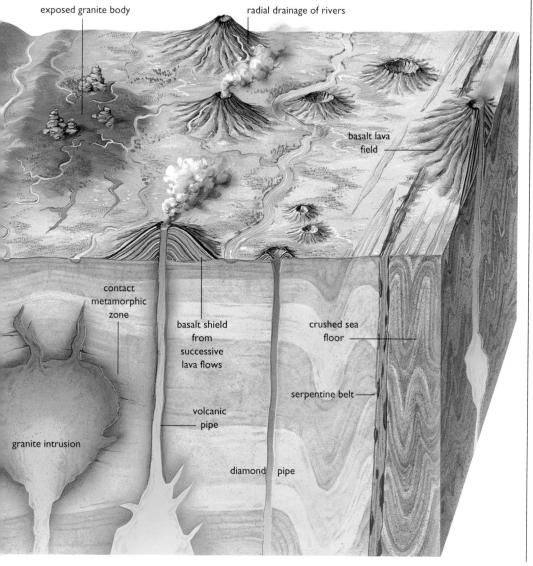

exposed granite body

radial drainage of rivers

basalt lava field

contact metamorphic zone

basalt shield from successive lava flows

crushed sea floor

serpentine belt

volcanic pipe

diamond pipe

granite intrusion

MINERAL IDENTIFICATION

Any collector, amateur or professional, can identify most minerals by using a few simple tests.

I dentifying minerals is easy and satisfying. The tests you need to carry out are based on fundamental mineral properties, and most involve no equipment at all. Others involve inexpensive equipment that you can use in the field or at home. Often, one or two tests will be enough to establish a sample's identity, although occasionally, you may need to take it to a professional for further testing.

The properties that define any mineral are as follows: hardness, solubility in acid, magnetism, specific gravity, color, streak, transparency, luster, sheen, fluorescence and phosphorescence, crystal system, habit, cleavage, and fracture. These properties depend on the arrangement of a mineral's atoms, rather than merely its chemical composition. For example, diamond and graphite are identical in chemical composition, being pure carbon, but are as different in their properties as any two minerals could be.

MINERAL *identification can usually be done in the field (top). Brazilianite and mica crystals growing together (right) are easily distinguished.*

Diamond is the hardest known substance, whereas graphite is one of the softest; diamonds are transparent and shine brilliantly, whereas graphite is opaque, dull, and black. These differences are all due to the structure of the carbon atoms within the minerals. Those in diamond have a cubic arrangement whereas the atoms in graphite have a hexagonal arrangement.

With practice, you will carry out most identification tests automatically. As you pick up a mineral sample for the first time you will notice its shape and color, and whether or not you can see through it. Perhaps it looks oily or resinous, or reflects light in a certain way. With each property you identify, you greatly reduce the range of minerals that your sample might be. If this all seems a bit daunting, remember that the common rock-forming minerals are few, and with a little practice, you should easily learn to recognize them.

DIAMOND AND GRAPHITE *(above) are chemically identical but have very different physical properties.*

IDENTIFICATION TESTS

Take your mineral specimen, or the rock containing the minerals that you wish to identify (provided they are big enough to see with a hand lens), and work your way through the following tests. By comparing your results with a list of standard mineral properties, you should be able to identify your specimen.

HARDNESS

A mineral's hardness is revealed by trying to scratch it with another mineral or an object of known hardness. A scale, grading from 1 (talc) to 10 (diamond), was established by the German mineralogist, Friedrich Mohs (1773-1839). Minerals with higher Mohs' numbers will scratch those lower on the scale. For convenience, a number of everyday objects of known hardness can be used (see table).

A word of warning—never use this test on good specimens as it leaves a permanent scratch. Also, don't mistake hardness for toughness. Many a good diamond has been destroyed in the mistaken belief that diamond, being the hardest known mineral, is able to

HARDNESS SCALE

1. Talc

2. Gypsum

fingernail (2.5)

3. Calcite

coin (3.5)

4. Fluorite

5. Apatite

glass (5.5)

6. Feldspar

steel knife (6.5)

7. Quartz

8. Topaz

emery cloth (8.5)

9. Corundum

10. Diamond

HARDNESS *Mohs' scale of hardness, from softest to hardest, combined with everyday objects you can use in the field. If an unknown mineral will scratch feldspar (6) but can be scratched by quartz (7), it has a hardness between 6 and 7.*

resist a good hammer blow. Instead, it will break into smaller fragments with a perfect octahedral cleavage.

THE ACID TEST

This is an easy field test for the presence of carbonate minerals, such as calcite, and carbonate rocks, such as limestone, marble, and chalk. Carefully place a drop of dilute hydrochloric acid on a fresh surface of the rock or mineral to be tested. Acid reacts with any carbonate to produce carbon dioxide gas so, if bubbles form in the acid, carbonate is present in the sample. Again, do not try this on good samples.

MAGNETISM

A simple test for the presence of iron in a sample is to use a magnet. Minerals with high iron content, such as pyrrhotite, are attracted by a hand magnet. Weak magnetic samples will cause a compass needle to rotate.

SPECIFIC GRAVITY

Specific gravity, or density, is the relative weight of a mineral compared to the weight of an equal volume of water. Unless you are experienced, you will need to do this test at home. However, it is well worth doing, as a mineral's specific gravity is a very reliable means of identification. If your specimen contains more than one mineral, this test is not applicable.

For this test you need a balance that can weigh the mineral normally in air and again suspended in water. The mineral's weight in air is divided by the difference between the two weights to obtain its specific gravity.

With a little experience, you will be able to estimate specific gravity by hand, distinguishing between light

minerals (specific gravity 1–2), such as sulfur and graphite; medium minerals (2–3), such as gypsum and quartz; medium heavy minerals (3–4), such as fluorite and beryl; heavy minerals (4–6), such as corundum, and most metal oxides and sulfides; and very heavy minerals (more than 6), such as cassiterite. Native gold and platinum are the heaviest minerals, with specific gravities of about 19.

ACID *will bubble when placed on a carbonate mineral.*

LODESTONE *(left) was once used for navigation because of its magnetic properties. Identically sized samples of rhodochrosite and calcite reveal their different specific gravities when placed on a scale (below). Calcite is clearly lighter.*

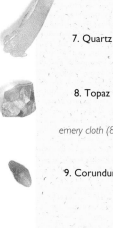

MINERAL IDENTIFICATION
by OPTICAL EFFECTS

Perhaps the first thing you notice when you find a mineral is its appearance in the light. Color, sheen, luster, and transparency all offer clues to its identity.

A mineral's color may not always be a diagnostic characteristic. This depends on whether the color is caused by elements essential to the mineral's composition (idiochromatic minerals), or by non-essential trace elements (allochromatic minerals). Idiochromatic minerals include rhodonite and rhodochrosite (pink, colored by manganese), malachite (green, colored by copper), olivine (green, colored by magnesium), and sulfur (yellow).

The color of allochromatic minerals (particularly non-metallic ones) is extremely variable, and will not identify them. For example, the minerals corundum, apatite, tourmaline, beryl, and fluorite are colorless and completely transparent when pure, but may be found in a variety of colors, depending on the trace elements present when the crystals were growing.

COLOR *alone will not identify fluorite, which is found in a variety of colors (below), but will identify malachite (top), which is always green.*

In these cases, other optical effects, such as streak, transparency, luster, sheen, and luminescence can be used to identify them.

STREAK
When a mineral is rubbed against an unglazed, white, porcelain streak plate (the back of a ceramic tile will do), it leaves a distinctive streak, or line of powdered mineral. The color of this streak remains constant regardless of trace elements. For example, the allochromatic minerals corundum, apatite, tourmaline, beryl, and fluorite all leave a white streak. Streak is very distinctive for the metallic minerals. For example, brassy yellow pyrite and chalcopyrite leave a greenish-black streak, black hematite produces a cherry-red streak, black pyrolusite produces a black streak, black wolframite leaves a brown streak, and black cassiterite leaves an almost white streak.

STREAK *is constant, regardless of a mineral's color. From left to right are cassiterite (whitish streak), chalcopyrite (greenish-black), and malachite (green).*

TRANSPARENCY
A mineral's transparency refers to the ease with which light can pass through it. There are three categories of transparency: "Transparent" minerals, such as quartz, topaz, and beryl, allow objects to be seen clearly through them. "Translucent" minerals, such as opal, jade, and chalcedony, allow some light to pass through, but an object would not be visible through them. "Opaque" minerals, such as malachite and hematite, allow no light to pass through. Minerals found in rivers tend to have abraded, frosted surfaces and these will need to be polished for the minerals to reveal their true transparency.

LUSTER

This refers to the appearance of a mineral's surface and is dependent on the way that light falling on it is absorbed or reflected. Lusters vary from "dull" (like kaolinite) to "adamantine" (diamond-like). Other distinctive lusters include "vitreous", or glassy (like quartz and beryl), "metallic" (like many of the metals, metal oxides and sulfides), "waxy" or "greasy", as if covered with a thin layer of oil (like turquoise), "resinous" (like amber), "pearly" (like pearl, moonstone, and talc), and "silky", as shown by minerals with a finely fibrous struc-ture (such as asbestos and "satin spar" gypsum).

SHEEN

Sheen is produced by the reflection of light from within a stone, and is, therefore, caused by the internal struc-ture, or inclusions within the mineral. Sheen must not be confused with color, nor luster, which is purely a surface effect. For example,

the body color of a precious opal may be white, grey, black, or colorless, but the magnificent rainbow effect known as "play of color" is a sheen caused by the refraction of light from the ordered arrays of tiny, silica spheres that make up the opal structure. Sheen effects are best seen in cut and polished stones, but are discernible in rough material.

There are a number of terms used to describe sheen. "Iridescence" is the rainbow effect seen on the inside of some shells and on the polished surfaces of labradorite feldspar. "Adularescence", otherwise known as "schiller", is the sheen of silvery-blue light seen in semi-transparent moonstone feldspar and some opal. "Chatoyancy", or cat's-eye effect, is the reflection of light from parallel fibers or oriented needle-like inclusions within the mineral. This appears as a single, bright line when the mineral is cabochon cut. It is seen in quartz that contains parallel asbestos fibers (known as cat's-eye quartz), silicified crocidolite asbestos (tiger's-eye) and cat's-eye chrysoberyl. "Asterism" is chatoyancy occurring in several directions. This is the star-like effect for which star sapphires and rubies are famous.

LUMINESCENCE

Not all optical effects are visible to the naked eye. Certain minerals, such as scheelite, fluorite, calcite, zircon, common opal, and diamond, may be optically excited when exposed to ultraviolet light. This is known as fluorescence, and as phosphorescence if the glow continues after the light has been switched off. In the darkness, these minerals glow in stunning violets, greens and reds, quite different from the colors they display in natural light. Collectors often make special cabinets to enjoy the full beauty of these minerals.

IDENTIFYING MINERALS
by PHYSICAL PROPERTIES

The visible form of a mineral is a demonstration

of its invisible atomic structure. As such, physical

properties provide excellent clues to a mineral's identity.

Many minerals can be identified by their external shape. First, look carefully at the crystal faces. Can you tell what shape they are and at what angles the faces meet? If so, you can determine the crystal system to which they belong. Crystals also have a distinctive appearance, or habit. Like people, they can be short and fat (tabular), tall and thin (acicular), or somewhere in between.

The crystal faces may have distinguishing features, such as lines (striations) or geometric pits and bumps, which are often specific to a particular mineral. Examination of broken surfaces also reveals

clues. Have they fractured irregularly or broken along a series of parallel flat surfaces (cleavage planes)? With practice, you will learn to recognize these properties.

CRYSTAL SYSTEM
Minerals will always crystallize into one of six crystal systems reflecting their internal molecular arrangement. Perfect crystals are rare in nature, but even a broken fragment or distorted crystal is enough to give some clues to its identity.

The six basic crystal systems are cubic, tetragonal, hexagonal, orthorhombic, monoclinic, and triclinic. These are shown below, with characteristic examples.

AGGREGATES, *or interlocking crystals, form in confined spaces, as seen in this gypsum specimen.*

HABIT
The size and shape of a mineral's crystals determine its habit. These range from isometric or equant (all faces equally developed), through pyramidal (crystal edges converge to a point), tabular, columnar, acicular (needle-like) to fibrous. Other habits include stellate (star-like), dendritic (tree-like), reniform (kidney-shaped), botryoidal (grape-like), and massive (with no distinctive shape).

Minerals in the same crystal system, or even the same mineral with different trace elements, can display vastly different habits. Ruby crystals, for example, are

THE SIX CRYSTAL SYSTEMS
with mineral examples.

| Pyrite | Vesuvianite | Beryl | Barite | Selenite | Amazonite |
| *Cubic* | *Tetragonal* | *Hexagonal* | *Orthorhombic* | *Monoclinic* | *Triclinic* |

usually tabular, while sapphire crystals are generally pyramidal or prismatic.

Crystals often grow in confined environments in between already formed crystals. As a result, they may become distorted or they may form an assemblage of interlocking crystals, known as an aggregate.

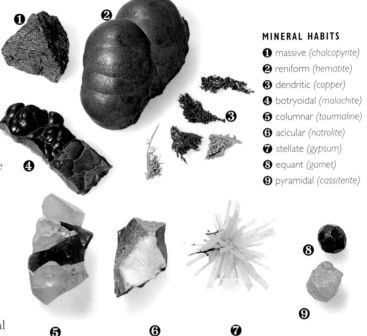

MINERAL HABITS

❶ massive *(chalcopyrite)*
❷ reniform *(hematite)*
❸ dendritic *(copper)*
❹ botryoidal *(malachite)*
❺ columnar *(tourmaline)*
❻ acicular *(natrolite)*
❼ stellate *(gypsum)*
❽ equant *(garnet)*
❾ pyramidal *(cassiterite)*

CRYSTAL FACES

Crystal faces are rarely flat and featureless, often being striated, patterned or deformed in distinctive ways. Quartz is usually striated across the width of the crystal while striations in tourmaline run along the length of the crystal. The octahedral faces of diamond crystals often show triangular pits known as trigons. Similarly, sapphires and rubies may show raised triangular hillocks, in both cases due to corrosion damage from the magma that carried them to the surface.

CLEAVAGE

Certain minerals, when struck with a hammer, will break, or cleave, along set planes of weakness related to their mineral structure.

Cleavage may be poorly defined (as in bornite) to perfect (mica and diamond) and may occur in one plane (mica), two planes (gypsum, pyroxene, amphibole, feldspar), three planes (galena, calcite, halite), four planes (fluorite, diamond) or even five planes (sphalerite).

Minerals will therefore cleave into sheets (mica, talc), prisms (pyroxene, amphibole), cubes (halite, galena), octahedra (fluorite, diamond), and rhombs (calcite). The ease of cleavage is also important, and can range from easy (mica) to very difficult (diamond).

Again, don't take to your finest pieces with a hammer. By looking closely, it is often possible to find silvery, reflective planes within transparent minerals, known as incipient cleavages. These often parallel a flat outer surface, indicating cleavage directions and their relationship to the crystallographic axes.

MICA *(above) has perfect cleavage along one plane. A magnification of the face of a diamond (above right) showing triangular pits, or trigons.*

FRACTURE

Minerals that do not cleave easily will fracture irregularly instead and the type of fracture can often be used to distinguish among mineral species. The most common type of fracture is conchoidal. This is the smooth, shell-like fracture seen in obsidian and quartz. Metals and tough minerals, such as jade, tend to have a hackly fracture, like broken cast iron. Arsenopyrite is an example of uneven fracture and kaolinite breaks with an earthy fracture, like clay or chalk.

COMMON FRACTURES *include (clockwise, from top left) uneven (arsenopyrite), earthy (kaolinite), and conchoidal (quartz and opalite).*

THE METALS

The discovery of metals led to great leaps forward for human civilization.

About 75 percent of the elements on the Periodic Table are metals. The most abundant are aluminum, iron, calcium, sodium, potassium, and magnesium, but these were not discovered by ancient civilizations because they are found only in compounds with other elements. The first to be discovered were the native metals, such as gold, silver, and copper, that occur naturally in a pure form. As each metal was discovered, societies were transformed.

Gold artifacts from Sumer date from 4000 BC, but gold was probably discovered at least 8,000 years ago. Strong and pliable, yet unbreakable, a native gold nugget could be honed to a fine edge or hammered into thin sheets.

Native copper, an attractive salmon–pink metal discovered about the same time, was stronger and harder than gold. It could be fashioned into tools and weapons as well as ornamental objects.

At some time before 4000 BC, a crucial discovery was made—molten metals could be combined (or alloyed) with one another when heated. The first metal alloy was bronze, and its discovery marked the birth of the Bronze Age. Made from roughly 90 percent copper and 10 percent tin, bronze is harder and more useful than either of its constituents. It facilitated the production of weapons and tools and expanded the potential for trade. People also realized that metals could be extracted from certain rocks by placing them in a very hot fire. This primitive form of smelting brought about the discovery of lead and mercury, as well as new sources of copper.

The last metal to revolutionize the lives of ancient people was iron. Although more difficult to extract than the other metals, its abundance and strength changed the face of civilization during the Iron Age. By 1100 BC, iron was in widespread use, creating vastly superior tools and weapons.

A BRONZE
statue of Hercules, from the second century AD. The green staining indicates the high copper content of bronze.

MODERN METALS

Modern technology has given rise to a range of new metals. Aluminum, a strong, lightweight metal that resists corrosion, is used widely for construction and packaging. Although abundant, its early discovery was impossible because of the vast amount of power required to refine it from its ore, bauxite.

Another important metal is titanium. Its light weight and high melting point make it ideal for use in rockets and planes, and it can be used as an alloy to improve the quality of other metals, particularly iron. Chromium, tungsten, and platinum are also important modern metals.

SOME METALS,
such as silver (left), are found in a pure form. Copper occurs naturally or is derived from the shiny compound "peacock ore" (top). Titanium is used in aircraft such as the Concorde (right).

METAL-BEARING ORES

The term "ore" refers to those minerals that form the raw product of a valued commodity. For example, the metal tin (Sn), is derived from the ore cassiterite (SnO_2). Ore deposits represent unusually high concentrations of raw minerals that are economically viable to extract and process. Most metals can be derived from a number of ore minerals, and are extracted by smelting in a carbon-burning furnace. The oxygen in the ores combines with the carbon to form carbon dioxide (CO_2), leaving behind the pure metal.

Colored staining on rocks can indicate ore deposits. Bright blue and green staining may indicate the presence of copper or nickel. Red, rusty-looking rocks indicate iron, while black staining reveals manganese. The metal ores tend to have a higher specific gravity than other minerals, and often show a metallic or sub-metallic luster.

Many of the minerals that make up the metal-bearing ores are spectacularly beautiful. Copper was first smelted from the attractive carbonates, azurite and malachite. Today, the principal ores of copper are chalcopyrite (a brassy yellow sulfide), bornite (called "peacock ore" because of its shiny purple tarnish), chalcocite and covellite.

Lead was first smelted from its carbonate ore cerrusite. It was used in the water pipes of Rome, and even for food and water vessels before its toxicity was understood. Now, the main ore of lead is the heavy, silver-grey mineral, galena.

Iron, our most important metal, is abundant and cheap.

GOLD FEVER

During the Middle Ages, alchemists were obsessed with the possibility of making gold from lead (right), its near neighbor on the Periodic Table. Despite elaborate efforts, all attempts were fruitless. Today, nuclear facilities can actually create the synthetic gold that so frustrated the alchemists. However, the cost of doing so is far greater than the current market value of gold.

In the face of fluctuating currencies, gold is accepted by all nations as a common and reliable medium of exchange and an important reserve asset.

NATIVE GOLD, *often found with quartz (right), was probably the first metal discovered. This golden torc (below) comes from pre-Roman Britain.*

People find gold in fields, veins, river beds and pockets. Whichever, it takes work to get it out.

ART LINKLETTER
b. 1912, North American
radio personality

and alloyed with copper to produce brass. Today, its primary ore is sphalerite, or "blackjack", usually found with ores of lead and copper.

Mercury, the only metal that exists as a liquid at room temperature, is extracted from the mineral cinnabar, although it is occasionally found in a native form as metallic drops. Used in pesticides and paints, mercury is highly toxic and persistent in the biosphere.

Hematite, the most common ore of iron, takes a mirror polish, making it a useful ornamental stone.

Silver occurs as ductile, twisted, branching masses of silvery native metal that tarnish to grey and black, or as the silver sulfide argentite.

Zinc was first smelted from its carbonate ore, smithsonite,

THE NON-METALLIC MINERALS

The non-metallic minerals have provided many of the basic needs of our society since its beginnings.

The world's most common minerals belong in this group and without them we would not have bricks, tiles, cement, plaster, ceramics, insulation, filters, fertilizers, and other chemicals. These minerals may contain some metallic elements but they are not used as a source of metals.

A number of non-metallic minerals are evaporites, meaning that their crystals develop during the evaporation of water in desert lakes. Examples of these include calcite, gypsum, halite, and the borate minerals. Beautiful crystals of these minerals may be picked up from dry lake beds. Evaporite crystals form very quickly and you can even grow your own.

The clay minerals, dull, soft, and generally unattractive, were probably the first to be used, and remain the basic materials for building, pottery, and ceramics. A clay brick from beneath the city of Jericho has been dated from between 8000 and 7000 BC, and clay bricks were also used in ancient Egypt, China, and in the Americas.

These early bricks were made by drying a mixture of clay and straw in the sun.

Calcite, the most common of the carbonate minerals, and gypsum, a soft evaporite mineral, were similarly important to the people of ancient Egypt and the Americas. It was discovered that if these minerals were crushed and mixed with water, they would harden into solid rock. This led to their widespread use in cement, plaster, and stucco. These carbonate minerals also make fine collection specimens. Gypsum often occurs as beautiful swallow-tail crystals or as massive alabaster which is equally interesting. Calcite, too, occurs as attractive crystals or massive non-crystalline forms, such as chalk.

In the days before refrigeration, the mineral halite, or common salt, was as valuable as gold itself.

The preservative qualities of salt were vital for the transport and storage of meats. Salt is an evaporite, forming in layers after the evaporation of salty water. Because of its low density, salt may rise, punching through overlying layers and forming huge pillars or domes. These can be mined in the traditional way, or dissolved by pumping water in and out through boreholes, to recover the salt. Apart from being a popular food additive, salt is

SPECTACULAR *non-metallic minerals include selenite (left) and chrysotile (above), an asbestos. This soapstone pipe (top left) was made about 800 years ago by Native Americans.*

SALT CRUST *On this Australian salt lake (left), a dead shrub has been blown upside down and encrusted with salt.*

Many other important non-metallic minerals make fine collection specimens. Barite, also known as "heavy spar" because of its high specific gravity, often occurs as large, transparent or whitish crystals. Another particularly attractive mineral, found in almost every color, is fluorite.

Talc, or "soapstone", is the softest of all minerals, with a hardness of 1. It has been used for carving since ancient times, but is now best known in the form of talcum powder.

The borate minerals are good examples of evaporites, and are found in desert salt pans. They include borax, the principal source of boron, and ulexite, also known as "television stone".

used in the manufacture of chlorine-based products and soda ash for glassmaking.

Another of the oldest known elements is sulfur, a soft, yellow, elemental mineral. When burnt, sulfur reacts readily with oxygen to produce the pungent gas sulfur dioxide, which reacts with water to produce sulfuric acid. Because of its association with active volcanoes, sulfur was known to the ancients as "brimstone" or "the fuel of Hell's fires". Most sulfur is converted to sulfuric acid and used in fertilizers. Its low melting point means that it can be mined from the surface by pumping superheated water underground through large pipes and drawing out the molten sulfur.

Graphite is an extremely soft (hardness 1.5) form of carbon. It is an invaluable industrial mineral because of its qualities as a lubricant, its resistance to corrosive chemicals, and its ability to conduct electricity. Graphite leaves a distinctive black streak and its name derives from the Greek word meaning "to write". The "lead" in pencils actually consists of a mixture

of graphite and clay, molded and baked at high temperatures.

Among the most infamous non-metallic minerals are those collectively known as asbestos. Fibrous in appearance, they include crocidolite, or blue asbestos, and chrysotile, a form of serpentine. Because their fibers don't burn or conduct electricity, they were used for fireproofing and insulation for many years, until the fibers were found to cause permanent lung damage when inhaled.

TELEVISION STONE *When ulexite (right) is polished, its crystals behave like optical fibers, transmitting images from one side to the other.*

GROW YOUR OWN SALT CRYSTAL

To grow your own salt crystals, stir salt into water in a small container, or glass, until no more will dissolve (using warm water will help). Simply allow this supersaturated solution to evaporate slowly and crystals will begin to form on the sides of the container. You may want to suspend a thread into the container, as the crystals will tend to grow on this.

To grow large crystals, continually remove the smallest crystals as they develop and re-dissolve them. This will ensure that your best crystals continue to grow.

SOURCES *of* ENERGY

Fossil fuels represent the warmth of the Sun locked within the Earth's crust. Uranium's energy stretches back to a time before the very formation of our Earth.

Alump of coal is compressed plant material from a prehistoric time, which may be burned today to release its stored energy. To appreciate the energy driving the technology around you, imagine a bright, sunny day millions of years ago. The scene is the edge of a swamp filled with strange-looking plants and insects. At that moment, a minuscule portion of the Sun's energy was captured and locked away to be released millions of years later, for the benefit of a species that had not yet evolved.

FOSSIL FUELS

Coal is classified as an organic sedimentary rock and is the fuel that fired the industrial revolution. As plants and trees are buried in an oxygen-starved environment and compressed, water and organic gases are driven off and the carbon content gradually increases. This process first produces peat, not considered true coal, containing about 80 percent moisture and gases. Further heating and compression produces a true coal, lignite (also known as brown coal). Continuing the process gives us bituminous, or black, coal. Yielding far more heat,

COAL FORMATION *(below, from left to right). In prehistoric times, dead vegetation was buried in a swamp, forming peat. As this was compressed and water driven off, higher grades of coal were formed. In the past, a "gusher" (top) was often the first sign of an oil strike.*

bituminous coal represents 90 percent of all coal mined. Its higher grades store well and burn with an almost smokeless flame. Anthracite is the highest-ranking form of coal, containing only about 5 percent water and gases.

Petroleum is made up of the microscopic remains of plants and animals buried in the fine muds of the sea floor. The fluidity of the petroleum depends on the length of the chains of hydrocarbon molecules. The shorter chains form the lighter fluids, kerosene, gasoline, and diesel, while the longer chains form the more viscous tars and asphalts. Petroleum migrates through porous formations, such as sandstone, and becomes trapped in reservoirs when it reaches impermeable layers such as shale or salt.

Natural gas is a mixture of the lightest hydrocarbons

peat

lignite

bituminous coal

anthracite

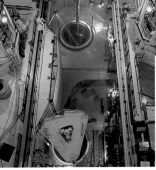

ENERGY NEEDS *Modern sources of energy include oil from North Sea oil rigs (above) and power generated by nuclear reactors (right). Large cities, such as New York (below right), consume enormous amounts of energy.*

found in the upper part of petroleum reservoirs. The pressure of natural gas in a reservoir formation is often enough to drive the oil and gas up the drill pipe, causing the famous "gushers" of old. These were dangerous and wasteful, and today's drillers pump high-density fluids (barite muds) into the hole to keep the gas pressure contained in the rock formation until the well is established.

Oil shales are organically rich, oil-bearing rocks that can be mined, then heated and processed, to yield petroleum and natural gas. At present, oil shales are not used, but they will soon become economically viable as liquid petroleum resources start to run out.

Uranium is an extremely heavy, unstable, naturally occurring metal, formed during the explosive evolution of stars. It breaks down to lighter, more simple

products over time, releasing enormous amounts of atomic energy. Controlled in a nuclear reactor, the heat given off by uranium can be used to drive conventional steam turbine generators. When the mass of uranium in one place exceeds a critical threshold, known as its "critical mass", all the available energy is released at once. This is the basis of the highly destructive atomic bomb. The principal source of uranium is the mineral uraninite or pitch-blende, a hard, black, heavy, radioactive ore.

ENERGY DEPENDENCE

These sources provide us with energy that we take for granted in our daily lives and it is virtually impossible to imagine living in the modern world without using any of the above-mentioned fuels. At present, however, we are burning up the Earth's fossil fuel resources at an

unsustainable rate. Unlike metals, which may be partially re-cycled, fossil fuels are nonrenewable. While coal reserves will probably last for another 300 years, some estimates suggest that known oil reserves will be exhausted within about 50 years.

The burning of fossil fuels also releases a great deal of carbon dioxide into the atmosphere, which has been linked to global warming, as well as sulfur dioxide and nitrogen oxides, which produce acid rain. Nuclear power, too, has dangers that we have yet to deal with satisfactorily.

To meet these challenges, we must develop means to reduce our consumption of energy. We must also continue to encourage and financially support research into alternative, renewable sources of energy, harnessing natural forces such as the Sun, wind, and tides.

GEMSTONES, ORNAMENTALS, *and* BUILDING STONES

The Earth is a treasure chest of rocks and minerals that are sought for their durability and intrinsic beauty. Some are prized for personal adornment while others are used for building.

The word "gemstone" refers to any rock, mineral, or organic substance suitable for personal adornment. This may be any uncommon, transparent, colorful, or unusually brilliant material. The first use of gemstones dates from prehistoric times when the wearing of personal adornments preceded even the wearing of clothes.

A gem's weight was once measured by comparing it to that of a carob seed. While these seeds have a relatively constant weight, a standard unit of measurement was eventually agreed upon. Known as a carat, it is equivalent to 0.006 ounces (0.2 g).

WHY ARE THEY PRECIOUS?

The three distinctive qualities that generally characterize gemstones are their beauty, durability, and rarity. Beauty is a gemstone's attractiveness to the beholder and is dependent on its optical properties. These are its color,

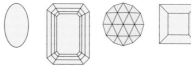

RAW GEMSTONES, *such as this tourmaline crystal in quartz (right), are often cut and polished to accentuate their natural qualities. Some popular cuts are (above, from left) cabochon, emerald cut, rose cut, and table cut.*

transparency, luster, sheen, refractive index, and dispersion (the ability to split white light up into its spectral colors).

Durability is a gemstone's ability to resist damage over time, an important property if it is being worn or handled. This is dependent on the hardness and tenacity of the material. The durability of certain gemstones has invested them with mystical significance and allowed them to pass from generation to generation.

Rarity is an essential quality of a precious stone and, may be more important in determining value than physical properties. Amber, opal, and pearl, for example, are very precious, but not particularly durable.

Of the 3,600 mineral species known to science, only about 100 possess all the attributes required in gems. Traditionally, diamond, ruby, sapphire, emerald, and opal are considered precious gemstones. Other well-known gems include topaz, aquamarine, spinel, garnet, and tourmaline.

Some stones are notable only for their striking colors or patterns, not being transparent, durable, or rare. Stones such as these are known as ornamentals, and examples include jasper, onyx, jade, malachite, rhodonite, and lapis lazuli. Organic gemstones are those formed as a result of living processes. These include amber (fossilized tree sap), coral, pearl, jet (coal), and shell.

TIMELESS BEAUTY *A lion pendant (top) made from amber more than 2,500 years ago. A selection of cut topaz stones (left). Stonehenge (right) was constructed about 4,000 years ago from sandstone blocks. Texture details of granite and gneiss (insets, far right).*

BUILDING BLOCKS *The ancient Mayan Temple of the Inscriptions (above), in Mexico, was made from limestone blocks. A marble quarry (right) near Tuscany, Italy.*

ROCKS FOR BUILDING

Many of the Earth's common rocks are cut for building stones and look spectacular when polished or carved. However, the fundamental building blocks of our society are calcite, the basis of cement, and the humble clay minerals, pressed into bricks and fired. Other building stones have been largely replaced by steel, reinforced concrete, and glass, and are now mainly used for finishing and decoration. They must be attractive and long wearing, with no iron minerals that will oxidize and rust with time.

Blocks of unfractured material are quarried with cable saws, cracked out with wedges, or broken free using small amounts of carefully placed explosives.

The enormous stones used in ancient structures, such as the pyramids of Egypt, or Stonehenge in England, had to be dug manually from quarries nearby because of the enormous difficulties involved in moving them.

Igneous rocks are often used as building stones because of their strength, ability to take a high polish, and resistance to weathering. These are generally known as granite (light-colored rocks, including true granites, porphyrys, and rhyolites), or black granite (all other darker-colored igneous rocks).

Metamorphic rocks, such as gneisses, are also favored for their attractive swirly, folded, or brecciated patterns. Slate, which splits easily into large, thin sheets, is used for roofing and floors. White, pink, black, or patterned marbles are particularly popular for carving.

Softer than granites and gneisses, they are easier to cut and work but less resistant to weathering and the corrosive effects of pollution. Some well-known structures, such as the Taj Mahal in India, are made of marble.

Sedimentary rocks, such as sandstones, are often attractive, with delicate patterning. Sandstone is favored because its bedding makes it easy to quarry and stonemasons have few problems working it. Its only drawback is that porous varieties are less durable. Limestones, particularly those containing fossil corals, shells, and other marine organisms, are most attractive and interesting when cut and polished. The pyramids and statues of the great civilizations of Egypt and Mexico were constructed from limestone blocks.

The book of Nature is the book of Fate. She turns the gigantic pages—leaf after leaf—never re-turning one.

The Conduct of Life,
RALPH WALDO EMERSON (1803–82), American essayist and philosopher

CHAPTER FOUR

THE LIFE FORCES

THE TREE *of* LIFE

To visualize the evolution of life forms through time, picture the spreading branches of a tree.

There is a complete unity to life. All the animals, plants, fungi, bacteria, and viruses that have lived on Earth are related by descent. Throughout the past 3.6 billion years, life has been growing, dividing, and developing to produce the myriad forms we see around us today. We can call this concept the Tree of Life. This four-dimensional tree grows through the three dimensions of space, and also through the fourth dimension of time.

The diagram on the facing page shows part of the tree extending only through the past 600 million years—life began a long time before this. The oldest life forms are at the bottom of the tree and time progresses toward the present at the top.

Only some of the major branches are shown.

By carefully studying fossils, we can trace back along the branches of the tree, find out when different branches divided, determine how the tree is structured, and also establish how organisms are related.

THE HISTORY OF LIFE

As far as we can determine, life first appeared on Earth about 3,500 million years ago and it started only once.

TWO BEETLES, *one living (top) and the other a 50-million-year-old fossil. Both show striking iridescent blue coloring, illustrating the continuity of life through time.*

While the exact mechanism by which the first life form came into existence is still unclear, once it had appeared, the processes of evolution began acting on it, resulting in a changing and complex diversity of plants and animals.

For most of its history, life has been very simple. For the

STROMATOLITE FOSSIL SECTION
(above) and living stromatolites (right) at Shark Bay in Western Australia. Their structure has remained basically the same since the early Precambrian.

THE TREE OF LIFE

Each line on the diagram (right) represents a group of organisms and shows its distribution through time and its relationship to other groups of organisms. Plants, animals, and even fungi and bacteria (not shown here), are truly our siblings. The geological periods are shown on the left and proceed from the oldest at the bottom to the present at the top. Their abbreviations are as follows:

T   Tertiary
K   Cretaceous
J   Jurassic
Tr Triassic
P   Permian
C   Carboniferous
D   Devonian
S   Silurian
O   Ordovician
Є   Cambrian
PЄ Precambrian

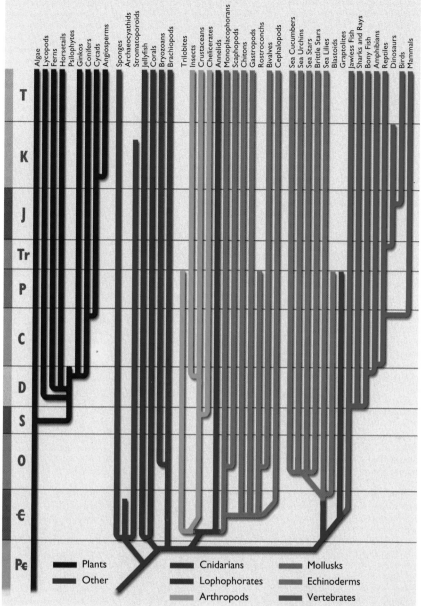

first 3,000 million years, it was no more complex than single-cell organisms that sometimes built colonies called stromatolites. About 600 million years ago, complex life forms evolved with multi-cellular organisms, similar to jellyfish, flourishing. The next important step, about 570 million years ago, was the development of animals with shells or hard skeletons.

Life spent most of its time (the first 3,000 million years or so) in the sea, and only comparatively recently, in geological terms, have life forms ventured onto land.

The first land plants occurred 410 million years ago; the first insects crawled on land 360 million years ago; and the earliest terrestrial vertebrates appeared some 20 million years later.

OLD SURVIVORS, BRIEF APPEARANCES

Even though life is always changing, some life forms have remained relatively unaltered for long periods. Such groups are commonly known as "living" fossils. Stromatolites in Shark Bay, Western Australia, are almost identical to those that lived thousands of millions of years ago. The small brachiopod *Lingula* has remained unchanged since its appearance 550 million years ago.

Most forms of life, however, appear and disappear relatively quickly. For example, the smallest dinosaur, *Compsognathus*, just 16 inches (40 cm) long, is known from a single specimen (above) found at Solnhofen, Germany. This is the only representative of a species that probably existed for a million years and whose total number would have been counted in the hundreds of thousands.

HISTORY *of* EVOLUTION

Fossils show that life has a complicated history and that organisms have become increasingly more complex.

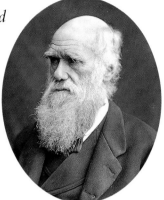

Throughout the vast expanse of time life has existed, it has altered in response to environmental pressures. The changing of life through time is known as evolution.

There are many unscientific explanations for the origins of life, generally based on the existence of a divine creator, or many creators. The first suggestions that life forms were related by descent occur in early Greek texts. The ancient Greeks noted certain physical similarities among organisms and assumed that these resulted from their relationship to one another,

CREATION THEORIES, *such as the story of Adam and Eve (below), were essentially unchallenged until the nineteenth century. French naturalist Georges Cuvier (right).*

but they were unable to explain the relationship.

Little advance was made in understanding the relationships of organisms until the mid eighteenth century, when Swedish naturalist Carl Linnaeus (1707–78) published his *Systema Naturae*, in which he set out a method of classifying plants and animals that is still in use. The Linnaean system places every species within a group, known as a genus, of similar plants or animals. Genera (the plural of genus) are placed, in turn, in larger groupings based on the

Heaven knows what seeming nonsense may not tomorrow be demonstrated truth.

Science and the Modern World,
ALFRED NORTH WHITEHEAD
(1861–1947), English philosopher
and mathematician

sharing of similar structures by their members. Linnaeus considered the order that he found in nature to be God's "ladder of creation", rather than being the result of an evolutionary history.

Advances in geology in the late eighteenth and early nineteenth centuries revealed that the Earth was a great deal older than had previously been believed. The study of fossils also revealed a number of perplexing facts. Modern organisms had not been around since the beginning of the fossil record and most organisms that had lived in the past were not alive in the present. Most types of organism appeared at some point in the fossil record, persisted for a period of time, then disappeared. New organisms appeared throughout Earth's history rather than being concentrated in a single appearance at the beginning, as would have been expected from a divine act of creation. Organisms also disappeared throughout time, although there seem to have been at least seven instances in the fossil record when huge numbers of organisms disappeared at the same time.

NATURAL SELECTION, *expounded by Charles Darwin (far left) in 1859 in* The Origin of Species *(left), is still regarded as the basic, most widespread mechanism by which evolution occurs. Variations evolve (below left) among closely related species, such as finches.*

By the mid nineteenth century, the accumulating evidence of biology (the similarity of organisms) and paleontology (the complex history of life) was directing the minds of intellectuals toward the concept of evolution. Erasmus Darwin (1731–1802), grandfather of Charles, wrote about the possibility of organisms being related by ancestry. French naturalists Etienne Geoffroy Saint-Hilaire (1772–1844) and Georges Cuvier (1769–1832) studied and documented similar structures in different organisms and Geoffroy believed these similarities were the result of an evolutionary

history. Despite such support, evolutionary theories were not generally accepted because no one had yet proposed a viable mechanism by which they could operate.

NATURAL SELECTION
Jean-Baptiste de Monet Lamarck (1744–1829) was the first biologist to propose such a mechanism: he suggested that organisms changed during their lifetimes to meet particular pressures or demands and that these changes could be passed on to their offspring. He suggested that the accumulation of such minor changes through many generations would lead to new species being formed, but his theory was widely discounted.

It was not until the work of the English biologists Charles Darwin (1809–82)

and Alfred Russel Wallace that a viable mechanism for evolution was proposed. Working independently, both Darwin and Wallace came up with the theory of natural selection. The theory drew on extensive scientific evidence relating to competition for resources among organisms, with their success or survival being dependent on their varied forms and the transmission of favorable traits from one generation to the next.

With the acceptance of natural selection as a valid scientific theory, evolution became the core concept of modern biology. The theory has since been supplemented by the science of genetics.

ALFRED RUSSEL WALLACE

While Darwin is most often cited as the originator of the theory of natural selection, the role of Alfred Russel Wallace (1823–1913) in the development of this theory should not be overlooked. Like Darwin, Wallace had spent long periods in Asia and South America collecting specimens, and his familiarity with nature led him to similar conclusions. Ironically, Wallace sent his manuscript describing natural selection to Darwin for comment. Darwin, who had been working in secret, was startled at the similarity of their ideas. The theory was eventually proposed under their joint authorship at a meeting of the Linnaean Society with neither present.

PROCESSES *of* EVOLUTION

*Millions of species of plants and animals, all with a common ancestry,
have evolved on Earth through many processes.*

Although it is widely accepted that evolution has taken place, the mechanism by which it operates is much less certain. Evidence of evolution comes in many forms. Related species of animals or plants can be shown to have the same or similar structure.

EVOLUTION: THE FACT

Deoxyribonucleic acid (DNA) is the fundamental chemical in life. It is a complex molecule found in every living being and is the "blueprint" or code that tells an organism how to build itself. DNA is inherited from the parents so there is great similarity between the structure of the DNA of parents and their offspring. Over a greater distance of relationship, those organisms that are closely related will have a greater similarity in their DNA than those whose relationship is more distant. By comparing the degree of similarity, we can determine how closely two organisms are related. In this way, it is possible to map the history of relationships among organisms.

FEATHERED DINOSAUR? *As much a dinosaur as a bird, Archaeopteryx (right), with its modern-looking feathers, provided a convincing link between the two groups and confirmed evolutionary theory. The molecule DNA (above) controls the form of all organisms.*

Fossils provide evidence in support of evolution by tracking the progress of life forms as they change through time. The classic example comes from Jurassic rocks of southern Germany.

When Darwin published *The Origin of Species*, he noted that one problem with the theory of evolution was the apparent lack of transitional forms in the fossil record. In 1861, miners near Solnhofen in southern Germany unearthed the first specimen of *Archaeopteryx*.

This specimen would have been described as a small dinosaur because of its dinosaur-like skeleton, except that the fossil clearly had impressions of feathers covering its body. Here was a link between birds and dinosaurs, two groups that had previously been thought to be separate.

The similarity of body parts (homology), the similarity of DNA sequences, and the changes in the fossil record make sense only in an evolutionary perspective.

MECHANISMS OF EVOLUTION

The most convincing mechanism for evolutionary change is natural selection, as proposed by Darwin and Wallace.

THE SCORPION *(left), like other organisms, produces more offspring than can possibly survive to adulthood. Offspring, such as the penguins below, show individual variation, even within the same family.*

ARMS FOR EVOLUTION

The front leg of a crocodile, the wing of a bat, the flipper of a whale, and the wing of a bird superficially look quite different from each other. On closer examination, however, these differences begin to disappear. For example, the arrangement of bones in the front limbs of these four animals is identical, even if the shape of those bones varies greatly. This common arrangement of bones, which extends also to humans, indicates that these limbs have all evolved from the same basic plan.

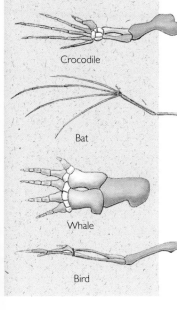

Crocodile

Bat

Whale

Bird

The theory results from three basic observations. First, each generation produces far more offspring than can possibly survive to adulthood and this leads to competition for resources. Second, all individuals vary in form, even siblings within a family showing slight differences. By chance, some variations within a population will be better suited to the prevailing environment and have a better chance of surviving to adulthood. Last, favorable traits of parents are passed on to their young.

The struggle among individuals for survival, the selection of the most fit individuals, and the passing on of favorable traits from one generation to the next allows a species to change through time to adapt to changing environmental pressures. Additional mechanisms have been proposed, but natural selection appears to be the most common means by which evolution proceeds.

THE TEMPO OF EVOLUTION

Darwinian evolution was thought to have been a gradual process that affected an entire species. By this model, called gradualism, one whole species was thought to evolve gradually into a new

one. This view went largely unchallenged until the 1970s when Harvard professor Stephen Jay Gould and fellow paleontologist Niles Eldredge proposed that evolution had progressed in short bursts followed by long periods of little or no change, a model called punctuated equilibrium.

Debate between the two camps raged throughout most of the late 1970s and early 1980s. Gradualism found particularly strong support from genetics and biochemistry. Punctuated equilibrium was best supported by the fossil record, where new species appear "suddenly", and persist for a time without change before going extinct. This pattern, which fits the punctuated equilibrium tempo of evolution, is the result of a new species evolving in small populations in isolation from its ancestors. It is now generally accepted that evolution has proceeded in both of these ways.

91

FORMATION *of* FOSSILS

*Preserved in a variety of ways, the remains of plants and animals
that lived millions of years ago reveal the secrets of life on Earth.*

There is no precise definition of a fossil. Generally, fossils are the remains of animals or plants, usually turned to stone, but this is not always the case. Mammoths frozen solid or insects trapped in amber are also considered to be fossils, even though their original composition has not been altered. While fossils are usually the remains of extinct prehistoric animals or plants, there are also fossil specimens of many animal and plant species that still survive. Pollen, excrement, tracks, eggs, and even the cast-off shells of living animals can also be fossilized.

The vast majority of fossils are impressions of a once-living organism preserved in stone. While there are a number of processes that will convert a living organism to a fossil, they generally conform

TRAPPED IN MUD, *the dragonfly (below) may eventually become fossilized like the beautiful specimen shown at left with a modern relative. Shells, such as this gastropod (far left), fossilize readily.*

to a set series of events. Initially, after the animal or plant dies, the soft parts (guts, muscles, leaves, and so on) rot away, leaving the hard parts (bones, teeth, or wood).

There are exceptional situations where the soft parts are also fossilized, but these are rare. Soon after the organism has been reduced to its hard parts, it is buried by sediment—usually in association with water—in soft mud on the bottom of a lake, or in silt dropped by a flooding river. Once buried, the remains are impregnated with water carrying dissolved minerals that slowly replace the original organic material, turning the remains to stone.

After a fossil has been formed, one more essential process must occur before it can be found: the rocks that entomb the fossil must be uplifted and eroded back to reveal the fossil's location.

"INSTANT" FOSSILS

A relatively common fossil found on many parts of the coast of northern Australia, *Thalassina* is a crustacean, a kind of lobster, that lives in burrows on tidal mudflats. Like all other crustaceans, it has to cast off its shell in order to grow. Throughout its life, a single *Thalassina* may produce a dozen or more shells. Each time it molts, the shell is buried at the bottom of the burrow and a new living chamber is excavated. Buried in mud, the cast-off shell can be fossilized in a very short time, perhaps less than a year. Some of these fossils are so young that the animals that shed them may still be alive.

The chess-board is the world; the pieces are the phenomena of the universe; the rules of the game are what we call the laws of nature.

A Liberal Education,
THOMAS HENRY HUXLEY
(1825–95), English biologist and writer

WHERE FOSSILS OCCUR

The distribution of living organisms is governed by many factors: whales are found in the open sea, dogs live on land, and some apes inhabit forests. After the death of an organism, its carcass is rarely transported very far, so if the remains are fossilized, these will usually be found where the organism died, most often where it lived.

The location of fossil sites is determined by three factors:

FOSSILIZATION *sometimes happens on a grand scale, such as occurred at Dinosaur National Monument, Utah, USA.*

the environment where the organism lived, the rock type in which it is preserved, and the current exposure of that rock. Only rocks of certain types are suitable for preserving fossils. Volcanic rocks or rocks formed deep within the crust of the Earth will not contain fossils. Similarly, rocks with a very coarse structure, such as conglomerates, will usually destroy the remains of any organisms before they can be fossilized. The best types of rock for preserving fossils are limestones or such fine-grained sedimentary rocks as shales and mudstones.

Regardless of the fossil-iferous nature of a rock unit, the fossils can be impossible to collect if the unit is not exposed. Mountainous areas where rocks have recently been uplifted and eroded back are good places to look. Some human-made rock exposures, such as quarries or road cut-tings, can be prime sites for collecting. But the forces of weathering and erosion that expose fossils will also, even-tually, destroy them.

HOW A FOSSIL FORMS *In stage one, the soft tissues of the animal are broken down, leaving only hard parts such as teeth and bones.*

OVER A LONG PERIOD, *the bones become buried under layers of sediment, and the original bones are replaced by minerals from groundwater.*

WITH THE SLOW MOVEMENTS *of the surrounding terrain, the rock holding the fossil is uplifted and gradu-ally makes its way to the surface.*

ONCE BACK NEAR THE SURFACE, *the fossil may be eroded out of its rocky tomb, or released by a fossil hunter, to disclose its information from the past.*

93

VARIETIES *of* FOSSIL

The range of fossil forms is astonishing,

not only in the diversity of organisms represented,

but also in the numerous types of preservation.

Most fossils are impressions of the original organism preserved in rock. The same effect can be created by taking a leaf, lightly pressing it into wet cement, and removing it. When the cement has dried, a "fossil" of the leaf remains.

In nature, the cavity left behind after the organism has rotted inside its rock tomb is often all that is recovered as a fossil. On rare occasions, the organic compounds from the organism decay to a carbon film that is left inside the natural mold. Sometimes the cavity, or mold, is filled with minerals deposited by water seeping through the rock.

In other cases, minerals are deposited from the water while the original organic matter is decaying, which results in petrification, or cell-by-cell replacement of the organic matter by minerals. In some cases, the resulting cast may be harder than the surrounding rock and the fossil will erode out of the rock and be found loose on the Earth's surface. Usually, replacement minerals are common elements from the surrounding environment,

PEARLY LUSTER *This Jurassic ammonite has its original mother-of-pearl coating, like that of modern oyster shells.*

but sometimes more exotic minerals form fossils. For example, in Australia, fossils are sometimes formed from opal.

OTHER FORMS OF PRESERVATION

There are numerous other types of preservation. Since the movie *Jurassic Park*, amber fossils have become very well known. Amber is a semi-precious mineraloid formed

FORMS OF PRESERVATION
Fern fronds (above) have been turned into a carbon film on a rock surface, while a tree trunk (above left) has been replaced by opal.

from the sap of ancient trees. In rare cases, as the sap oozed out of the tree, a spider, insect, or other small animal would become entombed in the sticky goo. When the sap hardened, the creature was perfectly preserved in exquisite detail.

Some fossils retain their original organic composition. The most common of these are calcareous shells, where the calcium carbonate shell of the living animal forms the fossil shell, but often

with some reorganiz-
ation of the individual
molecules. In some
cases, the mother-of-
pearl luster of the living
animal is preserved on
the fossil. Bone, too,
can retain parts of its
original composition,
but because the more
volatile fatty compounds
quickly degenerate after
the death of the animal,
any bony remains pre-
served this way are
usually chalky, brittle,
and crumbly.

Another exceptional
form of preservation
occurs when bodies are
buried in peat bogs. The
high acidity of peat pre-
vents bacteria and other
decay-causing organisms
from attacking the carcass and
the organism is preserved in a
process similar to that used to
tan leather. In such unusual
circumstances, the soft tissue,
bones, teeth, and even
the stomach contents may
be preserved.

The ultimate preser-
vation of ancient life is
when bodies have been
frozen solid, although it
is debatable if these can
be classed as fossils—
they are usually termed
sub fossils. Frozen
fossils" of mam-
moths, woolly
rhinoceroses, and
even people have
been found high on
mountains, or in the
permanently frozen parts of
northern Europe and Asia.
Some specimens preserved in

this way may be up to a
million years old but there is
no replacement of the original
organic material and the
specimen has not left an
impression in rock.

Usually, only the hard parts
of an organism, such as shell,
bones, or teeth, will
be fossilized.
In some rare
sites, how-
ever, be-
cause of a

PAST AND PRESENT
*Although preserved only as a
two-dimensional impression,
this fossil seedpod is clearly
similar to its modern relative.*

variety of factors, soft
tissue may be preserved
as well. These sites are
so important to our
understanding of the
evolutionary history of
various groups that they
have a special name,
Lagerstätten, from the
German word for
"mother lode".

Although fossils
show how life has
changed through time,
the record is imperfect
—99 percent of all the
different life forms that have
ever existed have left no
fossils of themselves. Of the
life forms that have produced
fossils, many are known from
a single example and most of
the rest are represented by
only a handful of specimens.
Clearly, this is an inadequate
record, but it is the only one
we have. While many details
of the story of life will never
be revealed, we can at least
deduce the major themes.

BONES AND INSECTS *A section
of dinosaur bone (above) has been
petrified and replaced with agate, while
a tiny mosquito (right) has been
preserved in perfect detail in amber.*

FOSSILS *in* LIFE

The only record we have of most of the animals

and plants that have ever lived on Earth is from their fossils.

Paleontologists have developed sophisticated and complicated techniques to decode the fossil record and learn something of how animals and plants lived in the ancient world. Usually, it is only the hard parts of an animal or plant that become fossilized. Particularly in the case of vertebrate animals, only parts of a skeleton may be found, but a small part of a skeleton is often enough to make a reconstruction of the whole animal.

From shells or a few fossilized teeth or bone fragments, the paleontologist first identifies the type of animal. This is usually straightforward because different types of animal each have certain types of shells, teeth or bones. Remains of a species will resemble those of close relatives so even when a new type of animal is discovered, it can often be recognized by its similarity to other species.

Once the fossil fragments have been identified, the complete skeleton can be reconstructed by filling in the missing portions, using the structure of its closest relatives

❶

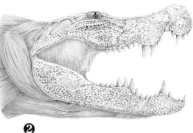

❷

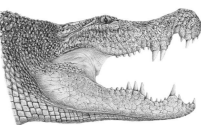

❸

as a guide. Imagine that you were trying to reconstruct a previously unknown '57 Ford from only the bumpers and a small piece of bodywork. Your approximation would be more accurate if you based your reconstruction on '56 and '58 Fords rather than on a '57 Chev or, even worse, on a '91 Toyota.

From a complete skeleton, a paleontologist can reconstruct the size, shape, and posture of the animal. Muscles are

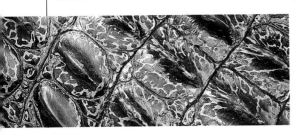

ASSEMBLING THE EVIDENCE

Reconstructing an animal from an original fossil ❶ *involves completing the bones and musculature* ❷*, then covering with appropriate skin* ❸*. Each of these steps is aided by comparison with details from living relatives, such as the crocodile skin (below left).*

located in similar positions in most vertebrates, and by looking for sites of muscle attachment on the bones, the paleontologist can reconstruct the musculature that gave the animal its form.

The last step is the addition of skin and color. Skin is rarely fossilized, so the paleontologist makes an educated guess as to what kind of skin an extinct animal might have had by looking at that of close relatives. Similarly, the color of extinct animals is seldom preserved, so this also has to be an educated guess. While the skin, fur, feathers, scales, or color may be the most noticeable aspects of a reconstructed animal, they are of minor significance compared with its size and shape. These aspects can be deduced fairly accurately from fossils.

EDUCATED GUESSWORK

A reconstruction of an extinct animal is only a model of what it might have been like. We can never be really sure, but a good reconstruction will present what we do know about the animal. Knowledge of extinct animals and plants changes with each new find

FROM A FRAGMENT

such as this shark tooth, a whole animal can be reconstructed. Many fossil sharks are known only from their teeth.

and subsequent reconstructions reflect this. For example, the first finds of the dinosaur *Iguanodon* were a few bones, teeth, and a mysterious spike. The teeth indicated that this animal was similar to the modern iguana but much bigger, so *Iguanodon* was reconstructed as a gigantic iguana with the spike on its nose.

When complete skeletons were found, it was clear that this animal could move on all four legs but probably spent a large amount of time standing on its hind legs and tail like a kangaroo. They also showed that the spike was not on the nose, but on the thumb. So *Iguanodon* was reconstructed in a pose similar to that of a giant kangaroo with spiked thumbs. We now know from

more detailed studies that *Iguanodon* did not rest on its tail, but carried it straight out behind. It is also thought that the animal probably spent most of its time on all four legs, but could run on its back legs when necessary.

Fossils tell us more than what an extinct organism looked like. Analysis of teeth, claws, and even the contents of the gut (which are sometimes fossilized) can tell us what the animal ate. The association of different fossils in a single deposit allows us to reconstruct their environment and their positions in food chains. Fossil trackways (a series of footprints) can tell

The universe is not only queerer than we imagine, it's queerer than we can imagine.

Possible Worlds,
J.B.S. HALDANE (1892–1964),
British geneticist

us a great deal about how animals moved. A series of fossils representing different growth stages of an animal reveals much about the development of individual members of that type of organism. In many cases, a relatively complete picture of an ancient ecosystem can be reconstructed from the fossils left behind.

RESTORATION OF THE IGUANODON.

CHANGING UNDERSTANDING

Reconstructions of extinct animals are modified with each new find. Early models of Iguanodon (above) pictured it as a giant lizard with a nose spike. Later illustrations (above left) improved Iguanodon's posture and moved the spike from its nose to its thumb. Even the most recent interpretation (left) may be modified after future finds.

97

IDENTIFYING *and* CLASSIFYING FOSSILS

Being the remains of living organisms, fossils are placed into groups in the same way that living organisms are classified.

All cultures have systems for naming familiar plants and animals, but these common names vary among cultures and geographic areas. The biological sciences require a naming system that is universal and consistent, so all living organisms that have been described scientifically have been given a two-part name, or binomial. The first part is the genus to which the organism belongs and the second is the species. This is like the Western system of people having a given and a family name, but in biology the order is switched so that we first find out to which group the animal belongs and then the species name.

In addition, all plants and animals are classified according to kingdom, phylum, class, order, and family. This system is the legacy of Carl Linnaeus. The concept was later expanded to include all known living organisms.

Like their living counterparts, fossils are identified as species, the smallest group in classification. Species are grouped in genera (the plural of genus), which are grouped in families; families are grouped in orders, classes, phyla (the plural of phylum), and kingdoms. For example, *Tyrannosaurus rex* is classified:

Kingdom	Animalia (animals)
Phylum	Chordata (animals with a dorsal nerve cord)
Class	Archosauria (dinosaurs)
Order	Saurischia (lizard-hipped dinosaurs)
Family	Tyrannosauridae (large, carnivorous dinosaurs with small arms)
Genus	*Tyrannosaurus*
Species	*T. rex*

TRACE FOSSILS *such as these 400-million-year-old eurypterid tracks (above) are given different names to the animals that made them. Beetles (above left) exhibit a huge range of diversity, making identification a challenging task.*

Because binomials are derived from Latin, Greek, or other languages, the convention is for them to be written in italics or to be underlined. The genus always starts with a capital letter but the species never does. Another convention is that a generic name can appear by itself (for example, *Tyrannosaurus*) but a species name must always be accompanied by the genus name (*Tyrannosaurus rex*).

LIVING ORGANISMS, *such as the Nautilus (left), and fossil organisms, such as the ammonite (below), are named using the same classification system.*

morphologically similar to each other but different from all other fossil groups.

CONFUSING THE ISSUE

The species concept presents paleontology with another set of problems. Juveniles can look quite different from adults, and eggs and trackways bear no resemblance to either. It can thus be very difficult to relate juveniles, adults, eggs, and trackways to the one species. In cases where juveniles and adults of the same species have been accidentally named as different species, there is a comprehensive set of rules that allows us to determine which name is correct. A well-known case of juvenile–adult confusion is where the dinosaur *Brontosaurus* (an adult) and *Apatosaurus* (a juvenile) were described as different species. When the mistake was realized, it was determined that *Apatosaurus,* the name given first, had priority.

Identifying trace fossils, such as eggs and trackways, is more difficult, so a different naming system has been devised for them. They are given a binomial, genus and species, but because we can rarely associate a trace fossil, or ichnite, with its maker, it is classified an ichnotaxa with ichnogenus and species. For example, large, three-toed footprints with sharp claws were almost certainly made by carnivorous dinosaurs, but they are given the name *Anchisauripus* rather than *Tyrannosaurus* or *Allosaurus.* Consequently, it is quite possible for an extinct animal to have been given four names: one for the juvenile, one for the adult, one for its footprints, and one for the type of eggs it lays. Without evidence to link them, we may never discover that these four names belong to fossils of the same animal.

After the generic name has been used in full once, it can then be abbreviated to the first letter in all subsequent references to species of the same genus (*T. rex*).

A species is defined as a group that can reproduce with other members of that group but not reproduce with members of other groups. This is the principle of reproductive isolation. Experiments on the reproductive isolation of fossils are impossible, so another method of defining fossil species is required.

In paleontology, species are identified by their shape (or morphology) so a species of fossil is a group of fossils

TYRANNOSAURUS REX *is probably the most widely known binomial. It means "tyrant-lizard-king".*

99

TRACKS, TRACES,
and MICROFOSSILS

While the fossil of an organism tells us much about the creature

it once was, trace fossils help establish its patterns of behavior.

In broad terms, fossils fall into two groups: body fossils (the remains of the organism itself), and trace fossils (signs and remains of an animal's activities, such as footprints, trackways, bite marks, feeding and dwelling burrows, nests, eggs, droppings, and stomach stones). Because conditions for preservation differ, the two types are rarely found in the same localities. Since we can seldom identify which animal made which trace fossil, the names of trace fossils differ from those of their makers.

TRACKS AND TRACES

Fossil footprints can tell us the animal's weight, and a trackway can suggest how fast it moved. Usually, the normal walking speed is indicated, because comparatively little of an animal's time is spent running. Trackways can also reveal if the animal lived alone, in small groups, or in large herds. Sometimes, we may even glimpse how those groups behaved. In Lark Quarry, near Winton, central Queensland, Australia, there is a trackway of more than 190 small dinosaurs stampeding at the approach of a single, large carnivorous dinosaur. This is a moment preserved from life 98 million years ago. Such sites are fossilized in what were sandflat or floodplain deposits

beside rivers and lakes. Other important places for dinosaur tracks include Glen Rose, Texas, and the Connecticut Valley, USA.

Trace fossil include the feeding burrows of invertebrate animals, each species of organism making a distinct type of feeding track. The burrows of underground dwellers may also be preserved. Some sediments become very mixed up by the actions of animals feeding and burrowing through them

and are termed "bioturbated" (literally, "mixed-by-life").

Sometimes, the eggs of an animal are fossilized in the nest. Although rare, such sites can tell us much about the reproductive and parental behavior of the animal. From a dinosaur hatchery in Montana, USA, we can say that at least one kind of dinosaur nested in enormous rookeries, that the young remained in the nests for a considerable time, and that the parents brought them food and warded off predators.

Fossilized animal droppings, or coprolites, tell us about the diet of an animal and something of its digestive system.

TRACE FOSSILS *Tubular structures (left) in a matrix of fibrous dolomite, are thought to be worm burrows. "Worm tracks" and wave marks (below) on a shallow bottom, in Lower Cambrian sandstone. The radiolarian (top left), highly magnified to show its intricate form, is one of many types of microfossil.*

FOOTPRINTS OF GIANTS

There are many sites worldwide where the fossilized footprints of dinosaurs and other animals are preserved. Among the first areas in North America found to have footprints were the brownstone quarries of New England. Much of the early work on footprints was

conducted by Edward Hitchcock (1793–1864), of Amherst College, Massachusetts, who thought the footprints were those of giant birds.

A more prolific site is the area around Glen Rose, Texas. Here, footprints, including many extensive trackways, were known only to local residents until a visit to the area in 1938 by Roland T. Bird (1899–1978).

Bird found a trackway in which a meat-eating dinosaur appears to be stalking a long-necked dinosaur. This significant find is now on display in the American Museum of Natural History, New York.

A RARE FIND, *dinosaur eggs (above), fossilized in the nest, have been discovered on several continents. These small stones (below), preserved alongside the bones of a giant bird, were once held in the bird's crop.*

A number of animals ingest stones to help with digestion or for ballast in water. These stones, which become smooth and rounded inside the animal's gut, are called gastroliths or stomach stones. Gastroliths are sometimes found in the body cavity of the fossil or alone in sediments where they were regurgitated after use.

Teeth marks of a predator or scavenger are sometimes seen on the fossilized bones of an animal and indicate which predators were eating them. In some cases, it's the teeth marks not of another species but of a member of the same species, possibly the result of a clash over a mate or territory.

MICROFOSSILS

Most people think of fossils as being visible to the naked eye, but the most abundant and useful types of fossil are too small to be seen without a powerful lens or microscope.

The variety of microfossils representing the plant and animal kingdoms is vast.

A number of different types of microscopic, single-cell organisms have hard shells that can become fossilized. Typical among these are dinoflagellates, radiolarians, and diatoms. Dinoflagellates have both "animal" and "plant" characteristics and leave fossils of a "shell" or cyst, typically between 20 and 150 thousandths of a millimeter long.

Radiolarians are larger, at between 100 and 2000 thousandths of a millimeter. Diatoms are single-cell algae that produce a "shell" of silica. These "shells" can be so abundant that they form the whole rock, called diatomite. Diatomite is composed of compacted diatom shells, regular in size

and shape. This makes it commercially useful for filtration in brewing and other industries.

Because a single tree can produce billions of grains of pollen and these can be scattered over a wide area, pollen grains are the most likely tree parts to survive as fossils. Plant spores and pollen can both be fossilized—they are very useful for reconstructing ancient climates and floras.

Parts of animals, such as the bony scales of some fish, are also classed as microfossils. Other types of microfossil, including conodonts, foraminifera, and coccolithophores, appear in the fossil field guide.

PLANT FOSSILS

*When plants emerged from the water and spread onto land
about 410 million years ago, they had many problems to overcome.*

Plants have a long history —algae are known from Precambrian rocks. However, until about 410 million years ago, plants were represented only by algae found in aquatic environments. Because of their fragility, algae are largely inconspicuous in the fossil record, except where they formed stacked algal mats called stromatolites, or where they produced calcareous skeletons similar to corals. Stromatolites are the most abundant macrofossils of the Precambrian, and various calcareous algae are reasonably common in Ordovician and Silurian deposits.

To survive on land, plants had to stand without the support of water surrounding them. They evolved in two ways: by developing a vascular system that transported water and nutrients around their tissues and also acted as a pressurized skeleton; and by developing woody stiffening compounds. Because these woody fibers were generally harder than other plant material, plants that developed them were much more likely to be fossilized.

The earliest land plants, Psilophyta, were little more than creeping root systems with vertical shoots and no

PLANTS *(dark green on diagram) diversified rapidly after they spread onto land in the Silurian. The dominant plants of today are the angiosperms, flowering plants, which first appeared in the Cretaceous.*

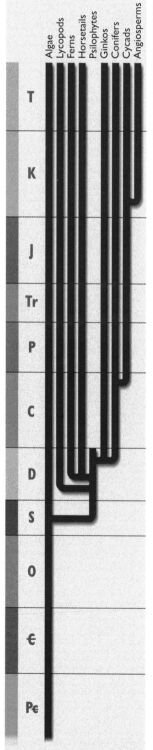

FOSSILIZED CONES *(top left) from the monkey puzzle tree—the one on the right has been sectioned and polished. The delicate form of a leaf (above) that grew in the Eocene.*

evidence of leaves. Ferns, Pterophyta, appeared in the Devonian. Their close relatives, the seed ferns (Pteridospermophyta), and lycopods, a group of tree-like plants, grew in such abundance by the Carboniferous that the earliest coal deposits were formed from their remains. Seed ferns are now extinct but modern ferns are familiar to us all. Despite their early success, lycopods are represented today by only three genera.

Cycads, a group of palm-like plants, became relatively common in the Mesozoic era, but today are represented by only a few species growing in tropical to warm temperate regions. Conifers, the group that includes fir and pine trees, dominated most of the Mesozoic and, together with the cycads, probably formed the bulk of the diet of plant-eating dinosaurs.

The plant world today is dominated by angiosperms, the

flowering plants, which include all grasses, and most trees, palms, and shrubs. Angiosperms appeared early in the Cretaceous, but did not become common until toward the end of that period.

Plant parts (leaves, seeds, roots, trunks, and so on) may be found as separate fossils and identified as different organisms. Until the various parts are found in association, this confusion cannot be addressed. For example, a single lycopod had one name for its trunk fossils (*Lepidodendron*), another for fossils of its roots (*Stigmaria*), a third for those of its leaves (*Lepidophyllum*), and a fourth for its cones (*Lepidostrobus*). *Lepidodendron*, the first name given, is now assigned to all parts.

Plant fossils are usually found in rocks where the environment was slightly acidic. Mudstones and shales, particularly where they are associated with coal deposits, are good locations for finding fossils of plant parts. In these fine-grained rocks, flat objects such as leaves have been laid down and preserved in detail. The accumulation of rock on top of the entombed fossil will usually have reduced it to an

FERNS HAVE THRIVED *for over 300 million years, retaining the same essential form. Compare the fossil ferns (above) and their living relative (right). The petrified logs (below) are from the late Triassic. Petrified wood is prized by collectors for its beauty and color.*

imprint, but often the original carbon content of the plant material is preserved as a film on the rock surface. In special cases, the waxy leaf covering, or cuticle, can be preserved and removed for examination.

The more robust parts of a plant, such as the trunk, branches, cones, or seeds, can withstand more rigorous environments, and fossils of these plant parts can be found in sandstones. In such cases, the original plant material has been completely replaced by minerals. This process, pro-

ceeding slowly, cell by cell, is called petrification. The result is a faithful reproduction of the plant material in minerals, the structure inside the individual cells being retained. Whole forests preserved in this way have been found in the USA in Yellowstone National Park, Wyoming, and Arizona. In Australia, the minerals in some petrified wood have been replaced by opal.

AN ETRUSCAN SACRED OBJECT

When one Etruscan chief was buried some 2,500 years ago, a section of the fossilized cycad *Cycadeoidea* was interred with him. This fossil is particularly well preserved, still showing scars where the fronds once grew from the main trunk. Although it is unlikely that the chief recognized the paleontological significance of the specimen, it was obviously important to him. We can surmise that the owner believed that some magical process had produced such an unusual form, giving the object mystical power. This specimen is now held in the Bologna Museum, Italy.

SIMPLE INVERTEBRATES

Fossils from groups of invertebrate animals with the simplest
level of organization demonstrate the developing complexity
of animal life.

The abundance of invertebrate fossils is the result of a number of factors: shells are hard enough to withstand fossilization; the animals usually live in high concentrations; and they often live in environments where fossilization is likely to occur.

Multicellular animals, or metazoans, first appear in the fossil record in the late Precambrian, although fossil tracks and burrows of these or similar animals are known from earlier rocks. These early animals are enigmatic—they are possibly early representatives of later groups such as jellyfish, annelid worms, and crustaceans, or they could belong to an early group that evolved, flourished, and became extinct before the beginning of the Cambrian.

Certainly, there are fossils found in the late Precambrian that appear to belong to no known metazoan group. These include the circular *Tribrachidium*, with three-fold symmetry that is seen in no other known group.

BRACHIOPODS *(above), a group of bottom-dwelling marine animals with two hinged shells, are abundant as fossils. Cambrian limestone (right) containing fossils of archaeocyathids.*

CAMBRIAN EXPLOSION

There are very few fossils from the beginning of the Cambrian, and these are from only a few types of animal. By the mid Cambrian, animals were abundant and diverse. This apparent explosion of life, known as the Cambrian Explosion, could be due to a number of factors. It could be that, because there were many environmental niches, organisms evolved rapidly to fill them. It could also be that the ability to form a hard shell (thus increasing the chance of producing a fossil) appeared simultaneously in a number of different groups in response to changed conditions.

Whatever the cause, and it is likely to be a combination of factors, by the mid Cambrian, there were representatives of most major groups and even of a few animals that have since become extinct.

Sponges (phylum Porifera) and their allies, the archaeocyathids and stromatoporoids, are multicellular animals, but they are not regarded as metazoans. All three groups first occur in the Cambrian and sponges survive today. The sponges are mostly represented by microscopic spicules—slender, pointed, crystalline structures—but all three groups leave macroscopic calcareous structures as fossils. These are usually either cup-shaped or cylindrical.

... [time is] the process of

decay and transformation,

just as it always has been.

Timebends: A Life,
ARTHUR MILLER (b. 1915),
American playwright and author

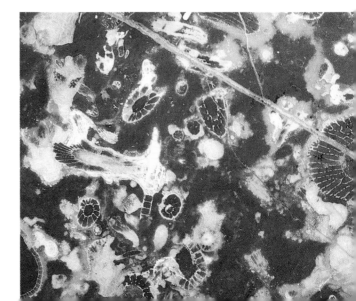

SPONGES AND CORALS
*are among the oldest
multicelled animals. A fossil
sponge (below left) is from
the Cretaceous. Great Barrier
Reef, Australia (left).*

Stromatoporoids, particularly, were important reef-builders from the Ordovician to the Devonian.

CNIDARIANS

Probably the most primitive group of metazoans is the Cnidarians, including jellyfish, corals, and hydroids. Cnidarians have two layers to their body walls and are arranged in a radial pattern. They have two forms in their life cycle, a free-swimming medusoid and an attached hydroid.

In different groups, different forms are emphasized or lost. In jellyfish, it is the free-swimming medusoid that is most familiar to us, but in corals, the attached hydroid, or polyp, is the only form, the medusoid stage having been lost. Cnidarian fossils are among the oldest fossil metazoans and, while jellyfish are rare as fossils, corals are abundant and widespread throughout the fossil record.

All remaining animals, vertebrate and invertebrate, have three layers in the body wall. The middle layer, the mesoderm, can form a body cavity or coelom. This allows for a far more complex level of organization than in Cnidarians. Primitively, animals with a coelom (coelomates) were probably bilaterally symmetrical and divided into segments along their length. Many coelomates retain this form of organization and, even in groups that have lost their segmentation, we suspect that they are derived from segmented ancestors.

LOPHOPHORATES

A relatively small group of coelomates that is well represented in the fossil record is the lophophorates. This is a group of filter feeders that includes bryozoans and brachiopods. These animals strain microorganisms from the water with a pair of coiled furry arms called lophophores.

Bryozoans, commonly known as cold water corals or lace corals, are a group of mostly marine colonial animals. Today there are more than 3,500 known species.

Brachiopods are known as lampshells because of their resemblance to Roman lamps. There are only 70 surviving species, most of which are living in marginal environments.

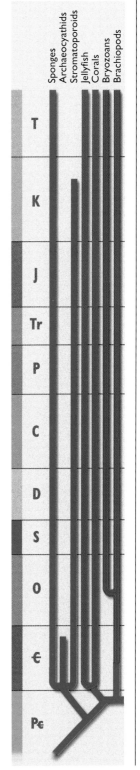

THE GROUPS *of invertebrate animals (sponges dark blue, Cnidarians light green, lophophorates burgundy) shown in the diagram (right) have relatively simple levels of organization. The ancestral link to all these groups also appears in dark blue.*

MORE INVERTEBRATES

Among animal species, those without backbones are by far the most numerous and they are widely represented in the fossil record.

A major group of invertebrates includes the annelid worms (segmented worms and leeches), the arthropods (crabs, shrimps, insects, spiders, and trilobites), and mollusks (snails, clams, and squid). All are united by having similar larvae and development patterns, and most are bilaterally symmetrical. Annelids and arthropods are clearly segmented but mollusks have lost most traces of segmentation, which suggests that they split from the group early in their history.

Annelid worms, which include the familiar garden and marine worms, are rarely fossilized because they have no hard parts.

ARTHROPODS

Arthropods have a good fossil record because they have hardened shells that fossilize easily. Further, because arthropods regularly cast off their old shells and grow new ones, a single individual may produce many shells in its lifetime, multiplying the opportunities for fossilization.

NATIVE AMERICANS *found trilobites (above) so appealing that they gave them a name meaning "little water bug in the rocks".*

Arthropods are easily identified by their jointed legs, which are moved by a series of internal muscles. It is this thin suit of armor that has allowed the arthropods to become so successful. It affords protection and supports the animal's weight while still allowing a wide range of movement.

Within the arthropods there are four classes of varying importance to the fossil record: *Trilobita, Uniramia, Crustacea,* and *Chelicerata.*

Trilobites are one of the most important fossil groups of the early to mid Paleozoic and their attractive fossils are much sought after by collectors. They are characterized by a multisegmented body of three basic parts: a broad head

RELATED GROUPS *The seemingly disparate groups (right) of arthropods (orange), mollusks (red), and annelid worms (dark blue) can be shown to have a common ancestor (also dark blue). Insects (left) are the most diverse group of living metazoans but they are rarely fossilized.*

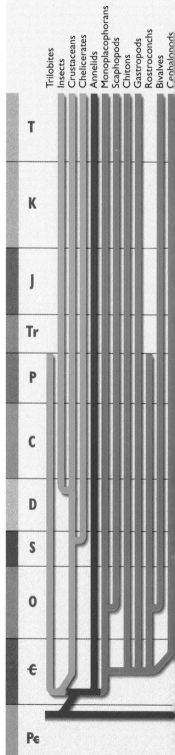

	Trilobites	Insects	Crustaceans	Chelicerates	Annelids	Monoplacophorans	Scaphopods	Chitons	Gastropods	Rostroconchs	Bivalves	Cephalopods
T												
K												
J												
Tr												
P												
C												
D												
S												
O												
€												
Pe												

MOLLUSKS

Mollusks are mostly marine invertebrates with some freshwater groups and a single terrestrial group, the land snails. Mollusks have a very good fossil record because most have hard shells. The success of mollusks is due largely to the protection given by their heavy shield-like shells. There are six main groups: monoplaco-phorans, chitons, gastropods, scaphopods (tooth-shells), bivalves (clams), and cephalo-pods (squid, octopus, nautil-oids, and ammonoids).

Gastropods are familiar as snails—marine, freshwater, and terrestrial. The helically coiled shells of gastropods are common fossils from the Cambrian to the present.

Bivalves are readily recognized as clams, oysters, and mussels. These two-shelled mollusks first appeared in the Ordovician, but their possible progenitors, the rostroconchs, are known from the late Cambrian through to the Permian. Bivalves are also known as pelecypods and lamellibranchs, both of which are old names now considered to be incorrect.

The most advanced mollusks are the cephalopods, including octopus, nautiloids, squid, and ammonoids. They have a single shell that can be straight, spiral, or some variation of these. In some groups, the shell is reduced or completely lost. The largest shelled cephalopods were some types of ammonite that could grow to more than 10 feet (3 m) in diameter but the largest cephalopod is the living giant squid, which reaches 50 feet (15 m) in length.

or cephalon, a body or thorax, and a tail or pygidium. Each body part can be divided into three sections (lobes). Trilobites became extinct at the end of the Permian.

Uniramia is a group of arthropods with unbranched limbs. It includes hexapods, or insects, onychophorans (small arthropods that superficially resemble caterpillars), and myriapods (centipedes and millipedes).

Insects, the most diverse group of metazoans in the world today, do not have a fossil record to match their current massive diversity. However, rare preservations, such as those in amber, indicate the major evolutionary paths of this group.

Crustaceans (shrimps, crabs, and lobsters) are mostly marine and have limbs that branch into two. The earliest representatives are about 550 million years old. Most crustaceans have relatively thin shells that readily disarticulate after death so they have been preserved only in exceptional situations.

MOLLUSKS

come in a variety of forms, including gastropods (above) and cephalopods (below).

ECHINODERMS *and* VERTEBRATES

More complex animals, such as the echinoderms and vertebrates, represent
some of the most fascinating organisms in the fossil record.

CRINOIDS
(left) are upside-down echinoderms attached to the sea floor by a stem with "roots". Sea stars (above) are one of the most important invertebrate predators of marine life.

The last major group of fossil animals on our Tree of Life consists of the echinoderms (including sea stars, sea urchins, and sea lilies), the protochordates (including graptolites), and the chordates, which include vertebrates (fish, amphibians, reptiles, birds, and mammals).

These animals are placed in one group because of numerous similarities. They have similar larval forms, show segmentation, and have either bilateral or five-part symmetry around a central axis.

ECHINODERMS

Echinoderms are distinct in the animal world in having five-fold radial symmetry (five similar parts arranged around a central axis) instead of bilateral symmetry, although they are probably descended from a bilaterally symmetrical ancestor. The echinoderm skeleton is composed of many small, interconnected plates made of calcite. These animals also have an internal water-vascular system—a series of fluid-filled canals and reservoirs through which water and food circulate. Externally, they are covered with spines. There are four main groups, all of them marine.

Echinozoa, including sea urchins (echinoids), and sea cucumbers (holothuroids), are mostly rounded or discoid. Echinoids gather their food in a variety of ways—there are active hunters moving over the sea floor, and burrowing forms that process huge amounts of sediment to extract microscopic organisms. Some echinoids have jaws powerful enough to allow them to burrow into solid rock. The earliest echinoids and holothuroids are from the Ordovician.

Asterozoa includes sea stars (asteroids) and brittle stars (ophiuroids). Both have a familiar form with five or more radiating arms, and both have a reasonable fossil record dating from the Ordovician.

Crinoids, or sea lilies, mostly live in deep water and have not been studied in great detail. Blastozoa is an extinct group of attached echinoderms that superficially resemble the crinoids. These two groups first appeared in the Cambrian.

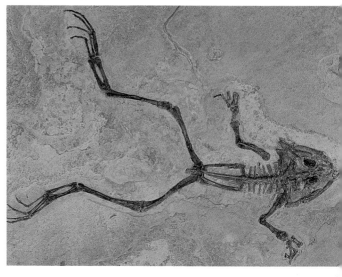

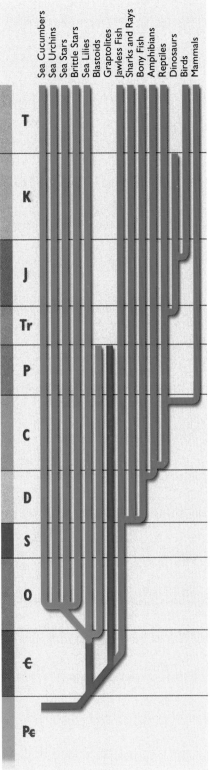

CLEAR DETAILS *of the skeleton and fin rays are visible in this small fossil fish. Bony fish first appeared in the Silurian.*

PROTOCHORDATES

Graptolites are colonial organisms that floated through the Paleozoic seas. These protochordates are most widely known from thin impressions of branches of colonies, like hacksaw blades drawn on rocks. Other members of this group are rarely fossilized.

CHORDATES

Chordates are bilaterally symmetrical animals with segmented body muscles in V-shaped bands (myotomes). They also have a stiffened rod (notochord) running along the back and a nerve cord above the notochord. In this basic form, primitive chordates possess no hardened parts that are likely to be fossilized and the fossil record of early

FOSSIL FROG *(left). These amphibians date from the Jurassic. Graptolites (below) first appeared in the Ordovician and went extinct by the end of the Permian.*

chordates is sketchy. The earliest recognized chordate is the tiny *Pikaia,* from the middle Cambrian.

After chordates developed hard parts, they became better represented in the fossil record as vertebrates. The earliest fossils of vertebrates are microscopic "scale-bones" from late Cambrian rocks, probably belonging to early jawless fish (agnathans), which proliferated in the Silurian and Devonian.

The cartilaginous skeletons of sharks and rays (chondrichthyans) do not fossilize well, but early chondrichthyans are known from the Devonian.

Other groups of fish have appeared and disappeared throughout evolutionary history. The group that contains the bulk of modern fishes—the ray-finned fish or actinopterygians—had its origin in the late Silurian.

The earliest terrestrial vertebrates were amphibians that resembled salamanders. The next big step in vertebrate evolution was the development of an egg that could be laid on land, thus freeing the parents from remaining close to water to reproduce. This appears to have occurred during the Carboniferous, and resulted in the evolution of reptiles, birds, and mammals.

THE SEEMINGLY DIVERSE GROUPS
of echinoderms (purple) and chordates (dark blue), including the vertebrates (light blue), can be shown, from studies of their development and morphology, to have a common origin in the early Cambrian.

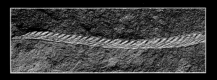

CHAPTER FIVE

UNLOCKING *the*
SECRETS *of* FOSSILS

*Unless you expect the unexpected you will never find
[truth], for it is hard to discover and hard to attain.*

Fragments,
HERACLITUS (c. 500 BC), Greek philosopher

STUDYING FOSSILS

This fascinating science not only reveals the secrets of the past, but has a variety of practical applications.

Paleontology is the study of fossils, a scientific discipline that has emerged from the long history of association between humans and relics of the past. Today, as the result of long intellectual struggle, fossils are readily recognized as the remains of ancient life forms.

Fossils have always been difficult to interpret. Native North Americans thought that the petrified tree trunks scattered around the landscape in Arizona were the bones of monsters, or weapons from battles among the gods. The ancient Egyptians used some fossils for road-making and carving, but they do not seem to have appreciated their origins.

As early as the seventh century BC, Ancient Greeks, including Xenophanes, Pythagoras, Xanthus, and Herodotus, observed fossils of marine shells and even a small fossil fish found inland in the

FIERCE RIVALRY
between Othniel Charles Marsh (above) and Edward Drinker Cope (left) led to the retrieval of huge collections of dinosaur specimens.

mountains and realized that these areas of land must once have been under the sea. Although Pliny the Elder (AD 23–79) recognized that amber was ancient pine resin, he also thought that fossilized shark teeth had magical powers helpful for those who court fair women.

During the Dark Ages and Middle Ages, fossils received little attention and were generally regarded as curiosities, oddities, or freaks of nature. While some, such as the Moslem philosopher Avicenna (980–1037), held more accurate ideas about fossils and the Earth's history, such views were far from universal. Leonardo da Vinci (1452–1512) recognized that fossils might once have been living organisms and went some way to explaining how they

could have been formed by burial in sediment. Anatomist Gabriello Fallopio (1523–62) thought that fossils were the result of movements and activities inside the Earth. This view, and the idea that fossils grew within the Earth by various processes, were widely held throughout the Middle Ages. Another concept that retarded a scientific understanding of fossils was that they were the remains of organisms killed in the Biblical Flood.

By the Renaissance, a more rational view of fossils was becoming prevalent. Scholars began to make fossil

PLINY THE ELDER *(left) was familiar with some types of fossil, including shark teeth. Native Americans thought petrified logs (above) were bones of monsters.*

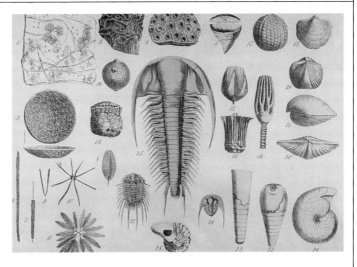

collections and to illustrate and describe them in printed works. The Scottish physicist and mathematician Robert Hooke (1635–1703) was the first person to make detailed studies of the fine structure of petrified wood with a microscope and to comment on the similarities, even at the most detailed levels, between fossilized wood and living trees. He was convinced that fossils must be the remains of once-living organisms.

The eighteenth century marked the foundation of the sciences of geology and paleontology, and by the nineteenth century the two were firmly established. Fossils showed that the world had changed and that numerous organisms had appeared and disappeared. They were instrumental in establishing evolution as a scientific fact—

Every great and commanding moment in the annals of the world is the triumph of some enthusiasm.

Nature Addresses and Lectures,
RALPH WALDO EMERSON
(1803–82), American essayist

BY THE LATE *eighteenth century, fossils were being collected for study by both scientists and amateurs.*

no longer were they poorly understood oddities but a record of the history of life.

During the nineteenth century, the great museums of the world competed for the best collections of natural objects and prized among these were fossils. In the latter half of the nineteenth century, two great American adversaries, Othniel Charles Marsh and Edward Drinker Cope, battled fiercely for the latest and largest dinosaur specimens for display in their respective museums. Both were wealthy and employed professional fossil hunters to scour the badlands of the western United States for specimens.

Today, paleontology has gone far beyond the esoteric collecting of fossils and interpreting the history of life. It is an active and vigorous science practiced worldwide by people working for universities, museums, geological surveys, and mining companies. It is of particular use in the mining industry, especially for the petroleum exploration industry, and is widely used in the assessment of modern environmental problems by providing evidence from environments of the past.

SHE SELLS SEASHELLS ...

Mary Anning (1799–1847) lived in Lyme Regis, Dorset, England. Her father owned a souvenir shop and, finding that the abundant fossil shells from the area fetched high prices, Mary began collecting them to sell. She inspired the tongue-twister "She sells seashells by the seashore".

In 1811, she found her first skeleton of an ichthyosaur (a dolphin-like reptile), and later dug up many other skeletons of Jurassic marine animals from the Age of Dinosaurs. Many fine specimens on display in the British Museum of Natural History and other museums around the world were found by Mary Anning.

THE PAST REVEALED

If we are to preserve the Earth's wonders and resources for future generations, we need to examine all the evidence and learn as much as possible from past calamities.

Fossils can be thought of as snapshots from the past, giving indications of what earlier environments were like. Such relics provide a chronicle of the evolution of the biosphere. And, like many historical documents, the fossil record holds important lessons for the present.

GLOBAL WARMING

One of the major crises confronting the world today is global warming, the raising of the temperature of Earth's atmosphere. Known as the greenhouse effect, this phenomenon is being caused by various human activities, chiefly the burning of fossil fuels. One of the important questions that confronts us is how to predict what will happen if the temperature of the atmosphere rises. We can invoke complicated computer models, which are only as good as the assumptions made in them, or we can look at the Earth's past, to a time when the atmosphere was hotter than it is now.

Measuring the past temperatures of Earth's atmosphere presents considerable difficulties, but the temperature of the oceans is a little easier to gauge. There is a correlation between the temperatures of

oceans and the atmosphere. Chemical analysis of certain minerals that were present in the shells of once-living creatures and that are now trapped in their fossils can be used for this purpose. Living animals trap oxygen molecules in their shells and the ratio of the two most common isotopes of oxygen are correlated to temperature. So, analysis of the oxygen isotopes of a shell indicates the temperature of the ocean at the time the animal was alive.

This type of analysis has been conducted on the fossil shells of animals dating back

CHEMICAL ANALYSIS *of fossil shells (top) reveals the temperature of the ancient world at different times.*

THE MAKING OF A DESERT

There are some frightening lessons from fossils, both with respect to natural changes and those wrought by human activity. Fossils reveal that much of northern Africa was covered by savanna

woodlands until comparatively recent times. Animals, such as elephants and hippopotamuses, roamed much of the area and their presence was recorded by early human inhabitants.

The nature of this region has been gradually changing over the past few million years, becoming drier and less hospitable to life. These changes have been accelerated by human activities such as grazing, fire management, and land clearing. As a consequence, there are now large areas of desert.

IN THIS CHANGING WORLD, *ancient rain forests (top) that once covered vast areas of Australia and other southern continents have been replaced by desert (left). Extensive glaciers (above) locked up enough water to lower the sea level, creating "bridges" over which species crossed to new lands.*

as Australia and Antarctica, now the two driest continents on Earth.

On the other hand, fossils tell us about life when the Earth's temperature was cooler than now. During past ice ages, for example, glaciers covered large parts of the Northern Hemisphere, extending as far south as the latitude of New York. Because more of the Earth's surface water was bound up in ice sheets, the sea level was lower and precipitation decreased. When the sea level fell, land bridges appeared where once there were shallow seas. These bridges allowed animals and plants to disperse into areas that were previously inaccessible to them.

It was the extensive land bridges formed during the last ice age (100,000 to 15,000 years ago) that allowed our species to spread to most parts of the globe, including the Americas and Australasia. In this cooler, drier world, deserts were much more extensive than they are now.

It is worth remembering that the radically different world of the last ice age was an average of 9° Fahrenheit (5° C) cooler than the world today. Most prognostications about the effects of global warming are based on an increase in global temperatures of a similar magnitude.

to the early Cambrian, giving us a fairly accurate measure of the temperature of the Earth's atmosphere since then. There are other ways to take the temperature of ancient atmospheres and oceans, and these are used for corroboration.

As well as indicating the temperature of ancient worlds, fossils also tell us about the life occurring at a particular period. In past times, when the world was warmer than it is now, forests extended over larger areas than they cover today. Warm-habitat plants

and animals spread to higher latitudes because the prevailing conditions were favorable to them. In general, a warmer world is a wetter world and the sea level rises as water is released from the melting of polar ice caps. Such conditions prevailed in the mid Cretaceous and again in the Eocene. During these times, rain forests covered areas such

PRACTICAL APPLICATIONS *of* PALEONTOLOGY

Fossils are present in many of the things we take for granted in the modern world, from building materials to the fuels we depend on.

It is easy to dismiss fossils as curiosities, or as merely the basis of an arcane science, but the study of fossils produces a vast body of information that has both direct and indirect economic value.

Fossil fuels, such as gas, oil, and coal deposits, are all formed from once-living organisms. The accumulated debris of a forest that was growing for many thousands of years before burial eventually produces coal. It is because of its organic content that coal and some other deposits, particularly some sea-floor sediments, are high in complex hydrocarbons.

When coal deposits are heated, volatile components are driven off and migrate through the sediments to be deposited elsewhere as oil or gas. The hydrocarbon chains in the gasoline that powers our cars, in the natural gas that heats our stoves, and in the oils that lubricate our engines were all put together by plants and animals millions of years ago. Most of the world's electricity is produced by coal-fired generators that burn the compacted residues of ancient forests. In a very real sense, our energy needs are filled by the fossilized remains of ancient worlds.

READING ROCKS

The rocks of the world were laid down, one atop the other, in grand sequences called stratigraphic columns. No rock unit, however, is distributed worldwide and most are very restricted geographically. So, while stratigraphic columns can be constructed for a particular area or region, it is difficult to correlate the layers of one stratigraphic column to those from another region except through their fossil content.

Unlike rock units, some plant and animal species are distributed over large areas, many even globally, so their fossils are potentially useful in correlating distant rock units. If the fossils are of organisms that evolved rapidly and of species that occurred in short, well-defined periods, the correlations should be quite accurate. If the species existed for a more extended period, precision may be compromised. It helps greatly if the fossil organisms are abundant and easy to find.

The rapid evolution, wide distribution, and abundance of many microfossils, such as

WINKLESTONE (above) is an ornamental stone that was formed of fossils. Similar decorative stone was used in building the Taj Mahal (right) in India.

THE LUXURIANT SWAMPS *of the Carboniferous (above) eventually became extensive coal deposits. Geological processing of coal produces oil deposits. In Kuwait (right), these were wasted by war.*

radiolarians, foraminifera, and conodonts, make them useful indicators for correlating rock units over large areas. Fossilized plant pollens and spores reveal a great deal about stratigraphic correlation in rocks younger than about 290 million years.

Correlation of rock units is economically important in the search for deposits of minerals, oil, gas, and coal. If a particular type of mineral deposit is found in rocks of a particular age, it is useful to investigate rocks of a similar age when seeking similar deposits.

BUILDING WITH FOSSILS

There must be few buildings in the world that do not, in some way, rely on the fossils of ancient organisms to keep them standing. Cement (powdered limestone) is perhaps the most commonly used material, either alone or mixed with aggregate to form concrete.

Most of the world's limestone deposits suitable for cement production are fossilized reef systems. Ancient organisms extracted calcium carbonate from the surrounding seawater to form their shelters, and we recycle their ancient dwellings to construct our own homes.

Decorative stone, principally marble, is also used extensively, particularly in bathrooms and kitchens. Marble is limestone that has been heated and subjected to enough pressure to reorganize the crystal structure of the original rock. Certain types of marble retain the fossilized remains of ancient

MICROSOPIC DIATOMS *(top far left) form diatomite, a rock used to filter beer.*

reef builders. It is always worth inspecting marble for signs of fossilized animals.

OTHER USES

While collectors pay well for spectacular specimens, fossils have many more practical applications. The most widely used material for the filtration of beer and similar liquids is diatomite, a porous rock composed of the fossilized shells of microscopic diatoms. The main source of superphosphate for fertilizers is sea-bird excrement known as guano. In some places, the guano is so deep and old that it is best thought of as fossilized bird droppings.

Black ivory, the tusks of mammoth fossils collected in Siberia, had numerous uses, including black keys for pianos. This resource was largely exhausted by the middle of the twentieth century, as were commercial deposits of particular types of amber that had been used in the production of varnishes and lacquers.

LIMITATIONS OF FOSSIL RESOURCES

All fossil resources are finite. They have taken thousands, often millions of years to form and, once depleted, they will take a similar period to be replenished. We are using fossil resources, particularly our limited fossil fuel deposits, at a much higher rate than they can be produced, so we need to develop other solutions to the problems these resources currently solve.

117

FINDING FOSSILS

With minimal equipment, proper care, and a little planning,
searching for fossils can be a satisfying hobby.

The search for and recovery of fossils is a rewarding pastime that requires physical effort, some basic research and knowledge, some simply acquired skills, and a minimum of special equipment.

MAKING PREPARATIONS

Fossils are not found in every rock, so some basic research is needed before embarking on a fossil-collecting exped-ition. It is important to find out not only where to search, but also what kind of fossil can be expected in a particular area, who owns the site, whether access is permitted, and if there are any partic-ular dangers, such as traffic at roadside sites, or tides at the seaside. Prime collecting localities are often listed by State mining departments and local geological surveys.

Amateur collectors who know the area are usually helpful and can often be contacted through rock-collecting and lapidary clubs. Tourist informa-tion centers, souvenir and rock shops, and regional museums also sometimes have local information.

Once you have identified a likely site, it is worth

surveying it for recent exposures—road cuts or landslips may have exposed some fresh material. Quarries have great potential because the ongoing work of the quarry continually turns

A HAMMER AND CHISELS
(top left) and eye protection are all that is needed in the field, but sledge hammers (left) and other specialized equipment are also options.

up new rocks. Re-member that quarries can be particularly dangerous places and that safety aspects should be thoroughly checked with the property owner before you venture in.

FINDING FOSSILS INSIDE ROCKS

It is relatively uncom-mon to find fossils exposed on the sur-face. Better specimens are usually obtained by breaking rocks open with hammers, cold chisels, or crowbars. When at a new site, experiment with some of the rocks to see how they break.

Usually, fossils are found on bedding planes, like book-marks between the pages of a book. The trick is to work out the best way to open a particular type of rock along its bedding planes. In some cases, it is easier to cut across the bedding planes; in others, it is

DETAILED FIELD NOTES
should be kept for all field activities. Keep information about site locations and access for future reference.

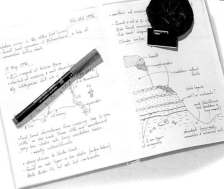

BRUSHES *can be used (left) to remove the loose debris that clings to your precious specimen. Often the best technique for finding fossils is to persevere, systematically splitting the rock at one particular site (center).*

etter to cut along. Only trial nd error will show the best pproaches to take for partic-lar types of rock.

Don't be too ambitious in he field. It might be better o take a fossil home still em-edded in lots of rock so that t can be removed carefully ater. Many good specimens have been destroyed by im-patient collectors removing too much rock in the field.

TAKING YOUR SPECIMENS HOME

Although fossils are made of rock, they should be treated like glass. Once you have cut away as much rock as is wise in the field, write a number on the fossil or surrounding rock with a felt-tipped pen for easy identification later, then wrap your prize in plenty of newspaper to protect it on the journey home.

Most important: don't be greedy. Never take more than you need for your collection. The more you collect, the less there will be for other enthu-siasts. As a courtesy to others, leave the site in the condition you originally found it.

Sometimes the facts are

of value in themselves, …

now and then someone

finds a key that opens

a whole new field.

The Molds and Man,
CLYDE CHRISTENSEN
b. 1905), Professor
of plant pathology

WHAT TO TAKE ON A FIELD TRIP

The most important equipment is protective gear such as eye goggles and, for powdery or dusty conditions, a face mask. Fossil-collecting sites are usually in rough terrain, so sturdy footwear is essential—steel-capped boots have saved many a toe from being crushed by falling rocks. Check weather reports and ensure that you have adequate protection from the Sun and the elements (sun-screen, broad-brimmed hat, long-sleeved shirt, and rainwear). A small first-aid kit is also a good idea.

A notebook and pen (take spares) allows you to record what you have found and where you found it. A felt-tipped pen will write on most rocks or fossils so you can immediately number specimens for later identification. Don't rely on memory and don't write important collecting information on separate scraps of paper that can become detached from the specimen and get lost. You might take maps of the area you are looking at to plot your finds and progress.

You will need packing material, such as newspaper, bubble wrap, and plastic bags, to transport your finds, and a sturdy knapsack will be useful.

Of course, you will also need tools to break the rocks to get at the fossils. A geologist's hammer and a range of cold chisels in different sizes is really all that is required. Crowbars, sledge hammers, picks, and shovels can all be useful, but remember that they are heavy and tiring to carry.

PREPARATION *and* CARE *of* FOSSILS

Fossil collecting begins in the field with the retrieval of specimens, but this is only the start of your adventure with paleontology.

Fossil specimens are usually brought home embedded in the rock matrix to protect them. The amateur paleontologist must clean and preserve the specimens collected, then identify, catalog, and store them.

The first step is to remove the surrounding rock with fine chisels, small hammers, and probing tools, such as those used by dentists, or even an electric engraving tool. This takes skill and patience.

The tools and techniques used will vary with the nature of the fossil and the matrix. Proceed slowly, using a variety of tools and techniques to determine the most appropriate for the type of fossil. The experience and guidance of other fossil collectors is invaluable at this stage. The golden rule is not to do too much—it is better to leave a specimen partly embedded in matrix than to damage it by taking risks in the preparation.

Once the specimen has been prepared, it may need to be hardened. One technique is to dissolve some water-soluble wood glue in water with a drop or two of detergent—10 percent solutions of glue are usually fine for most fossil work. This solution is

A SELECTION OF TOOLS, *including brushes and fine probes, is essential. Sometimes it may be necessary to glue specimens (right).*

dribbled onto the surface of the specimen where it forms a clear, hard skin. For porous, crumbly specimens, acetone-soluble glue dissolved in acetone is better—again, a 10 percent solution will be satisfactory. This solution will soak into the specimen and harden it throughout. Don't mix different types of glue as this can result in the formation of an insoluble cement that cannot be removed if further cleaning is required.

Often a specimen is broken when found or breaks during excavation or preparation. Once the individual pieces have been cleaned and hardened, they can be glued together again. Be sure that surfaces to be joined are clean

and fit together properly prior to gluing. Use an acetone-soluble glue so that mistakes can be undone if necessary.

Epoxy glues are useful for large specimens that need strong joints, but if a mistake is made, these glues are almost impossible to dissolve. A box of sand makes an excellent "pair of hands" to hold a fossil while the glue is drying.

TO IDENTIFY *your finds, compare them with illustrations in reliable books.*

CLEANING SPECIMENS *with a fine, pointed tool (below). Larger fossils may need to be protected in a plaster cast (left).*

IDENTIFYING FOSSILS
The levels to which hobby collectors wish to identify their finds will vary greatly. With this book, an amateur will be able to identify the major group to which a fossil belongs and, in some cases, the genus. For many amateur collectors, this level of identification is satisfactory.

To identify finds more accurately, buy or borrow books with illustrations and photographs of excellent specimens with detailed descriptions of each type of fossil. These are available through rock and fossil shops, local geological surveys, or mining departments. Again, the knowledge and resources of more experienced collectors will prove invaluable.

STORING FOSSILS
There are two basic types of storage: display storage for your more spectacular and interesting fossils, and collection storage for more mundane specimens. For both groups, humidity and temperature must be kept as low and as constant as possible. This means being careful when choosing lighting for a display cabinet—it should not heat the specimens. Wood is the perfect material for these cabinets because it helps to buffer the humidity around the fossils as well as providing some insulation against temperature extremes. Display cases can be fitted with locks to protect your collection against theft or damage from inept handling.

Collection cabinets are usually stacks of shallow drawers. Consider lining the bottoms of drawers with soft material, or placing your specimens inside small cardboard boxes within the drawers. This stops them from rolling around when drawers are opened and closed.

CATALOGING
Since collectors rapidly acquire many different types of fossil from a number of locations, it is important to establish a system for cataloging and identifying them—don't trust your memory. All fossils in a collection should carry a unique number, which can be written on the specimen. This number, plus the fossil's identification and collecting information, should be recorded on cards to be kept with each specimen. It is also a good idea to keep a central register of specimens detailing the number of each, its identification, collecting information, and details of its preparation history and any preservation treatments that have been carried out.

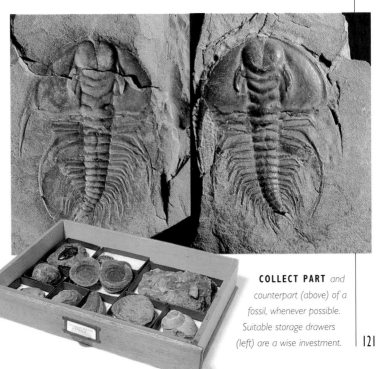

COLLECT PART *and counterpart (above) of a fossil, whenever possible. Suitable storage drawers (left) are a wise investment.*

SPECIAL TECHNIQUES

Although the amateur can prepare many types of specimen, some require special equipment, patience, skill, and more demanding techniques.

Many types of fossil can be prepared at home by amateur collectors with simple, readily available tools, but other preparation techniques are more complicated and call for equipment to which the average collector doesn't usually have access.

THIN SECTIONS

When fossils are sliced thinly with a diamond saw, paleontologists can study the internal structure of the organism. Further information can be retrieved from thin sections carefully ground to a thickness through which light can pass and mounted on microscope slides. Studying these by means of microscopes that polarize light can reveal details of the organism's structure and composition.

ACID PREPARATION

Some rocks, particularly those with high concentrations of calcium carbonate, can be dissolved in acid to release the fossils inside. Usually only weak acid, such as formic or acetic acid, is used. By this gentle process, specimens with extremely delicate or small features can be recovered without damage.

Acid preparation is also the easiest way to release microfossils from rock. To retrieve microfossils such as

ACID PREPARATIONS *involve carefully dissolving the rock surrounding the specimen (left) in weak acid and hardening the emerging fossil.*

THIN SECTIONS *of fossil bone (above left) reveal internal detail. The small mammal (above) has been prepared in resin and shows the original hair.*

radiolarians, which have shells that resist acid, stronger acids are used.

Conversely, acids can be used to dissolve the fossil. This is particularly useful where the fossil is fragile and the surrounding rock is impervious to acid attack and otherwise too hard to remove. By soaking the rock in an acid that dissolves only the fossil, the cavity where the fossil lies is cleaned out, then filled with latex, or some other molding compound, and the rock smashed away. The result is a perfect latex copy of the original fossil.

COPYING FOSSILS

There are numerous techniques for copying fossils. Basically, a mold is made of the fossil, usually with latex or silicon rubber. The fossil is removed from the mold, which is then filled with plaster of Paris or a hard-setting resin. A more basic technique used by many amateurs is to press the fossil into modeling clay to form a mold. Copies are then made with plaster of Paris. In recent years, the prices of silicon rubber molding compounds and casting resins have fallen to a level that is affordable by the average amateur. Experiment with making copies of your favorite fossils, but remember to use a suitable releasing agent between the fossil and the molding compound (soapy water or petroleum jelly are good), and try your technique on disposable objects first.

EMBEDDING IN RESIN
Particularly delicate fossils that rely on the surrounding rock matrix for support can be liberated by embedding them in resin. Although a simple procedure, it takes practice and patience. Once the

specimen is prepared from one side, a clear casting resin is poured over the surface and allowed to set. The block is then turned upside-down and the matrix carefully removed from the other side. Eventually, all that is left is the fossil, embedded in clear resin.

X-RAYS AND CT SCANS
In some cases, especially where a fossil is very delicate and of a similar hardness and composition to the surrounding matrix, the specimen is studied by X-ray or Computer-aided Tomographic-scanned images. X-rays are most useful for fossils that are essentially flat but those that are more three dimensional can be most easily studied by CT scans. The object is to see what the fossil looks like without removing it from the rock. In this way, structures inside the fossil, such as brain cavities or bone

A DELICATE FOSSIL
(left) prepared using acid to dissolve the surrounding rock, is revealed in exquisite detail.

COPIES OF SPECIMENS *can be made by first coating them in latex (left). Some fossils, such as the Devonian arthropod below, are best studied using X-rays.*

thicknesses, can be looked at and measured without damage. It is now possible to take CT-scan data and make a three-dimensional resin reconstruction of the fossil. In effect, this technique produces a perfect copy of a specimen that is still locked inside rock.

ULTRAVIOLET AND FLUORESCENT FOSSILS
Some fossils are preserved in minerals that glow under UV light. The fossil may be invisible to the naked eye until viewed under UV light. One example of this phenomenon is the remains of the dinosaur *Seismosaurus*. Uranium-rich minerals have been deposited in the fossilized bones, causing them to glow under UV light. These minerals were not present in the surrounding rock. The fossilized bones look similar to the surrounding rock, but under UV light, the difference between the two materials was obvious. This greatly assisted in preparing the specimen.

The true scientist never loses the faculty of amazement.
It is the essence of his being.

Newsweek, March 31, 1958
HANS SELYE (1907–82), Austrian-born American physician

CHAPTER SIX

ROCKS FIELD GUIDE

USING *the* ROCKS GUIDE

This field guide introduces a variety of landscapes and treasures of the Earth, revealing many of the fascinating secrets behind its long history.

Rocks abound in every setting and this field guide can be used to seek out some interesting landscapes or to look for some elusive gems hidden beneath the Earth's surface.

Semi-precious Stones

Semi-precious Stones

Orange grossular garnet crystals

Green elbaite crystals

Lead photograph shows ornamentals and gemstones. They are rough and/or cut. Larger rock formations are shown in a landscape setting.

Secondary photographs show forms of this rock or mineral and possible building, fine or applied art, or ornamental uses.

Garnet

Garnets are a related group of minerals whose chemical compositions can vary continuously from one to the other. Key members of this group, often cut as gemstones, include almandine (red to violet red), spessartite (yellow, rose, or orange to reddish-brown), pyrope (deep red), grossular (white, yellow, yellowish-green, brownish-red, orange, or brown to black), and andradite (colorless, yellow-green, or brown to black). This last group includes the most prized garnet—the emerald-green variety known as demantoid. The name garnet probably derives from the Latin *granatum malum*, for pomegranate. The inside of this fruit resembles red almandine and pyrope garnets.

A variety of cut garnets (above). Andradite garnet crystals in marble (below).

Pyrope ranks among the most popular of the garnets, and fine crystals have been mined and used in Czechoslovakia since the Middle Ages. Many forms of garnet do not occur as gem-quality crystals and are used industrially as abrasives.

Garnets are common worldwide, particularly in metamorphic rocks. Pyrope garnet forms in many magnesium-rich, ultrabasic, igneous rocks, including peridotites and serpentinites. Grossular and andradite garnets grow in calcium-rich metamorphic rocks, such as marble. Almandine garnet forms in iron-bearing, regionally metamorphosed rocks, such as schist.

Identification Minerals in the garnet group have a hardness of 6.5 to 7.5 and a specific gravity of 3.4 to 4.6. They are translucent to opaque, have a vitreous luster, and leave a white streak. They have very indistinct cleavage and break with a conchoidal fracture. Garnets belong to the cubic crystal system and display a variety of equant habits, particularly rhombododecahedrons.

· FIELD NOTES ·

Crystals form distinctive soccerball shapes.

All varieties of garnet are abundant in the USA. Other sources include Australia, Brazil, Sri Lanka, and the Czech Republic.

Tourmal[ine]

Tourmaline is a complex borosilicate of aluminum and other elements, noted for its beautiful, multi-colored, prismatic crystals. In fact, tourmaline exhibits a greater range of color than any other gem, with the spectacular watermelon tourmaline changing color from green to red along the length of the crystal.

The tourmaline family is made up of seven distinct groups: schorl (black), elbaite (many colors), dravite and buergerite (brown), rubellite (pink), chromdravite (green), and uvite (black, brown, yellow-green).

Tourmaline crystals display a number of very interesting properties. They are pleochroic, meaning that they appear differently colored when viewed through different

Watermelon tourmaline (above). A pink tourmaline crystal (left). Tourmaline gemstones (right).

Field Notes panels
 *Best Field Marks: A brief list of the most characteristic features of the rock or mineral to aid identification in the field.*

Locations: A brief guide to where these rocks and minerals occur. In the case of rocks, the geological environment is given. For minerals, a list of the best source countries is featured.

The text provides information on the formation of various rocks and their constituent minerals. In the case of minerals, each entry ends with the mineral's identifying characteristics (see Mineral Identification pp. 70-75).

The **illustrated banding** at the top of the page identifies either general categories of collecting rocks or rock sites—see the key below.

Volcanoes

Mt Augustine, Alaska, USA

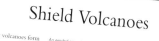

Volcanoes

Mt Kilauea, Hawaii, USA

Explosive Volcanoes

shape according to
osition. The more
ntains, the steeper the
h-silica andesitic
ussia), Japan, Alaska,
de of the Americas
occur above
llects and mixes
silica volcanoes
al mountains,
ert, California.
, Typically,
gullies
e mountain,

sive, and
natically

rminations
esent, they
ly different.
ated, the ends
and negatively
ast particles.
and in granites
metamorphic
ctacular sizes
ge of minerals,
l, and topaz.
maline often

After an explosion, a lake may form in the
resulting crater. Subsequently, a small cone
forms in the center of the lake, as in Lake
Toya, Japan, and Crater Lake, Oregon, USA.
Eventually, the small cone grows to the size of
the original volcano, and the next explosion
occurs. This pattern is recorded around Mt Fuji,
Japan. The growth and explosion of andesitic
volcanoes continues until subduction stops
feeding them magma.

*An 1831 sketch
(right) of a vol-
cano, Julia Island,
Sicily. Sunset
Crater (below)
Arizona, USA*

FIELD NOTES
Volcanoes along subduction
lines, as in Russia, Japan,
ka, Indonesia, New Zealand,
North and South America.
rater lakes can be seen
Lake Toba, Indonesia;
Crater Lake, USA;
ake Toya, Japan.

e minerals have a
ecific gravity of
nt to opaque, have
a white streak. They
eak with an uneven
idal fracture. They
the hexagonal crystal
lisplaying a prismatic
th vertical striations.

153

Shield Volcanoes

Hot-spot volcanoes form
from fast-running,
low-silica basalt
magma. On land, they have
low-angle cones and are often
referred to as shield volcanoes,
after ancient Roman shields.
When they form underwater,
they start with a steeper shape
because the lava freezes much
faster and does not travel as far.
The volcanic pedestal is formed
from fractured pieces of pillow
basalt (see p. 177). The shape
flattens to the shield form as the
cone builds above sea level, as
in the Hawaiian Islands.

A hot-spot volcano has a
limited life, forming as a plate
passes over a hot spot deep in the
mantle (see p. 43). The volcano
builds in size as the plate moves
steadily on. Once the plate has
moved sufficiently, a new volcano
will appear over the stationary hot
spot and the old one will become
inactive and eventually erode.
Continental hot-spot volcanoes

An eroded oceanic hot-spot volcano in Tahiti, Polynesia.

FIELD NOTES
Hawaiian Islands, USA
Yellowstone National Park, USA
Mt Erebus, Antarctica
Mt Kilimanjaro, Tanzania
Tristan da Cunha, Atlantic Ocean
Réunion Island, Mauritius
Lord Howe Island, Australia
Barrington Tops, NSW, Australia

erode to subdued hills, as can be
seen all along the eastern coast
of Australia. Oceanic hot-spot
volcanoes erode to sea level to
produce flat-topped pedestals
called guyots. These subside
below sea level as their load
depresses the ocean floor. This
series of events is clearly recorded in the Hawaiian Island chain
and surrounding reefs.

175

Field Notes panels
Locations: Places where these significant geological formations
can be found are listed. Plate tectonic addresses are given in some
cases to give a broader range of sites, particularly where common.

Collecting Rocks   128

*Granite, Rhyolite, Obsidian, Andesite, Basalt,
Breccia, Conglomerate, Sandstone, Mudstone,
Limestone, Chert and Flint, Evaporites, Marble,
Quartzites, Slate, Schist and Gneiss, Diamond,
Ruby and Sapphire, Emerald and other Beryls, Opal,
Chrysoberyl, Topaz, Garnet, Tourmaline, Peridot (Olivine),
Quartz, Spinel, Feldspars, Zircon, Hematite, Agate, Other
Chalcedony, Rhodochrosite, Rhodonite, Lapis Lazuli, Turquoise,
Malachite and Azurite, Jade, Veined Gold, Alluvial Gold, Silver,
Rocks from Outer Space.*

Rock Sites   172

*Explosive Volcanoes, Shield
Volcanoes, Columnar Jointing,
Pillow Basalt and Basalt Flows,
Sedimentary Remnants, River
Bends, Caves, Lava Tubes, Folded Rocks, Gorges
and Canyons, Glacial Valleys, Rift Valleys,
Deserts, Crossbeds, Geysers, Meteorite Craters.*

Collecting Rocks

Granite

Granite detail
(above). Carving
on the tomb
of Ramses II,
in Egypt.

Granite is a light-colored igneous rock, rich in quartz and orthoclase feldspar but poor in the ferro-magnesian (iron and magnesium) minerals. Because it cools for a long time underground, its large crystals are visible to the naked eye. Granite is structureless so weathers to spheres, called tors, in otherwise rolling countryside. These rocks form deep underground and as they rise, there is a great reduction in pressure and temperature. As a result, granite easily breaks down. Surface heating and cooling causes it to flake off, or exfoliate, in large sheets parallel to the ground surface.

Granite forms above subduction zones where two plates are colliding, and where heat melts the crustal rocks, (see p. 40). Convection holds the melt there. The granite cracks as it cool, and the cracks fill with the last of the melt. The resulting dikes may be either fine-grained aplite, or coarse-grained pegmatite. Pegmatite, which is produced from water-rich melts that allow easy movement of elements, forms crystals that can be larger than a person. Granite frequently occurs in the cores of old, folded mountain chains, often in association with metamorphic rocks. This is the signature of an old subduction zone.

A very tough rock, granite polishes to a fine mirror finish and is a popular building stone. Two of the more spectacular occurrences of eroded granite are Devil's Marbles, Australia, and Half Dome, Yosemite National Park, California, USA.

FIELD NOTES

👁 Light-colored with large crystals. Often block-jointed. May form smooth spheres or erode to sharp spires and crags.

🔨 Forms at continent-continent collision sites, so is found in the cores of old, folded mountains.

130

Rhyolite

Rhyolite is commonly pale gray, pink, or yellow. It usually forms from the melting of deep crustal rocks of granitic composition. In North America, such rocks are common in western Texas, New Mexico, Arizona, and Nevada. In western Texas, unusually fluid rhyolites flowed from fissures to cover thousands of square miles of land.

Rhyolite has basically the same composition as granite—its fine-grained structure is due to rapid cooling. It contains some large crystals, phenocrysts, formed early within the magma chamber. The many small crystals in rhyolite respond to flowing by aligning themselves in bands, an effect called flow-banding. Such patterned rocks are keenly sought after as a stone for building.

If charged with steam, rhyolite erupts noisily, ejecting clouds of ash and steam. If little steam is present, the magma will be far too stiff to flow easily and so rises directly out of the ground as mounds of hot rock.

When the magma cools too quickly for crystallization to

occur, glass-like obsidian is produced. If the cooling lava froths, a rock called pumice is formed. This variety of rhyolite is so porous and light that it can float on water—the only rock that is able to do so.

Gas cavities in rhyolite sometimes fill with silica precipitates, such as agate. When the rock is cut and polished, the resulting mosaic of banded rhyolite and agate makes pieces of great beauty that are popular with collectors.

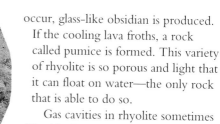

Rhyolite detail (above). Lava spire (right) in Arizona, USA.

FIELD NOTES

👁 Fine-grained, light-colored rock, often pink or gray. Frequently exhibits a flow-banding pattern.

⛏ Forms when molten granite erupts at the surface or forms intrusive bodies.

Obsidian

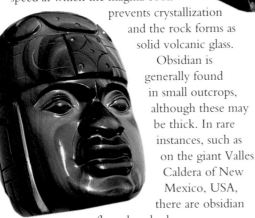

Like rhyolite, obsidian forms from the melting of deep, crustal, granitic rocks. In the case of obsidian, the speed at which the magma cools prevents crystallization and the rock forms as solid volcanic glass. Obsidian is generally found in small outcrops, although these may be thick. In rare instances, such as on the giant Valles Caldera of New Mexico, USA, there are obsidian flows hundreds of feet thick. The Glass Buttes, in Oregon, USA, are composed entirely of obsidian.

With its glassy luster and sharp conchoidal fractures, obsidian is a distinctive rock. There are several varieties of obsidian, distinguished by their color and sheen: pure black, light brown,

brown mottled with black, and black with a beautiful golden or silvery sheen. Snowflake obsidian is dotted with white patches where parts of the rock have begun to crystallize. The most prized obsidian of all is the rainbow variety, with its purple, green, and gold bands of sheen.

Because of its absence of crystals and conchoidal fractures, obsidian can be easily worked to razor-sharp edges, even sharper and finer than those of flint. It is also able to take an extremely high polish. As a result of these properties, obsidian was revered by ancient cultures. It was one of the major materials of barter, and was prized for the manufacture of sharp and delicate heads for arrows and spears. Today, obsidian is used throughout the world as a semi-precious stone for jewelry or decorative items.

Rainbow obsidian Olmec head replica (left). Obsidian detail (center). Aztec obsidian arrowhead (right).

FIELD NOTES

👁 *Generally black and glass-like, containing no crystals. Tends to form small outcrops, although these may be thick.*

🔨 *Forms where magma erupts at the surface and cools very rapidly.*

132

Andesite

Andesite is intermediate in composition between granite and basalt, so it has some small component of iron and magnesium, giving it a speckled, salt-and-pepper appearance. Andesite magmas are very viscous and set quickly, forming steep-sided volcanoes, such as Fuji, in Japan, and Anak Krakatau, Indonesia. These magmas tend to block volcano vents, causing explosions as the pressure builds.

Ignimbrite is a rock of andesitic composition that has formed in an unusual way. It usually contains some quite large crystals, but the major component is extremely fine particles of volcanic glass. It forms when gas dissolved in the lava suddenly boils as the roof of a magma chamber collapses. This causes the andesitic lava, which has been slowly crystallizing, to explode. The pressure blows some molten rock into tiny fragments that cool rapidly to fine dust or ash. Occasionally, fragments reach the ground while they are still aglow, and the particles are cemented into a solid rock called ignimbrite (meaning, literally, fire rock).

Andesite and ignimbrite are common where oceanic crust subducts under continental crust. In these conditions, melting basalt rises and mixes with melting rocks of granitic composition, as in mountain chains such as the Cascade Mountains of Washington and Oregon, USA, and the Andes of South America, from which andesite took its name.

Andesitic volcanoes are very destructive. In the Yellowstone area in Wyoming, USA, for example, several eruptions since the Pleistocene threw huge volumes of volcanic ash into the atmosphere that are each thought to have changed world climate. Small ignimbrite explosions have covered historic sites, such as the Roman city of Pompeii.

FIELD NOTES

👁 Speckled, usually brown or dark gray. Ignimbrite may contain large crystals.

➤ Extrusive igneous rock that forms at ocean–continent subduction zones, such as the South American Andes.

Victim of the Vesuvius eruption in Pompeii (below). Hornblende andesite detail (center).

Basalt

Basalt is the most common rock on the Earth's surface. It is a fine-grained, black, igneous rock, rich in silica and the ferro-magnesian minerals. Basalt occasionally contains large crystals of the green mineral olivine. In wet climates, ferro-magnesian minerals are susceptible to chemical weathering, and basalt weathers rapidly to clay.

Some black beach sands, such as those in Hawaii, are formed when hot basalt lava flows into the sea and is shattered into fragments as it suddenly chills. Basalt is typically the first lava

Amygdaloidal basalt detail (above).
Moai (below) at Anakena Beach, Easter Island.

to issue from any volcano. The majority of basalt is extruded at mid-ocean ridges from where it has formed 70 percent of the Earth's surface. Most basaltic ocean volcanoes, such as the Hawaiian Island chain, result from hot spots deep in the Earth. Islands closer to continents may be basaltic, although there is a transition to andesitic composition near continents and above subducting slabs.

As hot, flowing basalt cools, it forms a skin that distorts and stretches into rope-like shapes called *pahoehoe*. With further cooling, it slows and may crack into blocks called *a-a*. Basalt is also extruded through fissures on continents when they begin to rift. Basalt lava is very fluid and can flow for hundreds of miles, forming vast sheets. On continents, it is mostly found in areas that have undergone extension, or pulling apart, such as the Rio Grande Rift in New Mexico, or the Columbia River Plateau in the States of Washington and Oregon, USA.

FIELD NOTES

Black, fine-grained rock, occasionally with large olivine crystals.

Extrusive igneous rock often found on oceanic islands and rifting continents.

Earth's most common rock.

Breccia

Breccia is a rock composed of generally large, sharp fragments cemented together. These fragments may be produced by volcanic explosion, faulting, or sedimentary deposition. The sharpness of the fragments indicates that they did not travel far from where they fractured. Conglomerate, on the other hand, has rounded fragments, indicating significant travel. Breccia forms among volcanoes at convergent zones and wherever faulting occurs. It may also form where desert or alpine conditions cause fast erosion and the collection of debris in alluvial fans.

Mudflows are breccias made up of small particles mixed with water. They often result from volcanic debris falling on the steep flanks of snow-covered volcanoes. They also occur at the toes of alluvial fans in desert regions. Mudflows travel downhill mostly as slurries, and may set to the consistency of cement. They may be so dense that they can pick up and carry cars and large boulders. These sometimes move at such high speeds that they strip the bedrock clean of trees. A significant mudflow occurred in 1980 when Mt St Helens, in Washington, USA, erupted. Hot ash landing on snow caused a massive avalanche of debris and mud down the Toutle Valley, smashing everything in its path. Mudflow deposits are characterized by the chaotic mix of particles of all sizes and can turn V-shaped valleys into flat-floored valleys. Where the surrounding topography is steep, a flat-floored valley may indicate the presence of a mudflow.

Breccia detail (above). House (right) engulfed by a mudflow.

FIELD NOTES

👁 Breccia contains a mix of rock fragments of all shapes and sizes.

⛏ Breccias are found in fault zones, mudflows on the flanks of volcanoes and in mountainous deserts.

Conglomerate

A conglomerate is a sedimentary rock composed mostly of coarse fragments, but including a range of grain sizes. The fragments are well rounded, which indicates transportation by water. They are often deposited near mountains where gradients decrease, river velocity suddenly drops, and the river is unable to carry the coarse sediment any further. Conglomerates are common along present and ancient continental edges.

Conglomerates are common and accessible in desert alluvial fans, such as Death Valley, in California, USA. In ancient, giant alluvial fans, such as the Olgas of Australia and the Van Horn, West Texas, USA, conglomeratic deposits hundreds of feet thick can be found.

Large areas of conglomerate are produced by continental collision, where uplifting has resulted in mountain building. New rivers rise in these mountains and loose debris is swept into the river channels and carried downstream to the flat coastal areas. Later, this coarse material is covered by thick sand deposits. Many ancient sedimentary basins, such as the Sydney Basin, in Australia, record this history.

Other ancient environments represented by conglomerates include rocky beaches and the front of coral reefs, where coral that has broken off the living reef may form a slope of coral debris. As a result, fragments of shallow-water organisms may be found in conglomerates that have formed at great depths.

Look for conglomerates in desert areas where roads may skirt over alluvial fans and where recently deposited conglomerates have been cemented by minerals in the groundwater. These are quite common and easy to collect along the stream channels on the fan surface.

FIELD NOTES

👁 Composed of coarse, rounded fragments in a range of sizes.

🔨 Sedimentary rock that forms in rift valleys and near mountains. Common in rocky desert areas.

Hertfordshire pudding stone (center). Particles of various sizes in a conglomerate (above).

Sandstone

Sandstone is any rock made of particles that are sand-size, up to ¹⁄₁₂ of an inch (2 mm) in diameter. The vast majority is made of rounded particles of quartz, but it can contain feldspar and even fragments of rock. Sandstone is a very common sedimentary rock and is easy to find. It forms landscapes that reflect the orientation of its layers. Flat layers erode to cliffs as in the Grand Canyon, Arizona, USA, while folded sandstone erodes to peaks such as seen in the Rocky Mountains in the west of North America, and the European Alps. In deserts, sandstone cliffs can weather into stupendous arches and shallow caverns, as sand is flaked off the cliff face by wind and chemical erosion.

Since sand can accumulate in so many places, including rivers, beaches, lakes, offshore marine environments, and desert regions such as the Sahara, sandstones are found almost everywhere. Many features of a sandstone outcrop can be used to determine how the original deposition may have occurred. The fossil desert sand-hills exposed at Zion Canyon,

Utah, USA, for example, still show their original dune shape.

Sandstone is prominent in western USA, notably in Arches National Monument and the natural caves in which the Mesa Verde buildings are ensconced. It may be prominent in roadcuts or on the tops of small hills, where it forms resistant caps. Many vertebrate fossils are preserved in river and lake sandstone. The dinosaur graveyard at Dinosaur National Monument, in Utah, is in sandstone that accumulated during several flood events.

Sandstone detail (above).
Huerfano County Court House
(right), Colorado, USA.

FIELD NOTES

👁 *Even, medium-sized grains. Often forms in layers. Great variation of color.*

⚒ *Forms extensively in marine and land environments, in deserts, rivers, shorelines, and barrier islands.*

Mudstone

Mudstone is formed from tiny, clay-size particles. Like sandstone, mudstone is found just about anywhere on continents where still water once existed. Most mudstone collects in oceans where the water is calm enough for fine particles to settle. Thick deposits of mudstone are present in most deltas, where rivers enter still water. Layering occurs in thick mud deposits because the clay flakes, being flat, align themselves horizontally.

Mudstones are used in the manufacture of bricks and ceramics. Because they weather so easily, the best place to see them is in roadcuts or in desert areas where vegetation is sparse. Multicolored mudstones, called paleosols, represent ancient stacked soil horizons. They are found in desert areas and are easily noticeable by their alternating subdued reds, mauves, grays, and greens. An excellent example can be seen in the Painted Desert of Arizona, USA.

While mudstones may weather to subdued landscapes, turbidites, which contain some sand, may resist erosion and form more hilly topography. They are made of alternating layers of shale and sandstone. Turbidites form mainly beyond the edges of continental shelves when loosened material on the shelf edge slides down the continental slope into the ocean abyss. The downslope flows that form turbidites may attain speeds of more than 100 miles (160 km) per hour, and have been known to cut submarine communication cables. Turbidites may be squeezed up to become continental rocks but rarely form on continents. Minor turbidites are also found in deep lake deposits.

Turbidite detail (above). Banded mudstone (left), Oregon, USA.

FIELD NOTES

👁 *Composed of tiny clay particles. Gray to shades of red and distinctly layered.*

🔨 *Sedimentary rocks formed in undisturbed environments. Turbidites found on ancient ocean floors and in lakes.*

Limestone

Limestone is formed from calcium carbonate. Lime precipitates in warm tropical waters on shallow sea floors, where almost no other sediments cloud the water. Limestone rocks formed in the broad centers of flooded continents and along the edge of continental shelves where reefs were built. As a result, many limestones are composed of the skeletons of reef-forming animals. Freshwater limestone forms in tropical lakes or where hot solutions of calcium carbonate rise to the surface, such as in Yellowstone National Park, Wyoming, USA. As this water cools, the precipitates form flowstones.

The closely related dolomites are calcium magnesium carbonates, whose presence may indicate more arid conditions during deposition. Since such rocks are susceptible to solution, caves, fissures, and sinkholes are a frequent form of weathering. Limestone stores carbon dioxide in a solid state, so the amount of limestone deposited may bear a close relationship to the volume of this greenhouse gas in the atmosphere and its solution in water.

Limestone terrains frequently show the effects of chemical solution. Visually dramatic karst formations, named after the Karst region of the former Yugoslavia, are produced by limestone dissolution. The tower karsts of Asia are particularly striking examples of this type of scenery. Limestones are also prominent at the White Cliffs of Dover, England, and throughout central Texas, USA. Because of limestone's extreme solubility, it often contains underground streams and caves, in which stalactites and stalagmites form. Fossils are extremely abundant and easy to find in limestone.

Limestone detail (above). Pyramid of Kukulkan (left), Chichen Itza, Yucatan, Mexico.

FIELD NOTES
👁 Dense, massive rock. Usually light colored, but may be darkened by organic material. Fizzes in dilute hydrochloric acid.
🔨 Sedimentary rock forming in tropical marine waters and warm freshwater lakes.

Chert and Flint

Like quartz, chert and flint are composed of silicon dioxide, but because they form in the sedimentary environment, they are more likely to contain traces of other elements. All rivers entering the ocean carry dissolved silica. Oceans, already rich in silica from organic sources, consequently become super-saturated with silica, and an ultra-fine silica ooze precipitates in deep water. If no other sediment blankets the ooze, it consolidates to chert, which forms continuously in deep oceans. Where iron is present, red jasper forms. The term flint was used to describe workable nodules of chert that were found in the chalk of western Europe.

Because chert and flint are resistant to weathering, they may be left behind as nodules that accumulate on the surface of slowly dissolving limestone landscapes. Chert layers often outcrop as raised, resistant ridges. Both chert and flint are easy to find in stream channels, where they outlast most other pebbles. Chert pebbles are extremely compact and have no visible crystals. They bounce quite high when dropped on a hard surface and when two pebbles are knocked together, they make a high-pitched sound.

Chert and flint are the materials that formed the technological basis of some of humanity's earliest weapons and tools. These include delicate, razor-sharp, finely worked knives and heads for arrows and spears. Flint was also used to strike sparks to ignite gunpowder in early firearms.

Chert occurs widely in western Europe and North America. Marble Bar in Australia is a classic locality.

FIELD NOTES

Extremely tough rock.
May be plain or colorfully banded.
Dense with no visible crystals.
Associated with ancient
ocean floors. Resists erosion,
so often found as resistant ridges
or massive outcrops.

Ribbon chert detail (center). Flint spear heads (left and above right).

Evaporites

A n evaporite is the result of mineral-bearing water evaporating and precipitating crystals of its dissolved material. The common evaporites are gypsum and rock salt—gypsum frequently forms beautiful "desert roses". Evaporites are susceptible to later erosion and can dissolve under the surface, causing collapse. They form in terrestrial lakes and river environments, on the shores of arid seas, such as the Gulf of Aden, and in deep, closed basins. The entire Mediterranean Sea was a site of evaporite precipitation during the Miocene. Evaporites typically form in continental rifts when seawater pours in from one end. They are abundant in many Permian rocks around the world.

Being readily resoluble, evaporites are best preserved in deserts. Once dissolved, they precipitate as a white residue on the desert surface, which indicates that there may be crystals nearby. In general, evaporites are not very common. Rock salt is usually found only in desert lakes, such as Lake Eyre,

Australia, or Death Valley, California, USA. Gypsum may crystallize in dry lakes and appear as translucent, soft, waxy crystals, gray to pink in color.

In several events during the Tertiary, the Mediterranean Sea was closed at the Strait of Gibraltar. Each time, the entire sea evaporated, leaving behind thick salt deposits on the ocean floor. Being low in density, salt formations may become mobile when buried and rise toward the surface as giant domed structures called diapirs. These are major sites of oil accumulation.

Gypsum crystals (above). Gypsum "desert rose" (right).

FIELD NOTES

👁 Tend to be extremely pure and soft. May occur as large and beautiful crystals.

⛏ Deserts and ancient rift basins with high rates of ocean water evaporation. Salt may form underground diapirs.

Marble

Marble forms from metamorphosed carbonate rock, most usually limestone. It may be found in regionally metamorphosed areas along continent–continent collision zones and in the roots of folded mountain chains, in areas that were once shallow marine shelves where abundant coral reefs accumulated. Granite intrusions can also metamorphose limestone to marble. Examples of marble can be seen in areas such as the Alps in Europe, and Oregon Caves National Monument, USA.

Pure marble, largely calcite with minor amounts of impurities, is white, but depending on the level of metamorphosis and chemical impurities in the original limestone, different colors and crystal sizes may be present. Because it is soft and beautifully colored, it has long been valued as a stone for sculpting. Statues by such famous artists as Michelangelo and Bernini were worked in Carrara marble quarried in the Italian Appenines. Unusual textures and colors also make this

a valuable facing stone for buildings and tables. Some of the great buildings of antiquity, including the Parthenon in Greece and the Taj Mahal in India, are made of marble. Sadly, this material suffers greatly from acid rain and industrial pollution and many famous marble statues and buildings are now rapidly deteriorating.

If present in sufficient quantity, marble may weather into the same karst formations as limestone. The rock is easily weathered, so look for it in old quarries and along the sides of valleys that are cut into marine sedimentary rocks.

Bernini's "Ecstacy of St Theresa".

FIELD NOTES

👁 *Often white and uniformly crystalline, but sometimes veined and colored. Fizzes in dilute hydrochloric acid.*

⚒ *Found at continent–continent collision sites where old sea floors have been folded.*

Detail of polished marble slab (above center).

Quartzites

When quartz sandstone with a silica content of 95 percent or greater is metamorphosed, it becomes quartzite. Since sandstones form in so many lowland and marine sedimentary environments, quartzites are found in many metamorphic settings. Look for them in the roots of ancient folded mountain chains at continent–continent collision boundaries. Contact metamorphism also produces quartzite, so it can be found around granite intrusions. Quartz is a very stable mineral, so quartzite will persist through nearly any degree of metamorphism.

Because quartzite is very resistant to erosion and rarely supports vegetation, it forms exposed, rocky landscapes and rugged ridges. It can be easily seen in road cuts, stream channels, and on hillslopes, and usually stands out from the intervening schists. Sandstone crossbeds and bedding will often be preserved in quartzite, providing valuable clues about where the original sandstone came from. A famous quartzite deposit is Mt Arapiles, in Australia.

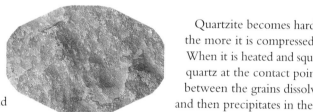

Quartzite becomes harder the more it is compressed. When it is heated and squeezed, quartz at the contact points between the grains dissolves and then precipitates in the spaces among the grains, increasing the density of the rock. As a result, it is tough and very resistant to cutting. It is therefore rarely used as a building stone. Although most quartzite is white, minor amounts of elements such as iron and manganese may produce red, green, or gray coloring. Some quartzite in Western Australia is believed to be 3,500 million years old, making it some of the oldest land crust on Earth.

FIELD NOTES

👁 *Commonly light colored. Massive with visible grains. Original bedding may be preserved.*

⚒ *Found at continent–continent collision zones where sandstones or cherts have been metamorphosed.*

Quartzite outcrop, Mt Narryer, Western Australia. Quartzite detail (above center).

143

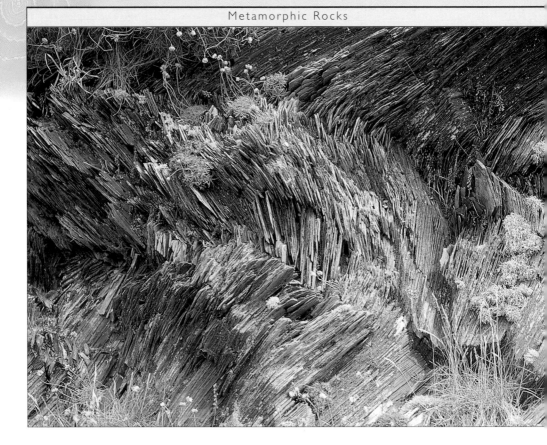

Slate

S late is metamorphosed mudstone that has been very strongly compressed. It is black to gray and mostly occurs at continent–continent collision boundaries. It is commonly found in the roots of old folded mountain chains, such as the Appalachians in the USA, and the Alps in Europe. It cleaves into sheets because all of its mica minerals are perfectly aligned at right angles to the direction of compression.

Slate detail (above). Slate tombstone (left) in Boston, USA.

Because it cleaves so easily, it sometimes produces sheets of enormous size.

Being very resistant to weathering, slate tends to be exposed in rough and craggy hills and breaks as brittle splinters along its cleavage planes. For centuries, the ability of slate to resist weathering, and even attack by acid rain in industrialized coal-burning England, made slate the preferred roofing. Tiles can be quarried, split, and installed on roofs easily, so slate was an inexpensive building material. Another popular use in former times was for writing slates and blackboards, which took their name from the black color of the slate. A major current use is for the tops of billiards tables, where weight and flatness are essential. The few remaining working slate quarries produce both tabletops and floor tiles. In a few locations, colored slate occurs in red, brown, green, and yellow, often with attractive streaking and texture.

Slate samples are easy to obtain from quarries and road-cuts in regional metamorphic areas throughout Europe.

FIELD NOTES

👁 Mainly black to gray. Cleaves into sheets. Resists erosion.

🔨 Forms at continent–continent collision zones, often at the roots of old, folded mountains. May be exposed as rough, craggy outcrops in hills.

Schist and Gneiss

Schist and gneiss are regional metamorphic rocks formed at depth in continent–continent collision boundaries. They are characterized by coarse-grained minerals, such as micas, visible to the naked eye. Schist often has a flaky, plate-like appearance, while gneiss shows alternating bands of dark ferromagnesian minerals and light minerals, quartz and feldspar.

Schist represents metamorphosed shale or basaltic rock and is largely formed from minerals that grow during metamorphism, such as muscovite mica and the semi-precious mineral garnet. Where sandstones and mudstones were present in layers, metamorphism turns the sandstone to quartzite and the mudstone to schist. Gneiss forms from either granitic igneous rock or sedimentary rock.

Because of its high mica content, schist may weather to subdued landscapes. Gneiss, which is more resistant to weathering, usually forms ridges and beds that appear as a craggy, rough landscape.

These rocks are among the most common metamorphic

rocks because they can form from most other rocks and are produced from deep burial when large volumes of rock are subducted. Some beautiful minerals grow in schist, notably garnet, which is red or brown and forms 12-sided crystals up to the size of tennis balls.

Talc, a common lubricating and dusting powder, is derived from schist that forms from basalt.

Both schist and gneiss exhibit parallel alignment of the mineral grains that grow during metamorphism. This gives them a layered appearance called foliation. When schist with a sedimentary component is exposed to increased temperature and pressure, it will metamorphose to gneiss. Both schist and gneiss are found around the Idaho Batholith, USA, and similar locations.

FIELD NOTES

👁 Coarse-grained rocks. Schist is flaky. Gneiss shows alternate banding.

🔨 Found in continent–continent collision zones. Schist erodes easily, but gneiss is more resistant, producing craggy landforms.

Gneiss detail (above center) and schist studded with garnet crystals (above right). **145**

Diamond

Diamond, the hardest natural substance, is highly valued as a rare and precious gem. Surprisingly, it is nothing more than crystalline carbon. It tends to be colorless or pale, although deep shades, known as "fancy colors", occasionally occur. The most sought-after of these colored diamonds is blood red. Less attractive industrial diamonds, known as "bort" and "carbonado", are used in drill bits and saws, and as abrasives and polishes.

Diamonds form under extremely high pressure deep at the base of old continents (known as cratons), such as occur in Africa, Siberia, India, and Australia. They may remain there for many millions of years until caught up as accidental inclusions in volcanic eruptions,

which can bring them to the surface in a matter of hours.

Miners mine diamonds from volcanic pipes or recover them from surrounding rivers.

Diamond crystals can be very large. The biggest crystal yet discovered is "The Cullinan", found in 1905 at the Premier Mine near Pretoria in South Africa. It weighed 3,106 carats and was cut into nine large and 96 smaller stones. The largest of all these stones is mounted in the British royal scepter.

As you are unlikely to find your own diamonds, the best places to see them are museums. The National Museum of Natural History in Washington, DC, USA, the Tower of London in England, and the Louvre Museum in Paris, France, all house spectacular diamonds.

Identification Diamond (C) has a hardness of 10, a specific gravity of 3.52. It is transparent to opaque, has an adamantine luster and leaves a white streak. It has a perfect octahedral cleavage, breaks with a conchoidal fracture, and belongs to the cubic crystal system. Its crystals are mostly octahedral.

Diamond crystals (center). Diamond crystal in rock (left).

FIELD NOTES

👁 *Extreme hardness (10) and adamantine luster.*

🏹 *Australia and South Africa are the main producers. Other sources include Brazil, Russia, Venezuela, India, Namibia, Angola, Ghana, and Borneo.*

Ruby and Sapphire

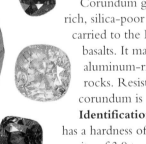

Rubies and sapphires are colored forms of corundum and the most popular colored gemstones used in jewelry today. In its pure form, corundum is colorless and somewhat rare in nature. Ruby is the red form of corundum, and its color is due to traces of chromium. All other forms of corundum are known as sapphire. These come in a range of colors, including blues, greens, and yellows, due to varying combinations of iron and titanium.

Corundum is the hardest gemstone after diamond and a high-quality ruby is more valuable than a diamond of similar quality and size. However, the value drops rapidly with the decline of color, size, and quality.

The color of corundum often occurs in patches or bands and gemstones must be cut carefully for an even appearance. Some display a star-like sheen known as asterism, due to the reflection of light from tiny, needle-like inclusions of rutile in the stone. These are known as star rubies or sapphires.

Corundum grows in aluminum-rich, silica-poor pegmatites and is carried to the Earth's surface by basalts. It may also form in aluminum-rich metamorphic rocks. Resistant to weathering, corundum is often found in rivers.

Identification Corundum (Al_2O_3) has a hardness of 9 and a specific gravity of 3.9 to 4.1. It is transparent to translucent, has a vitreous luster and leaves a white streak. It has no cleavage, breaks with an uneven, conchoidal fracture, and belongs to the hexagonal crystal system. Ruby crystals tend to be tabular to prismatic, while sapphire crystals are often barrel-shaped or pyramidal.

Sapphire crystal and gemstones (above).
Ruby crystal growing in rock (right).

FIELD NOTES

👁 Hardness (9) and horizontal striations on crystal faces.

🔨 Best locations for rubies are Burma, Thailand, and India. Sapphires are most abundant in Australia and Sri Lanka.

Emerald and other Beryls

Emerald is the name given to the highly prized green variety of the mineral beryl. The color is the result of chromium present during crystal growth. The other beryl gemstones are also given special names according to their color: aquamarine (blue-green and light blue), morganite (rose pink), golden beryl (golden yellow), heliodor (yellow to light yellowish-green), goshenite (transparent, colorless), bixbite (red), and bazzite (blue).

Beryl crystals grow, sometimes to gigantic size, in granite pegmatites, together with topaz, quartz, tourmaline, fluorite, and cassiterite. They also form in some regionally metamorphosed rocks. The largest single crystal of gem-quality emerald, weighing 7,025 carats, was found in Colombia in 1961. Massive, poor-quality beryl crystals up to 60 feet (18 m) long have been found. Emeralds were mined in Egypt around 1500 BC and Cleopatra is said to have possessed an emerald engraved with her portrait. Today, the finest-quality emeralds come from Colombia.

Identification Beryl ($Be_3Al_2Si_6O_{18}$) has a hardness of 7.5 to 8 and a specific gravity of 2.6 to 2.9. It is transparent to translucent, has a vitreous luster, and leaves a white streak. It has an indistinct cleavage and breaks with an uneven to conchoidal fracture. Beryl crystals belong to the hexagonal system and are usually prismatic with flat terminations, although they occasionally form as plates.

FIELD NOTES

- Six-sided crystals and hardness (7.5 to 8).
- Colombia is the best source of emerald. Other locations for beryls include Austria, Brazil, India, Australia, and the USA.

Uncut and cut crystals of aquamarine (center). Emerald crystals in rock with cut gem (left).

Opal

Opal is different from most precious gems because of its non-crystalline, or amorphous, nature. Opal comes in a variety of colors, the most valued being black. Other forms include white (milk opal), red (fire opal), or colorless (water opal).

The most striking feature of precious opal is the sheen effect it exhibits when turned in the light, known as "play of color". This is caused by minute spheres of silica that reflect and diffract white light. Smaller spheres produce only blues and greens, whereas larger ones produce the whole spectrum. Black opals highlight play of color most dramatically.

An opal's value depends on its body color, play of color, and soundness. A black opal, free from flaws and with a uniform pattern made up of bright, clear colors, including red, may be worth more per carat than diamond. Common opals do not exhibit play of color and, as a result, are valueless.

Opal forms in surface sedimentary environments when silica-laden waters pass through cracks, joints, and cavities precipitating silica gel. It occurs as thin veins, sheets, or nodular masses that sometimes display a botryoidal habit. Opal may also be found replacing shells, bones, plants or other minerals.

Identification Opal ($SiO_2 \cdot nH_2O$) has a hardness of 5.5 to 6.5 and a specific gravity of 2.1 to 2.2. It is transparent to opaque, has a vitreous, greasy, dull, or waxy luster, and leaves a white streak. Opal is allochromatic and often shows a brilliant play of color. It has no cleavage and breaks with a conchoidal fracture. Opal is non-crystalline and comes in a variety of habits, including massive, stalactitic, and botryoidal.

FIELD NOTES

👁 Play of color and slippery (greasy) feel.

⚒ Australia is the largest producer, with Lightning Ridge famous for black opals. Minor sources include Mexico, USA, and Brazil.

Black and white opals (center).
A polished piece of black opal (left).
A cut and polished fire opal (above).

149

Chrysoberyl

Chrysoberyl, once mistakenly considered a form of beryl, comes in various shades of yellowish- and brownish-green, due to traces of iron, titanium and chromium present during formation. It is the third hardest gemstone after diamond and sapphire.

The most prized variety of chrysoberyl is alexandrite, first discovered in the Urals, Russia, in 1830, on the 21st birthday of the Russian Czar, Alexander II. It is notable for its color change, appearing green in daylight but red under incandescent light. It is now considered to be one of the most valuable gemstones. Another notable variety is golden-yellow cymophane, also known as "cat's-eye" chrysoberyl. When cut as a cabochon, light is reflected as a silvery-white chatoyant line from the many fine, oriented inclusions.

Chrysoberyl grows as tabular crystals in granite pegmatites, together with beryl, tourmaline, garnet, and spinel. It also forms
150 in metamorphic gneiss and mica

schists. Because of its hardness, it resists weathering and is often found in alluvial deposits. The largest stone found (in Sri Lanka weighed 0.56 ounce (16 g). Alexandrite localities in the Urals have long since been depleted.

Identification Chrysoberyl ($BeAl_2O_4$) has a hardness of 8.5 and a specific gravity of 3.7. It is transparent to translucent with a vitreous luster and leaves a white streak. It has good basal cleavage and breaks with an uneven to conchoidal fracture. It belongs to the orthorhombic crystal system, with tabular or prismatic crystals, often twinned.

> **FIELD NOTES**
> 👁 *Hardness (8.5).*
> *Alexandrite changes from green to red under incandescent light.*
> 🔨 *Alluvial deposits in Sri Lanka. Mine sources include Brazil, Russia, Italy, Africa, Burma, and the USA.*

Cat's eyes (center) and a chrysoberyl crystal (above).

Topaz

Topaz occurs in a wide variety of colors, depending on the amount of flourine present during formation. It ranges from colorless, to pale green, light blue, pink, red, purplish, honey-yellow and brown. Dark orange topaz is known as "hyacinth". Some varieties of topaz, particularly the purplish ones, have been heat-treated to enhance their color.

Topaz was a rare and highly valued gemstone until the middle of the nineteenth century, when rich fields were discovered in Brazil. Today, it is very affordable and is extremely popular, particularly in its blue, pink, and honey-colored varieties.

Topaz forms at high temperature in igneous rocks such as granite pegmatites, quartz porphyry, or in veins and cavities in granitic rocks. It is associated with fluorite, quartz, tourmaline, beryl, apatite, and cassiterite. It often occurs as well-formed prismatic crystals that may weigh more than 220 pounds (100 kg). Topaz is also found as an alluvial concentrate.

One of the most distinctive features of topaz is its perfect, easy cleavage. Minute planar cleavage cracks, or incipient cleavage lines parallel to the base of the crystal, distinguish topaz from other colorless stones. Because of its cleavage, topaz requires careful handling when being cut and polished.

Identification Topaz ($Al_2SiO_4F_2$) has a hardness of 8 and a specific gravity of 3.5 to 3.6. It is transparent to translucent with a vitreous luster and leaves a white streak. It shows gold-yellow, cream, or green fluorescence. It has perfect basal cleavage and breaks with an uneven to subconchoidal fracture. It belongs to the orthorhombic crystal system with crystals forming vertically striated prisms.

FIELD NOTES
- Hardness (8) and perfect basal cleavage.
- Brazil is the world's best source of topaz. Other sources include Sri Lanka, Mexico, Japan, and Russia.

Topaz displaying typical crystal form (center and below).

151

Garnet

Garnets are a related group of minerals whose chemical compositions can vary continuously from one to the other. Key members of this group, often cut as gemstones, include almandine (red to violet red), spessartite (yellow, rose, or orange to reddish-brown), pyrope (deep red), grossular (white, yellow, yellowish-green, brownish-red, orange, or black), and andradite (colorless, yellow-green, or brown to black). This last group includes the most prized garnet—the emerald-green variety known as demantoid. The name garnet probably derives from the Latin *granatum malum*, for pomegranate. The inside of this fruit resembles red almandine and pyrope garnets.

A variety of cut garnets (above). Andradite garnet crystals in marble (below).

Pyrope ranks among the most popular of the garnets, and fine crystals have been mined and used in Czechoslovakia since the Middle Ages. Many forms of garnet do not occur as gem-quality crystals and are used industrially as abrasives.

Garnets are common worldwide, particularly in metamorphic rocks. Pyrope garnet forms in many magnesium-rich, ultrabasic, igneous rocks, including peridotites and serpentinites. Grossular and andradite garnets grow in calcium-rich metamorphic rocks, such as marble. Almandine garnet forms in iron-bearing, regionally metamorphosed rocks, such as schist.

Identification Minerals in the garnet group have a hardness of 6.5 to 7.5 and a specific gravity of 3.4 to 4.6. They are translucent to opaque, have a vitreous luster, and leave a white streak. They have very indistinct cleavage and break with a conchoidal fracture. Garnets belong to the cubic crystal system and display a variety of equant habits, particularly rhombododecahedrons.

FIELD NOTES
👁 Crystals form distinctive soccerball shapes.
⛏ All varieties of garnet are abundant in the USA. Other sources include Australia, Brazil, Sri Lanka, and the Czech Republic.

Tourmaline

Tourmaline is a complex borosilicate of aluminum and other elements, noted for its beautiful, multi-colored, prismatic crystals. In fact, tourmaline exhibits a greater range of color than any other gem, with the spectacular watermelon tourmaline changing color from green to red along the length of the crystal.

The tourmaline family is made up of seven distinct groups: schorl (black), elbaite (many colors), dravite and buergerite (brown), rubellite (pink), chromdravite (green), and uvite (black, brown, yellow-green).

Tourmaline crystals display a number of very interesting properties. They are pleochroic, meaning that they appear differently colored when viewed through different

Watermelon tourmaline (above). A pink tourmaline crystal (left). Tourmaline gemstones (right).

axes. Also, if both terminations of the crystal are present, they are morphologically different. If the crystal is heated, the ends become positively and negatively charged, attracting dust particles.

Tourmaline is mostly found in granites and pegmatites but also in some metamorphic rocks. Crystals may grow to spectacular sizes and are found with a wide range of minerals, including quartz, feldspar, beryl, and topaz. Being resistant to erosion, tourmaline often occurs in alluvial deposits.

Identification Tourmaline minerals have a hardness of 7 to 7.5 and a specific gravity of 3 to 3.3. They are transparent to opaque, have a vitreous luster and leave a white streak. They have poor cleavage and break with an uneven to conchoidal fracture. They belong to the hexagonal crystal system, displaying a prismatic habit with vertical striations.

FIELD NOTES

👁 Vertically striated, columnar crystals may be multi-colored or show different colors through different axes. Has electrical properties when heated or rubbed.

⛏ Sources include Afghanistan, Brazil, Russia, and the USA.

Peridot (Olivine)

Peridot is the name given to the mineral olivine when it is of gem quality. Olivine is an idiochromatic mineral, always occurring in a shade of green. The ratio of iron to manganese varies in this mineral, with the maganese end member known as forsterite and the iron end member known as fayalite.

Olivine is an essential rock-forming mineral, making up much of the Earth's mantle, where it combines with pyroxene to make up the heavy, coarse-grained, green rock known as peridotite. These rocks are brought to the surface by basaltic volcanoes and are occasionally blown out as volcanic bombs. Olivine also occurs in meteorites and was found in basalts recovered from the moon by *Apollo* astronauts.

Olivine is most often found in tiny granular masses, intergrown with other minerals. Large, gem-quality olivine crystals are extremely rare,

although small crystals are fairly common. These occur as short, columnar, or thick tabular forms as well as wedge-shaped terminations in basic and ultrabasic igneous rocks, such as basalts. They also form in some marbles.

Identification Olivine $(Mg,Fe)_2SiO_4$ has a hardness of 6.5 to 7, a specific gravity of 3.3 (forsterite) to 4.2 (fayalite), and leaves a white streak. It is transparent to translucent and has a vitreous luster. Olivine has an indistinct cleavage and breaks with a conchoidal fracture. It belongs to the orthorhombic crystal system, forming short, prismatic crystals, although it is usually found in granular masses.

FIELD NOTES

👁 Olivine is always a shade of green and often contains black chromite inclusions.

⛏ The major sources are Burma, and Arizona in the USA. Other sources include Brazil, Sri Lanka, and Russia.

A selection of cut peridot stones (far left). Detail of an olivine crystal (center). A peridot talisman (left) from ancient Egypt.

Quartz

One of the most common minerals on Earth, quartz, comes in a wide variety of colors and forms. The purest variety is the colorless form known as rock crystal. One of the most popular quartzes is the violet form, amethyst. Other varieties include citrine (yellow), smoky (brown to black), milky (white), rose (pink), sapphire quartz (blue), and morion (black). Rutile inclusions are common.

Quartz is an important rock-forming mineral and an essential component of acidic igneous rocks, together with feldspars, micas, amphiboles and pyroxenes. Quartz forms hexagonal prisms that are often horizontally striated and terminated by rhombohedra or pyramidal shapes. Crystals can grow to enormous sizes in pegmatites. A single crystal of

approximately 40 tons was found in Brazil, and one of 70 tons was found in Kazakhstan.

In ancient Rome, large rock crystals were cut and polished into balls, which rich citizens used to cool their hands in summer. A rock crystal ball weighing 106 pounds (48 kg) can be seen in the National Museum in Washington, DC, USA.

As a key rock-forming mineral, quartz is common in all geological environments and it makes up much of the dust in the air. As a result, any gem with a hardness less than quartz (7) will be worn down by exposure to the elements and is not generally considered to be truly precious.

Identification Quartz (SiO₂) has a hardness of 7, a specific gravity of 2.65 when pure, and leaves a white streak. It is transparent to opaque and has a vitreous luster. Quartz has no cleavage and breaks with a conchoidal fracture. It belongs to the hexagonal crystal system, usually forming prismatic, horizontally striated crystals.

Quartz stained by hematite (below).
Detail of rutilated quartz (center). A cut amethyst gemstone (right).

FIELD NOTES

👁 Crystals tend to be horizontally striated, hexagonal prisms, often terminated by rhombohedra or pyramidal shapes.

🔨 Common worldwide.

The best amethyst comes from Russia, India, and Brazil.

155

Spinel

The term spinel refers to a group of oxide minerals including magnetite, chromite, and the gem member also known as spinel. The name derives from the Latin *spina*, meaning spine or thorn, in reference to its sharp, octahedral crystals. Gem spinels occur in a wide range of colors, including shades of red, blue, bluish-green, green, and violet. Spinel has long been valued as a gemstone and, in the past, was often mistaken for ruby or sapphire. Although large, gem-quality crystals of spinel are quite rare, they tend to have fewer flaws than ruby and thus often came to be used by royalty. The best-known ruby-red gem spinel is the Timur-Rubin,

weighing 352 carats and included in the British Crown Jewels. Another famous spinel is the 2½ inch (5 cm) oval Black Prince's Ruby, which adorns the British Imperial State Crown. Spinel most commonly grows as well-formed octahedral crystals or twinned octahedra. It forms in basic igneous rocks, and in a wide variety of metamorphic rocks, including serpentinite, gneiss, schist, and marble. It also weathers into secondary alluvial deposits where it is often associated with rubies and sapphires.

Identification Spinel ($MgAl_2O_4$) has a hardness of 8, a specific gravity of 3.6, and leaves a white streak. It is transparent to translucent and has a vitreous luster. Spinel has imperfect cleavage and breaks with a con-choidal fracture. It belongs to the cubic crystal system, forming octahedral crystals that are frequently twinned.

> **FIELD NOTES**
> 👁 Sharp, octahedral crystals, often twinned. Hardness (8).
> Best sources are Sri Lanka and Burma. Minor sources include Italy, Germany, Russia, Thailand, and the USA.

Detail of a ruby-red spinel crystal (center). A variety of cut spinel gemstones (left and right).

Feldspars

Feldspars are aluminum silicates and make up more than 50 percent of the Earth's crust. They are the most common rock-forming minerals, being five times more common than quartz. They occur widely in all rock types and giant crystals are common in pegmatites. They form two major subgroups: the potash (potassium) feldspars, including orthoclase, microline, and adularia; and the plagioclase (calcium and sodium) feldspars, including oligoclase, albite, and labradorite.

A number of gemstones belong to the feldspar family. Moonstone is a transparent orthoclase which diffracts reflected light, creating a silvery-blue, cloudlike sheen called schiller. Amazonstone is a bright green variety of microcline with a silvery sheen. Sunstone is an oligoclase that reflects light from tiny, oriented, flake-like inclusions of goethite or hematite. Labradorite is a grey plagioclase with a beautiful iridescent sheen. Perfectly transparent, golden-yellow orthoclase may be faceted for jewelry, as may the pure colorless variety, adularia. With a hardness of 6 to 6.5, feldspar is not particularly durable, and tends to scratch and chip easily.

Identification Potash feldspars ($KAlSi_3O_8$) and plagioclase feldspars ($NaAlSi_3O_8$ to $CaAl_2Si_2O_8$) have a hardness of 6 to 6.5, a specific gravity of 2.5 to 2.7, and leave a white streak. They are transparent to translucent and have vitreous lusters. Feldspars have two good-to-perfect cleavages and break with an uneven fracture. The plagioclase feldspars belong to the triclinic crystal system and the potash feldspars to the monoclinic crystal system (with the exception of microcline, which is triclinic).

FIELD NOTES

👁 Various members show distinctive sheens. Two flat cleavage faces often apparent.

🔨 Worldwide. The best source of amazonstone is Russia. Moonstone common in gem gravels in India and Sri Lanka.

Moonstone cabochons (center).
An uncut amazonstone crystal (above).

157

Zircon

Zircon is a zirconium silicate that is colorless in its pure form, but comes in a variety of yellows, browns, and reds. It displays a subadamantine luster and, like diamond, has the ability to break up white light into its spectral colors, particularly in cut stones. Consequently, colorless zircons have long been used as diamond simulants. However, the birefringence, or double refraction, of zircon is so strong that when a cut stone is viewed with a hand lens, the edges of the rear facets appear double. Although it has a hardness of 7.5, zircon is extremely brittle, and the edges of cut stones chip easily. Zircon crystals grow in many types of igneous

A variety of zircon crystals (left and center). Cut zircon gemstones (right).

and metamorphic rocks, and are also found in sedimentary rocks and alluvial deposits weathered from the primary zircon-bearing sources. Most gem-quality zircon comes from alluvial deposits. Although most gem-quality crystals are small, low-quality crystals of up to 16 pounds (7 kg) have been found in Canada.

Zircons contain traces of radioactive elements that decay at a known rate and can be used to determine the mineral's age.

Identification Zircon ($ZrSiO_4$) has a hardness of 7.5, a specific gravity of 4.6 to 4.8, and leaves a white streak. It is transparent to translucent and has a sub-adamantine luster. Zircon has imperfect cleavage parallel to the prism face and breaks with an uneven fracture. It belongs to the tetragonal crystal system, forming prismatic and bipyramidal crystals, which are frequently twinned.

FIELD NOTES

Subadamantine luster, strong dispersion, double refraction, and brittleness.

The best sources of gem-quality zircon are alluvial deposits in Sri Lanka, Cambodia, and Thailand.

158

Hematite

Hematite is an iron oxide varying in color from dull brown to brownish-red, bright red, grey, or a lustrous black. Its name derives from the Greek, *haima*, meaning blood, because of its extremely diagnostic cherry-red streak.

Hematite is an important ore of iron. The earthy-red ochre varieties are used as a polishing powder known as rouge. They have also been used as a raw material for red paint since ancient times. Compact crystalline varieties, called specular iron, were once ground into highly polished flat pieces displaying a black metallic luster and used by the Aztecs as mirrors. Hematite is common, inexpensive, and is popular for jewelry. Its only drawback as an ornamental is its weight.

Common in many countries, hematite occurs in sedimentary, metamorphic, and igneous rocks. It forms as a hydrothermal or secondary mineral, as concretions, or by filling cavities and fractures.

Hematite may grow as tabular or rhombohedral crystals. The tabular crystals sometimes form rose-shaped aggregates, known as iron roses, which are highly sought after by collectors. Other habits are massive, crusty, granular, earthy, radiating-fibrous, and reniform (known as kidney ore). The hardness of hematite varies from 6.5 for the crystalline massive varieties, to as low as 1 for the fibrous and earthy varieties.

Identification Hematite (Fe_2O_3) has a hardness of 6.5 (in crystalline form), a specific gravity of 5.0 to 5.3, and leaves a cherry-red streak. It is opaque, with a dull, metallic luster and breaks with a conchoidal fracture. Its crystals are hexagonal (trigonal) and it occurs in a variety of habits.

Polished hematite stones (center). A necklace made from hematite beads (below).

FIELD NOTES
👁 Distinctive cherry-red streak. High specific gravity (5.3). Compact varieties may be attracted to a hand magnet.

🔨 Common worldwide, including sites in North America, Europe, and Australia.

159

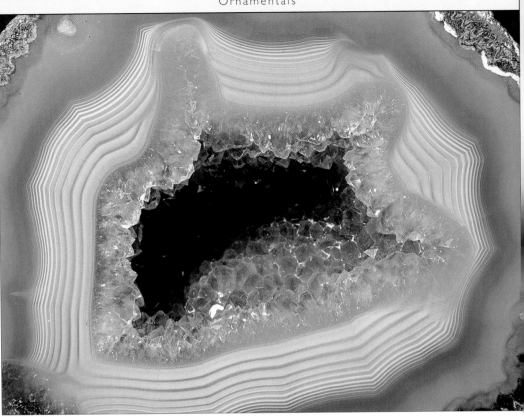

Agate

The cryptocrystalline quartzes, or chalcedony, comprise a wide group of minerals made up of tiny, interlocking microcrystals of quartz. Its members are the most visually diverse of any group, in terms of both color and habit. Collectors and jewelers have given them a wide variety of names, depending on their color and pattern.

Chalcedony precipitates from silica-bearing groundwater in rock cracks and cavities. Agates consist of brightly colored, thin, parallel bands that follow the contour of the cavity where the silica gel solidified, and this concentric arrangement is best seen in sawn and polished slabs.

Agate and quartz crystals formed in a rhyolite geode cavity (above). Agate detail (center).

Sometimes, if the cavities are not completely filled, the centers may contain crystals of amethyst, rock crystal, or smoky quartz.

Agates are named according to their appearance. Blue lace agate has bands of delicate translucent, mauve-blue and opaque white. Cloud agate has several dark, translucent centers set in a cloudy white background. Ruin agate is an interesting rare form where agate-filled cavities have been shattered by earth movement and then the broken pieces have been recemented by chalcedony of a different color. Moss agate is a transparent chalcedony with green, moss-like inclusions of chlorite. Onyx is a black-and-white-banded agate, and sardonyx has reddish-brown and white bands. Other varieties include star agate and ogle-eyed agate.

Agate was prized by the peoples of ancient Sumeria and Egypt, who used it for ornaments, receptacles, amulets, and charms. Artists in ancient Greece and Rome carved agate cameos and intaglios, using the different-colored layers to accentuate aspects of the design.

FIELD NOTES

👁 Agates are distinguished by characteristic colors and banding.

⚒ Forms in cracks and cavities, often in volcanic rocks. Like all cryptocrystalline quartz, they are found worldwide.

Other Chalcedony

There are many unbanded varieties of chalcedony that are popular with collectors and jewelers. Some of these include pale blue or yellow chalcedony; a beautiful orange-red translucent variety known as carnelian; a reddish-brown variety called sard; and plasma, a dark green chalcedony. Heliotrope is an interesting form of plasma, with numerous red spots that give it the common name bloodstone. Chrysoprase, a bright apple green due to the presence of nickel, is the most highly sought after variety. It is sometimes referred to as "Australian jade", because of its appearance and the fact that its most important sources are mines in Queensland, Australia.

Jasper is a mixture of chalcedony, quartz, and opal. It is opaque and comes in a variety of colors, including red, green, and brown, or in interesting combinations of these.

The use of colored jasper, chalcedony and agates dates back to Greek and Roman times when they were drilled and carved into numerous ornamental objects. In the Urals, in Russia

and the Ukraine, boulders of jasper weighing hundreds of pounds have been sculpted into beautiful objects. The popularity of chalcedony for carving and sculpture is largely due to its toughness and ready availability in large, uncracked lumps.

Identification Cryptocrystalline quartz (SiO_2) has a hardness of 7 and a specific gravity of 2.6 to 2.9. It is transparent to translucent, has a waxy, vitreous, or dull luster, and leaves a white streak. It has no cleavage and breaks with a conchoidal fracture. It most often occurs as botryoidal crusts and in geodes.

Detail of banded jasper (center). Cut and uncut specimens of carnelian (below), a variety of chalcedony.

FIELD NOTES

👁 *Under a microscope, chalcedony reveals itself to be either a fine crystalline aggregate, or made up of layers with a reniform surface.*

🔨 *Forms in cracks and cavities. Found worldwide.*

161

Rhodochrosite

Rhodochrosite is a manganese carbonate that comes in various shades of pink and red. It may be found as crystals but it more commonly occurs in a massive, granular, stalactitic, globular, nodular, or botryoidal habit. In these forms, rhodochrosite is often finely banded in hues of translucent to transparent pink and opaque white. These beautifully colored forms of rhodochrosite are often carved into decorative objects. Only a few stones are known to have been cut from extremely clear crystals.

Rhodochrosite is found in medium-temperature hydrothermal veins associated with copper, lead, and silver sulfides, and in altered manganese deposits. It is fairly common as a secondary mineral in the oxide zone of sulfide minerals, and may be used as an ore of manganese when available in large enough masses. When exposed to the air, rhodochrosite will develop a thin, dark oxidation crust.

The main source of rhodochrosite is San Luis in Argentina, where the local silver mines were worked by the ancient Incas. It is also mined at Capillitas near Andalgala and Catamarca east of Tucumán in Argentina.

Identification Rhodochrosite ($MnCO_3$) has a hardness of 4 and a specific gravity of 3.4 to 3.7. It is translucent, has a vitreous luster and leaves a white streak. It has one perfect cleavage and breaks with an uneven to conchoidal fracture. Rhodochrosite belongs to the hexagonal (trigonal) crystal system, but is more often found in granular, massive, reniform, or stalactitic forms.

Large rhodochrosite crystals (center) are rare. A polished slice of rhodochrosite (below).

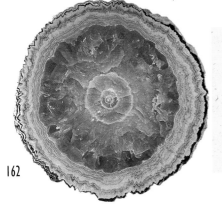

> **FIELD NOTES**
>
> 👁 Pink or red. In nodular form it shows distinctive pink and white banding. Soluble in warm hydrochloric acid.
>
> ⚲ Main source is San Luis in Argentina. Other sources include Romania and USA.

Rhodonite

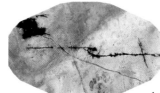

Rhodonite is a manganese silicate that, like rhodochrosite, derives its name from the Greek *rhodos*, meaning rose. As the name suggests, its color varies from pink to various shades of red, with cardinal red being the most prized. It has been used for decorative purposes since the nineteenth century and has recently become fashionable as a gemstone.

Large, transparent rhodonite crystals suitable for cutting into gemstones are extremely rare. Generally, rhodonite grows in massive cryptocrystalline aggregates, often containing black spots, bands, or fine veinlets of manganese oxide. Such inclusions stand out strikingly against the mineral's pink hues. This opaque, compact form of rhodonite has the greatest use in jewelry, being ideal for cabochons, necklace beads, and ornate carvings.

Rhodonite occurs in ore veins and forms through metamorphism of rocks rich in manganese, such as deep marine sediments and impure limestones. Although it is often associated with the oxide ores of manganese, rhodonite itself is not considered an economical manganese ore.

Major deposits of rhodonite are located in the Urals, at Sverdlovsk, Ukraine, where the mineral is extremely popular. Rich deposits also occur in Australia, particularly at Broken Hill, where large red crystals are found associated with the lead–zinc lode.

Identification Rhodonite ($MnSiO_3$) has a hardness of 5.5 to 6 and a specific gravity of 3.3 to 3.7. It is translucent, has a vitreous or pearly luster and leaves a white streak. It sometimes shows dark red fluorescence. Rhodonite has two perfect cleavages and breaks with an uneven fracture. It belongs to the triclinic crystal system, but generally occurs in massive and granular aggregates, or as stalactitic encrustations.

FIELD NOTES

👁 Pink or red coloring with characteristic black veining.

⛏ Major deposits are located at Sverdlovsk, in the Urals in Ukraine. Crystals are found at Broken Hill in New South Wales, Australia.

Detail of polished rhodonite (center). Naturally occurring rhodonite (right).

Lapis Lazuli

Lapis lazuli is a rock containing a number of minerals. Its quality and value is determined by the color and abundance of the blue mineral lazurite. This mineral is a feldspathoid of the sodalite family and varies in color from deep blue to azure or greenish-blue. Other minerals occurring in lapis lazuli include hauyne, sodalite, wollastonite, pyroxenes, amphiboles, and calcite. Traces of pyrite pepper the rock with an unmistakable, golden-yellow

Lapis lazuli detail (center). Sumerian panel (left) made of lapis and shell.

sparkle. Lapis lazuli forms in regional and contact metamorphic rocks associated with calcite and pyrite.

References to lapis lazuli occur as long ago as 2650 BC, in the Sumerian epic, "Poem of Gilgamesh". In ancient Egypt, it was used by the Pharaohs and fabulous examples were found in the tomb of Tutankhamen. The oldest and most famous lapis lazuli deposits in the world are the mines of Sar-e-Sang in the mountains of Badakhshan Province in Afghanistan. These deposits have been worked for some 6,000 years and still produce the best lapis lazuli.

Identification The primary mineral in lapis lazuli, lazurite $(Na,Ca)_8(Al,Si)_{12}O_{24}(S,SO)_4$, has a hardness of 5.5, a specific gravity of 2.4 to 2.5, and leaves a light blue streak. It is opaque and has a greasy, dull luster. Lazurite has one imperfect cleavage and breaks with a conchoidal fracture. It belongs to the cubic crystal system but crystals are rare. Lazurite generally occurs in massive and compact forms, or as fine, granular aggregates.

FIELD NOTES

👁 Blue rock peppered with golden-yellow pyrite crystals.

🔨 The best lapis lazuli comes from Afghanistan. Other sources include Chile, Tadjikstan, Colorado, USA, and the Pamirs region of Central Asia.

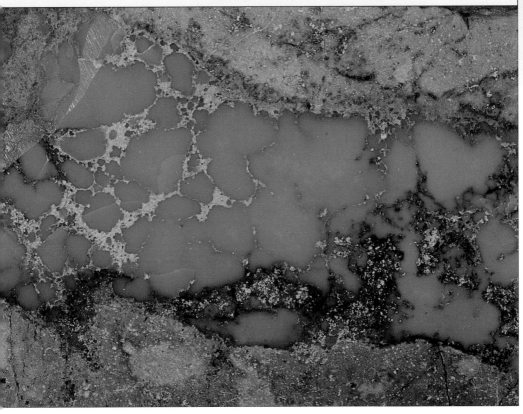

Turquoise

Turquoise is a hydrated phosphate of copper and aluminum. Its color varies from bright blue, colored by copper, to blue–green, colored by traces of iron.

Turquoise is opaque and often mottled with brown veinlets of limonite or black manganese oxide. It rarely forms crystals, more often occurring in massive, granular, crypto-crystalline, stalactitic and concretionary habits. It may be confused with the other aluminum phosphates—variscite, wardite and lazulite.

Turquoise forms in arid areas as a secondary mineral in the weathered zone of aluminum-rich igneous and sedimentary rocks. It forms crusts on the weathered rocks or fills cavities.

Turquoise has been used as a gemstone for thousands of years, dating back to ancient Egypt. It is usually cut as cabochons or used for carving. The ancient Aztecs used small tiles of turquoise to decorate elaborate masks. Turquoise is sensitive to heat so great care must be taken with cutting or polishing. If it is heated to 480°F (250°C), it will turn an unattractive green.

Identification Turquoise ($CuAl_6(PO_4)_4(OH)_8 \cdot 5H_2O$) has a hardness of 5 to 6, a specific gravity of 2.6 to 2.9, and leaves a white streak. It is opaque and has a greasy, waxy luster. Turquoise has no cleavage and breaks with a conchoidal fracture. It belongs to the triclinic crystal system but crystals are rare. It generally occurs in a massive form, as compact veins and crusts.

FIELD NOTES

- Bright blue-green with veinlets. Greasy luster.
- Best source is the Ali-Mirsa-Kuh Mountains in Iran. Another good source is the USA, particularly Arizona, Colorado, Nevada, New Mexico, and Utah.

An Aztec turquoise mask (left). Turquoise detail (center). A turquoise earring (above).

165

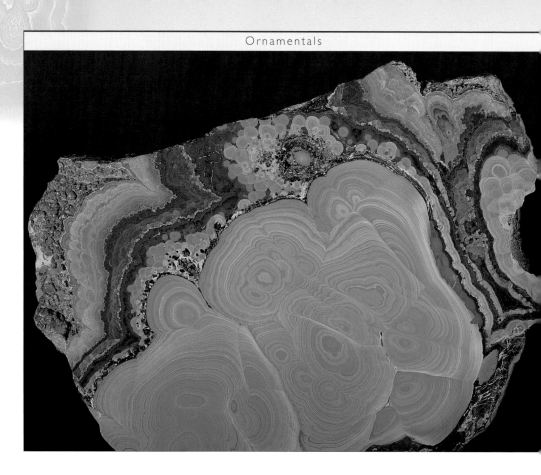

Malachite and Azurite

Malachite and azurite are carbonates of copper that generally form together. Malachite is a banded, rich green mineral, while azurite is deep azure blue. They were originally used as copper ores before their ornamental applications were realized.

Azurite was important in the ancient Orient as a blue pigment in mural painting, and today it remains important in paint production. Its use in jewelry is limited because, with a hardness of 3.5 to 4, it is too soft.

Malachite was popular with the Greeks and Romans, and was often worn in the form of amulets to ward off evil spirits. It was a popular decorative stone at the court of the Russian Czars. The majestic malachite columns of St. Isaac's in Leningrad are from this period.

Malachite and azurite both occur commonly as stalactitic, nodular, or botryoidal masses, although azurite may be found as tabular crystals. Both are very common in the oxidized zone of copper deposits, together with iron oxides and other secondary copper minerals, such as cuprite, chalcocite, and chrysocolla.

Identification Malachite $Cu_2CO_3(OH)_2$ has a hardness of 4, a specific gravity of 3.3 to 4.1, and leaves a pale green streak. Azurite $Cu_3(CO_3)_2(OH)_2$ has a hardness of 3.5 to 4, a specific gravity of 3.7 to 3.9, and leaves a light blue streak. Both are translucent to opaque, with a vitreous to dull luster. They break with an uneven conchoidal fracture and have a monoclinic crystal structure. Malachite crystals are prismatic while azurite crystals are tabular or columnar. Both occur more commonly in granular and massive forms.

FIELD NOTES

👁 Malachite is an opaque, banded green, while azurite is a deep azure blue. They are usually found together. Both react to hydrochloric acid.

🔨 Sources include Australia, Namibia, Russia, and USA

Polished malachite (above) from Zaire, Africa.
Detail of unpolished blue azurite (center).

Jade

The term jade refers to two separate minerals: nephrite (a member of the amphibole group) and jadeite (a pyroxene). Because of their incredible toughness, these minerals have developed great cultural and historical significance, being used for stone axes, hammers, fish hooks and other implements.

Nephrite varies in color from black through dark green, brown, yellow, and white. Jadeite may be green, yellow, white, pink, purple, orange, bluish, brown, or gray. The emerald-green variety of jadeite, known as imperial jade, is highly sought after. Ornamental nephrite and jadeite occur in massive habit and are difficult to distinguish from each other visually—in fact, they were considered the same mineral until the nineteenth century.

Both nephrite and jadeite are made up of microscopic, inter-locking crystals making them the toughest naturally occurring minerals. They can withstand enormous pressure and are more elastic than steel.

Nephrite and jadeite form during the high-pressure, low-temperature metamorphism of basic or ultrabasic igneous rocks.

Identification Nephrite $Ca_2(Mg,Fe)_5Si_8O_{22}(OH)_2$ has a hardness of 5 to 6, a specific gravity of 2.9 to 3.1, and leaves a white streak. Jadeite $(NaAlSi_2O_6)$ has a hardness of 6.5, a specific gravity of 3.3 to 3.5, and leaves a white or gray streak. Both are translucent to semitransparent. They lack cleavage and break with a hackly fracture. They belong to the monoclinic system but generally occur in massive form or as granular aggregates.

FIELD NOTES

Jadeite and nephrite are best distinguished from one another by their specific gravity.

Best sources of jadeite are China, South America, and Mexico. Best sources of nephrite are Canada and New Zealand.

Carved nephrite knives (above) from New Zealand. Detail of polished nephrite (center) from New South Wales, Australia.

167

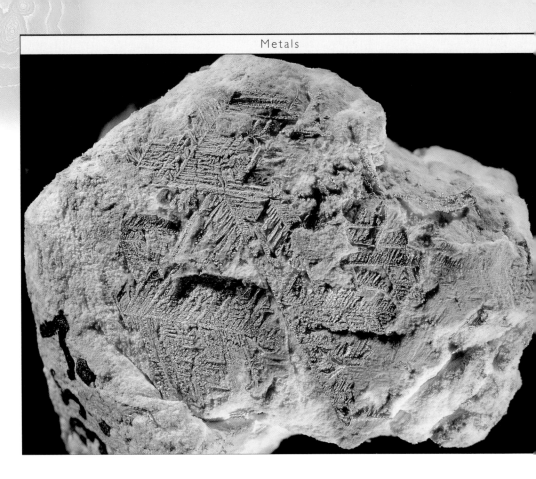

Veined Gold

Gold is a precious metal that resists forming compounds with water or oxygen. As a result, it usually occurs in an uncombined metallic form in ore-bodies. Like silver, it is referred to as an elemental, or native, metal.

Native gold is a bright, rich yellow and is resistant to tarnish. It is sometimes confused with pyrite or chalcopyrite (known as "fool's gold"), but can be easily distinguished by its golden-yellow streak. Pyrite and chalcopryite leave greenish black streaks.

Gold will sometimes mix with other metals such as silver, copper, rhodium, iridium, and platinum, which may change its color. For example, when gold contains silver, it is much paler, or if it contains copper it is redder.

Gold jug (left) from the tenth century. Veined gold in quartz (center).

Gold forms as a native metal in hydrothermal igneous veins. It may be associated with quartz, and sulfide minerals such as stibnite, chalcopyrite, arsenopyrite, pyrite, pyrrhotite, tellurides, and silver minerals. Gold sometimes crystallizes as cubes or octahedra, but more usually as irregular or dendritic masses. It has also recently been discovered that gold may be precipitated in soils by bacteria and other organisms.

Occasionally, gold appears as thick encrustations within the quartz veins. Generally, however, the gold occurs only as small specks and, in many cases, the gold particles are too small to be seen, remaining locked up within the sulfide minerals. During processing, these rocks have to be crushed and ground to expose the gold, which can then be dissolved using mercury or cyanide. With mercury, gold forms a heavy amalgam, that can then be separated from the treated ore. In the cyanidation process, gold reacts with sodium cyanide to form sodium cyano-aurite, which can then be treated to extract the gold.

> **FIELD NOTES**
>
> 👁 *Distinguishable by high specific gravity, softness, malleability, and yellow streak.*
>
> ⚒ *The Witwatersrand mines of South Africa produce a third of the world's gold. Other sources are Australia, Russia, and the USA.*

Alluvial Gold

Because of its high specific gravity and resistance to erosion, gold will often weather from vein deposits. The grains and flakes of gold will then find their way downhill, eventually ending up in river deposits or sedimentary rocks formed from these deposits. While these grains are usually tiny, larger lumps, known as nuggets, are sometimes found. Because gold is so malleable, the nuggets are often rolled or worn into rounded shapes.

Gold nuggets are rarely larger than pebbles, but there are some famous exceptions. The largest pure nugget, weighing 156 pounds (70.9 kg) was the "Welcome Stranger" found at Moliagul, Victoria, in Australia in 1869. The "Holtermann Nugget", found in 1872 at Hill End, Australia, and weighing 630 pounds (286 kg), is often named as the largest gold nugget. However, this is not technically correct. It was actually a slab of slate containing 220 pounds (100 kg) of veined gold.

Panning is the age-old method of searching for alluvial gold, although extraction processes have become more sophisticated. Whatever the method of extraction, the principle is much the same—dense gold particles are separated from the lighter sand and gravel particles.

Identification Gold (Au) has a hardness of 2.5 to 3, and a specific gravity of 19.28 (when pure). It is opaque, with a metallic luster, and leaves a golden-yellow streak. It has no cleavage and breaks with a hackly fracture. Gold belongs to the cubic crystal system and grows as crystals or dendritic masses in veins.

> **FIELD NOTES**
> Grains, flakes, or nuggets of soft, golden-yellow material that will tend to concentrate in the bottom of the pan.
> Gold can be panned wherever streams or rivers drain away from gold deposits.

Gold nugget (above) from Mt Kari, Papua New Guinea. Gold nuggets (center). An 1869 sketch (right) showing gold panning in California, USA.

169

Silver

Silver, like gold, occurs as a native metal, although it is more often found combined with the sulfides of lead, zinc, and copper (galena, sphalerite, and chalcopyrite). In its native form, silver usually occurs as star-shaped or tree-like aggregates, as dendrites and wire-like forms, or as compact masses. It occasionally crystallizes as cubes or octahedra.

Silver forms as a primary mineral in hydrothermal, supergene deposits and in veins, usually associated with lead, zinc, or copper. It is very soft and is usually alloyed to make it stronger. The best known alloy is sterling, which is 92.5 percent silver and 7.5 percent copper, and has long been valued for its work-ability and resistance to corrosion. The main application for silver are for coinage, jewelry, medicine, chemistry, and photography. Because of its thermal and electrical conductivity, it is also important in electrotechnology.

The first significant silver mines were those of the pre-Hittites of Cappadocia in eastern Anatolia, and by 2000 BC, lead ores were being smelted to obtain silver. Today, the largest producer of silver is the Guanajuato Mine, in Mexico, where silver has been extracted since AD 1500. More than half the world's silver reserves are held in Mexico, USA, Canada, Peru, Kazakhstan, and Russia.

Identification Silver (Ag) has a hardness of 2.5 to 3 and a specific gravity of 9.6 to 12 (when pure). It is opaque, has a metallic luster, and leaves a glossy white streak. It has no cleavage and breaks with a hackly fracture. Silver belongs to the cubic crystal system, but crystals are rare, forming as octahedrons or hexahedrons. Silver more often occurs as wires, dendrites, or plates.

> **FIELD NOTES**
> 👁 High specific gravity.
> Softness, malleability, and color.
> Guanajuato Mine in Mexico is the world's best source.
> Also North America and Russia.
> Fine dendritic and wire-like crystals are found at Köngsberg in Norway.

Viking amulet made from silver (above).

Silver crystals (center).

Rocks from Outer Space

Meteorites are bodies of material that, while traveling through space, e trapped by the Earth's gravitaonal field. If they survive their urney through the atmosphere, ey strike the Earth's surface. Of ousands of meteorites that strike the arth each year, fewer than 10 are generally corded. The rest land in oceans or deserts.

As meteorites enter Earth's atmosphere they artly melt. As they slow down, their surface olidifies again, forming a dark, glassy fusion rust. Four distinct types of meteorite are found. he first, composed completely of nickel and on, are known as irons or siderites. If cut and olished, the nickel and iron appear as light and ark parallel bands. A gigantic, 36.5-ton siderite housed in the American luseum of Natural History.

The second type are stones or erolites. Composed of silicate aterial, these have an oxidized rust and consist largely of yroxene and olivine. The third oup are composed of both metal nd silicate and are known as stony ons or siderolites.

The fourth group are tektites— splashes of molten meteoritic and crustal material from large impacts. Because they are predominately crustal in composition, however, they are not always considered to be true meteorites.

Meteorites are important because they are likely to represent samples of planetary material and their compositions are used to estimate the average composition of other planets as a whole. The irons and stony irons may contain iron, cobalt and nickel sulfides, carbides, phosphides, and sometimes graphite. Crater structures so large that they are visible only from a satellite tell us that the Earth has been struck by giant meteorites in the past.

FIELD NOTES

Look for the presence of a fusion crust, and the presence of nickel-iron alloy.

If you recover an object that fell from the sky, submit it to a museum or university for expert examination.

An australite (center), a tektite from Australia. A meteorite (above) recovered from the Arizona crater, Flagstaff, USA.

Rock Sites

Explosive Volcanoes

Volcanoes vary in shape according to their magma composition. The more silica the magma contains, the steeper the volcano will be. So the high-silica andesitic volcanoes of Kamchatka (Russia), Japan, Alaska, Indonesia, and the western side of the Americas are all steep. These volcanoes occur above subducting slabs where silica collects and mixes with basalt magma. Most high-silica volcanoes produce ash and form soft, conical mountains, such as occur in the Mojave Desert, California, and Sunset Crater, Arizona, USA. Typically, these have radial drainage—many gullies running straight down all around the mountain, as seen at Mt Yoti, Japan.

All high-silica volcanoes are explosive, and their perfect cone shape changes dramatically upon explosion. Some of the mountain may be left, as when Mt St Helens exploded in Washington State, USA, or only the perimeter of the cone may be left, as when Mt Hakone erupted in Japan.

After an explosion, a lake may form in the resulting crater. Subsequently, a small cone forms in the center of the lake, as in Lake Toya, Japan, and Crater Lake, Oregon, USA. Eventually, the small cone grows to the size of the original volcano, and the next explosion occurs. This pattern is recorded around Mt Fuji, Japan. The growth and explosion of andesitic volcanoes continues until subduction stops feeding them magma.

An 1831 sketch (right) of a volcano, Julia Island, Sicily. Sunset Crater (below) Arizona, USA.

FIELD NOTES

Volcanoes along subduction lines, as in Russia, Japan, Alaska, Indonesia, New Zealand, North and South America. Crater lakes can be seen at Lake Toba, Indonesia; Crater Lake, USA; Lake Toya, Japan.

Shield Volcanoes

Hot-spot volcanoes form from fast-running, low-silica basalt magma. On land, they have low-angle cones and are often referred to as shield volcanoes, after ancient Roman shields. When they form underwater, they start with a steeper shape because the lava freezes much faster and does not travel as far. The volcanic pedestal is formed from fractured pieces of pillow basalt (see p. 177). The shape flattens to the shield form as the cone builds above sea level, as in the Hawaiian Islands.

A hot-spot volcano has a limited life, forming as a plate passes over a hot spot deep in the mantle (see p. 43). The volcano builds in size as the plate moves steadily on. Once the plate has moved sufficiently, a new volcano will appear over the stationary hot spot and the old one will become inactive and eventually erode. Continental hot-spot volcanoes

An eroded oceanic hot-spot volcano in Tahiti, Polynesia.

FIELD NOTES

Hawaiian Islands, USA
Yellowstone National Park, USA
Mt Erebus, Antarctica
Mt Kilimanjaro, Tanzania
Tristan da Cunha, Atlantic Ocean
Réunion Island, Mauritius
Lord Howe Island, Australia
Barrington Tops, NSW, Australia

erode to subdued hills, as can be seen all along the eastern coast of Australia. Oceanic hot-spot volcanoes erode to sea level to produce flat-topped pedestals called guyots. These subside below sea level as their load depresses the ocean floor. This series of events is clearly recorded in the Hawaiian Island chain and surrounding reefs.

175

Columnar Jointing

Columnar jointing is one of the best known geological structures. Columns, usually with five or six sides, can measure from 2 inches (5 cm) to 10 feet (3 m) across. Columnar jointing occurs when hot lava or welded volcanic ash cools and contracts.

To release the contraction stresses, triple cracks develop from points of chilling on the top surface. The angles between the cracks are about 120 degrees and they influence each other, joining into polygons. The cracks penetrate into the rock, eventually meeting similar cracks initiated by cooling at the bottom.

The resulting basalt or ignimbrite columns are usually oriented at right angles to the cooling surfaces. Horizontal surfaces tend to have vertical columns, but when lava flows cool against sloping creek banks, the columns will be inclined, indicating the topography beneath. When the cooling pattern is distorted by nearby lava tubes or steam vents, some columns develop in radiating shapes that suggest flowers.

Thick ignimbrite can develop columns up to 1,000 feet (300 m) tall. Basalt lava thins as it flows, so columns up to 50 feet (15 m) are more usual.

Teleki's East African expedition encounters a columnar basalt ravine (left). Devil's Tower (right).

FIELD NOTES

Devil's Tower, Wyoming, the Palisades, New York, and along the full length of the Columbia River Gorge, Washington and Oregon, USA. The Giant's Causeway, Ireland. Cape Raoul, Tasmania, Australia.

Pillow Basalt and Basalt Flows

When basalt magma flows into water, the outer surface chills, becoming solid, while the inside remains hot and continues to flow. As the front of the flow freezes, magma bursts out of its new basalt tube and surges forward before chilling again. The top shape of the flow is rounded, much like a long pillow, and the spaces between the tops are V-shaped. As new pillows flow over layers of earlier pillows, they conform to the shape between the old tops. These new pillows will then have V-shaped bottoms and rounded tops.

Pillows form where oceans spread, so pillow basalt is a very common rock form, although usually hidden beneath the oceans. Pillow basalt along the Columbia River Gorge, Washington State, USA, was formed by a flow of basalt that interrupted rivers, causing lakes, which then filled with basalt in this pillow form. Most of the underwater flows near volcanic islands are pillow-shaped, so it is common to see them around such coastlines.

Basalt flows that chill in air have two typical forms. Slow air-cooling causes a thin skin, which is then stretched and wrinkled as the flow continues. The resulting ropy texture is called *pahoehoe* lava. Further cooling thickens the skin, so cracks develop, and the lava surface becomes blocky, and is called *a-a* lava. With cooling downslope, there is a transition from ropy lava to fractured blocky lava. This is visible in all surface basalt flows and around any active volcano.

Pillow basalt (right) forming on the slopes of an underwater volcano in Indonesia.

FIELD NOTES
✦ Craters of the Moon lava field, Idaho, and Columbia River Gorge, Washington, USA.
Volcanoes National Park, Hawaii.
Around the coasts of Japan, New Zealand, Tahiti, Hawaii, Italy, and the west coast of South America.

Typical ropy form of lava (left) called pahoehoe.

177

Sedimentary Remnants

Erosion is Nature's sculptor, carving some of her best art in flat-lying layers of sedimentary rock by isolating small parts of once-continuous beds. Water enters vertical cracks that are generated when the layers of sediment flex, and weathering widens them until most of the layer is removed. This process creates mesas and buttes that erode further to natural bridges, arches, pinnacles, and pillars, some capped by balanced rocks. Seaside cliffs may also erode in this way, creating such formations as the Twelve Apostles, in Victoria, Australia.

An 1869 engraving of buttes in Colorado (center) by John Wesley Powell. A natural arch (below left), Utah, USA.

Mesas and buttes are common in central Australia, and North and South America. Some of the most impressive eroded landforms can be seen in Utah and Colorado, USA. In Arches National Park, Utah, many closely spaced, intersecting vertical fractures divide the thick Entrada Sandstone into thin vertical slabs. The fracturing results from the presence of a layer of salt beneath the sandstone. The soft, buoyant salt flows with pressure, and in doing so, removes support from beneath sections of the slabs. Unsupported sections fall down, forming natural bridges, caves, and arches.

At Bryce Canyon, Utah, USA, quite different patterns form when silty and limey lake deposits are eroded by rain. The result is myriad banded, pastel-colored spires that form a spectacular natural amphitheater

FIELD NOTES
Monument Valley,
Arches National Park,
Natural Bridges National Park,
Bryce Canyon, Utah, USA.
Venezuela, South America
The Twelve Apostles, Victoria,
and the Bungle Bungles,
Western Australia.

River Bends

When water flows across a plain with almost no gradient, small local rises can deflect the flow from the average downhill direction. This leads to meandering streams. In low-gradient areas, these streams will not cut very deeply into the land surface.

Most meandering streams flow in loose sediment, where the position of the stream channel is constantly changing. Erosion on the outside of bends is accompanied by deposition on the inside of bends, and the bends creep both sideways and downstream. This occurs mostly in mid-plate regions, affecting rivers such as the Amazon, in South America, and the Darling, in Australia. The Alatna River, in Alaska, USA, has spectacular, tight bends that increase the actual length of the river dramatically.

In areas of strong tectonic uplift, such as the Rocky Mountains, in Colorado, USA, streams can become deeply incised in the bedrock. These have very abrasive bedloads, allowing rapid down-cutting into the relatively soft sediment of the surrounding area. Deep entrenchment depends on uplift, but also requires soft bedrock, or

the process ceases as soon as a hard barrier occurs in the river, slowing erosion to less than the uplift rate.

Entrenched meandering rivers change their position little, as is evident at the Goosenecks on the San Juan River, Utah, USA. The pattern of bends has not changed since the river first began.

East Alligator River (above left), Australia.
Goosenecks (above), San Juan River, USA. 179

Caves

Limestone caves form when calcium carbonate dissolves out of limestone. Water entering narrow cracks in the limestone enlarges them to passageways, and sometimes to ballroom-size caverns. Many levels may develop in the one cave system, leaving upper caves dry. Some caves are formed by wave action around the perimeters of lakes, and may have been inhabited by animals and humans through time.

Water leaking into dry caves evaporates, leaving calcite on the cave surface. Beautiful

Drapery formations in Carlsbad Caverns, New Mexico, USA.

shapes form as ornamentation on the cave walls, floors, and ceilings. Cave decorations include stalactites, stalagmites, columns, draperies, flowstones, oolites (cave pearls), and helictites (or mysteries, the formations that project sideways from walls and other formations). Coloring in caves is the result of impurities in the groundwater, with iron oxide producing most of the yellows, browns, and reds.

Cave systems can be vast. The Mammoth–Flint Ridge cave system in Kentucky, USA, consists of 190 miles (306 km) of connected passages and chambers. One of the world's deepest caves, extending 1 mile (1.6 km) underground, is the Gouffré de la Pierre St Martin, on the border of France and Spain. Papua New Guinea also has enormous caves, formed in thick, inclined limestone layers. One of these, Atea Kananda, is just under a mile (1.5 km) deep.

Stalagmites and stalactites in Jenolan Caves, NSW, Australia.

FIELD NOTES

Carlsbad Caverns, New Mexico, USA

Mammoth–Flint Ridge cave system, Kentucky, USA

Jenolan Caves, NSW, Australia

Gouffré de la Pierre St Martin, French/Spanish border

Atea Kananda, Papua New Guinea

Lava Tubes

Basalt flows can become hollow inside. When flowing basalt begins to cool, the interior cools more slowly than the outer skin. This results in the top of the flow becoming hard while the inside is still able to move. Should the lava supply dwindle, the interior of the lava tube may drain and what remains is an empty tunnel.

Lava tubes are relatively rare, but many stretch for several miles. They can have the dimensions of a large railway tunnel, or be quite small, just a few feet (a meter or so) across. Sometimes, the lava has flowed along a creek bed, so that the lava tube is an isolated tunnel, such as the Undara lava tubes in Queensland, Australia. Ornamentation is common in lava tubes, with solidified dribbles of lava and spatter from popping bubbles decorating the walls.

Lava stream in tube, Surtsey Island, Iceland.

FIELD NOTES

Undara lava tubes, Queensland, Australia

Thurston Lava Tube, Big Island Volcanoes NP, Hawaii, USA

The Shoshone Ice Caves, Idaho, USA

Family caves of Rapanui people, Easter Island

Sections of the roof may collapse giving access to the tube, and eventually, the entire roof may collapse, forming a long depression. Lava tubes often have flat floors, created when later flows drained through the cooling tube. Sometimes, several flows will fill the tube completely, leaving horizontal layers. Occasionally, benches are seen along the sides of the tubes, revealing past "flood" levels. In cold areas, ice may form in lava tubes and persist all year round.

Lava tubes may also be found on any recently formed islands, such as Hawaii and Tahiti. On Easter Island, the family caves in which the Rapanui people stored relics, are, in fact, lava tubes. In Hawaii, the Thurston Lava Tube, complete with stairs and interior lighting, has been opened to the public.

Folded Rocks

Sediment deposited in water forms rocks with uniform flat, horizontal layers. Subsequent geological events may fold these layers, changing their angle. Erosion working on inclined sediments makes different scenery from that formed in unfolded sediments. Compare the scenery produced by the horizontal layers of the Grand Canyon, Colorado, USA, with that produced by the sloping layers of the European Alps, or the Andes, in South America.

When continents collide, horizontal compression can incline rock layers at angles up to 90 degrees. Folding on a continental scale forms fold mountains. The European Alps and the Himalayas are examples of currently active continental collision folding, while the Appalachian Mountains of the USA are the eroded remnants of an ancient continental collision.

Localized folding of rocks may occur when buoyant masses of magma and salt

rise through overlying sediment layers, forming circular domes. Rocks also fold when dragged along a fault. These folds often reveal the movement of the fault as seen along the San Andreas Fault, in California, USA.

Folds can be open, such as the gently sloping folds near Barstow, in California, USA. They can also be more tightly folded, such as seen in the dramatic folds exposed in the Jurassic limestone of Stair Hole, at Lulworth Cove, in Dorset, UK. Here, the once-horizontal beds have been folded into spectacular S-shapes. Very small, tight folds develop in deeply buried rock layers when they become warm and plastic.

FIELD NOTES

✦ Andes, South America
Zagros Mountains, Iran
European Alps
Rocky Mountains, North America
Ural Mountains, Russia and Ukraine
Stair Hole, Dorset, UK
Himalayas, Nepal

Tight folds in Hammersley Gorge (center), Western Australia. Open folded hills in north-west Argentina (below).

Gorges and Canyons

Gorges are deep, steep-sided slots, cut below the surrounding countryside by water. Special conditions are required to produce the deep floor and steep sides, as valleys usually widen faster than they deepen. The existence of a gorge indicates either active uplift, or some recent event, such as a fault or a volcanic eruption. Canyons cut into hard metamorphic rocks maintain their shape well.

The Grand Canyon in Arizona, USA, developed from the slow uplift of the Colorado Plateau. The Colorado River kept pace with the uplift and still maintains its base level. The Grand Canyon keeps its remarkable shape because it is located in arid country, where erosion of the gorge sides is slow. Waimea Canyon on Kauai Island, Hawaii, is a volcanic canyon, cut into soft ash and occasional lava layers by heavy rainfall.

Cheddar Gorge (right), UK. The Colorado River, USA (below).

FIELD NOTES

Waimea Canyon, Kauai Island, Hawaii, USA

Grand Canyon, Arizona, USA

Verdon Gorge, Provence, France

Cheddar Gorge, UK

Katherine Gorge National Park, Northern Territory, Australia

Yangtze Gorges, China

Canyons can form from the widening of fractures in sandstone, as occurred in the Blue Mountains, in NSW, Australia. Joints formed some 80 million years ago, and were widened into gorges by recent uplift.

183

Glacial Valleys

As glaciers grind their way through valleys, rocks become embedded in their bases and scrape a characteristic U-shaped path. The width of a valley glacier does not change downvalley, as do rivers, so glacial valleys are uniformly wide between side tributaries. Loose rock fragments are continuously falling into the valley, mostly down into the gap between the ice and the valley sides, ensuring that erosion of the valley sides keeps pace with the valley bottom.

Smaller tributary valleys carry smaller glaciers, and so wear down more slowly. As a result, they often end abruptly, well up the main wall of the valley. These are called "hanging valleys" and the glaciers that created them are known as "hanging glaciers". The ice and rock debris of a hanging glacier avalanches onto the main glacier, depositing rocks along its edge, and sending shattered ice across its surface.

Retreating glaciers melt back up their valleys, past hanging glaciers. Hanging glaciers persist longer, having greater elevation and so continue to enter the main valley after the main glacier has melted past. Their terminal moraines, or rock piles collect on the floor of the main valley, forming rock fans.

FIELD NOTES

Glacial activity occurs at high altitudes and high latitudes.
Glacier National Park, British Columbia, Canada
The fiords of Norway
The Andes, Chile and Argentina
The Himalayas, India and Nepal
The European Alps

A precariously balanced rock, deposited by a glacier (left), Mer du Glace, French Alps. Briksdalsbreen Glacier (centre), Norway.

Rift Valleys

Rift valleys form mid continent, directly above divergent convection zones. They are the first step in continental break-up. Continental rifting begins when a dome develops and the surface cracks. Three splits form, radiating from the center at roughly 120 degrees to each other. These intersecting rift valleys extend in length and gradually widen further.

Fissures open as the rift valleys form and basalt lava rises to create a floor in the rift, well below sea level. High scarps are common features of rift margins and drainage from surrounding areas creates lakes on the rift floor, such as Lake Victoria and the several other lakes of the East African Rift. Volcanoes develop on rift floors, creating beautiful and unusual volcanic wetland scenery.

The East African Rift, the Red Sea Rift, and the Gulf of Aden Rift are three arms that originally formed over a dome at their point of intersection. When one rift reaches the ocean, sea water enters and evaporation causes salt to be precipitated. This process results in the buildup of evaporite deposits. In the East African Rift, major volcanic activity blocked off the

A rift valley at Almannagjá, Thingvellir, in Iceland.

FIELD NOTES

East African Rift, Africa
Red Sea Rift, Africa
Gulf of Aden Rift, Africa
Baikal Rift, Russia
Rhine Graben, Germany
Oslo Rift, Norway
Rio Grande Rift, New Mexico, USA
Iceland Rift

East African arm of the rift from the ocean, making the salt deposits accessible.

The East African Rift valley contains some of the earliest traces of human development. It has been suggested that rifting in Africa created a series of rapidly changing environments which, in turn, provided the conditions for humans to evolve.

Deserts

A desert is a region where there is very little available water. This includes areas such as Antarctica, as well as the dry, sandy regions people more often recognize as deserts. Low rainfall in deserts often results in sparse vegetation, with landforms standing out in sharp relief, giving a clear picture of the geology of the region.

Many deserts occur mid-continent because the winds have released all their moisture by the time they reach so far inland. These dry winds erode desert landscapes into spectacular shapes and build vast sand dunes. Variable wind directions create arcuate, curved, sand dunes, but if wind direction is consistent, straight sandhills up to 75 miles (120 km) long form, as in central Australia. Strong winds strip sand from among pebbles,

"A Sand Wind on the Desert" (below), 1821, in northern Africa. Gibson Desert wildflowers (below left), Western Australia.

leaving a layer of pebbles exposed on the surface. These are often coated in iron oxide and have a red-brown polish called desert varnish.

Some deserts, such as the Atacama Desert in Chile, are entirely natural. Here, dry offshore winds from the Andes Mountains blow across the region and out to sea. They are so constant that rain has not fallen there in living memory. In other cases, the activities of human habitation have contributed to desertification.

> **FIELD NOTES**
> ✺ Kalahari Desert, Botswana
> Sahara Desert, North Africa
> Atacama Desert, Chile
> Central Australian deserts
> Sonoran, Great Basin, Mojave, and
> Chihuahuan Deserts, USA
> Gobi Desert, Mongolia and China
> Thar Desert, India and Pakistan

Crossbeds

Crossbeds are inclined layers seen within otherwise horizontally deposited beds of sandstone. When bedding is horizontal, the differences in color and composition between consecutive layers of sandstone and mudstone are obvious. In the case of crossbed layers, however, the compositional difference between the layers is not nearly so apparent.

Crossbeds are formed by the movement of sand in dunes by wind or water. Sand grains roll or bounce up a dune, then collapse down its lee side as an avalanche, adding a discrete layer—a crossbed. Between the deposition of each sand layer, fine dust or mud is deposited in the lee of the dune. Later dunes may then cover the earlier dunes.

When the grains cement into rock, the thin, fine layer allows the sandstone to break along the crossbed surfaces, particularly when compression has turned the fine sediment to mica. Erosion works at different rates on layers

The distinctive pattern of crossbedding in Navajo Sandstone (left and below).

of various hardness, revealing the crossbeds.

Wind-deposited dunes have undulating tops, and sandstone formed in this way reveals the wind-blown shape of desert dunes. River-deposited beds have flat tops, and the crossbeds slope from top to bottom of each bed. During a flood, the river picks up sediment, but after the peak level, this is dropped. Large volumes of sand are then deposited quickly with the rapid fall in stream velocity. Sand is dumped on the river bottom, slumps down dune faces, and one sand wave covers another, forming flat crossbedded layers.

FIELD NOTES

Crossbeds are found on all sedimentary basins
Zion Canyon, Utah, USA
Blue Mountains, NSW, Australia
The Old Red Sandstone, Devon, UK
The Karoo Sandstone, South Africa

Geysers

The term geyser comes from the Icelandic word *geysir*, meaning spouter or gusher. A geyser is the spectacular exit of water and steam from a subterranean cavity through a vent in the ground. The continuous discharge of water from geysers is probably not possible, although steam jets issuing from hot ground areas are related and some in Iceland and Hawaii are harnessed to generate geothermal power.

Geysers occur only in volcanic areas with hot rock close to the surface. They are most common above subducting zones and hot spots, where temperatures near the surface exceed boiling point. Water discharge is cyclic, and is produced by a sequence of events unique to each geyser.

Tall geysers occur only under special conditions when water steadily fills a cool cavity near the surface. Beneath this cavity, and connected to it, is a hot-walled cavity that receives the overflow from the upper cavity. The walls of the lower cavity are well above boiling point and they turn the overflowing water to steam, which generates a vast and sudden increase in volume.

The water in the upper cavity is then forcefully ejected by the steam. Once the water is gone, the steam is free to escape, no more steam is made, pressure falls, and the show is over. Before the next performance, the system must rebuild to flash point.

Explorer John Wesley Powell (left) at Yellowstone in 1869. Beehive Geyser (below), Yellowstone, USA.

FIELD NOTES

Yellowstone National Park, Wyoming, USA
(300 geysers, including
Old Faithful, which shoots
every 90 minutes)
Hawaii, USA
Rotorua, New Zealand
Iceland

Meteorite Craters

A meteor describes any material traveling through space. When such an object strikes the surface of a planet, it is known as a meteorite. There are craters made by meteor impacts all over the Moon, Mars, and Mercury, and on all other dry planets and satellites of the solar system. The Earth has had its share of these, but plate tectonics and erosion continuously erase the record. As a result, major craters still visible tend to be in old, dry areas.

Because meteors strike the Earth at such high velocity, their craters are much larger than the meteors that made them. Meteor Crater in Arizona, USA, is ¾ mile (1.2 km) in diameter and 600 feet (180 m) deep, but is thought to have been made by a meteorite only 100 feet (30 m) in diameter traveling tens of thousands of miles per hour on impact. This event took place 25,000 years ago, and since that time, most of the rim of the original crater, now about 100 feet (30 m) high, has been eroded, even in such dry conditions as prevail in Arizona.

The high compressional shock of a meteor impact creates radiating supersonic waves. The heat of impact fuses rock, forming

Gosse Bluff, Central Australia, a 130-million-year-old crater with a giant "shattercone" in the foreground.

FIELD NOTES

✦ Meteor Crater,
Arizona, USA
Wolfe Creek, Henbury, and
Gosse Bluff, NT, Australia
The Acraman Craters,
South Australia
Chicxulub Crater,
Yucatán, Mexico

glass. Deeper rock is shocked, producing an unusual cone-in-cone structure, characteristic of high-impact sites. Much material is ejected on impact, including chemicals vaporized from the meteor. Some material from the Acraman Crater in Australia has been found more than 160 miles (250 km) from the impact site.

189

Every truth has two sides; it is well to look at both,
before we commit ourselves to either.

"The Mule", *Fables*
AESOP (c. 620–560 BC), Greek fabulist

CHAPTER SEVEN

FOSSILS FIELD GUIDE

USING *the* FOSSILS GUIDE

This field guide introduces some common fossil types

as well as special sites where finds of great significance have been made.

Whether you want to get out into the field and feel the thrill of finding your own specimens, or just understand more about fossils, this guide provides the amateur with a useful introduction.

This panel refers to the biological classification of the fossil group.

Mollusca: Cephalopoda

Oxytracheras (ammonite), Jurassic

Mollusca: Cephalopoda

Ammonites: Asteroceras (large shells) and Promicroceras (small shells)

Nautiloids and Ammonites

Cephalopods are the most active and highly developed marine carnivores. Although many forms had coiled or straight shells, some, such as octopus and squid, appear never to have developed major skeletons. These animals have complex eyes and brains, tentacles with sucker pads, and parrot-like beaks with which they consume their prey. Cephalopods use jet propulsion to move through water. The oldest known octopus is from the late Cretaceous of Palestine.

Ammonites, which are now extinct, and nautiloids were perhaps the most agile and intelligent invertebrate carnivores, living in ocean waters of all depths. Since these animals lived in the water column rather than on the sea floor, the rocks in which their shells are

found may not actually reflect the environment in which they lived. Ammonites and nautiloids had straight or coiled chambered shells, in which the old living chambers were either empty or lined with mineral (cameral) deposits that acted as ballast.

siphuncle spiral tube connecting chambers

cameral chambers

living chamber

Living Nautiloid

Color diagrams supplement the text by showing a cutaway of a basic fossil structure. These may include a depiction of the living animal.

section of nautiloid

FIELD NOTES

Cretaceous limestones, Texas and Kansas, USA, and Europe

Triassic rocks, California, USA

Devonian rocks, New York, USA

Permian limestone, central Europe

Cretaceous lagoonal shales (dwarf forms)

Jurassic rocks of the Himalayas

€ O S D C P Tr J K T

Older chambers were separated by walls called septae that left distinct suture marks where they joined the outer shell. In nautiloids, these are seen as a simple sigmoid curve, but in ammonites, there are many types of complicated, jagged suture lines. Detailed lineages of ammonite evolution have been arrived at

by studying the suture patterns.

The abundance of ammonites and their presence in many types of sedimentary rock makes them one of the most useful biostratigraphic indicators of all. Coiled cephalopods are very common in the middle and late Paleozoic and the Mesozoic. Ammonites became extinct at the end of the Cretaceous. The small numbers of nautiloid surviving after this time make them relatively rare in Cenozoic rocks.

Nautiloids and ammonites were creatures of open tropical seas, and are abundant in limestones from tropical reefs. They may also be found in shales both from deeper water and from restricted lagoons. Some of the more interesting forms are dwarf species that presumably lived in the hyper-saline waters of such lagoons, but most are found in limestone.

Like the bivalve mollusks, the shells were made of the pearlescent calcareous mineral aragonite. In most fossil shells, the aragonite has been converted to calcite and the pearly luster has been lost, but in some forms, the shells retain usually preserved in shales, the shells retain their beautiful luster. Unfortunately, the shells of most ammonites were so thin that they are

heteromorph ammonite

216

Field Notes panels

Collecting Sites: A list of a few choice locations around the world where these fossils can be collected, giving information on the geological nature of the area where most relevant. For more detailed site localities, contact your nearest club or society.

€ O S D C P Tr J K T

Timeline: From Cambrian to Tertiary. A bar across the timeline indicates when these fossils were living— darker shading equals greatest abundance. Letters refer to Geological Periods outlined on p. 87.

The text provides information on the biological evolution of various fossil forms and what to look out for in the field.

This panel indicates the Geological Period and environment of the site/s.

The illustrated banding at the top of the page identifies either general categories of fossils or sites of particular importance—see the key below right.

Jurassic–Cretaceous Continents

■ Apatosaurus and Diplodocus bones, Colorado, USA

Jurassic–Cretaceous Continents

■ Centrosaurus bone bed in Alberta, Canada

Dinosaur Sites

years, from the late Triassic Cretaceous, dinosaurs Their fossilized remains ery continent, including tribution is skewed to ns. One of the most rt of North America. usually a poor place for g the Mesozoic Era, much of western d by the flood plains hat drained into an s were home to other animals. osaur Triangle, Utah do, t e

Centrosaurus bone bed excavation.

FIELD NOTES

✴ Dinosaur National Monument, Utah, USA
Cleveland-Lloyd Quarry, Utah, USA

🏛 American Museum of Natural History, New York, USA
British Museum (Natural History), London, UK
Royal Tyrrell Museum, Drumheller, Alberta, Canada

€ O S D C P Tr J K T

such as *Diplodocus, Apatosaurus, Camarasaurus*, and *Barosaurus*, but there are other plant-eaters, such as *Stegosaurus, Dryosaurus*, and *Camptosaurus*, as well as meat-eaters, such as *Allosaurus* and *Ceratosaurus*. This unusual abundance is a result of bodies collecting in a sandbar as they were washed downstream in a huge river. Dinosaur National Monument is open to the public and many fine specimens can be

seen, still partly embedded in the quarry face. Other sites in the Dinosaur Triangle include the Cleveland-Lloyd Quarry south of Price. Younger, Cretaceous-age deposits to the west and north of the Dinosaur Triangle contain a different set of dinosaurs. Dinosaur Provincial Park in Alberta, Canada, has been set aside to protect its vast fossil deposits. Coupled with the Royal Tyrrell Museum near Drumheller, this area is a mecca for dinosaur enthusiasts because of the beautiful specimens that are on display in the museum or have eroded out of the ground. The Alberta specimens come from toward the end of the dinosaurs' reign and include a variety of strange duck-billed dinosaurs and various types of horned dinosaur.

In one bone bed, lie the remains of thousands of individuals of a horned dinosaur similar to *Centrosaurus*. This species appears to have lived in huge herds, perhaps comprising tens of thousands of individuals, that migrated across the continent in search of food. These migrations entailed dangerous river crossings during which many animals died, their remains swept away by the river. The carcasses collected where the flow of water slowed, producing the bone beds we find today.

ssils. und as erving the ern so cation. autiloids, lying in the in the Atlas se are often and are ining shell is occur in the y a fraction of gh some

The skull of *Camarasaurus* (top), and a *Triceratops* skeleton (right).

241

Color field sketches supplement the text by illustrating some basic fossil types.

Field Notes panels

✴ **Location:** The site or sites where these significant fossils have been found. These are usually inaccessible to amateur collectors.

🏛 **Collections:** Institutions such as museums and universities where significant finds can be viewed.

€ O S D C P Tr J K T

Timeline: A bar across the geological timeline shows the age range of the fossils. Where this is a specific site, an arrow indicates its age. The letters refer to the Geological Periods (see p. 87).

Secondary photographs or illustrations show some of the fossil finds from this particular site or type of site.

Collecting Fossils   194

Fossil Sites   226

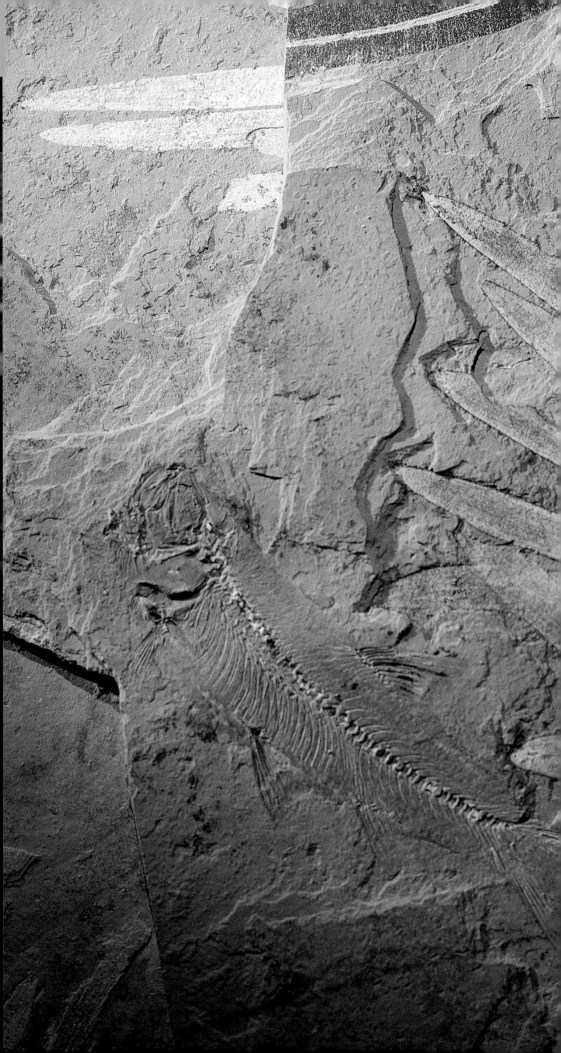

Collecting Fossils

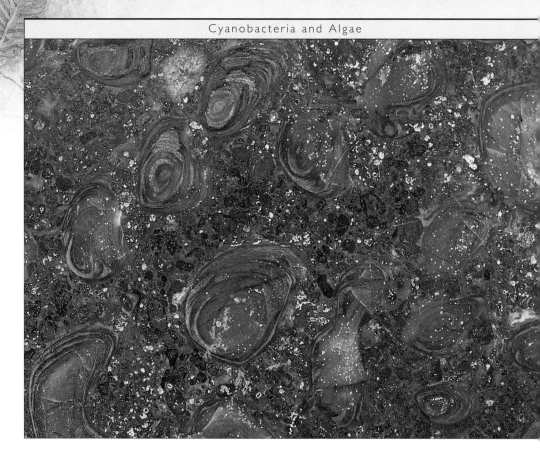

Stromatolites

S tromatolites are layered structures produced by the growth of so-called algal
mats, primarily of various sorts of algae and
cyanobacteria, which, like plants, photosynthe-
size their food. They are among the oldest
fossils, some dating back more than 3,500 million years. Ancient stromatolites lived in waters
with a range of salinity. Needing light, they are
limited to shallows where sunlight can penetrate.

Stromatolites are prokaryotic (simple-celled)
organisms and their evolution has been very
slow. Many forms lived during the Precambrian,
creating some of the earliest reefs, but today,
they are limited geographically and morphologically. Good examples of living stromatolites
are found in many
regions, such as the hot
springs in Yellowstone
National Park. Fossil
stromatolites may be
common in carbonate
rocks younger than
3,500 million years, but
are not common after
the early Paleozoic.

fossil stromatolit

Look for stromatolites
in Precambrian carbonate rocks of southern
Canada, South Africa, in the Altyn Limestone o
Montana, and in the Alamore Formation of
West Texas, USA. Younger stromatolites can b
found in lake deposits of the
Green River Formation in
Wyoming, and in the Canning
Basin of Australia. Look for
road cuts or weathered vertical
surfaces where the delicate layer
of stromatolites can be seen in
cross-section as domes or bul-
bous forms. They also occur as
layered planar structures with
interlayered carbonate and silica
Some stromatolites are mineral-
ized and beautifully colored.

Living Stromatolite

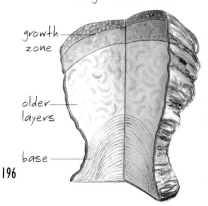

growth zone

older layers

base

196

FIELD NOTES

Van Horn, Texas, USA
Waroona Group,
North Pole, Western Australia
Manitounuk Island,
Hudson Bay, and Beresford Lake,
Manitoba, Canada
Living examples:
Green Lake, New York, USA
Shark Bay, Western Australia
Є O S D C P Tr J K T

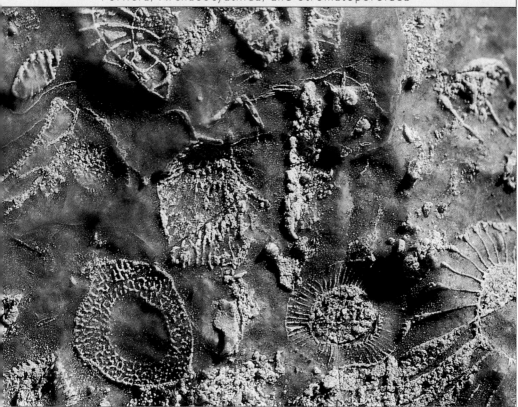

Sponges and Relatives

The simplest multicellular organisms are the sponges and related forms, such as stromatoporoids and the early Cambrian archaeocyathids. Sponges, which still thrive today, have a two-layered body with an internal skeleton composed of soft spongin, or of microscopic calcite or silica particles (spicules). Most sponges live in marine waters from shallow to deep. Tall, vase-like, or branching sponges are found in calm water, while shorter, encrusting forms live in areas with fast currents.

Sponges have changed little in the past 600 million years and are found throughout the fossil record. These do not include the familiar bath sponges, as they are too soft to fossilize. Double-walled sponges,

such as archaeocyathids, flourished only in the early Cambrian and then became extinct. Stromatoporoids (Cambrian to Cretaceous) formed layered calcareous skeletons that resemble sheets or cabbage heads.

Although relatively rare in the fossil record, sponges may be locally abundant. Whole sponges are found in Paleozoic limestones, but the best place for whole, easily recoverable skeletons is in shale. Siliceous spicules are present in many lime-stones. Most sponges are preserved only as single spicules—the siliceous types can be extracted from limestone by dissolving the matrix in weak acid. Some siliceous and calcareous sponges are preserved as entire fossils, ranging from pepper-corn-size forms up to some the size of clothes baskets.

hexactinellid sponge

hyalosponge

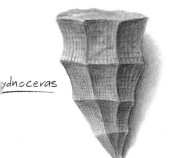

ydnoceras

FIELD NOTES

Late Carboniferous shales, central North America
Lower Cretaceous limestones, UK
Jurassic limestones, Germany
Permian Reef, Texas–New Mexico
Devonian limestones, UK and Pennsylvania, USA
Ordovician limestones Kentucky, USA
Cambrian limestones, Nevada, USA

€ O S D C P Tr J K T

197

Corals

Fungia

scleractinian
Micrabacia

The phylum Cnidaria consists of jellyfish, corals, sea anemones, and the Anthozoa or "flower animals". These relatively simple animals have complex folds (mesentaries) in their gut cavities that are frequently reflected in their skeletons. They have a single opening, or mouth, to the gut cavity where food enters and solid wastes are eliminated. Cnidarians are carnivores, and immobilize or kill their prey with specialized stinging cells (nematocysts) on their tentacles.

Although some fossil jellyfish are preserved as impressions from as long ago as the late Precambrian, it is the corals that are most frequently found as fossils. They have a dense, calcium carbonate skeleton and occur either as massive colonies of thousands of cloned individuals, or as single, usually cone-shaped corralites, commonly called horn corals. Modern corals live in relatively clean, warm (usually tropical) sea water of normal salinity, and may form reefs that cover vast areas. Ancient corals also seem to have preferred warm, tropical ocean environments. Unlike their colonial cousins, solitary corals are often found in shales, indicating that they preferred soft, muddy bottoms. But horn corals are also found, along with the colonial forms, in areas that once had hard sea floors. Primitive tabulate and rugose corals lived

FIELD NOTES

Most middle and late Paleozoic limestones
Lower Carboniferous rocks, UK
Late Carboniferous shales of mid North America
Carboniferous rocks, Missouri, USA
Devonian limestones, New York, USA, and Devonian rocks, Kentucky, USA

€ O S D C P Tr J K T

Living Coral Polyp

tentacles

mouth

hard skeleton

198

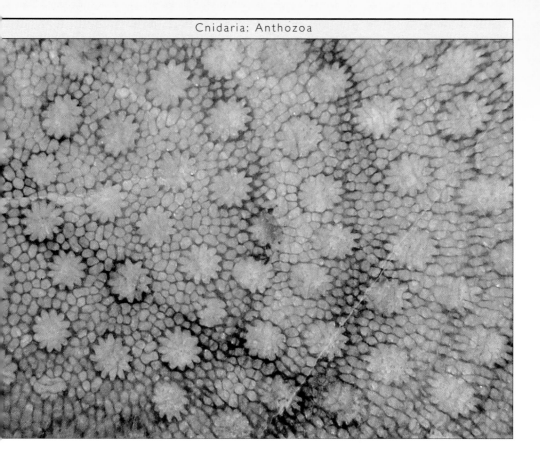

uring the Paleozoic, while only the more dvanced scleractinid corals re found in Mesozoic and Cenozoic rocks. The tube-haped tabulate corals requently resemble a series of oined organ pipes or pan pipes. Their name comes from the imple horizontal divisions tabulae) that block off older

rugose coral

ortions of the skeletal tubes during the growth of the individual coral. Rugose and scleractinian corals have vertical, radially aligned walls (septae) that support the mesenteries and project into the oral living space. These two major groups differ rincipally in the arrangement and number of their septae. Rugose corals are often ound as horn corals, although they lso occurred in colonial form, while abulate corals are always colonial.

Corals are among the most ommon fossils on Earth. Rugose nd tabulate corals are abundant in Paleozoic limestones and shales but are much easier to clean and recover from hales, where they simply weather out. cleractinid corals are rare in the Mesozoic

but are fairly common in Cenozoic limestones, where they are mostly found as massive reefs, although solitary scleractinian corals may be found. Solitary and colonial rugose and scleractinian corals occur as whole body fossils and are relatively easy to recognize because of their numerous radial septae. The most abundant fossil corals are scleractinian corals in the reefs that make up many tropical islands. By standard definition, any corals older than 10,000 years are fossils, so it is not difficult to find fossil scleractinian corals exposed on these islands in great abundance. Living corals have a symbiotic relationship with colonies of algae in their tissues, which help provide them with oxygen.

scleractinian coral

rugose coral
Arachnophyllum

199

Reef Communities

The massive deposits that were once reefs are an abundant source of fossils for the amateur collector. Large numbers of soft-bodied and skeleton-producing organisms inhabit reefs, although only the skeletal remains may be preserved. Reefs can be up to several thousand miles long, or as small as a few square feet, and stand on hard and stable sea floor. They are usually regions of incredibly rich biodiversity in which organisms are ecologically linked in a complex and intricate food web.

The kinds and shapes of animals that live in reef communities may be distributed across the reef, each inhabiting sections at the depth best suited to it.

Although modern reefs are dominated by the more advanced scleractinid corals, the composition of ancient reefs has varied a

belemnite

trilobite

great deal through time. For example, Cretaceous reefs are commonly formed of a type of bivalve called rudists, and Permian reefs may be mainly composed of brachiopods, sponges, and even foraminifera. The earliest Cambrian reefs were mostly composed of archaeocyathids, but middle and late Cambrian reefs are almost entirely made up of stromatolites.

Although small "patch" reefs, such as those oysters build, may form in temperate waters, large accumulations of calcium carbonate skeletal debris are really only possible in warm, tropical, ocean waters. Most reef organisms live within the photic zone—the top level of the water column where light can penetrate—and require clean, non-stagnant water of normal salinity.

Since reefs are composed of vast numbers of organisms, it

FIELD NOTES

Carboniferous, Illinois, USA

Middle Paleozoic rocks, England and Scandinavia

Middle Paleozoic carbonates from the Great Lakes, USA, to Arctic Islands

Edwards Formation, Texas, USA

Tropical islands

Petroleum Museum, Midland, Texas: reconstruction of a Permian Reef

Є O S D C P Tr J K T

200

coral
community

brachiopod

crinoid

seems difficult to discuss evolution and extinction in them. How-ever, studies have shown that individual reefs have a period of development and growth and a finite lifespan, measured in tens of thousands of years, much like an individual organism.

We also know that the composition of reefs has changed through time, reflecting the tempo and mode of evolution of reef-dwelling organisms. Reefs, especially accumulations of organic debris, are quite common in environments with high concentrations of calcium carbonate. They

are particularly good sites for fossil-collecting, because of the high likelihood of finding a wide variety of different fossils.

When collecting from ancient fossilized reefs, it is worth considering the structure of the reef when it was alive. The best fossils of reef-building organisms are usually found at the edge farthest from the seaward side of the reef complex. On the seaward side, the activities of waves, especially during storms, smashed shells or skeletons into small pieces, so complete specimens are rare. The remains here consist of coarse breccia formed mostly of broken shells.

Behind the reef, in the lagoon, if there were one, conditions were quieter, but only a few skeleton-producing organisms lived there. Although excellent specimens are sometimes found in exceptional circumstances, normally there will be little more than a strand of broken shells gently washed from the reef itself.

201

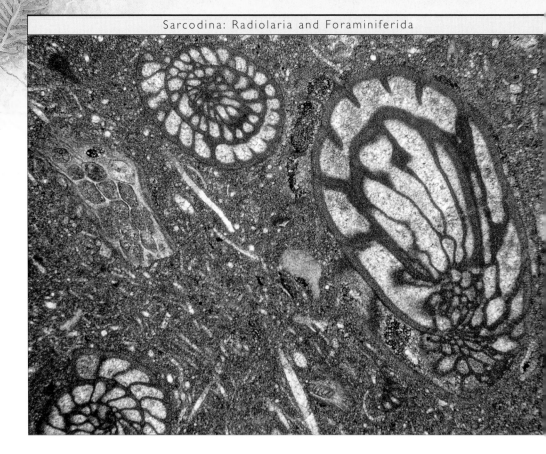

Microfossils

Although for the amateur, collecting microfossils is a challenge, many find it a rewarding pastime. Most microfossils are so small that they can be seen only under magnification. There are many types, but most common microfossils are the shells of single-celled organisms, such as foraminiferans and radiolarians. In spite of being the smallest skeletons on Earth, they are among the most intricate and detailed of any organism, often complex assemblies of glassy girders and spikes.

Radiolarians, with siliceous skeletons, and foraminiferans, also known as forams, with calcareous shells, are found in both fresh and sea water.

Deep-sea muds are almost entirely composed of radiolarian skeletons. The evolution of many forams is recorded in deep-sea sediments, and they are useful in dating strata for geological purposes, such as oil exploration.

Forams and radiolaria are found in many limestones and are also preserved in deep-water shales. Fusulinid forams the size of rice grains are very common in some later Paleozoic rocks. Many chert formations, such as the Arkansas Novaculite, seem largely made of chert derived from radiolarians. These can be recovered in the residue after dissolving limestone, and forams after washing shales.

When present, fusulinids are easy to see because they look like rice grains. Other microfossils may be present in shales and limestones. Some forams are as large as small coins.

globigerinid foram

quinqueloculinid foram

Actinomma radiolarian

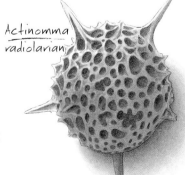

FIELD NOTES

Devonian limestones, Iowa and Oklahoma, USA

Jurassic rocks, Montana, USA

Pleistocene rocks, California, USA

Carboniferous shales, Texas, USA

Silurian limestones, Oklahoma, USA

Silurian rocks, Tennessee, USA

Eocene rocks, Alabama, USA

Chalk of the UK coast

e O S D C P Tr J K T

Conodonts

C onodonts are microscopic, up to
⁵⁄₁₆ inch (8 mm), phosphatic tooth-like
structures found abundantly in Paleozoic sedimentary rocks. After hundreds of years
of debate, the discovery of a conodont-bearing
animal in Scotland indicates that they are the
remains of early fish-like vertebrates. They are
found in many different types of sedimentary
rocks, representing a wide variety of marine
environments, so the original animals must have
been tolerant of wide environmental variation.
Up until now, all we have known about these
structures is that certain types appear in groups
known as associations and that these associations
change through time; in fact, conodonts make
very important index fossils for
much of the Paleozoic. Changes in
their shape and associations
presumably reflect the evolution
of the conodont-bearing animals.

Ozarkodina

Conodonts
are very common
in Paleozoic limestone. If this is
dissolved in weak acid, phosphatic conodonts
may be left in the residue. Because these are very
small, examine the residue with a microscope or
strong hand lens. Conodonts are particularly
abundant in Ordovician through Carboniferous
rocks. They also appear in mudstones
and can be removed by soaking
these in detergent and water.

Look for shiny, tooth-like
structures in the
residue. Some
are as simple
as long cones,
but most
have elaborate
blades and
cusps. Extreme
heat blackens
conodonts, so
color indicates
degree of heat
exposure.

FIELD NOTES

Ordovician and Silurian rocks,
Missouri, USA

Carboniferous rocks, Oklahoma,
Iowa, and Missouri, USA

Harding Sandstone, Colorado, USA

Ordovician shales, Minnesota, USA

Ordovician through Permian
rocks, Arkansas, USA

Devonian rocks, Iowa, USA

Є O S D C P Tr J K T

terospathodus

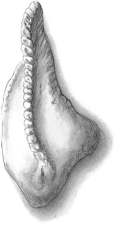

Palmatolepis 203

Brachiopods

The bodies of brachiopods are surrounded by two shells, or valves, that are joined along a common hinge, as in bivalve mollusks, such as clams. Unlike bivalve mollusks, brachiopods have dorsal (brachial) and ventral (pedicle) valves, while bivalve mollusks have left and right valves. So for unspecialized brachiopods, the plane of body symmetry passes through the center of the valves, with each side being a mirror image of the other.

Depending on the group, brachiopod shells are either chitino-phosphastic (inarticulate), or calcareous (articulate). Inside the shells are complex sets of muscles, arranged like pulleys, that both open and close the shells.

Brachiopods usually grip the substrate with a fleshy structure called a pedicle, but many extinct forms had spiny shells that were cemented to the sea floor. Frequently the shells have a fold on one valve that fits into a groove (sulcus) on the other. As adults, brachiopods are attached, but some inarticulate forms burrow.

Although solely marine, ancient brachiopods occupied a variety of oceanic environments—some Permian reefs are largely formed of interlocking, spiny forms. Brachiopods may be found attached to sea floors or isolated in shale that represent what were originally very muddy environments. Modern inarticulate brachiopod forms burrow in sand or mud, often on mudflats that are exposed at low tide. All brachiopods are filter feeders.

First appearing in the Cambrian, they rapidly diversified into many lineages, with a wide variety of

Rhynchopora

Microspirifer

Meristella

FIELD NOTES

Carboniferous and Permian limestones, UK

Paleozoic limestones and shales, central Oklahoma, USA

Devonian rocks, New York, USA

Glass Mountains, Texas, USA

Paleozoic limestones, Appalachian Mountains, USA

Cambrian limestones, Ohio, USA

Є O S D C P Tr J K T

hell shapes. Among the most interesting are the wing-shaped spiriferids. The greatest brachiopod diversity occurred during the Paleozoic. They declined dramatically at the mass extinction on the Permian–Triassic boundary.

Brachiopods survive today, but they are now limited to cool and temperate waters, most commonly around Japan, Australia, New Zealand, and the North Atlantic coastline of North America. They tend to live in deeper waters. Fossil brachiopods range in size from few millimeters to more than 10 inches

Megastrophia

(25 cm) in length, but most forms are 1–3 inches (2–7 cm). They are common as fossils in Paleozoic shales, sandstones, and limestones, and are important biostratigraphic index fossils worldwide.

Although very common in Paleozoic rocks, they can be found in much smaller numbers in Mesozoic and Cenozoic rocks. More often than not, brachiopods are found with both valves articulated, since at death the shells tend to stay closed and together. Those preserved in mudstones may be somewhat flattened by compaction, but are the easiest specimens to extract, since the clay can be washed away.

Many brachiopods had exaggerated surface folds (plications), which probably served to strengthen the shells. When brachiopods are exquisitely preserved, delicate spines can be found on the valves, particularly in the Permian productid brachiopods. In well-preserved specimens, the delicate, calcareous brachidium may be preserved within the shell—this is the structure that supported the spiral, ribbon-like, filter-feeding lophophore during life.

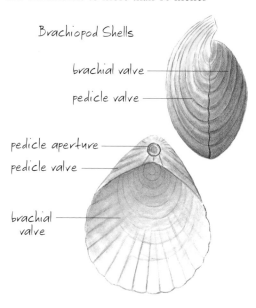

Brachiopod Shells

brachial valve

pedicle valve

pedicle aperture

pedicle valve

brachial valve

205

Bryozoans

The "moss" animals are unfamiliar to most people, but they are common animals that live in colonies and are found on many seashores. Unlike the corals, they have a true mouth and anus, and a ciliated filter-feeding mechanism called a lophophore. Yet they are tiny animals, only about ¹⁄₂₄ inch (1 mm) long. Bryozoans prefer shallow ocean water, but are found at depths of up to 18,000 feet (5,500 m). Most colonies are only about 1¼ inches (3 cm) across, but some fossil forms are up to 2 feet (60 cm) wide.

Most bryozoan colonies are fixed, but some can move slowly around. In the Cambrian, bryozoans quickly diversified into a number of twig-like, fan-like and encrusting forms. They are very common in carbonates and shales. In some shales they are the most abundant fossil—representing what were once vast undersea meadows of the twig- and fan-like forms. These tend to be well preserved in Paleozoic limestones and shales.

The best places to look for bryozoans are where the surface has weathered. The branching twig-like forms are especially common in Ordovician rocks. Lacy or fan-like forms are abundant in the early Carboniferous and are best found on the weathered surface of limestones. On each bryozoan, look for tiny pin-pricks, which are the openings in which the bryozoan animals lived. Modern bryozoans are common in tropical and temperate climates but because of their small size, they can be extremely difficult to see.

detail of Fenestrellina

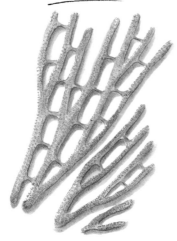

Archimede

FIELD NOTES

Silurian through Permian rocks, Kansas, USA

Ordovician rocks, Minnesota and Kentucky, USA

Eocene, Mississippi and North Carolina, USA

Carboniferous shales, Texas, USA

Devonian shales and limestones, UK

Є O S D C P Tr J K T

206

Graptolites

Graptolites, an extinct group of colonial floating (planktonic) organisms, are quite unlike any living forms. We now place them in the phylum Chordata, with the vertebrates, but they were very unusual. Some may have been attached to the sea floor, but during the early Paleozoic, most floated in vast numbers, perhaps on or close to the ocean surface. They probably filtered planktonic microorganisms.

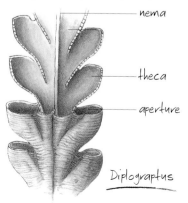

Climacograptus

Most of what we know about graptolites today comes from thin carbon films left in many Paleozoic shales and limestones, although some have been removed as three-dimensional structures from fine-grained limestones. A colony of graptolites is made up of many branches (stipes) with different arrangements of little cups (theca) in which the animals lived. They are important index fossils and are quite common around the world in early Paleozoic rocks. From the

Ordovician through the Silurian, numbers gradually dwindled. Graptolites are most plentiful and easiest to find in thinly layered black shales that are easy to break apart, and in some thinly stratified deep-water limestones. Open the matrix along the bedding planes and look for thin serrated lines that reflect light well. In limestones, look for serrated black strips of carbon. Dendroid graptolites built complex, branching colonies, while simpler colonies of graptoloid forms were suspended by floats (nema).

FIELD NOTES

Ordovician rocks, British Columbia and Ontario, Canada, and UK

Ordovician shales, Sweden and New York, USA

Silurian shales, Marathon Basin, Texas, USA

Silurian rocks, New York, Oklahoma, and Nevada, USA

€ O S D C P Tr J K T

— nema

— theca

— aperture

Diplograptus

207

Trilobites

Trilobites were the most numerous and successful marine organisms of the early Paleozoic. These segmented "pill-bug"-like arthropods ranged in length from several millimeters to 3 feet (90 cm). They had many legs, each with a set of gills, and most had sophisticated, multifaceted eyes. Like most arthropods, trilobites could grow only by shedding their old skins. Consequently, many of the trilobite fossils that are found are actually shed external skeletons and not the trilobite animals themselves.

Olenoides

Calymene (rolled up)

The name "trilobite" is derived from the three lobes into which each body segment is divided—two lateral pleural lobes and an axial lobe. They may also be divided into three longitudinal sections, the cephalon (or head), the thorax (made up of variable numbers of hinged segments or

somites), and the pygidium (or tail), made up of from one to 30 fused somites. The cephalon is formed from individual segments joined at facial sutures, which split apart during growth. The edges of the shell may be smooth or have a variety of spiny projections.

Most trilobites lived in shallow ocean waters, and on reefs. It has been proposed, however, that some of the spiny trilobites may have been capable of swimming. Trilobite tracks and trails, reflecting a wide variety of their activities, have provided some of the best examples of the daily activities of these extinct organisms. Their skeletons are found in all types of sedimentary rock, from limestones to shales.

Trilobites are relatively common in Cambrian, Ordovician, and Silurian rocks throughout the world. By the Devonian, they had declined to the point of being relatively rare finds.

FIELD NOTES

Atlas Mountains, Morocco

Early Paleozoic rocks, northwest Scotland

Ordovician and Silurian rocks, Illinois, USA

Cambrian rocks, Utah and Virginia, USA

Arbuckle Mountains, Oklahoma, USA

Cambrian, British Columbia, Canada

€ O S D C P Tr J K T

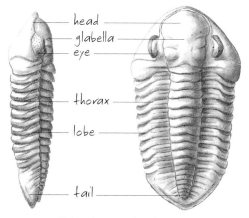

head
glabella
eye

thorax

lobe

tail

Trilobite exoskeleton

dimensions, with the skeletal material intact. Trilobites were gregarious animals and are frequently found in large numbers, either in deposits from storm activities or on bedding surfaces. It is not unusual for them to be locally abundant in Cambrian and Ordovician rocks as deposits or debris left by storms. It is also not unusual to find enrolled trilobites, curled up upon themselves, apparently a defensive behavior.

The oldest known published scientific paper on trilobites dates back to 1698. Trilobites are particularly popular with amateur collectors, some of whom collect them exclusively. Good specimens can be found in rock and fossil shops, but inspect carefully before you purchase. In some cases, large, complete specimens have been pieced together from parts collected separately. More than 1500 species of trilobite are known, and many are yet to be described.

Dicranurus

In the late Carboniferous and Permian, they are extremely rare. They are most likely to be found in limestones and shales.

When preserved in shales, trilobites are usually flattened, and often the original shell has been destroyed, leaving only an external cast. In some shales, however, entire skeletons are preserved in excellent detail, allowing X-rays to be taken. Specimens in limestone are frequently preserved in three

209

Insects

Insects are small, mobile organisms with jointed external skeletons made of chitin, a complex sugar. They are the most abundant form of multicellular animal life in the terrestrial realm. Insects live in a bewildering array of environments, from the base of an eyelash to Antarctica. The largest number of insects is found in the tropics, and this is the ancient environment best represented by fossil insects. Members of the phylum Arthropoda, insects evolved from centipedes in the Silurian. Their bodies are divided into three segments: head, thorax, and abdomen.

Despite their great abundance, insects rarely fossilize because of their size and the delicacy of their skeletons. Yet for all their rarity in the fossil record, the inclusion of insects in fossil tree sap (amber) has resulted in fossils of the most remarkable preservation. This can be so perfect that muscle fibers

and even DNA fragments can be extracted for study. Some sites, such as the Green River Shale in Wyoming, are famous for insects preserved in delicately layered shales.

To find insects in shale, look for small fragments of wings or bodies that have a slight shine. Use a hand lens to make certain. Most amber does not contain insects, so check any pieces carefully. Some of the largest fossil insects were Carboniferous and Permian cockroaches, sometimes more than 20 inches (50 cm) long. Insects are the only invertebrates that developed the ability to fly.

Libellulium

FIELD NOTES

"Baltic Amber", Samland Promontory, Russia

Green River Shale, Wyoming, USA

Cretaceous amber, California and Alaska, USA, and Canada

Miocene amber, Mexico

Carboniferous shales, North American mid-continent

Coal Measures, UK

Є O S D C P Tr J K T

snakefly

Other Arthropods

In addition to familiar insects and trilobites, there are many other members of phylum Arthropoda, which includes all animals with jointed, chitinous, external skeletons. As well as living forms, such as spiders, scorpions, lobsters, shrimp, crabs, and horseshoe crabs, there are interesting extinct forms, such as the so-called sea scorpions or Eurypterids (broad, winglike animals). Eurypterids included the largest known arthropods and in their day were probably some of the most effective and lethal carnivores. Like their living relatives, they inhabited a variety of environments, from fresh and brackish water to shallow marine.

Eurypterids are often found in dark shales, probably representing brackish marine environments. A variety of early arthropods, including the Eurypterids, had pincers. Modern horseshoe crabs are good examples of primitive arthropods. Eurypterids are common in Silurian and Devonian rocks. They are often preserved as carbonized outlines in shales and limestones. Look for animals with large pincers, segmented abdomens, and long, tapering tails called telsons. True crustaceans, such as crabs and shrimp, are found either as carbonized outlines or in three dimensions, especially those crabs with a thick shell. Arthropods with pincers range in size from mites less than ¼8 inch (0.5 mm) long, to giant Eurypterids more than 10 feet (3 m) in length.

Aeger

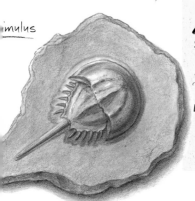

Limulus

FIELD NOTES

Mazon Creek, Illinois, USA

Alum Shale, southern Sweden

Silurian rocks, Scotland, Norway and New York, USA

Cambrian rocks, Wisconsin and Missouri, USA

Devonian shales and limestones, New York, USA

and throughout Europe

€ O S D C P Tr J K T

211

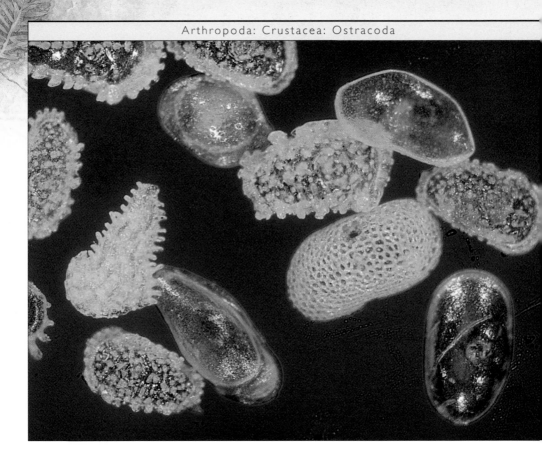

Ostracods

Ostracods are small, bean-shaped crustacean arthropods, related to the lobsters, shrimp, and crabs. Like clams or brachiopods, they have two shells, joined by a dorsal hinge. The shell encloses a subtly segmented body with a full set of appendages. Ostracods are usually up to ⅙ inch (between 0.5–4 mm) in length, so use a hand lens or microscope for detailed study.

Ostracods are omnivorous and occur in both fresh and marine waters to a depth of 9,000 feet (2.8 km). They are usually associated with the bottom sediments (benthic), or are found

palaeocopid ostracod

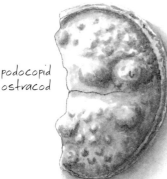

podocopid ostracod

living on the stems of plants. A few forms are planktonic and a few burrow in mud. They are one of the most numerous of all crustaceans and their fossils are very common throughout the geological record. Most species are widely distributed and have a short range in time, so they are a major biostratigraphic tool. They occupy a range of environments in terms of temperature and salinity.

The tiny bivalve shells are composed of chitin and calcium carbonate. They are joined along the upper edge and frequently have thin places that look like eyes. Many ostracod shells are highly decorated with nodes, swellings, ridges, and grooves, although some are completely smooth. Fossil shells are easiest to find in limestones, shales, and marls representing both marine and freshwater environments. The largest ostracods are up to ¾ inch (2 cm) in length. The first freshwater ostracods appeared in the coal-forming Carboniferous swamps

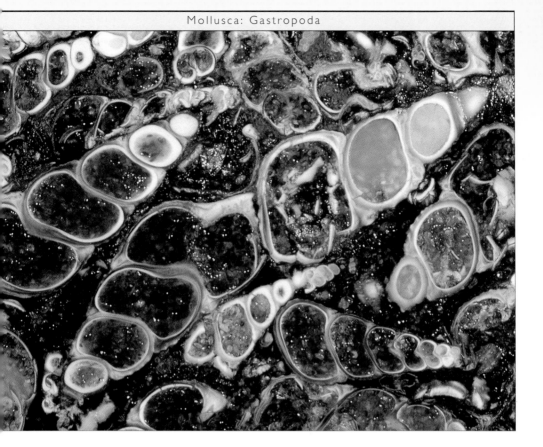

Gastropods

Gastropod means "stomach foot" and these mobile mollusks use their muscular "foot" to propel themselves. They ave a mouth and true eyes. Most gastropods crete a single, whorled, calcareous shell that ossilizes readily. Ecologically, they run the amut from carnivores to herbivores. Many astropods have a hardened radula, type of toothed tongue, that ey use to scrape away at food. astropods are the only group f mollusks that have successlly adapted to life on land, snails and slugs. lost fossil and ving species, owever, are arine or eshwater. Marine varieties ved in many nvironments, most in hallow water, but some have een recovered from depths of ore than 16,000 feet (5 km). he most ancient gastropod shells ow no coiling, but subsequent orms began to coil on a single

Planorbis

plane, similar to the shelled cephalopods. Later forms have a complex, three-dimensional growth that results in some form of spire. The most significant evolutionary changes within the group concern the twisting or torsion of the body organs, related to shell whorling, and the development of lungs in terrestrial forms.

Neptunia

Gastropods are usually preserved as entire shells and, to a lesser extent, as empty molds in certain limestones. Sometimes, even the original colors are preserved. A complete specimen may also include the flat calcareous operculum, or door, that covered the aperture, or main opening, during life. Some fossil gastropods are found joined to fossil crinoids, having once fed on the fecal debris produced by the crinoid.

FIELD NOTES

Early and middle Paleozoic limestones, Germany

Paleozoic limestones, Appalachian Mountains, USA

Carboniferous shales and limestones, Indiana and Illinois, USA

Cambrian limestones, Missouri, USA

Mississippian limestones, Belgium

Cretaceous limestones, mid USA

€ O S D C P Tr J K T

Turritella

213

Bivalves

Pitar

Also known as the pelecypods, bivalves include oysters, clams, and mussels, and have bodies encased between two calcareous shells, or valves, that are joined along a flat hinge plate by an elastic ligament. Superficially, bivalves bear a resemblance to brachiopods and the two are often confused by amateurs. In brachiopods, which also have two valves, one shell is usually larger than the other. Unlike brachiopods, bivalve mollusks have a plane of symmetry that passes between the shells, making the left and right valves, in most forms, mirror images of one another. Bivalves have a set of muscles for closing the shells, but they open automatically when the muscles relax. Where the shells join at the beak, or umbo, there are ridges, or teeth, of various types that help to hold the shells closed while the animal is alive.

Bivalves are entirely aquatic and are found in fresh and ocean waters. Most forms are attached and immobile as adults, but some are capable of limited movement by "jet propulsion". They live in many environments, from the quiet, calm, deep ocean, to freshwater lakes and turbulent streams. They are abundant in shallow marine waters, where they live on hard or soft surfaces or burrow through soft sediment. They first appear in the Cambrian and are abundant in Mesozoic and Cenozoic rocks.

One of the most successful and best preserved groups is the oysters, which are particularly abundant in Cretaceous rocks around the world. Their thick, durable shells may even be preserved through ancient storms that ripped up the oyster and deposited them in beds that mimic oyster reefs.

Bivalve evolution has been well documented with many detailed studies on Cretaceous oysters, and bivalves are often used as important time markers.

Ostre

FIELD NOTES

Cretaceous limestones, central Texas, USA

Jurassic limestones, UK

Triassic rocks, California, USA

Cretaceous limestones, Kansas, USA; France and UK

Early Paleozoic rocks, Ohio and New York, USA

Jurassic rocks, Idaho, USA

€ O S D C P Tr J K T

214

Goniophora

Since they live in many environ-ments, preserva-tion of their shells is likely in many different kinds of stone. The shells are made of multiple calcareous layers of the mineral aragonite, the mineral that gives the luster to mother-of-

Lyropecten

earl. Over time, natural processes often convert he aragonite to calcite and destroy the luster.

Unlike brachiopods, many bivalves are found isolated, single shells, because the shells open ter death when the ligaments relax. Burrowing rms have a greater chance of being found with

both valves intact. Some bivalves can even burrow into rock and hard wood.

Bivalve shells may be only a few millimeters in diameter, or more than a foot (30 cm) across. Look for entire shells especially among oysters and forms with thick valves. Also look for molds of shells—many shells are dissolved after being encased in rock and only the void is left behind. Many fossil bivalve shells have small holes drilled in them—these may have been made during attacks by either gastropods or sponges.

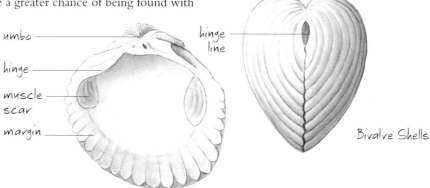

umbo

hinge

muscle scar

margin

hinge line

Bivalve Shells

215

Nautiloids and Ammonites

Cephalopods are highly active and very well developed marine carnivores. Although many forms had coiled or straight shells, some, such as octopus and squid, appear never to have developed major skeletons. These animals have complex eyes and brains, tentacles with sucker pads, and parrot-like beaks with which they consume their prey. Cephalopods use jet propulsion to move through water. The oldest known octopus is from the late Cretaceous of Palestine.

Ammonites, which are now extinct, and nautiloids were perhaps the most agile and intelligent invertebrate carnivores, living in ocean waters of all depths. Since these animals lived in the water column rather than on the sea floor, the rocks in which their shells are found may not actually reflect the environment in which they lived. Ammonites and nautiloids had straight or coiled chambered shells, in which the old living chambers were either empty or lined with mineral (cameral) deposits that acted as ballast.

siphuncle. spiral tube connecting chamber

cameral chamber

living chamber

Living Nautiloid

Older chambers were separated by walls called septae that left distinct suture marks where they joined the outer shell. In nautiloids, these are seen as a simple sigmoid curve, but in ammonites, there are many types of complicated, jagged suture lines. Detailed lineages of ammonite evolution have been arrived at

section of nautiloid

FIELD NOTES

Cretaceous limestones, Texas and Kansas, USA, and Europe

Triassic rocks, California, USA

Devonian rocks, New York, USA

Permian limestone, central Europe

Cretaceous lagoonal shales (dwarf forms)

Jurassic rocks of the Himalayas

€ O S D C P Tr J K T

216

heteromorph
ammonite

y studying the suture patterns.

The abundance of ammon-
es and their presence in many
pes of sedimentary rock makes
em one of the most useful bio-
ratigraphic indicators of all. Coiled
phalopods are very common in the
iddle and late Paleozoic and the Meso-
ic. Ammonites became extinct at the
d of the Cretaceous. The small numbers of
autiloid surviving after this time make them
latively rare in Cenozoic rocks.

Nautiloids and ammonites were creatures
f open tropical seas, and are abundant in
mestones from tropical reefs. They may also
e found in shales both from deeper water
d from restricted lagoons. Some of the
ore interesting forms are dwarf species that
resumably lived in the hyper-saline waters of
ch lagoons, but most are found in limestone.

Like the bivalve mollusks, the shells were
ade of the pearlescent calcareous mineral
agonite. In most fossil shells, the aragonite
as been converted to calcite and the pearly
ster has been lost, but in some forms,
sually preserved in shales, the shells retain
eir beautiful luster. Unfortunately, the shells
f most ammonites were so thin that they are
rarely preserved as fossils.
Usually, they are found as
internal molds, preserving the
delicate suture pattern so
important in identification.

Groups of straight nautiloids,
often hundreds at a time lying in the
same orientation, are found in the Atlas
Mountains of Morocco. These are often
sold in nature stores and rock shops and are
frequently polished so that any remaining shell is
destroyed. The smallest ammonites occur in the
dwarf faunas and adults may be only a fraction of
an inch (3 or 4 mm) across, although some
coiled ammonites more
than 9 feet (3 meters)
in diameter have
been found.

ammonite
Cophinoceras

ammonite
Dactylioceras

217

Plant Fossils

Isolated spores in Ordovician rocks mark the first appearance of plant life in previously untenable terrestrial environments. Much hardier than their aquatic ancestors, land plants developed tough skeletons to stand against wind and the forces of gravity. It is those tough skeletal materials, which first appear in late Silurian and early Devonian rocks, that come to us today in the form of vast coal deposits and in a fragmented but plentiful fossil record. Over a long period, plants also evolved methods of reproduction that relied on water as well as on the wind, insects, mammals, and birds.

Land plants occupy almost every terrestrial environment, but the chances of fossilization are greater in low-lying swampy areas in temperate climates than they are in the tropics, where plants are more abundant. Tropical plants are rarely preserved because rapid bacterial action destroys the material before it can be buried.

Dicroidium

Rhacopteris

The earliest plants were simple photosynthetic stems with no branches, topped by spore-bearing structures that barely poked up into the sunlight. They still needed to be in water for some parts of their reproductive cycle. In a steady succession of advances through the Paleozoic and into the Mesozoic, land plants developed many innovations, including woody tissues that allowed them to grow tall, vascular tissues that allowed liquids to move up and down the stems, as well as leaves and branches that increased the area available for photosynthesis

FIELD NOTES

Carboniferous coals, Appalachian Mtns, USA

Carboniferous rocks, Illinois, USA, and throughout UK

Petrified Forest NP, Arizona, USA

Cretaceous sandstones and shales, Argentina and Rocky Mountains, USA, Canada

Permian rocks, India

Є O S D C P Tr J K T

218

he oldest plants reproduced asexually, their pores being blown through the air. Eventually, plants reproduced sexually, their seeds made rtile by pollen carried by wind or insects.

Plant fossils are very common, especially in Carboniferous and Tertiary rocks. The great coal swamps date from the Carboniferous, and much of the coal mined today comes from this period. Plant fossils can usually be found in deposits associated with coal beds. Many Tertiary rocks have poorer grades of coal where these fossils are better preserved. Plant fossils are common in any rocks that represent sediments deposited in the terrestrial environment. So look for fossil leaves and stem parts in sandstones representing rivers and streams and in shales that represent ancient lakes and river flood areas.

Unlike animals, plant fossils are usually found as separate portions, entire plants being a great rarity in the

fossil
deciduous leaves

fossil
pine cone

fossil record. To make matters worse, different plants may have nearly identical leaves, branches, or roots, so many plant fossils are given names based only on shape and not on real botanical relationships. Plants may be preserved as carbonized impressions in shales or nodules, or as three-dimensional casts of trunks.

In some coals that are calcified, very old fossil plant material is preserved in such detail that it can be extracted and studied under a microscope. Unfortunately, some of the prettiest fossil plant material has the worst level of preservation, with no original detail remaining.

fossil
Eucalyptus

219

Echinoderms

Echinoderms are attached or mobile organisms with an internal skeleton made of interlocking calcite plates (echinoderm means "spiny skin"). In some individuals there may be hundreds of separate calcite plates, each a single calcite crystal. They are unique among animals in having an internal hydraulic system, or water vascular system that pressurizes their thousands of inflatable tube feet. The attached forms are filter feeders, while the mobile forms, such as sea stars and sea urchins, may be carnivores, herbivores, or deposit feeders.

The oldest forms seem to have been attached and limited to ocean waters of normal salinity, living on hard bottoms, usually in vast numbers, or attached to floating pieces of wood.

crinoid

Later unattached forms either lived on soft or hard bottoms or burrowed underneath soft sediments. They are generally indicative of normal ocean waters.

In the Cambrian and Ordovician, there was wide variety of unusual attached and unattached echinoderms that became extinct. It has been suggested that one form, the mitrates, were ancestors of vertebrates, but this is highly unlikely.

The crinoids, which survive today, typify the attached forms with their root-like holdfasts (stems) made of poker-chip-like columnals, and head (calyx) formed of articulated arms joined to the cup-shaped body.

Look for echinoderm fossils in shales and especially limestones. Although it is not unusual to find entire sea urchin fossils, entire articulated stemmed forms are extremely

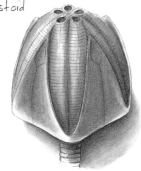

blastoid

FIELD NOTES

Ordovician rocks, Sweden, Canada, and Ohio, USA

Silurian limestones, UK

Cretaceous limestones and shales, central Texas, USA

Silurian and Devonian rocks, New York and Illinois, USA

Carboniferous limestones Appalachian Mountains, USA

Є O S D C P Tr J K T

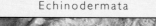

rare. Shortly after death, these fragile animals were usually disarticulated into many small polygonal calcite plates and columnals. Isolated columnals are among the most common

echinoid Tylocidaris

fossils in many Paleozoic limestones, and in some cases, the entire limestone is made of countless columnals. In shales, articulated specimens are less likely to be found, but single calcite plates and entire calyces are more common and may be in good condition.

Expect to find more columnals than other body parts. The columnals themselves may have many different shapes, from the ubiquitous round to pentagonal or even star-like shapes. The central cavity (lumen), through which living tissue passed, may be very small, or most of the diameter of the columnal, or it may also be star-shaped.

Unfortunately, it is nearly impossible to identify a crinoid from the columnals alone. Sea stars are very rare as fossils. Sea urchins begin to show up in

abundance in the late Paleozoic, and by the Cretaceous are very common fossils. Regular sea urchins have a symmetrical body, usually round, and represent forms that lived and moved about on the sea floor. It is not unusual to find isolated plates and spines of regular sea urchins in Carboniferous and Permian marine shales. Irregular sea urchins are bilaterally symmetrical and are streamlined for burrowing in soft sediments. Burrowing sea urchins are found in Cretaceous shales as entire body fossils. Their horizontal burrows may be wrongly identified as bones.

echinoid Micraster

brittle star Aganaster

221

Vertebrates: Fish

Vertebrates are highly mobile, complex organisms with internal skeletons. The oldest vertebrates are fish, and the earliest fish are the jawless agnathans, which had heavy head skeletons, but only a cartilaginous internal skeleton. Closely related are the placoderms, the first jawed fish, also with heavy head shields, and the cartilaginous chondrichthyians, including modern sharks and rays. The most derived fish (osteichthyians) have bony internal skeletons and include all modern bony fish as well as the early ancestors of land-dwelling vertebrates.

The first fish appeared in freshwater environments but rapidly spread from lakes to rivers to lagoons and then to open seas. By the Silurian, fish occupied all water depths from lakes and streams to deepest oceans, so expect to find fish fossils in nearly any environment. With the exception of placoderms, all major groups of fish are still alive, although older groups are reduced in number and diversity. Lampreys and hagfish are all that remain of the agnathans, but these have lost their head shields. Sharks and rays have tooth-like bones in their scales and their numerous generations of teeth are common fossils.

Bony fish are now the most numerous. The lone surviving

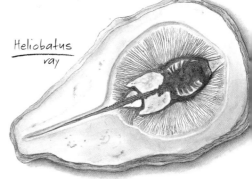

Heliobatus ray

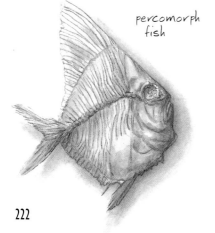

percomorph fish

FIELD NOTES

Green River Shale, USA

Old Red Sandstone, UK

Niobrara Formation, central USA

Permian shales, central Texas, USA

Chalk Marl, Sussex, UK (coprolites)

Harding Sandstone, Utah, USA

Cretaceous limestones, central and southern USA

Holzmaden, Germany

Є O S D C P Tr J K T

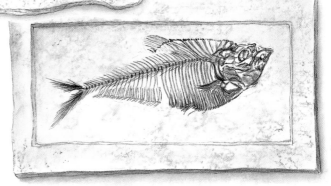

shark tooth

...ember of the group of bony fish that ...ve rise to land-dwelling animals, the ...oelocanth, was discovered in the 1930s ... deep water off the African coast. Most ...ony fish respire with gills, but some forms ...ve lungs and can breathe air.

As abundant as fish are, they are relatively ...re as fossils. The bony teeth of sharks fossilize ...ell and are common in some environments. ...therwise, fish are so easily broken up after ...eath that they make ...oor candidates for ...ssilization. In some ...inor dark shales, ...sh bones can be ...ery common. Since ...ost fish are active ...wimmers, their ...ossils are likely to be ...pread through a ...ariety of rocks. Look for them ... shales, especially marine black shales ...r shales deposited in freshwater lakes. ...ossil bones may be abundant in lake ...ales, where they are preserved on ...edding planes. Fossil fish fecal ...aterial, coprolites, may be locally ...ommon in Permian shales of brackish

or fresh water. Bones may also be concentrated in sediments on lake bottoms, where they have been protected from decay by lack of oxygen. Whole fish are more common in lake shales. In rare instances, in certain limestones, whole fish are preserved, uncrushed, in three dimensions. Many such fish from South America are available in rock stores. In such cases, the limestone can be delicately dissolved leaving an intact, articulated skeleton that looks almost modern.

Priscacara

cast of Diplomystus

223

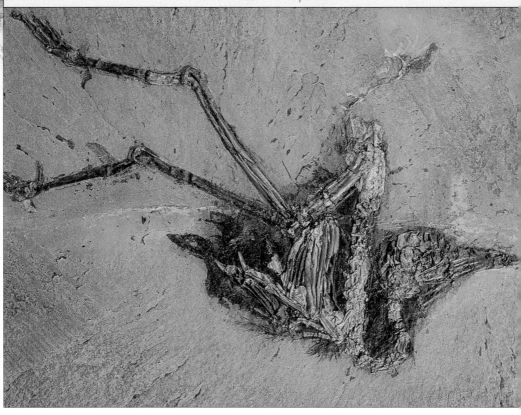

Other Vertebrates

The higher vertebrates are among the largest and most active animals on Earth. They have a bony internal skeleton and are well adapted for living and moving around. Not only do they inhabit the land surface, but vertebrates fly, burrow, and some, such as seals, whales, ichthyosaurs, and plesiosaurs, have even moved back to living in the sea. In the Devonian, the first land-dwelling animals, the semi-aquatic amphibians, evolved from bony fish. In the Carboniferous, the first animals that could live on land without a larval stage or needing water for fertilization, appeared. These were the reptiles, and in the Triassic, one major branch gave rise to the mammals. The other branch, representing all living reptiles, went on to spawn the great lineages of giant reptiles, flying and aquatic reptiles, and the humble lizards and snakes. All major lineages of terrestrial vertebrates survive today, although not necessarily in their early forms or diversity.

Higher vertebrates have occupied nearly all possible environments. Amphibians seem to have preferred tropical realms. Ancient reptiles, although mostly cold-blooded, are found in a variety of environments, reflecting their ability to adapt to extremes. Mammals have been able to move into very cold environments because of their ability to generate body heat.

In general, the fossil remains of higher vertebrates are uncommon for many reasons, the major one being that the land surface is not conducive to preservation. Although they may

possum teeth

Mesohippus

FIELD NOTES

Green River,
Wyoming, USA
Badlands, South Dakota, USA

Because of the rarity
of vertebrate specimens,
most countries generally
impose restrictions on
their collection
by amateurs.

Є O S D C P Tr J K T

e abundant in certain places, they are usually difficult to find, difficult to remove correctly from rock, and are often fragmented. For these reasons, collecting fossil vertebrates requires technical skills and sophisticated preparation devices and storage facilities.

Arguably, the best place to look at fossil vertebrates is in museum collections, where they have been carefully prepared for display. Vertebrate remains are likely to be found in any rocks that represent terrestrial or marine environments, but since vertebrates are rarely preserved, the search may be lengthy. When one is found, it means there may be other bones in the vicinity.

Look for higher vertebrates in association with shallow marine rocks, with lake deposits, and in the bases or sides of old river channels. Cave deposits may yield cave-dwelling vertebrates. Bones are rarely preserved in ancient soil deposits

kangaroo toe-bone

rodent jaw (lower)

Mastodon

because chemical processes in soils tend to destroy them. Bone might seem hard, but it is readily destroyed. Fossil bone is very delicate and should be stabilized with preservative agents. Large vertebrates should be removed only by experienced people.

The vertebrate parts most likely to be fossilized are teeth, which are made of dense enamel. Ancient mammals are well known from their fossil teeth. Many reptilian and amphibian teeth are similar and, when found in isolation, may be difficult to identify. The most unusual vertebrate fossils are those found frozen in the permafrost that stretches across the northern hemisphere from Asia into North America.

225

Fossil Sites

The Ediacara Fauna

There has been life on Earth for 3,600 million years, but early single-cell creatures left few fossils. The earliest fossils, 3,500 million years old, are bacteria from Australia and we know that more complex animals existed 1,000 million years ago because we have found their burrows.

The earliest fossils of multi-cellular organisms are between 700 million and 570 million years old. These soft-bodied animals take their collective name, the Ediacara Fauna, from the Ediacara Hills in South Australia, where they were found in aston-ishing abundance in 1947. Isolated specimens had been found earlier in England and Africa, and similar collections are now known from England,

Dickinsonia costata, a segmented worm.

Wales, parts of Europe, southwest Africa, the USA, Canada, and Russia.

Ediacaran faunas are found in what were once shallow marine environments, possibly intertidal areas such as mudflats or tidal pools, where animals became stranded. Early work in Australia recognized them as members of modern groups. Altogether, about 30 species, thought to be animals such as segmented worms, jellyfish, and sea pens, were recognized, as well as a few seemingly unrelated oddballs.

Jellyfish comprise the largest group within the Ediacara Fauna with about 15 recognized species. *Mawsonia* is one of the larger and more common at about 5 inches (13 cm) in diameter. It is named after Sir Douglas Mawson, an Australian paleon-tologist who collected some of the first Ediacara specimens.

There are three species of segmented worm in the Ediacara Fauna, including *Dickinsonia*, about 3 inches (7.5 cm) long. Close inspection reveals what appears to be a central gut lobe, but no eyes or mouth. There are also three species of soft coral, called sea

ens, colonies of which look like feathers up to 24 inches (60 cm) long.

Among the "weirdos" in the Ediacara Fauna Tribrachidium, a circular animal about 1 inch (2.5 cm) in diameter, with three radiating "arms" across its upper surface. Another oddity Parvancorina, more ellipsoid in shape and up to 1 inch (2.5 cm) long with a broad, anchor-shaped ridge on the upper surface. It has been suggested that Parvancorina may be an early arthropod.

Attempts to understand Ediacaran organisms tried to fit them into previously known groups, but while some Ediacaran fossils

resemble modern animals, closer inspection reveals structural details that exclude them. Furthermore, although differing in form, Ediacaran fossils follow a basic plan, which suggests that they may all be related in a single major group that has no modern descendants.

Another suggestion is that the Ediacaran fossils are the remains of lichens, a composite of fungi and algae common in modern terrestrial environments. They are also known in fresh-water and shallow marine environments. While soft-bodied animals, such as jellyfish, are unlikely to leave the types of impression seen in Ediacaran fossils, lichens, stiffened by chitin supports, could. Some Ediacaran organisms, however, appear to have lived in water depths that are too great for lichens, which require sunlight.

Tribrachidium (above) and a jellyfish (left).

The true identity of the Ediacaran organisms may never be known but their fossils tell us that 570 million years ago, life was already quite complex.

229

The Burgess Shale Fauna

During the Cambrian, life diversified rapidly from a few relatively uncompli- cated forms to a vast number of quite complex organisms. Although rapid by geo- logical standards, this process took almost 60 million years to develop fully. While the rudiments of this explosion of life can be understood from the fossils of hard-shelled organisms, it is the rare occasions where soft- bodied organisms are fossilized that better illustrate how dramatic it was. The best known soft-bodied fauna of the Cambrian comes from the Burgess Shale in British Columbia, Canada.

The Burgess Shale Fauna was discovered on the side of a mountain in 1909 by the famous American paleontologist Charles Doolittle Walcott (1850–1927), during a geological survey. The fauna dates to the middle of the Cambrian, about 540 million years ago, and contains more than 140 species of animal, most less than an inch (2.5 cm) or so in length. The reason so many different types of delicate organisms were preserved seems to be that the area was originally in very deep water just beyond the continental shelf.

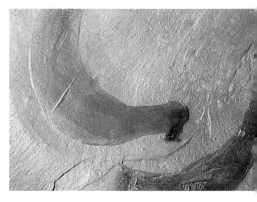

Animals living on that shelf would occasionally be swept over the edge and settle into the soft, fine-grained muds at the bottom where the water was too deep for scavenging animals to destroy their delicate carcasses.

One of the truly astonishing features of the Burgess Shale Fauna is that it contains many types of organism that probably became extinct by the end of the Cambrian. These were not simply different species of known types of organism, but whole body plans as different from each other as crabs are from spiders. While many of

FIELD NOTES

Burgess Shale, British Columbia, Canada

American Museum of Natural History, New York, USA

Smithsonian Institution, Washington, DC, USA

€ O S D C P Tr J K T

The Burgess priapulid Ottoia *(left) in its burrow.*

The grasping organs of Anomalocaris *(below).*

These organisms appear to be types of arthropod, there is also a large number of organisms whose wider relationships are obscure. In fact, there are more basic types of organisms in the Burgess Shale Fauna than there are in the world today, a feature that challenges much of our under-standing of the development of life.

Traditionally, we have accepted that life gradually gets more complex and diversified through time, but the Burgess Shale Fauna teaches us that the development of life has occurred as a selection process, with only a few types of organism surviving from earlier faunas

Marrella
splendens,
arthropod

that were once much more diverse. Although the Burgess Shale Fauna is the most widely known of the Cambrian soft-bodied faunas, there are other such faunas now recognized from around the world, including China, the USA, and Australia. These all tell the same strange story as the Burgess Shale—that by the mid Cambrian, life was amazingly diverse.

One of the most interesting animals from the Burgess Shale is *Anomalocaris,* a carnivore up to 2 feet (60 cm) long. It seems to have been composed mostly of soft tissue and, being large, it readily disintegrated after death. Initially, various pieces were described as different animals—the grasping organs were thought to be prawns. Recent finds, including complete specimens, reveal they all belonged to one animal.

The Hunsrückschiefer Fauna

One of the most important fossil faunas from the middle Paleozoic era is the Hunsrückschiefer Fauna from Bundenbuch, Wissenbach, and Gemünden in the German Rhineland. These fossils come from the Hunsrück Shales, which are lower and middle Devonian in age. The Hunsrückschiefer Fauna includes sea stars, trilobites, other arthropods, and cephalopods.

What is amazing about the Hunsrückschiefer and Burgess Shale faunas is that, as well as the more typical hard elements, the soft parts of organisms are preserved along with whole organisms consisting entirely of soft parts. Fossil specimens from the Hunsrückschiefer Fauna are preserved as pyrite within the shale and reveal exquisite detail when X-rayed. Usually, only the hard parts of an organism are fossilized, so the soft anatomy, particularly of organisms that are now extinct, can never be properly understood from most fossil remains. From such rare cases of fossils of the soft anatomy, we gain valuable insights into the complete organism. For example, study of cephalopod specimens from the Hunsrückschiefer Fauna

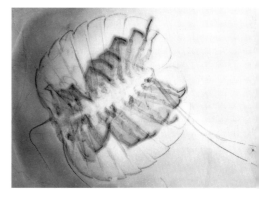

An X-ray of Cheloniellon calmani, *an unusual arthropod.*

reveals that some types carried their shells on the outside of their bodies while others had a layer of soft tissue surrounding the shell. Such detail can rarely be deduced solely from the fossil remains of the animal's hard parts.

In the Hunsrückschiefer Fauna, remains of some organisms not usually fossilized are preserved. *Mimetaster* is a bizarre arthropod that accounts for about half the known specimens of the Hunsrückschiefer Fauna. Curiously, despite its abundance

FIELD NOTES

Bundenbuch, Wissenbach, and Gemünden, Germany

Senckenberg Museum, Frankfurt, Germany

Institut für Paläontologie, Bonn, Germany

€ O S D C P Tr J K T

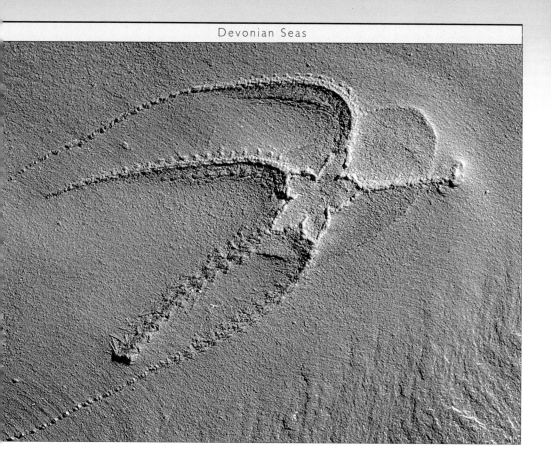

here, *Mimetaster* is known from nowhere else. It has eyes on stalks and two pairs of strong legs. Another strange arthropod is *Vasconisia*, which has a two-part shell covering much of its body. It does not appear to have eyes, but has three pairs of walking legs on its head. Two pairs of extra appendages near the mouth seem to have been used for manipulating food. *Mimetaster* was probably a deposit feeder, processing sediments for microsopic organisms, while *Vasconisia* was probably a carnivore or a scavenger.

While these two unusual animals seem to be related to one another, their wider affinities are obscure. They are possibly related to *Marrella* from the Burgess Shale fauna and they seem

to represent a whole group of arthropods seen only in faunas with exceptional preservation. The key point about deposits such as the Hunsrückschiefer and the Burgess Shale faunas is that they provide unique windows on a broad spectrum of life at a particular moment of time, including organisms without hard parts to leave fossils and the soft anatomy of others. This makes them so important to our understanding of the history of life that they have been given the name *Lagerstätten*, meaning "mother lodes".

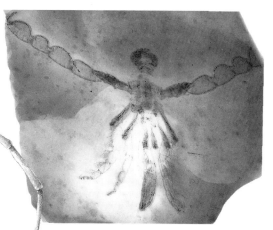

Mimetaster *(left)*. An X-ray of Palaeoisopus problematicus *(above)*, one of two known species of sea spider. **233**

Mazon Creek

The Carboniferous, divided in the USA into the Mississippian and Pennsylvanian sub-periods, saw the development of the first significant forests. Vegetation was so abundant that it produced the first major coal deposits, from which the Carboniferous takes its name. These forests were capable of supporting complex ecosystems.

Unfortunately, coal deposits are not particularly good locations for preserving fossils, but associated sediments often are. Such is the case in Illinois, in the area called Mazon Creek. Here, some 300 million years ago, a river delta ran through an extensive swamp. In many respects, Mazon Creek would have been like modern Louisiana, except that it would have been warmer, the whole location being only a few degrees from the equator at that time.

Mazon Creek is special because the fossils from the area are in a particularly fine state of preservation. These organisms were quickly buried in mud at the bottom of the river system, and bacterial action, while decomposing the organic material, also generated a hardened zone around the remains. These are now found as concretions, particularly hard balls of rock, which, when split open, reveal exquisitely preserved organisms. Such nodules or concretions are often found in soil dumps after strip-mining.

There are numerous exposures bearing concretions scattered over Grundy, Will, Kankakee, and Livingston counties in Illinois. It is certainly worth inspecting road and rail cuts, cliffs, quarries, and other excavations in these areas. Concretions are also found associated with the mines of LaSalle County. The abundance and exceptional preservation

FIELD NOTES

✦ Mazon Creek, northeastern Illinois, USA

🏛 Illinois State Museum, Springfield, Illinois, USA
Field Museum of Natural History, Chicago, Illinois, USA
Burpee Museum of Natural History, Rockford, Illinois, USA

Є O S D C P Tr J K T

A Mazon Creek fern, Neuroptis (above). A spider-like arachnid (right): rarely fossilized. 14 orders of spiders have been found here.

234

Tullimonstrum *(left)*, Octomedusa pieckorum *jellyfish (below). The delicate tentacles are not usually preserved.*

f fossils from Mazon Creek has made them favored specimens in collections.

The most bizarre and enigmatic organism to be recovered from Mazon Creek is a cigar-shaped, segmented animal with a spade-like tail and a shield-like snout with a toothed claw. Called *Tullimonstrum gregarium* after its finder, Francis Tully, these strange beasts still resist all attempts to place them within any known group. The curious *Tullimonstrum* has become the official state fossil for Illinois.

The Mazon Creek Flora contains more than 400 plant species from about 130 genera. Dominant among these plants are horsetails, ferns, and club mosses. The Mazon Creek Fauna, consisting of more than 320 species, can be divided into two parts, the Essex and Braidwood faunas. The Essex Fauna represents the animals that would once have lived in the shallow bays of the river system, while the

Braidwood Fauna consists of terrestrial and freshwater creatures from the area. Animals recovered from the Essex Fauna include jellyfish, worms, clams, snails, shrimp, and fish, while the Braidwood Fauna includes insects, millipedes, centipedes, scorpions, spiders, ostracods, shrimp, horseshoe crabs, fish, and amphibians.

Coprolites are also found in Mazon Creek nodules and more exceptional specimens include young lampreys with the yolk sac still attached. The mixture of marine and freshwater organisms is thought to be the result of storm surges bringing marine creatures into the delta system.

235

The Karroo Beds

The Permian and Triassic witnessed one of the most important developments in the history of life: the evolution of mammals from reptilian ancestors. While obviously descended from reptiles, modern mammals have a significantly different structure. The links between the reptilian grade and the mammalian grade remained poorly understood until the significant fossil beds of the Karroo Basin in southern Africa were studied systematically from the late 1890s to the 1930s.

The Karroo Basin, a massive structure covering most of what is now South Africa, consists almost entirely of Permian and Triassic sediments. Earlier sediments in the basin reveal that there were glaciers to the north, but later sediments indicate a warmer, more seasonal environment. Throughout the Permian and Triassic, the Karroo Basin would have been a complex of rivers draining into a southern sea. The animals living there evolved from reptiles to mammals and their fossilized remains are quite abundant through the basin. Found in older sediments towards the bottom were remains of reptiles that are beginning to show mammalian affinities—animals such as the dicynodonts with two dog-like fangs at the sides of their mouths, and the wolf-like *Lycaenops*. In common with mammals, these mammal-like reptiles had one major hole in the side of their heads to allow for the attachment of jaw

Skulls of gorgonopsian (top) and dinocephalian (above), two groups that demonstrate links in the transition between reptiles and mammals.

FIELD NOTES

Karroo Basin, South Africa

South African Museum, Cape Town, South Africa

British Museum (Natural History), London, UK

Є O S D C P Tr J K T

236

muscles but, in common with more primitive reptiles, they had jaw made up of our major bones with a single bone in the ear.

Because an almost continuous record of animals living in the area over a period of about 50 million years is preserved in the sediments of the Karroo Basin, the evolutionary history of many groups can be tracked accurately from their fossils. By the time the latest sediments were formed, the primitive mammal-like reptiles of the Permian had been replaced by forms more closely resembling true mammals—in animals such s *Thrinaxodon*, the jaw comprised, principally, a single bone and the other reptilian jaw bones performed a new role as xtra bones in the ear.

Oudenodon skull (left), after preparation. Large Bradysaurus skeleton (below) being excavated.

Mammal-like reptiles and their descendants, reptile-like mammals, dominated the Karroo Basin for most of the Permian and Triassic, but towards the end of the Triassic, a new group of animals emerged that would dominate terrestrial habitats for the next 160 million years. Early dinosaurs, such as the 40-foot (12-meter) long *Euskelosaurus*, are found in the youngest sediments of the Karroo Basin. It is not clear why, with such a promising start, mammals should have given way to dinosaurs in the late Triassic, but for the entire reign of the dinosaurs, mammals were rarely larger than a modern cat and were relegated to small, peripheral habitats.

One of the most famous paleontologists to work the Karroo Beds was Robert Broom, a Scot who later discovered the first fossils of the early hominid *Australopithecus*. 237

Holzmaden and Solnhofen

For most of the Jurassic, large parts of western Europe were covered by warm, shallow seas, and associated with these seas are two most important fossil sites. Holzmaden, near Stuttgart, Germany, is early Jurassic, while Solnhofen, in Bavaria, dates from toward the end of that period. At both sites, the fossils are recovered during stone-quarrying operations.

Fossils of marine creatures from the Jurassic, such as the dolphin-like ichthyosaurs, long-necked plesiosaurs, and short-necked pliosaurs, are found in many places, but rarely as complete skeletons. At Holzmaden, however, complete articulated specimens are abundant, usually with every detail of the bones faithfully preserved.

Horseshoe crab from Solnhofen.

Some specimens are so perfect that they have stomach contents and even unborn young inside females—at least one unfortunate ichthyosaur has been preserved in the act of giving birth. Occasionally, the skin and body tissues of the animals are also preserved, showing complete outlines and certain details of internal structure. Such rare preservations offer unique insights into the biology of these long-extinct creatures—we

FIELD NOTES
✵ Quarries near Holzmaden, Germany
Quarries around Solnhofen, Germany
🏛 Museum Hauff, Holzmaden, Germany
Eichstätt Museum, Bavaria, Germany
Senckenberg, Frankfurt, Germany
Є O S D C P Tr J K T

now know that ichthyosaurs had a dorsal fin and gave birth to live young at sea rather than coming ashore to lay eggs.

Many types of fish and invertebrates are also known from Holzmaden, all preserved in the same exquisite detail. One specimen, a petrified log some 30 feet (9 meters) long, is completely encrusted in crinoid up to 6 feet (1.8 meters) long. This breathtaking specimen

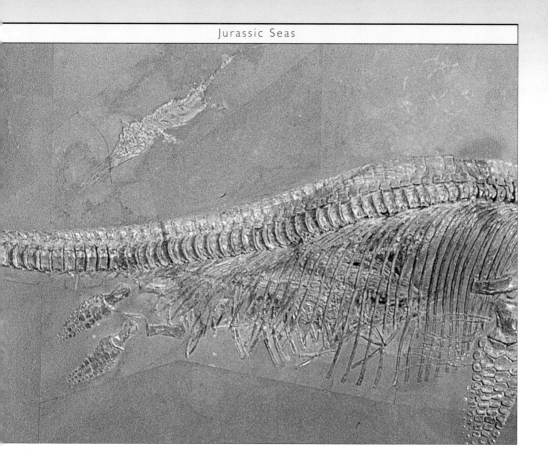

overs an entire wall of the Museum Hauff, which is located near the deposits. Holzmaden specimens are relatively common and are on display in many natural history museums around the world.

Holzmaden represents the bottom of a large, shallow sea, while Solnhofen represents quiet lagoons behind extensive coral and sponge reefs. In this environment of soft, fine sediments, the remains of animals living in and around the lagoons are well preserved. The sea creatures from Solnhofen are very diverse, including jellyfish, worms, bivalves, ammonites, prawns, shrimp, lobsters, barnacles, crinoids, horseshoe crabs, echinoids, sea stars, and fish. Horseshoe crab fossils are often found by following tracks made as they crawled to their last resting place.

From the land come the fossils of insects, plants, small

The flying reptile Rhamphorynchus (above) and a reconstruction of Archaeopteryx (right), both from Solnhofen.

dinosaurs, lizards, crocodiles, and flying reptiles (pterosaurs). But perhaps the most important fossils from Solnhofen are the seven amazing specimens of *Archaeopteryx*. These show a small dinosaur with two wings, making it the first bird—clear impressions of feathers cover its body. If it were not for the exceptional preservation qualities of the Solnhofen limestone, it is unlikely that impressions of the feathers would exist, and the unique place *Archaeopteryx* holds between birds and dinosaurs would have been more difficult to understand.

239

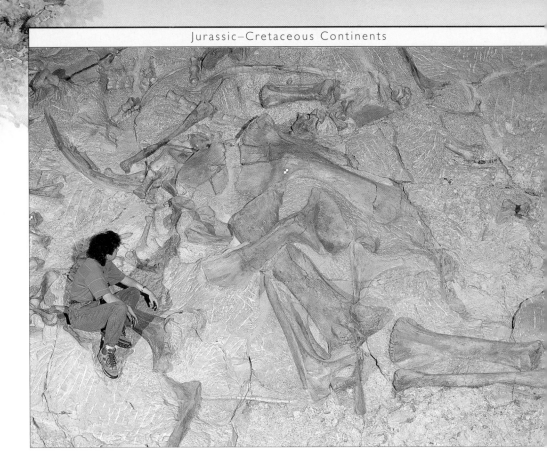

Dinosaur Sites

For 160 million years, from the late Triassic to the end of the Cretaceous, dinosaurs ruled the Earth. Their fossilized remains have been found on every continent, including Antarctica, but their distribution is skewed to favor a few special regions. One of the most prolific is the western part of North America. Dinosaurs lived on land, usually a poor place for creating fossils, but during the Mesozoic Era, the Age of the Dinosaurs, much of western North America was covered by the flood plains of enormous river systems that drained into an inland sea. These flood plains were home to many different dinosaurs and other animals.

Centrosaurus *bone bed excavation.*

An area known as the Dinosaur Triangle, between Vernal and Price in Utah and Grand Junction in Colorado, is particularly rich in significant dinosaur deposits. Most of these are Jurassic in age along with some Triassic and Cretaceous deposits. Perhaps the most well-known site is Dinosaur National Monument, east of Vernal. In this one quarry the remains of nearly 100 individuals, representing 10 species, have been found. Most are types of long-necked dinosaur, such as *Diplodocus*, *Apatosaurus*, *Camarasaurus*, and *Barosaurus*, but there are other plant-eaters, such as *Stegosaurus*, *Dryosaurus*, and *Camptosaurus*, as well as meat-eaters, such as *Allosaurus* and *Ceratosaurus*. This unusual abundance is a result of bodies collecting in a sandbar as they were washed downstream in a huge river. Dinosaur National Monument is open to the public and many fine specimens can be

FIELD NOTES

✴ Dinosaur National
Monument, Utah, USA

Cleveland-Lloyd Quarry, Utah, USA

🏛 American Museum of
Natural History, New York, USA

British Museum (Natural
History), London, UK

Royal Tyrrell Museum,
Drumheller, Alberta, Canada

Є O S D C P Tr J K T

een, still partly embedded in the quarry face. Other sites in the Dinosaur Triangle include he Cleveland-Lloyd Quarry south of Price.

Younger, Cretaceous-age deposits to the west nd north of the Dinosaur Triangle contain a lifferent set of dinosaurs. Dinosaur Provincial Park in Alberta, Canada, has been set aside to rotect its vast fossil deposits. Coupled with the Royal Tyrrell Museum near Drumheller, this rea is a mecca for dinosaur enthusiasts because f the beautiful specimens that are on display in he museum or have eroded out of the ground.

The Alberta specimens come from toward he end of the dinosaurs' reign and nclude a variety of strange duck- illed dinosaurs and various types f horned dinosaur.

In one bone bed, lie the remains of thousands of individuals of a horned dinosaur similar to *Centrosaurus*. This species appears to have lived in huge herds, perhaps comprising tens of thousands of individuals, that migrated across the continent in search of food. These migrations entailed dangerous river crossings during which many animals died, their remains swept away by the river. The carcasses collected where the flow of water slowed, producing the bone beds we find today.

he skull of Camarasaurus *(top),* nd a Triceratops *skeleton (right).*

241

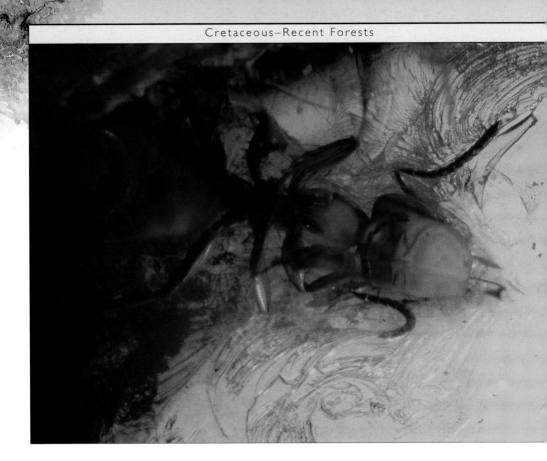

Amber Fossils

Amber is resinous tree sap that has hardened. The trees that originally produced the sap were usually conifers, but some angiosperms also exuded sap that was converted to amber. Technically, amber is not a mineral, but in many cultures, it is classed with precious stones for use in jewelry and ornaments. Last century, amber was melted down to produce high-quality lacquers and varnishes. People have long been attracted by its beauty. A wedge-shaped piece was found in a 10,000-year-old burial site in Denmark. Most amber is less than 70 million years old, but some types are 100 million years old.

As old, hardened tree sap, amber can be thought of as a fossil, but the most widely recognized fossils associated with amber are the insects and other small animals that occasionally became trapped in the sap while it was still viscous. The vast majority of

Chrysopilus, *a fossil fly in amber.*

amber fossils are insects but other organisms, such as spiders, centipedes, and even small lizards, are found preserved in this way. Many aspects of amber fossils are unique, and their importance cannot be overstated. An animal trapped in amber is preserved in exquisite detail, unparalleled by other forms of fossil preservation. Usually, even microscopic hairs on the most minute of insects are faithfully preserved without any crushing or distortion. Amber fossils also provide a detailed record for groups of organisms that are very delicate and rarely preserved in other ways. Insects and spiders are very poorly represented in the fossil record and what fossils are known of representatives of these groups are usually badly

FIELD NOTES

Cliffwood, New Jersey, USA

The Baltic Coast

The Dominican Republic

American Museum of Natural History, New York, USA

British Museum (Natural History), London, UK

Smithsonian Institution, Washington, DC, USA

€ O S D C P Tr J K T

242

rushed and distorted. Without the amber fossils of insects and spiders, little would be known about the evolutionary history of either group.

While amber fossils represent one of the most ideal forms of fossil preservation, it is not perfect. Once trapped in the tree sap, the organism decays and dehydrates leaving a carbonized mass inside a perfect mold of the original organism. In some cases, insects in amber have been dissected, and carbonized films representing the remains of major muscle groups and internal structures have been identified. However, despite the fantastic stories in the film *Jurassic Park*, we have not been able to retrieve DNA from the food of ancient insects. Small fragments

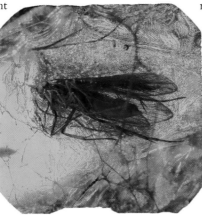

Ants in amber.

Amber with a 35–40-million-year-old moth.

of DNA from some amber insects have been identified, making it possible to compare their ancient DNA with that of contemporary relatives and calibrate the rate of change. Paleontologists have recently been able to reactivate bacterial spores from inside 40-million-year-old bees trapped in amber.

Many fine specimens of insects in amber are available for purchase through rock and museum shops. The buyer should, however, be wary, as amber fossils are easily faked using living insects and synthetic amber-like resins.

Although there are tests available to distinguish real and synthetic amber, the best advice for the amateur is to deal only with reputable outlets and to avoid unusually cheap specimens.

While very little amber contains insects, such fossils are known from many sites around the world, including the coast of the Baltic Sea, the Isle of Wight, and New Zealand. Amber is usually associated with coal and shale deposits. **243**

The Age of Mammals

ossil deposits representing the age of mammals are usually more common than those from the age of dinosaurs, even though dinosaurs were around for more than twice as long. Younger fossils are better represented than older ones, mainly because older fossil deposits are more likely to have eroded or to have been covered by younger sediments.

Worldwide, there are many fine and unusual deposits of mammal fossils. One of the most fascinating is the Eocene site, Grube Messel, near Darmstadt in Germany. Messel is for vertebrates what the Burgess Shale and the Hunsrückschiefer faunas are for invertebrates—one of those extremely rare situations where the soft parts of organisms were preserved along with hard skeletons. About 150 years ago, quarrying work began at Messel for brown coal and oil shales from which kerosene and other petroleum products were extracted.

Small wallaby skull from Riversleigh.

Fossils were found during these activities and removed to various museums. It was found that when one side of these fossils was carefully prepared and embedded in resin, delicate removal of the remaining rock from the other side could reveal not only the articulated skeleton of the animal, but sometimes also the skin, fur, feathers, internal organs, and gut contents. On occasion, beetles are found with the brilliant, iridescent colors of their wing covers preserved intact.

Messel represents what was once a rain forest area with a diversity of plant and animal

FIELD NOTES

Grube Messel, near Darmstadt, Germany

Riversleigh, Queensland, Australia

Senckenberg Museum, Frankfurt, Germany

Queensland Museum, Brisbane, Australia

Є O S D C P Tr J K T

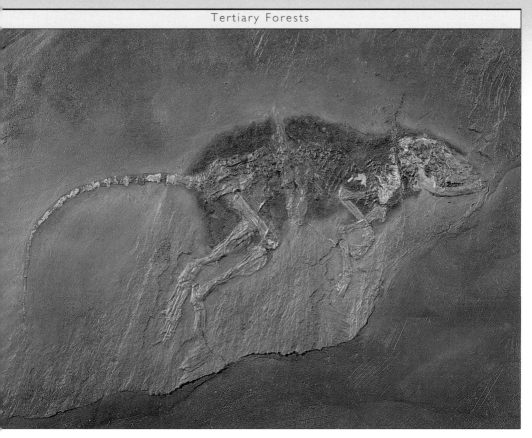

ife. Apart from the many species of plant, this site has produced fossil insects, fish, frogs, turtles, reptiles, birds, and a huge variety of mammals.

On the other side of the world, Riversleigh, in Queensland, Australia, provides a unique and exceptional window on the development of vertebrate life in Australia. It is remarkable because of the abundance of fossils found there and their near-perfect preservation, although animal soft tissue is not preserved in these specimens.

In the early Miocene, 25 million years ago, Riversleigh was a rain forest growing on an extensive area of limestone and teeming with animals. As the limestone dissolved in the water on the forest floor, animals or skeletons that fell into pools and ponds gradually became encased in limestone, an excellent preserving medium. They can be released by dissolving the surrounding rock in mild acid, leaving behind skulls, teeth, and bones as perfectly preserved as the moment the animal died. Fossil insects, crustaceans, snails, fish, lungfish, frogs, crocodiles, snakes, turtles, lizards, birds, and a variety of mammals, including egg-laying mammals, marsupials, and bats, have all been recovered from Riversleigh.

The ancient platypus Obduradon.

Riversleigh (above), North Queensland, Australia, has produced an abundance of new fossils. Bandicoot skull and jaw (left).

245

Tar Pits

I n the heart of metropolitan Los Angeles is
a unique and remarkable fossil deposit, the
Rancho La Brea Tar Pits. These disclose a
relatively complete record of literally thousands
of animals and plants that lived in the area
during the past 40,000 years.

The Los Angeles Basin contains significant
reserves of oil, to the extent that there are
working oil derricks in the heart of downtown
Los Angeles. The area is also tectonically active
and the energy from this activity has cooked
portions of the oil deposits into a thick, gooey
soup and assisted in the transport of this material
through the rock units. At Rancho La Brea,
these natural asphalts periodically break through
to the surface where they form pools. Surface
pools of asphalt act like adhesive flypaper and
are literally capable of holding an
elephant. Once stuck in the tar,
animals and plants are quickly
buried, and the petroleum-rich
sediments are an excellent preservative for the hapless creatures.

The variety of life recovered
from Rancho La Brea is remarkably diverse, including many types
of plant, insect, ostracod, bivalve,
gastropod, and many different

The skull of Canus dirus, th
*dire wolf, which was foun
in large number*

vertebrates. Famed for its beautifully preserved
large mammals, including bison, horses, saber-
tooth cats, wolves, coyotes, giant sloths, camels,
antelopes, and bears, the site has also yielded
other vertebrates, including small
birds, reptiles, and amphibians.

More rarely,
elephantine
mammoths and
mastodons were
found at Rancho
La Brea as well as
deer, a tapir, a jaguar,
and a peccary.

While the site has produced
an amazing diversity of animals,
there is an unusual twist about

FIELD NOTES

Rancho La Brea Tar Pits,
Los Angeles, California, USA

Los Angeles County
Museum of Natural History,
California, USA

George C. Page Museum,
Los Angeles, California, USA

Є O S D C P Tr J K T

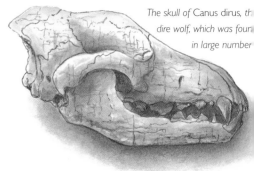

246

which ones are prominent. Predators, such as dire wolves (larger than, but similar to, the living gray wolf), saber-tooth and other large cats, together outnumber the large prey animals by more than 6:1. Usually, the ratio of predator to prey would be the other way round with prey outnumbering predators by about 20:1. It appears that Rancho La Brea was a death-trap for predators. One can imagine that a large prey species, such as a bison, hopelessly mired in the tar would be an irresistible attractant for numerous and varied predators who, in their attempts to gain a quick and easy meal, also became trapped in the sticky grave.

By about 11,000 years ago, the larger animals, including saber-tooth cats, native horses, and bison, had disappeared from the area. A short time later, in paleontological terms, a new animal appeared in the deposit. While only one specimen of this animal, a human, has been recovered, a quantity of human artifacts has also been found at Rancho La Brea.

By about 9,000 years ago, when this luckless individual was living in what is now the Los Angeles area, the animals and plants were essentially the same as those that we would recognize from the area today.

Skeleton of Smilodon *(left), the saber-tooth cat. Massive bone deposits at Rancho La Brea (above).*

247

Early Fossil Humans

Of all the organisms preserved in the fossil record, no group fascinates us more than those that lead directly to ourselves. The fossil record of our ancestors, while not abundant, is complete enough to show clearly our common ancestry with apes and our evolution.

It was Charles Darwin who correctly suggested that Africa was the cradle of humanity. Fortunately, the eastern half of Africa has been rifting apart for the past few million years, thus providing the right kinds of rockbed to preserve human fossils at the time when apes, including humans, were evolving away from the other primates. In the early Miocene, about 18 million years ago, a baboon-sized primate called *Proconsul* appeared in Africa.

Proconsul has features that clearly indicate that it was more ape-like than other primates and it appears to represent a common

ancestor for both humans and other apes. The human (hominid) and the African ape branches of the family tree seem to have split about seven or eight million years ago, but there are few fossils from this period. The earliest recognizable hominid, *Australopithecus ramus*, was found in Eritrea in 1994. This fossil is 4.5 million years old, and for the next 2.5 million years, other species of *Australopithecus* roamed Africa. Mostly shorter than 5 feet (150 cm), *Australopithecus* had a brain larger than that of a chimpanzee but smaller than a modern human. The faces of these creatures were more human-like than those of any other apes. *Australopithecus* has been found in a number of eastern and southern African sites, including Olduvai Gorge (Tanzania), Hadar (Eritrea), Koobi Fora (Kenya), and Swartkrans (South Africa). Footprints 3.5 million years old from Laetoli (Tanzania) indicate that *Australopithecus* walked fully upright, as do modern humans.

A second type of hominid, *Homo habilis*, appears in some of the sites where *Australopithecus*

FIELD NOTES

Olduvai Gorge, Tanzania

Koobi Fora, Kenya

Lake Turkana, Kenya

Hadar, Eritrea

Swartkrans, South Africa

National Museum of Kenya, Nairobi, Kenya

National Museum of Ethiopia, Addis Ababa, Eritrea

€ O S D C P Tr J K T

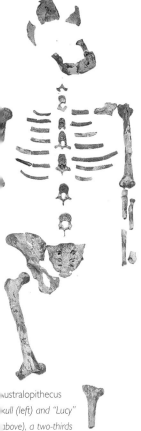

Hominid footprint trail (below), left in volcanic ash in Laetoli, Tanzania.

Australopithecus skull (left) and "Lucy" (above), a two-thirds complete, 3.2 million-year-old Australopithecus skeleton, found in Eritrea.

has been found, particularly Olduvai Gorge and Koobi Fora. This is the earliest member of the genus to which we belong.

Homo habilis was generally much larger than *Australopithecus,* with a larger brain and a more vertical face. It was also the first hominid to leave Africa—fossils have been collected from sites in the Middle East—but it was *H. erectus,* the next species of *Homo* to appear, that really began to explore the world.

The oldest specimens of *H. erectus,* found in Africa, are about 1.5 million years old; more modern specimens have been found in Asia and Europe. *Homo erectus* seems to have been the first user of fire, with hearths reported in China, Hungary, and France. *Homo erectus,* including the more popularly known Peking Man, Heidelberg Man, and Java Man, disappears from the record about 300,000 years ago. The only surviving hominid, *Homo sapiens,* went on to dominate the world.

A skull of Homo erectus.

249

Frozen Fossils

The ivory of mammoths from Siberia has been traded extensively in both China and Europe for perhaps the past thousand years. In 1707, Evert Ysbrand Ides, a Dutchman involved in this trade, reported that the frozen head and foot of a mammoth had been recovered from the icy tundra. Since then, the frozen remains of as many as 24 mammoths have been retrieved from all over northern Siberia, as well as frozen woolly rhinoceros, bison, and an array of other animals.

These animals date back to the last ice age, which ended 10,000 years ago. It was once thought that larger animals became trapped in crevasses in the glaciers, which then collapsed in on the hapless victims. More recent research shows that these animals tended to live where there was sandy ground that became boggy when thawed. Perhaps, during an exceptional summer, the ground

Woolly mammoths (above) were common in northern latitudes during the Pleistocene. A frozen mammoth leg (left).

FIELD NOTES

✳ Numerous sites in Siberia
The Italian Alps
🏛 Paleontological Institute, Moscow, Russia
University of Innsbruck, Austria
British Museum (Natural History), London, UK

Є O S D C P Tr J K T
| | | | | | | | | |

thawed and the animals became mired, only to be deep frozen the following winter. Being essentially packed in ice, the carcasses of these animals are remarkably well preserved— claims that the meat is still fit for human consumption are probably exaggerated (although there are reliable reports of dogs eating it and of carcasses being

250

scavenged by wolves and foxes). The fur (or "wool") of these animals has also been preserved, along with the internal organs and stomach contents—one frozen mammoth was found to have been eating wild thyme, poppies, and buttercups just before its death.

Frozen animals are often found on river banks where the action of the river has eroded the tundra to expose the buried carcasses. This led to early suggestions that the mammoth was a burrowing creature that would die if it broke through the surface and was exposed to light and air. Natives of northern Siberia sought out these specimens, not only to collect their tusks for trade, but also to retrieve their bones, which they fashioned into bowls, cups, and small ornaments.

Frozen fossils are usually associated with what is now permanently frozen ground, such as the tundra in northern Siberia. However, a dramatic find was made in 1991 in a glacier high in the Alps between Italy and Austria. The remains of a frozen man, nicknamed Ötzi, had become exposed during the

spring thaw. Ötzi was beautifully preserved along with his belongings, which included leather leggings, a loin cloth, a fur cap, a grass raincoat, and a jacket made of alternate strips of brown and golden fur. This 5,250-year-old traveler, with three broken ribs, appears to have been caught in a blizzard. He seemed poorly equipped for the environment in which he died and may have been fleeing some catastrophe.

This 5,250-year-old man (above) was found frozen in the Italian Alps in 1991. He was found complete with his axe (above) and other possessions of extraordinary workmanship.

251

From the time the first dinosaurs emerged, their history was one of expansion and diversification.

JOHN HORNER
(b. 1946), American paleontologist

DINOSAURS

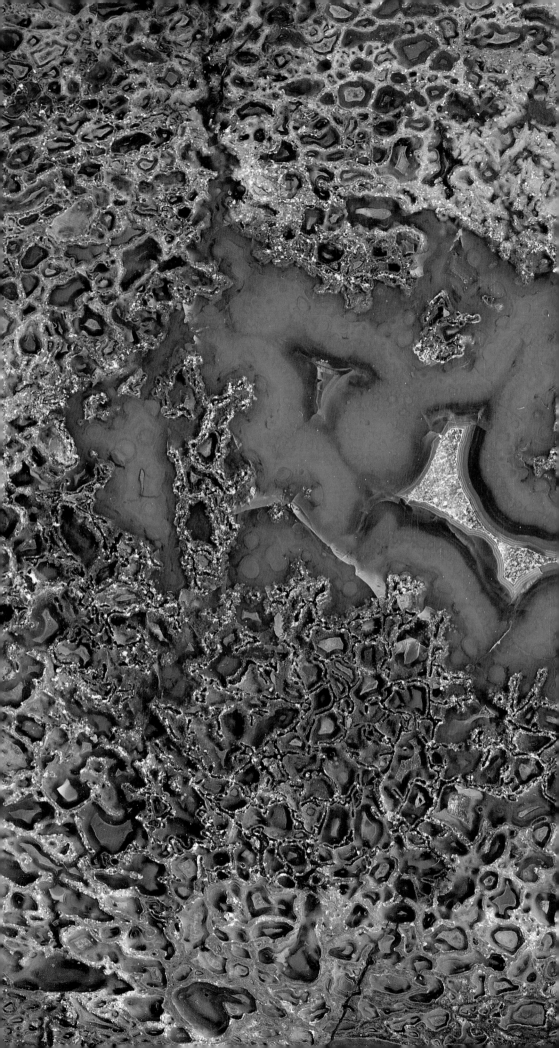

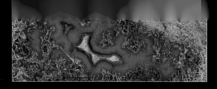

CHAPTER ONE

READING *the* PAST

> Time present and time past / Are both perhaps present in
> time future / And time future contained in time past.
>
> *Burnt Norton,*
> T.S. ELIOT (1888–1965), American-born English poet

DELVING *into*
the DINOSAUR PAST

Over almost two centuries the science of paleontology has painted for us an

increasingly clear and diverse picture of the world that dinosaurs lived in.

To many people, the very word "dinosaurs" conjures frightening images of colossal predatory beasts roaming ancient landscapes, the undisputed masters of the Earth. This popular—and, in the case of most dinosaurs, very inaccurate—perception no doubt helps to explain the peculiar fascination that these long-vanished creatures hold for us. There are, however, many other groups of animals that we know, from the fossil record, to have been contemporary with the dinosaurs, and many of these were every bit as spectacular and impressive as any of the dinosaurs. Indeed, animals larger than any of the dinosaurs—some species of whales—swim in today's oceans. While they, too, appeal to our sense of wonder, dinosaurs no doubt still have a stronger hold on our imagination.

CHANGED PERCEPTIONS

Our fascination with dinosaurs derives, at least in part, from the slowly unfolding history of their discovery and the gradual unearthing of the truths of their existence.

From the early years of the 19th century, museums began to fill with huge skeletons, carefully, but often wrongly,

THIS PAINTING *by Charles Wilson Peale (1741–1827) shows sophisticated technology being used in a fossil dig in the United States, in 1799.*

reconstructed from bones and other fossils recovered from sites all around the world. These remains of animals from a previously unrecorded past were brought to life again in petrified form. It was as if the fledgling science of paleontology had proved that the dragons and monsters of folklore and myth really did once exist.

In the 180 years or so since humans first learned of the existence of dinosaurs, our understanding of them and the worlds they inhabited has increased hugely. And with this growth in knowledge has come an increase in respect. We no longer think of dinosaurs in the way that earlier generations did—as

evolutionary mistakes that were selected for extinction to make way for more sophisticated animals. We now realize that they were an extremely successful and diverse group of animals that occupied all the lands of the world for 160 million years. The reign of humans on Earth pales in comparison with this long dominance.

DINOSAUR DIVERSITY

The diversity of dinosaurs as a group is now widely understood. Although a number of dinosaurs, including some of the best known, were huge, most were not, and many were small animals. In fact, the average size of a dinosaur was little bigger than that of a

modern sheep. Up to the present, researchers have named around 860 different types of dinosaurs, from bantam-sized insect-eating creatures to huge, lumbering beasts that weighed tens of tons. There were dinosaurs with horns, plates, spikes, clubs, frills, crests, and sails. Some had teeth like steak knives that could shred flesh, while others had batteries of flattened teeth for grinding plants to a paste. A number of dinosaurs had no teeth at all. Some were sleek and agile and probably capable of wolf-like speeds, while others were elephantine, with legs like tree-trunks that supported immense bodies.

The number of dinosaurs that have been discovered, studied, and named is now very extensive, and new discoveries are still coming to light. There are, however, many types of dinosaurs that we will probably never know about. All that we do know comes from fossil remains. Because fossils form only under certain conditions, and because many dinosaurs probably lived in environments where these conditions did not apply, no fossils have been found as clues to their existence.

PALEONTOLOGY

The science of paleontology is the study of fossils. Until relatively recently, the main focus of paleontological research into dinosaurs had been to work out how they were related to each other and where they fitted into the greater story of life. More recently, however, paleontologists have been delving more deeply into questions of how dinosaurs lived, and just what were they like as living animals.

The fossil clues that paleontologists have to work with are surprisingly varied. Bones readily fossilize if the conditions are right, and sometimes complete dinosaur skeletons are found intact. On rare occasions, muscles, skin, and other soft tissue can also fossilize. Dinosaurs have also left their footprints, eggs, and dung, all of which provide clues about the animals that created them. Though far from complete, these discoveries have given us an ever-expanding picture of what the Earth and its inhabitants were like in the age of dinosaurs.

ONE OF THE LARGEST *of all the dinosaurs, Tyrannosaurus (left) dwarfed its contemporaries. Compsognathus (right), was a midget by comparison. It grew no taller than a modern chicken.*

TELLING GEOLOGICAL TIME

Rocks that have built up in layers over millions of years have provided the vital clues to the age of the Earth and its successive life forms.

Unraveling the history of the Earth has been the task of geologists who have been studying the rocks of the world for the past 250 years. They have built up a coherent story by examining how rocks form and how they have come to be placed in relation to each other.

LAYERS OF ROCK

The rocks of the Earth's surface are layered one on top of the other, like a stack of books. It follows, then, that the rocks situated at the bottom of the pile must have been laid down before the rocks closer to the top. By working on this principle, geologists are able to work out the relative ages of rocks by observing how the different types of rocks are arranged with respect to each other. By systematically mapping all the known rocks of the world and working out their relative positions, geologists have assembled what is known as the stratigraphic column. This is a register, or diagram, of the relative ages of different types of rocks.

A FOSSILIZED CRAB *(top left), found in Jurassic deposits in Australia.*

The stratigraphic column spans almost the full 4,600-million-year history of the world. This is a huge collection of information so, in order to make it easier to understand, geologists have divided it into a number of sections. These sections are what we call the geological eras, periods and epochs. For example, the Jurassic period is a section of the

DIFFERENT STRATA *of reddish sandstones, shales, mudstones, and siltstones can be distinguished in these spectacular cliffs in Arizona's Grand Canyon.*

CHARLES HAZELIUS STERNBERG *led his family of three sons in a fossil-collecting business. At the feet*
of Charles Sternberg lie the fossil remains of Albertosaurus libratus, collected in 1917.

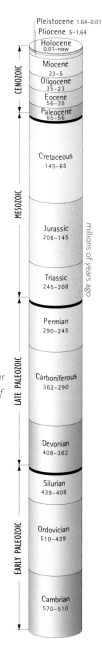

CENOZOIC	Pleistocene 1.64–0.01
	Pliocene 5–1.64
	Holocene 0.01–now
	Miocene 23–5
	Oligocene 35–23
	Eocene 56–35
	Paleocene 65–56

MESOZOIC
Cretaceous 145–65
Jurassic 208–145
Triassic 245–208

LATE PALEOZOIC
Permian 290–245
Carboniferous 362–290
Devonian 408–362

EARLY PALEOZOIC
Silurian 439–408
Ordovician 510–439
Cambrian 570–510

millions of years ago

stratigraphic column that is younger than the Triassic period that lies underneath, and older than the Cretaceous period that sits above it. The Jurassic period represents a segment of time in the history of the Earth that began 208 million years ago and finished 145 million years ago. Periods are grouped into geological eras. For example, the Triassic, Jurassic, and Cretaceous periods are grouped together into the Mesozoic era. The periods in turn are divided into smaller segments known as epochs and stages.

Times are calculated by looking at the degree of decay that is displayed by particular elements found in certain types of rocks. The longer the rock has been in existence, the greater the decay that will have taken place. These techniques provide "absolute" time or age, which scientists measure in millions of years. When combined with information from the stratigraphic column, they allow us to give dates to other rock units. It comes as no surprise that the dates given

by absolute dating techniques agree with the order of dates given to us from the stratigraphic column.

FOSSILS IN ROCKS

The world has existed for 4,600 million years, and fossils have been found dating back 3,800 million years, but evidence for complex life forms does not appear until around 600 million years ago. Fossils dating back longer than this are relatively scarce.

However, a more abundant supply of more recent fossils has allowed scientists to plot the course of evolution and the development of life. As various types of animals and plant forms have come into existence and become extinct, they have left their fossils behind in the rocks within the stratigraphic column.

Because living things do change through time, their fossils can be used to date rocks and to make comparisons and correlations between rocks over large geographical areas. For example, dinosaur fossils are found only in rocks of the Mesozoic era, which extends from 245 to 65 million

THIS TIMELINE *shows the order and duration of the different geological eras and periods in the Earth's history. The dinosaurs lived only during the Mesozoic era, appearing late in the Triassic period and becoming extinct at the end of the Cretaceous.*

years ago. Any rock in which a dinosaur fossil is found has to be from the Mesozoic era. A particular type of dinosaur, of course, is more restricted in its time range; identifying the dinosaur can help to narrow down even further the age of a kind of rock.

Unfortunately, however, dinosaur fossils are relatively rare. The shelly fossils, such as those of clams and snails, are more abundant and widespread, and are therefore more useful for this kind of dating.

259

THE FORMATION *of* FOSSILS

Fossils are the vital clues on which the laborious but fascinating detective work of paleontology is based.

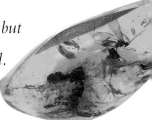

Fossils are records, written in stone or rock, of life through the ages. Anything that was once alive can leave fossil traces, but some organisms are better candidates for fossilization than others. Usually, only the hard parts of a plant or animal end up as fossils. Muscles, skin, and internal organs are rarely preserved. The shells of animals such as clams and snails and the bones of vertebrates are much more likely to be preserved than are the bodies of soft animals such as worms and jellyfish. Indeed, the fossil record of these creatures is almost nonexistent. In certain instances, footprints, eggs, and dung can also fossilize.

FOSSIL PROCESSES

There are a number of ways that fossils can form. Most fossils, however, involve watery environments and result from the burial of an organism's remains in the sediments of a river, lake, or sea. Once the soft tissues have rotted away, the bones or shell become encased in the surrounding muds and silts. As time passes, these sediments harden into rocks, and the bones or shells that are trapped within create an impression of their living

THIS AMBER contains the fossilized remains of a fly. Most fossils preserved in amber are of insects.

form. Sometimes the actual remains are totally replaced, cell by cell, with minerals that wash through the enveloping rock. This process is called "petrification." In other cases the whole bone is dissolved, leaving behind a hole—a natural mold in the rock that can later fill up with minerals

Other fossils are created in less usual ways. Insects and small animals can become trapped in tree sap that eventually hardens into the semiprecious stone amber and seals in a perfect copy of the entombed animal. Sometimes, the mineral silica

A FOSSILIZED TREE forms part of a fossil forest at Lulworth Cove, in Dorset, UK. The doughnut shape is the fossilized remains of a collar of algae. These fossils are from the Jurassic—they are betwen 162 and 135 million years old.

AMATEURS AT WORK

Not all fossils are found by professional paleontologists. Fossil collecting is an absorbing and popular hobby for many amateur enthusiasts, who sometimes make the important finds that lead to breakthrough discoveries. William Walker was a case in point. He was an amateur fossil collector who, in 1983, came upon an enormous fossil claw while fossicking in a quarry in Surrey, in southern England. He took his find to the British Museum of Natural History in London, where paleontologists soon realized that it belonged to a previously unknown dinosaur. A team of paleontologists went to the quarry and started digging. They eventually excavated a relatively complete skeleton of the new dinosaur, which they named *Baryonyx walkeri*. *Baryonyx* means "heavy claw," and *walkeri*, of course, is a tribute to the man who discovered it.

FISH *are the oldest vertebrates, but their fossils are relatively rare. Plant fossils are more common, especially in Carboniferous and Tertiary rocks. The palm and fish fossils (left) are from the Green River Formation in Wyoming, USA. The diagrams (below) show stages in the formation of dinosaur fossils.*

n fill the impressions in the
ck left behind by an animal,
sulting in a fossil shell or
eleton that glitters with the
e of precious opal. On rare
casions, the scalding ashes
m a volcano can encase a
pless animal. The resulting
ssil is a hole in the shape of
e trapped creature.

By far the greatest number
fossils are the remains of
elled creatures that lived in
allow seas. Corals, clams,
ails, and a host of other
vertebrate animals make up
e bulk of the world's fossil
llection. More rarely, plants
n become fossilized. Coal,
r example, is the fossil
mains of whole forests.
nly rarely, though, do any
aces of plant structure
rvive. These are destroyed
 the coal is compressed to
ss than one-hundredth the
ickness of the once-living
ants that comprise it.

AND ANIMALS
he remains of animals that
nce lived on land are
ssilized even more rarely
an those of plants. To be
ndidates for fossilization,

these animals need to have
died close to or in a water
course that floods and buries
its prize in muds and silts. The
fact that, at least as far as we
know, all dinosaurs lived on
land explains the scarcity of
their fossil remains and makes
it all the more likely that we
will never know just how
diverse they really were.

Animals that walked or ran
across floodplains or tidal flats
have left a record of their
passing as fossilized footprints.
Sometimes the trackways of
whole herds of animals are
preserved in this way. And
in some cases, complete
rookeries of dinosaur nests
have been inundated and are
now preserved as fossils.

Now let us turn to our

richest geological

museums, and what a

paltry display we behold!

On the Origin of Species
CHARLES DARWIN (1809–1882),
English naturalist

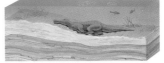

BELOW THE SURFACE *of a lake, a dead dinosaur's flesh rots away or is eaten by aquatic creatures.*

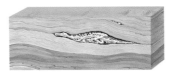

LAYERS OF SILT *build up over the dinosaur's bones and prevent them from being washed away.*

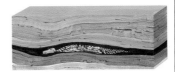

WEIGHED DOWN *by sediment, the dinosaur bones are slowly replaced by minerals.*

MILLIONS OF YEARS *later, seismic disturbances bring the fossilized bones near the surface.*

IDENTIFYING *and* CLASSIFYING DINOSAURS

Both living and extinct animals are classified by scientists according to the similarities and differences between them.

Even before humans appeared on the scene, animals, in order to survive, had to develop some of the skills of the naturalist. They had, for example. to learn to classify the plants and animals around them into "safe" and "dangerous," "edible" and "inedible," and "approach" and "avoid." Basic classification, then, is fundamental to what we do, not only as humans, but as living beings.

TAXONOMY

Biologists use a method of classifying living things which reflects the relationships between them. This system of classification is known as taxonomy. It was developed by the 18th-century Swedish naturalist Carl Linnaeus (1707-1778), who published his ideas in a book, *Systema Natura*. Linnaeus's approach involved two revolutionary initiatives. First, he assigned to all known plants and animals a two-part name—the biological binomen. The first part of the name is the generic name—it identifies the genus. A genus is a collection of closely related species. The second part is the species name—a means of identifying a population, or group, of individual organisms that are distinguished by the fact that they can interbreed with each other but not with other living things. The second breakthrough by Linneaus was the idea of ranking similar organisms according to their degree of similarity. Similar species are grouped into a genus, similar genera are grouped into families, families are grouped into orders, and so on. The higher we go in this hierarchy, the less similarity there is between individual members of the group.

Eighty years after Linnaeus developed his system, Charles Darwin's theory of evolution would give added sense to theses classifications, by suggesting that organisms are related because they share a common descent. The more recently organisms have diverged from each other the more similar they appear.

THESE THEROPOD FOOTPRINTS, *recognizable by the imprint of three large toes, are preserved in sedimentary rocks at Kalkfeld in Namibia.*

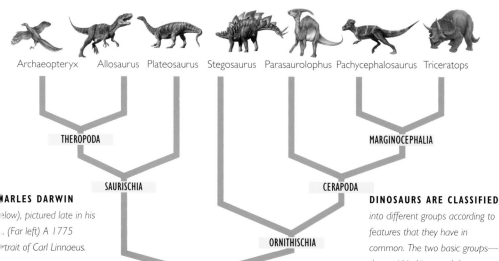

Archaeopteryx Allosaurus Plateosaurus Stegosaurus Parasaurolophus Pachycephalosaurus Triceratops

THEROPODA

MARGINOCEPHALIA

SAURISCHIA

CERAPODA

ORNITHISCHIA

DINOSAURIA

ARLES DARWIN
*elow), pictured late in his
. (Far left) A 1775
trait of Carl Linnaeus.

DINOSAURS ARE CLASSIFIED
*into different groups according to
features that they have in
common. The two basic groups—
the ornithischians and the
saurischians—are distinguished
by having markedly differing
hip structures.*

**OSSILS AND
LASSIFICATION**

lassifying organisms known
nly from fossils presents
me problems. First, we
nnot demonstrate which
dividuals could mate
ith others. Therefore, the
sis of the concept of
pecies" has to be changed.
paleontology, species are
efined by fossils that are
stinctly different in their
ructure from other fossils or
ving organisms.

Ranking fossils into genera,
milies, orders, and other
oups depends on skeletal
atures that are shared with
her fossils. The more
atures that two fossils share,
e more closely related they
e. Members of species are
sentially identical. Members
the same genus share many
atures, while members of
milies share fewer.

A recent improvement on
this system of classification
is the recognition that
evolutionary novelties can
indicate relationship. A fish, a
mouse, and a lizard all have
bones, but this tells us little
about how they are related.
The fact that the mouse and
the lizard both have four
walking limbs tells us that
they are more closely related
to each other than either is to
the fish, because the fossil
record reveals that "legs" are a
more recent evolutionary
advance than "fins."

About a dozen unique
characters identify dinosaurs.
Many of these are subtle, but
some are readily apparent.
Unlike their predecessors,
dinosaurs had a hip
configuration that allowed
the legs to move in a
backward–forward motion
under the animal. This
conferred a number of
advantages on dinosaurs,
including a more energy-
efficient way of moving and
the possibility of attaining
greater speeds. Another

common feature was a crest
on the upper arm bone. This
allowed the arms to be pulled
together with greater power.

The classification of
footprints, eggs, and other
non-body fossils of dinosaurs
presents other problems. It is
only rarely that we can match
footprints with a particular
dinosaur. Eggs, too are
difficult to classify unless the
remains of embryos, juveniles,
or adults are found in direct
association. For the sake of
simplicity, a separate set of
names is given to footprint,
egg, dung, and other trace
fossils. It is quite possible that
three different names have
been given to the same
dinosaur's bodily fossils, its
eggs, and its footprints.

A NEST *of oviraptorid eggs, found in the Gobi Desert in
Mongolia. Eggs are often hard to match with the dinosaur that laid them.*

WHAT DINOSAUR FOSSILS *can* TELL US

Everything we know, or can conjecture, about dinosaurs

and how they lived is based on what fossil remains can reveal.

Fossils are the remains of once-living organisms. It is the paleontologist's job to reconstruct the life of extinct animals based on the fossils they have left behind. Dinosaur fossils are among the most intensively studied fossils of all.

BONES AND SKELETONS
The most common dinosaur fossils are individual bones and, more rarely, complete skeletons. From these finds, paleontologists are able to construct theories and draw conclusions about the evolution of dinosaurs— what different species were like in life, and how they were related to each other and to other creatures that lived at the same time.

Although rare, skeletons present a more complete picture than separate bones. Complete skeletons have been found of only very few dinosaurs. However, most of the major groups of dinosaurs include at least one member for which a skeleton is known. Skeletons help us to construct the missing pieces of other dinosaurs that are known only from fragmentary remains, or even single bones.

Reconstructing any ancient creature from a collection of fossil remains is a difficult task. It is essential to combine only like with like, and not to

THESE HADROSAUR BONES, *dating back to the late Cretaceous, are in the Dinosaur Provincial Park in Alberta, Canada.*

generalize from one type of dinosaur to another. For example, to combine an isolated plate from an armored dinosaur with the shin bone of a small carnivore and the ribs of a long-necked herbivore would result in a strange hybrid that resembled no dinosaur that ever lived. Such mismatching, though, has sometimes occurred.

FEATURES IN COMMON
Bones and other fossil remains paint a cumulative picture of the evolutionary changes that dinosaurs experienced over time. Coupled with evidence of age, gained from the radiometric dating of rocks, changes of bone structure can be used to reconstruct dinosaurs' evolutionary history.

The starting point of this construction is the phylogenetic analysis. Paleontologists carefully note individual features of the bones of different dinosaurs and study how these features are distributed. The more closely two dinosaurs are related, the more features their bones should have in common. Of particular interest are features that are evolutionary novelties—new features not seen in the ancestors. For example, a crest on the arm bone (the delta pectoral crest) is found in all dinosaurs but in no other group of animals. This suggests that dinosaurs are more closely related to each other than any of them is to their immediate ancestors or to other animals that lack this crest. The more features we find that have a similar distribution, the more faith we can place in the groupings of dinosaurs.

REBUILDING PROCESS

Bones and skeletons are also our starting point in rebuilding the appearance of an extinct creature. To begin with, the size of a bone will reflect the size of its original owner. The paleontologist must be conscious that the features of these bones are clues to the ways in which they served living animal. For example, bones from the "hands" of dinosaur that walked on all fours will be more robust than the same bones of a relative that walked with its hands free. Again, sharp claws are

THIS FEATHER FOSSIL, *dating back to the early Tertiary, was found in the Green River Formation, Wyoming, USA.*

for slashing or holding, blunt claws are used for walking on. Meat-eaters require sharp teeth for ripping flesh; plant-eaters need grinding teeth to pulp their food.

Bones also give important clues about the soft parts of a dinosaur that have not fossilized. Muscles attach to bones and leave scars. Careful study of the size and position of these scars can reveal the way in which the animal moved a limb and how strong it was. Dinosaurs' brains were encased in bone, so, even though the brain is never fossilized, the space in which it was housed can give a good idea of what the living brain was like. Nerves and blood vessels coursed through various bones, leaving behind holes that tell of their passage.

Diseases and injuries suffered by an animal during life can also be reflected in bone fossils. An extensive list of diseases—including various cancers, arthritis, and gout—have been identified in dinosaurs from bone fossil evidence. Injuries detected include broken bones and gouges from fighting with members of their own species or with predators.

There is also a lot to be learned from the arrangement of bones where they are discovered. An intact skeleton reveals a quick burial after death, whereas a scattered collection of bones may indicate that the carcass was scavenged. Isolated bones may have been carried off by a predator or washed away from the rest of the skeleton in a stream or flood.

CLEAR IMPRESSIONS *of the skin and bony tendons of a hadrosaur from the late Cretaceous are preserved in this fossil (left) from Utah. The cell structure of a fossilized Jurassic dinosaur bone (below) is visible in this specimen from the Morrison Formation in Colorado, USA.*

RARER FOSSILS

Many important insights into how dinosaurs lived can be gleaned from non-bone fossils such as eggs, dung, footprints, and trackways.

The rarest of dinosaur fossils preserve soft tissue—feathers, skin, muscle, or, very rarely, internal organs. These delicate structures are easily destroyed and exceptional circumstances are required for them to fossilize.

Feathers are most famously known from some of the specimens of *Archaeopteryx*, which was first discovered in 1860. More recently, however, a suite of early birds and birdlike dinosaurs have been found in China with feathers and featherlike structures still attached. In these cases, the carcasses of the animals were preserved in extremely fine-grained sediments and were unaffected by scavengers. Perhaps after they died, their carcasses fell to the beds of lakes or seas where there was little or no oxygen, thus preventing scavengers from reaching the bodies. The occurrence of feathers associated with the skeletons of small theropod dinosaurs is crucial to our understanding of the origin of birds.

Skin, or impressions of skin, has been found with several dinosaurs. It reveals that most had a scaly covering, similar to that of crocodiles or of some lizards. Skin impressions are preserved in cases where a dinosaur fell

SINORNITHOSAURUS,
an early Cretaceous dinosaur, was discovered in Liaoning Province, north-eastern China, in 1999. This fossil showed evidence of featherlike structures on the body.

By this theory innumerable transitional forms must have existed.

On the Origin of Species,
CHARLES DARWIN (1809–1882),
English naturalist

into a fine mud that hardened soon after contact.

The small theropod *Scipionyx*, from Italy, provides the best example of preserved internal dinosaur organs. In this exceptional juvenile specimen, the liver, intestine, and various muscles have been preserved. Some specimens from Liaoning, in north-eastern China, also retain some internal organs, and a number of skeletons, such as the remains of *Seismosaurus*, retain small stones, called gastroliths, that were swallowed by the animal. These indicate the shapes and location of parts of the digestive system.

NESTS, EGGS, AND EMBRYOS

While fossils of dinosaur eggs and embryos have been known for over 100 years, it is only within the last couple of decades that they have been studied in detail. They have revealed a wealth of information about dinosaur reproduction, development, and behavior.

Whole rookeries of dinosaur nests—found in the United States, Argentina, and Mongolia—show that some dinosaurs nested in huge groups and that they returned to their nesting grounds year after year.

In many surprising ways, dinosaur nesting behavior resembles that of modern birds. Spacing of nests, for example, is determined by the length of the adult dinosaur. This reflects the way that nest spacing in modern communal nesting birds is set by the size of the adult bird. Studies of dinosaur nests reveal that the young of some dinosaurs stayed in the nest for a certain time after hatching, and that parents must have tended to them and fed them during the period. Other types of dinosaurs appear not to have given parental care to their offspring. They seem to have deserted the eggs as soon as they

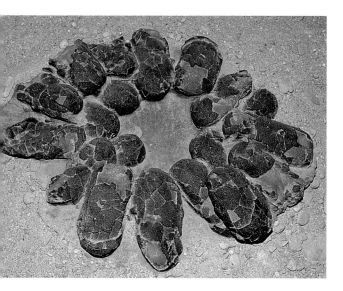

THE 1920s, *a number of nests, more than 70 million years old, of Oviraptor ⅃gs were discovered in Mongolia. Many of the eggs were still intact and some ntained the fossilized remains of tiny embryos.*

SAUROPOD TRACKMARKS
These herbivores walked on four feet. The large prints are from the back feet.

SMALL THEROPOD TRACKMARKS
These small carnivores left delicate, birdlike tracks.

CERATOPSIAN TRACKMARKS
These herbivores walked on four legs. The front feet made the smaller prints.

LARGE THEROPOD TRACKMARKS
These large carnivores were bipedal. Their back feet each had three toes.

ere laid, leaving the young fend for themselves.

THER FOSSILS
 me of the most intriguing nosaur fossils are the mains of dung. These fossils, own as coprolites, can ow what dinosaurs ate, and n give an idea of the size of e anus and the structure the lower digestive tract. owever, coprolites provide tle direct evidence that links em to the dinosaurs at produced them. While ere are analyses that suggest hich dung belongs to which nosaur, it is unlikely that ese identifications can ever positively confirmed. nother feature of coprolites that they are frequently ociated with dung beetles at burrowed under the dung d filled their burrows with nosaur feces.

Footprints and trackways ve been found for most of e major dinosaur groups, d they provide important

clues to the movement and behavior patterns of their makers. The spacing between footprints in a trackway indicates both the size of the animal and the speed at which it was traveling. A number of trackways at a site that point in a similar direction suggests that some dinosaurs moved in groups. In those rare sites where multiple trackways exist, the composition and structure of a herd can be determined. In some cases a dramatic tableau of dinosaur life has been preserved— showing, for example, evidence of a predator scattering a herd of smaller dinosaurs or stalking larger prey. However, associating footprints and trackways with the dinosaurs that made them is an imprecise science.

NOSAUR EGGS *were small in ation to the animals' body size. This is ause larger eggs would have had lls too thick for hatchlings to break.*

Oviraptor's egg

Emu's egg

Possible ornithischian egg

DINOSAUR HUNTERS
of the PAST

*A frenzy of fossil hunting that began in the 1870s
led to a spate of exciting dinosaur discoveries.*

EDWARD DRINKER COPE *probably named more reptiles, both living and extinct, than any other researcher.*

In 1859, Charles Darwin published his *On the Origin of Species*, in which he propounded his theory of evolution—the idea that life forms had changed through time and that all living things were related by descent. As the theory of evolution became widely accepted, at least among members of the scientific community, in the late 1800s—and the findings of paleontologists were seen as the most compelling support for it—the race to find and study dinosaurs became a major focus of scientific endeavor, especially in the United States.

AN INTENSE RIVALRY

The competition to find and name new dinosaurs led to an acrimonious rivalry between two greats of American paleontology. Othniel Charles Marsh, of Yale University, and Edward Drinker Cope,

OTHNIEL CHARLES MARSH *is pictured here with a team of fossil hunters. Marsh is standing in the center of the back row. Marsh and his arch-rival Edward Drinker Cope between them named more than 130 dinosaurs, including most famous North American species.*

of the Academy of Natural Sciences in Philadelphia, started their professional careers as friends, but soon they were bitterly competing against each other in the search for and study of new fossils. Both independently wealthy, they funded their expeditions into the American West. In some cases, they paid off other paleontologists, literally turning up at their sites, purchasing their fossils, and taking them back to the East Coast for study.

The two men even bought fossils from under each other's noses and employed spies in one another's camps. In their frenzied attempts to beat each other to the newspapers with new descriptions, they often telegraphed brief, sketchy, and sometimes misleading

accounts of their finds from the field. They frequently ventured into areas that were still considered dangerous frontiers. Within days of the Battle of Little Big Horn, in June 1876, for example, Cope and his team were hard at work excavating fossils just a few miles away from the site of the recent conflict.

The results of this intense feud were mixed. On the positive side, many of the now more familiar dinosaurs—such as *Apatosaurus, Diplodocus, Stegosaurus, Allosaurus,* and *Triceratops*— were revealed to the world by Cope and Marsh parties between 1870 and 1890. But on the negative side of the ledger, the result of their very

ndignified public feuding
vas the decision made by
ne United States government
o withhold public funding
f paleontology for 25 years.
'here is no doubt, however,
nat the discoveries that were
nade by Cope and Marsh laid
ne groundwork for future
xploration in some of the
nost important fossil-bearing
ocalities in North America.

OTHER AMERICANS

Others carried on the work
egun by Cope and Marsh
n North America. The field
vork of Barnum Brown and
Henry Fairfield Osborn of the
merican Museum of Natural
History was of considerable
gnificance. Among the finds
or which they are remem-
ered is that of *Tyrannosaurus
x*, which they found in
Iontana in 1905. Brown and
)sborn worked mainly in the
estern United States, but
ey also collected in western
anada, especially along Red
eer River, in what is now
lberta. These expeditions
ere conducted by flatboat.

After Brown and Osborn,
harles H. Sternberg—whose

passion for fossil collecting
dated back to childhood—and
two of his sons, Charles M.
and Levi, continued to scout
the late Cretaceous deposits in
Alberta. Among the dinosaurs
discovered by the Sternbergs
were *Albertosaurus, Edmontonia,
Styracosaurus* and *Lambeosaurus*.

OUTSIDE AMERICA

The rush of discoveries that
began in about 1870 with the
expeditions of Cope and
Marsh is often regarded as a
first golden age of dinosaur
paleontology. The majority of
its early finds were made in
North America. This changed
in 1907 when giant dinosaur
bones were discovered at
Tendaguru, in what is now
Tanzania. Dr. Werner
Janensch, curator of fossils at
the Berlin Museum, was sent
to Tendaguru, where he
assembled a huge field party
of almost 500 people. Many
fine specimens were found,
including the massive skeleton
of *Brachiosaurus* that is still on
display in the Berlin Museum.

Among the last discoveries
of this first golden age were
those made in Mongolia and

China. Beginning in 1922,
the first motorized expeditions, led by Roy Chapman
Andrews, were sent to central
Asia by Osborn and the
American Museum of Natural
History to search, not for
dinosaurs, but for evidence of
the oldest humans. Although
these expeditions failed in
their primary task, they yielded
a wealth of dinosaur finds,
including the first dinosaur
eggs and remains of *Oviraptor,
Protoceratops,* and *Velociraptor.*

This first golden age ended
in the 1930s. After that, and
although dinosaur exploration
continued, paleontologists
became preoccupied with
other issues. Another golden
age, which is still with us,
commenced in the 1970s.

The great inviolate place had an ancient permanence.

The Return of the Native,
THOMAS HARDY (1840–1928), English novelist

CHAPTER TWO

THE WORLD *in the*
AGE *of the* DINOSAURS

THE TRIASSIC PERIOD

*The first dinosaurs appeared sometime during the late
Triassic period, roughly 228 million years ago.*

The environment in which the first dino-saurs lived would be unrecognizable to us. It was a world in which there was only one major landmass, where there were dry, red landscapes and forests without a single flower.

Animals at one end of the world would have looked more or less like animals at the other, because there were no seas to stop them spreading across the globe. But by the end of the Triassic, many features of today's world were in place: Forces were tearing the supercontinent apart, and more familiar plants and animals were appearing. As well, significant variations were developing in animals and plants found in different places. By the end of the Mesozoic, there would be a world that was outwardly similar to ours, but much of what made it look "modern" got its start in the Triassic.

Since the 1960s, plate tectonics has been one of the primary paradigms in geology. According to plate tectonics, the crust of the Earth is divided into broad, rigid, but constantly moving, plates that "float" on the more plastic layers of the Earth's mantle. Wherever plates interact, we find intense geological activity—earth-quakes, growing mountains, and volcanoes. As a result of

plate movement, the Earth's continents are constantly in motion, a phenomenon known as continental drift.

PANGEA, THE SUPERCONTINENT

At various times in the past, all the Earth's landmasses have been joined. One of those periods spans the boundary between the Paleozoic and Mesozoic eras, when today's continents were joined in the single landmass of Pangea. North America, Europe, and much of Asia formed the northern part of the supercontinent, and the southern part consisted of South America, Australia, Africa, India, and Antarctica. At the beginning of the Triassic period, Pangea

extended from the South Pole to the middle of the Northern Hemisphere, and it gradually drifted northward. At the end of the Triassic, Pangea was centered on the equator. Consequently, climates changed, growing gradually drier and warmer.

Scientists agree that global climates were seasonal during the second half of the Triassic, with alternating warm-cool and wet-dry cycles. World-wide climate was probably warmer and drier than today, with a broad arid belt in the middle of Pangea and more humid conditions toward the northern and southern ends. Many late Triassic rocks represent ancient sand dunes, and they tend to be red as a result of oxidized iron—an indication of arid conditions, according to some paleo-climatologists. Evaporites— minerals formed when salty water evaporates—were common in the late Triassic.

VEGETATION
Needle-trees, similar to living Norfolk Island pines, and monkey-puzzle trees, some of which were very tall, grew during the Triassic. We can see remains of these conifer forests in places such as

WASSON BLUFF (above), in south-eastern Canada, was the site of important finds of prosauropod fossils in the late 1990s. (Right) Erosion pins are installed at Wasson Bluff in June 1999.

...etrified Forest National Park ...n Arizona. Ferns, including ...ree ferns, were common and ...iverse; and cycads—thick-...eaved plants that outwardly ...esembled palms—were also ...ommon. However, there ...vere no flowering plants.

FAUNA

...When continents collide, ...iant mountain ranges arise. ...his is still happening today ...n the Himalayas, where India ...s pushing into the rest of ...Asia. It also occurred when ...angea formed, but by the ...ime the dinosaurs appeared, ...hese mountain ranges were old and weathered down. As a result, and also because climates were broadly uni-form throughout Pangea, there was little to prevent animals from spreading far and wide. If you could go back to Pangea in the late Triassic you would see a range of animal life. On land, there would be herds of small, usually bipedal dinosaurs, as well as small, shrewlike early relatives of mammals and crocodiles that looked more like reptilian wolves. In the water, you would see various crocodile-like animals, among them large amphibians and distant relatives of true crocodiles.

Later in the Mesozoic, as Pangea gradually broke into separate landmasses—the result of plate tectonics—more diverse forms of animal life began to appear.

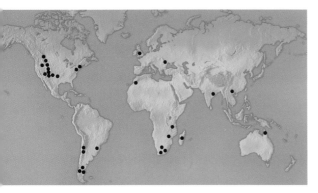

THE SUPERCONTINENT Pangea (above) was the Earth's only large landmass during the Triassic, although forces that would break it up were already at work. Sites where remains of Triassic dinosaurs have been found (left).

273

THE JURASSIC PERIOD

Throughout the Jurassic, changes occurred that resulted in a much greater diversity in landforms, flora, and fauna.

Changes occurred very gradually during the Jurassic. In the early Jurassic, world conditions were very similar to those of the late Triassic. In fact, some scientists make no distinction between these periods, often discussing them as though they were one. In the early Jurassic, the world was still generally warm and arid, especially near the equator, and there was little difference in land animals from one region to another.

THE JURASSIC LANDSCAPE *was much less arid than the Triassic one, thanks to generally warmer and more humid climatic conditions. More expansive forests grew, and plant groups that were present in the Triassic diversified greatly.*

DRIFTING APART

Change, however, was under way. At the very end of the Triassic, the slow but inexorable breakup of Pangea started. The ancestral Atlantic Ocean began to form as North America separated from Europe and Africa. If you visit Dinosaur State Park in Connecticut, you can see an extraordinary sight, thousands of footprints made by dinosaurs that lived in an early side valley of what would become the ancestral Atlantic. By the end of the Jurassic, we see separations, not only between the Americas and the Old World, but also between the world's northern and southern landmasses. What would later become the southern continents—South America, Australia, Africa, Antarctica, and India—were to remain in contact for the rest of the Jurassic and for much of the Cretaceous. The broad landmass they formed is known as Gondwana. The northern part of the former Pangea is now called Laurasia.

EXPANDING OCEANS

Scientists generally agree that both the North and South poles were free of ice throughout the Jurassic. It also seems probable that during periods of increased tectonic activity there was some slight expansion in portions of the oceanic crust. So, the lack of polar ice increased the amount of water in the

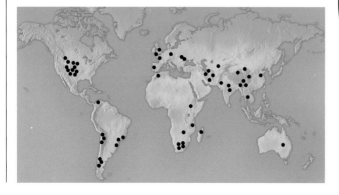

DURING THE JURASSIC, *Pangea slowly broke up to form the northern continent of Laurasia and the southern continent of Gondwana (above). Sites of finds of Jurassic dinosaur fossils (left).*

THE SEA *has eroded joints in the hard Jurassic rock in this cliff face, adjacent to Lulworth Cove, in Dorset, southern England, and then eroded softer rock behind, to create the formation known as the Stairhole.*

JURASSIC DINOSAURS

Jurassic conditions were conducive to the spread of reptiles, and many species of dinosaurs appeared during this period. By the end of the Jurassic, marked differences were beginning to develop between species inhabiting the northern and southern continents.

The late Jurassic, however, was predominantly the era of the giant sauropods, and it was at this time that they achieved their greatest diversity. Other plant-eating dinosaur groups—including ornithopods and, in some places, stegosaurs—were also present. Theropods, too, continued to diversify. There is reason to suspect that the fossil record of smaller theropods from the Jurassic does not truly reflect either their diversity or their numbers.

:eans, and the expanding sea ɔor dispersed the water more idely. As a result, sea levels ound the world rose during e Jurassic, and large sections the continents were ɔoded. This in turn added to e breakup of landmasses that ctonic activity was causing; ʒpanses of water now parated what had been ɔntinuous stretches of land.

ℐARM AND HUMID
he world was uniformly arm during the Jurassic, though slightly cooler than ɪring the Triassic. In

contrast to the variable Triassic seasons, seasons during the Jurassic probably varied only slightly. However, after the early Jurassic, climatic differences probably became more accentuated, largely because of the increased fragmentation of landmasses. Everywhere was warm, but some areas became more humid and received greater rainfall than others.

There were probably still no flowering plants during the Jurassic. Although there is evidence to suggest that the group that included flowering

plants was present at this time, it seems that these did not evolve flowers until the late Cretaceous. Forests, however, flourished and spread in the warm, wet Jurassic climate. They continued to be dominated by needle-bearing conifers, cycads, tree ferns, and ginkgoes.

THE CRETACEOUS PERIOD

The Cretaceous period, which began 144 million years ago and lasted for 80 million years, forms a bridge in time between the earlier Mesozoic and the Cenozoic, the age of mammals.

By the beginning of the Cretaceous period, the Earth was beginning to take on many of the features that are familiar to us today. As the continents continued to move farther apart, groups of plants and animals took on more regional characteristics. The fragmentation of landmasses also had an effect on the climate. As the Cretaceous progressed, climates around the globe gradually became more seasonal, and the annual variation in rainfall and temperature slowly became more pronounced.

FLOWERING PLANTS *appeared for the first time during the Cretaceous period. Plant-eating dinosaurs cleared areas of conifers and cycads, creating spaces that were conducive to the development of these plants.*

Some scientists believe that the changes in the dinosaur fauna, and its increasing variety, were a response to the expanding diversity of flowering plants in the local flora.

THE FIRST FLOWERS

The most significant biotic change that occurred during the Cretaceous was the emergence of flowering plants. They first appeared early in the period and were more abundant in disturbed habitats where dominant conifers and cycads had been removed. By the end of the Cretaceous, there was a great diversity of flowering plants, and some familiar-looking groups, such as the water lilies, magnolias, and sycamores, had appeared. However, there were still no grasses—they did not arrive until the Cenozoic.

The arrival of flowering plants had a cascading effect on all other groups of organisms. There is evidence that complex, mutually advantageous relationships existed early in the period between plants and insects. Insects such as colonial bees, for example, relied on the plants for food, while the plants in turn relied on the insects for pollination.

A DIVERSITY OF DINOSAURS

There was also a significant shift in the nature of plant-eating dinosaur faunas in some parts of the world. Long-necked sauropods continued to be diverse early in the Cretaceous, but the numbers of these huge dinosaurs declined later throughout the period. By the later Cretaceous, the dominance in the northern continents had shifted to the ornithopods and ceratopsians. This latter group of horned animals was among the last groups of dinosaurs to evolve.

FLUCTUATING SEAS

Sea levels throughout the world rose and fell a number of times during the latter half of this period. North America was essentially cut in half by a shallow sea that extended from present-day Hudson Bay to the Gulf of Mexico. Western North America was connected to eastern Asia, and some groups of dinosaurs—such as the ceratopsians, the tyrannosaurids, and the pachycephalosaurids—were unique to these two regions. Today's landmasses of South America, Antarctica, Madagascar, and India may have been closely linked, and all shared several unique groups of dinosaurs—such as the titanosaurid sauropods and abelisaurid theropods—during the Cretaceous.

Dinosaurs are also known to have existed in Australia during the Cretaceous. At that time, Australia was much

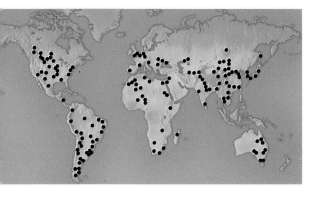

THE CONTINUING BREAKUP *of the world's landmasses during the Cretaceous (below) led to a greater diversification of species. Cretaceous dinosaur sites (left) are more numerous than those from the two preceding periods.*

...oser to the South Pole than ...is today and would have ...xperienced extended periods ...darkness, as Antarctica still ...oes. Some of the Australian ...retaceous dinosaurs, most ...otably *Leaellynasaura*, had ...nlarged orbits, which ...uggests that they had large ...ves that were specially ...dapted for night vision.

...E SEVEN SISTERS CLIFFS *in ...st Sussex, southern England, are ...pical of the white chalk cliffs that were ...rmed during the Cretaceous period.*

A Cataclysmic Event

At the end of the Cretaceous period, important changes were occurring around the globe that would dramatcially affect life on Earth. Sea levels were falling and temperatures everywhere were dropping slightly. Some parts of the world were experiencing extensive volcanic activity. Perhaps most significant of all, however, was a single extra-terrestrial cataclysmic event— a large asteroid or comet hit

the Earth, with devastating consequences.

Any or all of these pheno-mena may have played a role in the major extinctions that occurred at the end of the Cretaceous, in which more than half the world's animals, including all of the Mesozoic dinosaurs, died out.

DINOSAUR ORIGINS

Sometime during the middle Triassic, one of the most successful archosaur lineages appeared—the dinosaurs.

Archosaurs are a group of animals that included the last common ancestors of living birds and living crocodilians. They were present in the early Triassic, but it was not until the middle of the period that they began to dominate the Earth's dry-land habitats.

The first archosaur would have looked like a strange cross between a crocodile and a dog. Although the ancestral archosaur remains undiscovered, we can get a glimpse of what it probably looked like with *Euparkeria*, a small animal known from the Triassic of South Africa. *Euparkeria* measured about 20 inches (50 cm) from tip to tip. We believe it was a predatory animal, with sharp teeth and powerful jaw muscles.

Although not warm-blooded in the sense that birds and mammals are, the earliest archosaurs were probably more agile and active than other reptiles of the era. Like modern crocodilians and birds, they probably had a four-chambered heart and the ability to drag their limbs under their body while walking.

AMMONITES *were shelled marine carnivores of varying shapes and sizes. They evolved more than 500 million years ago, and became extinct, along with the dinosaurs, at the end of the Cretaceous.*

ARCHOSAUR GROUPS

Early in their biological history, the archosaurs split into two groups. In one of these groups, the quadrupedal nature of the early archosaurs remained dominant. Some of these animals grew to be quite large, and may have been the dominant predators in some places during the middle Triassic. Later, the group became dominated by animals that were semiaquatic—these were the ancestors of the crocodiles and alligators that we see today.

The other group adopted a different approach toward predation. The members of this group remained small, but the length of the hindlimb increased. Eventually, some members became bipedal, walking mainly on the hind-limbs and using the forelimbs for grasping. The ancestral dinosaur was such an animal.

Although we have no fossils from the true ancestor of the dinosaurs, primitive dinosaurs, such as *Eoraptor*, can give us

STAGES *in the development of a bipedal stance.*

❶ *The ancestors of dinosaurs sprawled like lizards.*

❷ *Some reptiles, such as crocodiles, can pull their limbs under their body.*

❸ *All dinosaurs could stand erect, supported by legs tucked beneath the body.*

me idea of what it was
ke. The first dinosaur was
obably no larger than a
eep. It was most likely
edatory. It differed from
her reptiles both in its
pedal stance and in its
pright posture. Most living
ptiles "sprawl"—their limbs
oject from the sides of the
dy, and their bellies are
ose to the ground when
ey walk. As they move,
e body is thrown into a
ries of S-shaped curves.

Early archosaurs could, to
me extent, draw their limbs
to a vertical posture, but
nosaurs evolved their hind-
mbs into a bipedal stance.
he head of the thighbone
emur) was turned inward,
that the shaft projected
wnward, not outward,
om the hip socket. Because
this, the hip structure
volved in a particular way. In
her reptiles, the hip socket
a solid cup, because the
mur is pulled inward by the
p muscles.

In the case of dinosaurs,
e femur is pulled upward
y the hip muscles. As a
sult, the hip socket is open
d bears a prominent shelf
f bone along the top rim.
he belly was kept far from
e ground, and the trunk
emained straight when the
imal moved.

This development is of
ital importance. In reptiles
ch as lizards the muscles that
ove the limbs also control
reathing—lizards cannot
reathe and walk at the same
me, and the distance they
an run without having to
op is very limited. But
eorientation of the hindlimb
 dinosaurs meant that
ifferent muscles controlled
alking and breathing, so that
inosaurs could do both

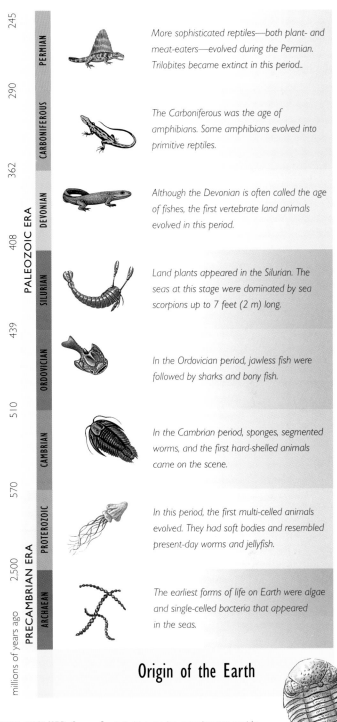

More sophisticated reptiles—both plant- and meat-eaters—evolved during the Permian. Trilobites became extinct in this period..

The Carboniferous was the age of amphibians. Some amphibians evolved into primitive reptiles.

Although the Devonian is often called the age of fishes, the first vertebrate land animals evolved in this period.

Land plants appeared in the Silurian. The seas at this stage were dominated by sea scorpions up to 7 feet (2 m) long.

In the Ordovician period, jawless fish were followed by sharks and bony fish.

In the Cambrian period, sponges, segmented worms, and the first hard-shelled animals came on the scene.

In this period, the first multi-celled animals evolved. They had soft bodies and resembled present-day worms and jellyfish.

The earliest forms of life on Earth were algae and single-celled bacteria that appeared in the seas.

Origin of the Earth

LIFE EVOLVED *from a few primitive marine organisms to a wide variety of marine and land animals in the 4,000 million years before dinosaurs appeared. (Right) A trilobite.*

simultaneously. This allowed them to travel much greater distances without stopping.

The oldest known dinosaur fossils were uncovered from 228-million-year-old rocks from Argentina and Mada-

gascar. The fossils from Madagascar represent primitive prosauropods, and those from Argentina are closely related to early theropods such as *Herrerasaurus* and *Eoraptor*.

THE RULE *of the* DINOSAURS

For 150 million years, the greater part of the Mesozoic era, dinosaurs were the dominant land animals on Earth.

For the first third of the Triassic, archosaurs were only minor components of the fauna. They were overshadowed by the synapsids, close relatives of mammals. By the end of the Triassic, the synapsids were small creatures overshadowed by the archosaurs—especially the dinosaurs. The dinosaurs continued as the dominant land vertebrates for the remainder of the Mesozoic.

TRIASSIC DINOSAURS

The earliest dinosaurs were bipedal predators, much like the early theropods *Eoraptor* and *Herrerasaurus*. Most of the known Triassic theropods were outwardly similar, the largest being approximately 6 feet 6 inches (2 m) long. The dominant theropod lineage of the time, known as the coelophysids, included the *Coelophysis*, which was found in New Mexico.

Plant-eaters appeared early. The early sauropodomorphs, the prosauropods, are known from the start of dinosaurian history: One of the best known Triassic dinosaurs is the

CAMPTOSAURUS *was a bird-hipped herbivore of the late Jurassic. Remains of this dinosaur, which grew to 20 feet (6 m) long, have been found in Europe and North America.*

prosauropod *Plateosaurus,* from Germany. We also have evidence for exclusively plant-eating primitive ornithischians. *Lesothosaurus,* from southern Africa, is an example.

Although later sauropodomorphs and ornithischians were diverse, and differed greatly from the theropods, the earliest herbivores still retained some features of the earliest dinosaurs, in that they were relatively small and could move on two feet.

INCREASING DIVERSITY

During the Triassic and early Jurassic, when there was only one major landmass and the

The astonishing claim that birds are dinosaurs cannot be ignored by fellow palaeontologists.

Sunday Times, March 17, 1974

climates were relatively uniform, dinosaurs moved quite easily from one region to another. As a result, dinosaur finds from the late Triassic and early Jurassic generally tend to represent very similar groupings, wherever they are from. They consist typically of one or a few small theropods; a prosauropod, which is usually the largest dinosaur of the group; and a small, bipedal ornithischian.

As the Jurassic progressed, theropods continued to diversify. Most of those that have been discovered were relatively large animals, but a few smaller theropods were also found.

We know, however, that there must have been a wide diversity of small theropods, because the first bird, *Archaeopteryx,* is from the late Jurassic. Most of the small theropods that were closest to birds are known only from the Cretaceous. If they shared a common ancestor with

WHY SO LONG?

We will never know for certain why dinosaurs enjoyed such a long dominance. Some argue that their advanced sytem of locomotion, which allowed them to breathe while walking or running, gave them an edge over other Triassic groups, including the synapsids, which did not evolve a completely upright posture until much later. Others contend that dinosaurs were simply filling an ecological void caused by the extinction of the dominant tetrapods of the early Triassic. Neither group, they maintain, was "better" than the other. Dinosaurs simply managed to survive whatever catastrophe befell the dominant early and middle Triassic vertebrates and to radiate before the other groups could.

irds, then these groups must lso have been present in the urassic, even though their ossils remain undiscovered.

CHANGING HABITS
he largest herbivorous ertebrates of all time, the auropods, were the most ommon plant-eaters of the te Jurassic and early Cretaceous. They seem to ave been most diverse during he late Jurassic, but the argest known forms lived uring the early Cretaceous.

Although sauropods still xisted at the end of the Cretaceous in some parts of he world, they were less ommon in the middle and te Cretaceous.

Ornithischians diversified roadly during the Jurassic. During the late Jurassic, ertain groups of armored

thyreophorans—including the stegosaurs—were common throughout North America, Eurasia, and Africa. Primitive ornithopods also appear during the Jurassic, but they were not major components of the fauna.

During the Cretaceous, the structure of herbivorous dinosaur communities under-went a radical shift. Sauropods, for example, often became minor components and the ornithopods became dominant ones. Late in the Cretaceous, ankylosaurs and, in some locations, ceratopsians, were very common.

REGIONAL VARIATIONS
As the continents diverged throughout the Mesozoic, dinosaur faunas around the world became increasingly distinctive—North American

groupings, for instance, no longer looked like South American or Asian assemblages. The sauropods, for example, which were common throughout all parts of the world during the Jurassic, had become common only in Madagascar, South America, and India by the late Cretaceous.

Some groups do not appear ever to have had a worldwide distribution. The ceratopsians and pachycephalosaurs, for example, are known only from western North America and from eastern Asia. These regions, which were connected to one another during the late Cretaceous, were, however, largely isolated from the other parts of the world.

IORE SPECIES *of dinosaurs evolved during the Cretaceous period than uring the Triassic and Jurassic combined. This group shows how diverse ese animals had become by the Cretaceous. They are, from left, riceratops, Corythosaurus, Pachycephalosaurus, Saltasaurus, uoplocephalus, and* Tyrannosaurus.

THE PTEROSAURS

Those animals that have the ability to glide or fly have some distinct advantages over their ground-bound relatives.

Lots of organisms travel through the air. Some—including many plants and a few invertebrates, such as spiders—use the wind to spread their seeds or young. The ability to actively move through the air—to fly or glide—has evolved only a few times, but many of the groups that have developed this skill have become hugely diverse. Flying or gliding allows broad dispersal and opens niches not available to non-flyers. The insects, of course, are the most successful such group, but several gliding and flying groups have appeared among the vertebrates.

AIRBORNE VERTEBRATES

The first true vertebrate flyers—animals that are capable of generating lift with their wings—were the pterosaurs. They first appeared in the late Triassic and they survived right to the end of the Cretaceous. Pterosaurs were archosaurs. Although they were probably close relatives of dinosaurs, they were not, as is often popularly supposed, real dinosaurs.

Pterosaurs are often called pterodactyls because of the structure of their wing. "Pterodactyl" means "wing finger," and the wing did, indeed, consist largely of a single finger. Pterosaur arms had four fingers. The first three were small, but the fourth was of an enormously length. A membrane of skin extended from the tip of this finger to either the side of the body or the hindlimb. A few pterosaur fossils preserve the imprint of the wing membrane and show that it was not just a thin flap of skin; rather, it was given support by slender collagen rods that would have kept it relatively rigid.

Pterosaur wings were thus similar to bat wings in that the flight surface was skin supported by the hand, but whereas pterosaurs relied on a single finger from the hand, bats use three or four. An additional skin membrane stretched between the animals' hindlimbs.

LARGE AND SMALL

The earliest pterosaurs were crow-sized animals. They had jaws filled with sharp teeth and probably fed on a variety of small animals, including vertebrates and insects. They had long, slender tails. More advanced pterosaurs differed from their Triassic ancestors in several ways—the tail was greatly shortened, the teeth were lost, and toward the end of the Cretaceous, these animals became very large. In fact, some of the last pterosaurs were the largest known animals ever to take to the air and fly. *Quetzalcoatlus*, from the late Cretaceous of North America, may have had a wingspan of up to 33 feet (10 m)—greater than the wingspan of some types of fighter aircraft!

Throughout the Mesozoic, the pterosaurs filled a large number of roles. Some retained the small size and toothy mouth that they had inherited from their ancestors but others modified their anatomy to acccommodate different needs. A number of them, including *Pteranodon* from the Cretaceous of North America, which had a wingspan of 23 feet (7 m), may have lived like modern gulls or albatrosses, soaring over the ocean in search of fishes. Other pterosaurs had heads that were shaped like those of sandpipers or flamingoes.

One pterosaur fossil of the Triassic—*Sordes pilosus*, from Kirghizia in eastern Europe—is preserved with the remains of short, hairlike fibers around the body. Some believe this was an external covering, similar to down. This is why some recently reconstructed pterosaurs have a "fuzzy" look about them.

A PTEROSAUR *of the late Jurassic,* Rhamphorhynchus, *with its distinctive long tail, grew about as big as a modern-day seagull.*

A RHAMPHORHYNCHUS *fossil (left)
and a* Pterodactylus *fossil (below).
Both these pterosaurs are from the late
Jurassic of Germany, but they are from
different groups. Rhamphorhyncoids
retained their long tails and remained
small. Pteradactyloids had short tails
and some grew very large.*

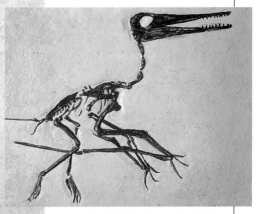

HEADS AND TAILS

Some later pterosaurs had bizarre crests on their skulls. The reason for these is not known, but there are several possibilities. Head ornaments could have been used as social signaling devices. Indeed, in some pterosaurs, two crest shapes are known, suggesting a difference between males and females. But crested pterosaurs also tended to have short tails, and it is thought that some long-tailed pterosaurs used their tails to help steer while flying. In fact, the late Jurassic pterosaur *Rhamphorhynchus* had a diamond-shaped keel at the tip of its tail. Some experts think crests may have helped short-tailed pterosaurs to steer. A flying model of *Quetzalcoatlus* was built during the 1980s, and engineers steered the model by turning the head, relying on the crest to control the direction of flight.

MOVING AROUND

There is some disagreement about how pterosaurs moved on the ground. Most researchers believe they were quadrupeds; some maintain they were bipedal. The four-footed view is supported by the structure of the hindlimb and wing membrane, as well as by footprints believed to have been formed by walking pterosaurs. They show what may be the impressions of both feet and folded wings.

We do not know how pterosaurs evolved flight. The first known pterosaurs in the Triassic already had a complete flight apparatus. We do not have the range of transitional forms that connect birds with their dinosaurian precursors. Most researchers assume that the precursors of pterosaurs were tree-dwelling archosaurs that jumped between trees. However, fossil evidence for this is scarce and inconclusive.

MARINE REPTILES

The return to a life in water has been a recurring theme for many different groups of reptiles.

No sooner had reptiles adapted to a life out of water than they started returning to a life in the seas. Time spent foraging in the productive shallows gradually led them to become increasingly proficient in the water. Structures needed for life on land—such as efficient respiratory and water-control systems—were no doubt an asset in this new environment.

ICHTHYOSAURS AND SAUROPTERYGIANS

The ichthyosaurs and sauropterygians appeared in the Triassic, and their careers as dominant marine predators lasted at least 150 million years. The earliest members of these groups were already so adapted to an aquatic life that the identity of their terrestrial ancestors has yet to be established. The ichthyosaur tail became shaped like that of a fast-swimming fish, the head merged with the body as it does in dolphins, and the teeth and jaws were well adapted to a diet of fish and cephalopods.

Many groups of sauropterygians became very successful marine predators. The strange

THE GREAT WHITE SHARK *is one of the most powerful, and feared, predators in today's oceans. It is a descendant of the ancient giant lamnid sharks that first appeared in the world's oceans during the Cretaceous.*

placodonts acquired heavy bones and strong, crushing teeth, and seem to have fed upon shellfish. Nothosaurs evolved a flattened skull with powerful jaw muscles on the end of a long, flexible neck which could be swiped rapidly sideways through the water to catch agile fish. Nothosaurs used their forelimbs as well as—or even instead of—their tail for propelling themselves through the water.

The descendants of the nothosaurs—the plesiosaurs—made their appearance in the very early Jurassic. In plesiosaurs all four limbs became paddles which were used for swimming

OPHTHALMOSAURUS, *a late Jurassic ichthyosaur, was remarkable for its huge eyes. It probably fed at night.*

through the water, and the tail was greatly reduced.

The two major groups of plesiosaurs modified the nothosaur feeding system to opposite extremes. The necks of long-necked plesiosaurs grew to almost ridiculous proportions—the elasmosaurs of the Cretaceous had necks with more than 80 vertebrae. The head was small, and could be moved quickly when catching prey.

In contrast, the pliosaurs strengthened the large skull of their nothosaur ancestors so it could handle large prey—and because these large prey were attacked head on, the flexible neck was shortened and strengthened to stabilize the massive skull. Species such as *Pliosaurus* and *Kronosaurus* were some of the largest predators of all time.

FOSSIL SKELETONS of the Cretaceous ichthyosaur Platypterygius (right) have been found in most parts of the world. This marine creature grew 23 feet (7 m) long. In the ichthyosur fossil below, a newborn young can be discerned just near the base of the mother's tail.

TURTLES, CROCODILES, AND LIZARDS

Turtles have made two major incursions to the sea. One was in the Jurassic, while the other started in the Cretaceous and has lasted to modern times. Most turtles have been medium-sized animals, feeding on bottom-dwelling animals and plants. During the Cretaceous, however, a number of species became very large. All turtles lay eggs; the hatchlings spend their early years far out to sea, moving back to the adult feeding grounds between 5 and 20 years later. This life cycle may explain why turtles survived the mass extinction at the end of the Cretaceous. Even if all the adults had died, there would have been at least five years' worth of young animals waiting to recolonize the habitat. Crocodiles, too, started a return to the sea in the Jurassic. The teleosaurs were highly adapted for a life at sea: They appear to have preyed upon fish, squid, and even other reptiles. They adopted a form of the underwater flight also employed by plesiosaurs and turtles, where the hindlimbs were used as underwater wings.

Lizards are successful today as small land-living animals, but they, too, have produced several marine lineages. The varanids (goannas and monitors) are the largest modern lizards—yet in the late Cretaceous a group of them returned to the sea to become the spectacular mosasaurs. Even today there are several species of varanid, including the water monitor and the Komodo dragon, that are quite at home in the ocean. The marine iguana of the Galapagos is perhaps the best example of a lizard returning to a life in the sea.

SHARKS

Sharks are not reptiles, but their history has been an important part of the marine reptile story. When reptiles first started to become marine predators, the large sharks were sluggish and not very good swimmers. By the Cretaceous, however, new groups of sharks—the carcharinids (reef and whaler sharks) and the lamnids (white and mako sharks)—had appeared. The lamnids are warm-blooded and are fast, powerful hunters. When the large pliosaurs died out in the middle of the Cretaceous, their place was taken by huge lamnids, even more powerful than the great white shark of today.

KRONOSAURUS, which is known from Queensland, Australia, was a pliosaur of the early Cretaceous. It grew more than 40 feet (12.5 m) long, twice the length of a modern great white shark.

OTHER LAND VERTEBRATES

Throughout the Mesozoic era, many interesting groups of animals, including some that are still alive today, existed alongside the dinosaurs.

For most of the Triassic, dinosaurs—and, more generally, archosaurs—were a minor part of the land fauna. During the early Triassic, synapsids were the most diverse group of large-bodied vertebrates on land.

MAMMAL BEGINNINGS

The class Synapsida now includes mammals, but during the early Triassic it comprised a large number of bizarre creatures that we used to call "mammal-like reptiles." Today scientists no longer include the early synapsids in the class Reptilia. However, when they first appeared during the Paleozoic era, they did look rather reptile-like,

especially as their limbs sprawled out to the side. The synapsids of the early Triassic were more sophisticated. In them, advanced features that we see in living mammals—such as specialized teeth—were blended with more primitive characteristics found in ancestral amniotes—such as jaws with more than one bone and a less advanced way of moving.

As the Triassic progressed, synapsids became smaller and more mammal-like. Synapsids of the latest part of the Triassic looked a great deal like modern shrews. Their cheek teeth had multiple cusps, their ears had multiple bones, and each side of their

jaws had only one bone. As well, they probably had hair. True mammals did not appear until the Jurassic, but these late Triassic synapsids probably lived much like small mammals.

Synapsids were present throughout the Mesozoic, but from the late Triassic through to the end of the Cretaceous, they remained small. The largest of them was no bigger than a modern domestic cat. The first true mammals—members of the group that included living monotremes, marsupials, and placentals—appeared during the Jurassic, and although small, they were probably diverse. Nevertheless, they were not the predominant land vertebrates they would become during the Cenozoic era.

SNAKES *first appeared during the Cretaceous, and the oldest known snake, which is 80 million years old, is known from Cretaceous rocks in South America. The fossil below is an undescribed Tertiary species from Messel in Germany.*

THE JAWS *and teeth of modern crocodiles (left) bear a striking resemblance to those of synapsids, such as Dimetrodon (below). Dimetrodon, however, was not a reptile but a distant relative of today's mammals.*

REPTILES

Other groups that were common in the Triassic have no close surviving relatives. Included among them were the rhynchosaurs. These were bizarre parrot-beaked, plant-eating reptiles, which were distantly related to the archosaurs. They are common in some late Triassic deposits. However, there is no fossil evidence to indicate that they survived beyond the Triassic. Other lizard-like reptiles, such as the procolophonids, may have been distant relatives of modern-day turtles.

Members of the order Crocodyliformes were very common and diverse during the Mesozoic. Many people think of these animals as "living fossils," because fossil crocodyliforms from the Mesozoic often outwardly resemble modern crocodilians—the alligators, crocodiles, and gharials. It is true that many Mesozoic crocodyliforms appear to have been "crocodile-shaped," but it would be incorrect to suggest that they have remained unchanged to the present day.

The earliest crocodyliforms were probably exclusively land-dwellers, and they had longer limbs and deeper skulls than their present-day counterparts. They may have ambushed their prey, much as the earliest archosaurs did. Throughout the Jurassic and Cretaceous, there was a variety of crocodyliforms. They included several lineages that adapted to life in the open sea, complete with limbs modified as flippers and, in a few groups, a tail that bent downward to accommodate a tail fin, much like that of an ichthyosaur. The first true crocodilians appeared during the late Cretaceous and, until the Tertiary, they lived alongside several other crocodyliform groups.

Other reptilian groups were common during the Mesozoic. Sphenodontia today includes only one species—the tuatara (*Sphenodon punctatus*) of New Zealand. During the Triassic and Jurassic, however, sphenodonts were very diverse and

DIMETRODON *was a synapsid—a mammal relative—that lived in the Permian period.*

included some semiaquatic groups. Although most non-dinosaurian reptiles of the time looked like lizards, true lizards did not appear until the Jurassic.

Lizards were very diverse during the Cretaceous and included some large terrestrial predators and one of the most important groups of marine reptiles, the mosasaurs. A particular group of legless lizards—the snakes—appeared during the Cretaceous.

There is fossil evidence that turtles, including some aquatic turtles, existed in the late Triassic and the Jurassic. This is not surprising: Turtle shells are extremely durable, which makes them excellent candidates for fossilization. Modern turtles are remarkably similar to their ancient counterparts.

However, true sea turtles—the ancestors of today's sea turtles—did not appear until the Cretaceous.

287

DEATH *of the* DINOSAURS

Theories abound, but mystery still surrounds the extinction of the dinosaurs at the end of the Cretaceous period.

Dinosaurs dominated the landscape for most of the Mesozoic, and, in a sense, they are still diverse today—they live on in the birds, which are their direct descendants. However, the animals popularly thought of as dinosaurs ceased to exist at the end of the Cretaceous and within a few million years, large mammals and birds were filling the roles once played by giant nonavian theropods and duckbills. Why did these animals disappear?

Just what caused the extinction of the nonavian dinosaurs is still hotly debated. Today there are very few places on Earth where the Cretaceous–Tertiary—often called the K/T—boundary is preserved in a sequence of land or freshwater sediments. We have a good idea about what happened in the marine realm, but only a few dinosaurs—in the form of aquatic birds—lived in the sea. So we are forced to generalize from what the few Cretaceous–Tertiary sites reveal and apply it to the whole world.

AN ANCIENT PUZZLE

Even events of recent times, observed by large numbers of people and recorded on videotape, are subjects that evoke heated controversy. The assassination of the United States president John F. Kennedy, which occurred less than half a century ago, is a case in point If we cannot know for certain what happened then, what chances have we of solving a mystery that is millions of years old, with only the evidence of what is probably very incomplete fossil record?

As far as we can tell, up to 70 percent of species of marine organisms became extinct at the end of the Cretaceous. Marine invertebrates were particularly affected. Prominent groups, such as ammonites—relatives of today's nautilus and squids—disappeared entirely. The extinctions also claimed many species of marine reptiles: Mosasaurs and plesiosaurs also disappeared.

SUDDEN OR GRADUAL?

We know less about what happened on land, but it is clear that all the nonavian dinosaurs disappeared at the end of the Cretaceous. So too did the pterosaurs and many groups of smaller vertebrates.

Some researchers have argued that the disappearance

AN IMPACT *that occurred 300,000 years ago resulted in the 3,000-feet (900-m) wide Wolfe Creek Crater in Western Australia's Wolfe Creek Crater National Park.*

DRAMATIC EXAMPLE *of the Cretaceous–Tertiary boundary (above) can be seen in this hillside north of Saltillo, Mexico. This meteorite (right), which is believed to have come from Mars, is 4,500 million years old.*

POSSIBILITIES

Many theories have been proposed to explain the extinction of the nonavian dinosaurs. These include poisoning from the first flowers, the destruction of eggs by early mammals, radiation poisoning from a distant supernova, and widespread plagues. All of these explanations, while they may seem plausible, leave many important questions unanswered. Flowering plants, for example, had evolved tens of millions years before dinosaurs became extinct. Mammals, too, had shared the land with dinosaurs for well over 100 million years. Most seriously, however, these theories fail to come to terms with the mass extinctions that occurred at the end of the Cretaceous—why so many groups of organisms, apart from dinosaurs, suffered at this time.

f nonavian dinosaurs occurred very suddenly, nd that several lineages ied out within the space f a few thousand years—a elatively brief time in erms of the Earth's history. Others, however, contend hat the extinction appened more gradually, nd that some groups isappeared well before the Cretaceous–Tertiary boundary. The evidence we have, which is restricted to only a few places, is not sufficient to resolve this question. While it seems likely that the marine invertebrates disappeared rather suddenly, the extinction of land animals may have been a more gradual process.

THE HOBA METEORITE, *from Namibia, is the largest meteorite yet found. It is between 410 and 190 million years old.*

CURRENT THEORIES

Most present-day paleontologists subscribe to one or more of three major theories to explain the Cretaceous–Tertiary mass extinction. All three have good evidence to support them, and all three may have been important factors, reinforcing each other in a vicious cycle of environmental devastation.

The first involves climatic changes that were already under way during the Cretaceous. Global temperatures fell at the end of the Cretaceous, and seasonal variations became more pronounced. Differences in summer and winter temperatures, especially at high latitudes, increased markedly. This phenomenon may have been partly the result of major changes in sea levels, which would certainly have increased the amount of habitat that was available for marine organisms.

Rising sea level changes, too, may well have resulted in increased fragmentation of terrestrial habitats. Stretches of forests that were formerly continuous, for example, may have become broken up. This in turn may have fragmented

PROFESSOR ROBERT ROCCHIA, *in his laboratory in France in 1993, holds 65-million-year-old samples of Cretaceous chalk and Tertiary limestone from the Cretaceous–Tertiary boundary.*

large concentrations of animals, resulting in smaller populations, which would be more vulnerable to environmental changes.

However, while climate and changes in sea levels could clearly affect the survival or extinction of living species, they would seem unlikely to bring about a sudden demise. If, as many researchers maintain, dinosaur extinction was sudden, other factors must have played a part.

The second major theory involves extensive volcanic eruptions. Several parts of the world at the end of the Cretaceous were experiencing a huge amount of volcanic activity. The most spectacular evidence for this is the Deccan Traps, a massive set of flood basalts in India.

THIS SEM *(Scanning Electron Micrograph) of magnetite in rock lends support to the theory of asterod impact at the end of the Cretaceous. (Right) A volcanic eruption in the Galapagos Islands.*

The third, and most dramatic, theory postulates the impact of a comet or asteroid at the very end of the Cretaceous. That an impact occurred is supported by several lines of evidence. Most convincing is the existence of certain elements, such as iridium, that are enriched in sediments laid down at the Cretaceous–Tertiary boundary. These elements are rare in the Earth but are common in extraterrestrial materials. Particles of shocked quartz—minerals that have been subjected to intense pressure—are also found in the boundary sediments. Geologists now believe we have found the crater caused by this impact in the Yucatàn Peninsula in Mexico, although it is buried deep underground.

Many of the environmental effects caused by volcanic activity and asteroid impact would be very similar. Both cause large amounts of dust and ash to fill the upper atmosphere, preventing sunlight from reaching the surface and impacts on the survival of plants. Any significant loss of plant life would certainly have had a cascading effect on other organisms. Plant-eating animals would obviously have suffered, as would carnivorous animals that preyed on them.

There is evidence for a temporary disturbance in plant populations in North America at the Cretaceous-Tertiary boundary, because at that point we find a sudden increase in fern spores. Ferns tend to become very common while other plants, such as angiosperms and conifers, are killed off. This suggests that something caused large portions of North America—near the impact site in the Yucatàn Peninsula—to be stripped, quite suddenly, of most vegetation. Flowering plants and conifers came back in the Tertiary, but the large plant-eating dinosaurs were no longer there to eat them.

The solution to the mystery of the mass extinction may continue to elude us. It is quite possible that all three factors cited in currently favored theories played an important part. There are certainly good reasons to

Our little systems

have their day;

They have their day and

cease to be.

In Memoriam,
ALFRED, LORD TENNYSON
(1809–1892), English poet

suggest there is a link between climate changes, volcanic activity, an asteroid impact, and mass extinctions, but the solid evidence that would clinch the argument does not yet exist. One thing we can agree on is that the early Tertiary world was very different from the late Cretaceous one. The only dinosaurs that seemed to have survived into the Tertiary were the feathered ones that flew across the Cretaceous-Tertiary boundary.

GLOBAL WARMING

As well as blocking the rays of the sun, the vast clouds of dust and ash that result from both an asteroid impact and volcanic eruptions can also trap ultraviolet radiation within the atmosphere, causing global warming. Volcanic eruptions usually include emissions of greenhouse gases, such as carbon dioxide, which can further enhance this warming. Even if it lasted only for a relatively short time, a sudden increase in temperature could in turn have contributed to extinctions by creating an environment that was unsuitable for many animals. Even more dramatic effects of an asteroid impact—such as giant tidal waves, global wildfires, and acid rain—have also been proposed, but there is no conclusive evidence that these occurred.

THE SURVIVORS *of* MASS EXTINCTION

Large numbers of animal species survived the cataclysmic events

at the end of the Cretaceous.

THIS SMALL MAMMAL, Purgatoriu
survived the cataclysmic events that
occurred at the end of the Cretaceous.

The mass extinction that occurred at the end of the Cretaceous destroyed over half the Earth's animals. The most familiar victims of the extinction were the nonavian dinosaurs and several important groups of marine invertebrates, such as the ammonites. Often ignored, however, are the important groups of animals that survived. They raise interesting questions about exactly what happened at the boundary of the Cretaceous and the Tertiary.

AQUATIC ANIMALS

The group that seems to have suffered least from changes at the Cretaceous–Tertiary boundary was the bony fishes. In both marine and freshwater settings, these animals appear to have maintained their former diversity.

There is little evidence to suggest that some other important groups that were dependent on fresh water— such as amphibians, freshwater turtles, and crocodylians— became any less diverse than before. This is curious, because scientists have long assumed that acid rain was one of the most harmful consequences of the asteroid impact that occurred about that time. Researchers believe that materials ejected from the crust by this impact would have interacted with atmospheric water to form acids that fell to earth as rain. But, strangely, the groups that have suffered most from the effects of acid rain in modern times—the freshwater fishes and amphibians—fared better than most in the events at the boundary of the Cretaceous and the Tertiary.

MAMMALS AND BIRDS

We cannot be certain about how badly mammals suffered at the Cretaceous–Tertiary boundary—or, indeed, whether they were affected at all. We do know that mammal species did increase in diversity early in the Tertiary. It also appears that some mammal groups became extinct at the end of the Cretaceous. Some researchers however, argue against this. They maintain that, rather than becoming extinct, these groups simply evolved into the forms for which we have fossil evidence in the Tertiary

One factor that may have saved many mammals was their size. Cretaceous mammals were small and may well have avoided the effects of climatic, volcanic, and other changes by burrowing into the ground and hiding.

Among flying vertebrates, pterosaurs died out completely but dinosaurs left their mark in the form of their direct descendants, the birds, and in

AS YET *we do not know for certain*
why many animals became extinct,
while others survived the
Cretaceous–Tertiary boundary.

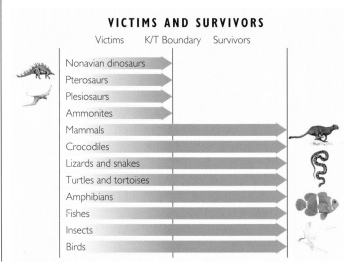

VICTIMS AND SURVIVORS

Victims	K/T Boundary	Survivors
Nonavian dinosaurs		
Pterosaurs		
Plesiosaurs		
Ammonites		
Mammals		
Crocodiles		
Lizards and snakes		
Turtles and tortoises		
Amphibians		
Fishes		
Insects		
Birds		

LANDSCAPES *such as Death Valley, California (above), characterize much of the post-Cretaceous world. Mammals that survived were smaller than many modern mammals (right).*

their more distant relatives, the crocodiles and alligators. However, not all avian groups outlived the Cretaceous. One very diverse group, the enantiornithines, which were the dominant birds of the Cretaceous and existed on all the continents, does not seem to have survived into the Tertiary.

THE FOSSIL RECORD

In recent times, biologists have been debating whether the fossil record accurately reflects the extent to which the diversity of birds and mammals changed across the Cretaceous–Tertiary boundary. According to the fossil record, these groups, already diverse in the Cretaceous, later became even more diverse, with large numbers of mammal and bird lineages appearing early in the Tertiary. This suggests that these animals adapted to the new conditions and diversified, with mammals, especially, filling the roles played by nonavian dinosaurs in the Mesozoic.

Some molecular biologists question this pattern. If we assume that changes in genes occur at a roughly constant rate over time, we can estimate the time at which living groups diverged from each other by counting the number of differences in their genes. Using this approach, some biologists have calculated that divergences between living mammal and bird groups occurred deep in the Cretaceous—long before these groups appear in the fossil record. This suggests that, while large numbers of bird and mammal lineages were present during the Cretaceous, there is no trace of them in the fossil record.

It is perfectly possible that the fossil record is incomplete. It is equally possible, though, that there are problems with the way biologists have been calibrating the "molecular clocks" that they use to help them calculate the time that divergences occurred. Further research may eventually reveal the truth.

293

TODAY'S DINOSAURS

The evolutionary link between present-day birds and long-extinct dinosaurs was one of the most exciting scientific discoveries of recent times.

Birds are living descendants of the dinosaurs that disappeared at the end of the Mesozoic era, 65 million years ago. Look at footprints left behind by a bird, and you will usually see the imprints of three toes spreading out from the rest of the foot. Now look at the footprints left by Mesozoic theropod dinosaurs, and you will see a similar pattern. Is there a reason for this?

A DINOSAUR ANCESTRY

The idea that birds are living dinosaurs is not a new one. Some of the most highly regarded anatomists of the late 1800s thought birds were the descendants of dinosaurs but, for most of the 20th century, scientists thought they were descended from some other kind of archosaur. It was not until the 1970s that birds began to be restored to their dinosaurian perch. Nowadays, a dinosaurian ancestry for

birds is just as well supported as a mammalian ancestry is for humans.

Perhaps the most famous fossil of all time is that of *Archaeopteryx*, the earliest known bird. Seven skeletons have been found, all from the late Jurassic lithographic limestones of Solnhofen, in southern Germany.

Archaeopteryx preserves a mixture of features that made it a "missing link" between birds and other reptiles. The jaws have teeth and the tail is long and bony—both reptilian features—but at least in some of the specimens, there are clear impressions of feathers on the body. Some specimens of *Archaeopteryx* were at first misidentified as the small theropod *Compsognathus*, because the impressions of feathers were very faint.

The first *Archaeopteryx* skeleton was found in 1861, only two years after the publication of Darwin's *On the Origin of Species*, which gave the scientific community powerful evidence that species changed over

time. And it was a critical discovery for those studying the origin of birds—modern birds are so modified for fligh that it is difficult to link them to any earthbound group of animals. *Archaeopteryx* was a primitive enough bird to still retain many features of the nonavian relatives of birds.

DISCOVERY AT DINNER

The prominent late 19th-century scholars who believe in birds' dinosaurian ancestry based their conclusion on skeletal similarities between birds and dinosaurs, especially in the hindlimb. Birds and dinosaurs both have a hole in the hip socket, and the ankle and foot of a chick loo much the same as those of a theropod dinosaur. Accordin to legend, Thomas Henry Huxley (1825–1895) first made the bird–dinosaur connection at a formal dinne after a day spent in the museum examining fossil dinosaur bones. The main course was poultry and, as Huxley ate, he noticed on his plate features that he had seen earlier in the museum.

Early in the 20th century, the idea that birds were derived from dinosaurs fell out of favor. Anatomists pointed out that, despite their shared features, birds and theropods differed in one crucial respect: Birds have a very large set of collarbones,

IN LATE 1996 *a new small theropod dinosaur, which was described as Sinosauropteryx, meaning "Chinese lizard wing," was discovered in China. It had hairy fibers covering much of its body—from head to tail, along the sides, and along the arms and legs. It is not yet clear whether these fibers were feathers.*

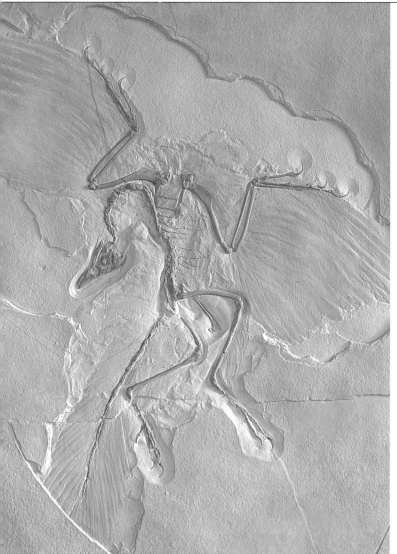

THE ILLUSTRATIONS *below show stages in the evolution of birds from dinosaurs. In the course of this evolution, the jaws and teeth gave way to a toothless beak, the bony tail was lost, and the nature of the hips changed. The four-toed hind foot, though modified, was retained.*
❶ *Compsognathus*
❷ *Archaeopteryx*
❸ *A living bird*

or clavicles, that are fused together to form the wishbone. No dinosaurs then known had a collarbone. Scientists at that stage believed that once a structure is lost during the process of evolution, it cannot be regained. Working from this premise, they argued that dinosaurs could not have given rise to birds. All the features they shared must have evolved convergently. The detailed similarities in the hindlimb and hip were viewed simply as being adaptations to the task of standing on two legs. The first dinosaurs that had clavicles were discovered in the 1920s, but the discovery largely went unnoticed for many decades.

A THEORY REAPPRAISED

The turning point came in 1964, when John Ostrom of Yale University discovered the remains of a small theropod, *Deinonychus*, in lower Cretaceous rocks of Montana. Ostrom was struck by a number of curious similarities between *Deinonychus*—and other small theropods—and primitive birds. The construction of the dinosaur's hands and birds' feet was very similar. *Deinonychus* had a flattened half-moon-shaped bone in the wrist that limited movement of the hand, much like a similar element of the bird wrist. The bones of the pelvis were also very similar in

shape. *Deinonychus*, then, had numerous striking features in common with birds. Based on his work with *Deinonychus*, Ostrom in the 1970s resurrected the hypothesis that birds were derived from theropod dinosaurs.

A New System of Grouping

Beginning in the 1980s, modern cladistic analysis—a system of classification developed in the 1950s by the German biologist Willi Hennig, in which all organisms that have a common ancestor are grouped together in a "clade"—was applied to fossil vertebrates. The first "cladistic" study to include birds and dinosaurs was published by Jacques Gauthier, now of Yale University, in 1986. Gauthier's analysis confirmed Ostrom's belief that small theropods such as *Deinonychus* were the closest extinct relatives of birds. To date, all such cladistic analyses strongly support a close relationship between birds and theropod dinosaurs.

Like birds, all dinosaurs have an inturned femoral head and open hip socket. Again like birds, all theropods have thin-walled hollow limb bones, complex air sacs in the skull and vertebral column, a three-toed foot, and a hand dominated by the thumb, index finger, and middle finger. As we look at smaller groups of theropods, we see the forelimb and hand become increasingly

birdlike, with the complete loss of the fourth and fifth fingers and the development of a specialized wrist. The tail becomes stiffened and reduced in length, and in those theropods closest to birds, including *Deinonychus*, the pubis points down or back, not forward. As well, we now know that many groups of theropods not only have collarbones but also true wishbones.

Do Only Birds Have Feathers?

Until quite recent times, feathers were considered to be exclusive to birds, including *Archaeopteryx*. During the course of the 1990s, however, several new discoveries from north-eastern China have proved otherwise. A fossil locality in Liaoning province began to yield the remains of small theropod dinosaurs, some of them with curious fibrous structures surrounding the body.

The first of these dinosaurs to be announced was *Sinosauropteryx*. This was an animal about the size of a turkey that was very similar to

Compsognathus, and it preserved a halo of short hairlike structures, which, it is now thought, may be the precursors of true feathers. In some of the theropods discovered at Liaoning, including *Beipiaosaurus* and *Sinornithosaurus*, short fibers, much like those of *Sinosauropteryx*, have been preserved, but in two others, *Protarchaeopteryx* and *Caudipteryx*, the feathers are unambiguous—they have a central shaft (rachis) as well as fibers (barbs).

As a result of these discoveries, we can no longer regard feathers as belonging exclusively to birds. *Sinosauropteryx* and *Compsognathus* are relatively primitive coelurosaurian theropods, which means that feathers, or their precursors, were present on many groups of theropods, even though these are not often preserved. We can no longer simply draw a line that separates bird and theropod; modern birds are clearly living members of the Dinosauria, just as humans are living members of the Mammalia.

JOHN OSTROM

John Ostrom is one of the most distinguished living paleontologists. He was a professor and curator of vertebrate paleontology at Yale University's Peabody Museum of Natural History for many years, and he was one of the driving forces behind the "dinosaur renaissance" of the early 1970s, in which the old image of dinosaurs as overgrown reptiles was replaced by an image of more dynamic, energetic animals. Ostrom published many landmark papers during his career, including descriptions of the small theropod *Compsognathus* and important analyses of the origin of flight, based largely on first-hand observations from the primitive bird *Archaeopteryx*. His description of *Deinonychus* stands as a turning point in the history of vertebrate paleontology.

DEINONYCHUS *was a ferocious predator. In this painting (left) two members of the species spar in foreground while others in the pack attack a* Tenontosaurus. *(Below) A fossil skeleton of* Sinosauropteryx.

THE ORIGINS OF FLIGHT

The knowledge that birds are dinosaurs has interesting implications for our understanding of the origins of flight. Paleontologists used to believe that all flying or gliding vertebrates—bats, birds, pterosaurs, sugar gliders, and the like—evolved from tree-dwelling animals that jumped from one perch to the next. As some of these animals developed the ability to glide, they would have been able to reach more distant targets. And as some developed the capacity to generate lift—that is, to actually take off and fly—they further enhanced their range and maneuverability. However, at least as far as we know, none of the theropods that were related to the ancestry of birds was a tree-dweller. How, then, did the capacity for flight arise?

THIS RECONSTRUCTION *of Deinonychus, with its characteristic long, low skull, is in the Natural History Museum in London, UK.*

The first possibility is that flight did evolve from arboreal creatures, but that fossils of these tree-dwelling ancestors have not yet been discovered. The second possibility is that flight arose from small, swift, ground-dwelling animals. According to this theory, the ancestors of birds gained an advantage in their pursuit of prey by being able to increase their strides, first by gliding, and then by flying. The answer may long elude us—we must await further discoveries before we can solve the puzzle of the origins of flight.

While dinosaurs, as we usually think of them, died out at the end of the Cretaceous period, the class Dinosauria did not become extinct at that time. It contains more than 9,000 species of living birds, and it remains one of the most diverse groups of vertebrates alive today.

CHAPTER THREE
MEET *the* DINOSAURS

… the dinosaurs, those surprising travelers from the Mesozoic, have returned today, thanks to the bone hunters.

Dinosaur Impressions,
PHILIPPE TAQUET, French paleontologist

DINOSAUR FEATURES

Bones are the key to our understanding of dinosaurs. Through them, we can identify the features that distinguish dinosaurs from other animals.

Dinosaurs, like all other animals, are identified and united by the common possession of key features. In the same way that we recognize mammals because they have fur or birds by their feathers, we can recognize dinosaurs because they have unique features. However, because all our knowledge of dinosaurs comes from the fossils of their skeletons, their unique features must be found in their bones. And similarly, different groups within the dinosaurs are recognized by their bony features.

LOOKING AT BONES

The skulls of vertebrates contain two bones in the palate called vomers. In dinosaurs, these reach from the front of the snout back to the level of the antorbital fenestrae (holes in the skull in front of the eyes). In most other animals, the vomers are not this long.

Moving down to the shoulder blades (the scapulae), we find that dinosaurs had a socket that faced backward where the arm attached. This feature was perhaps related to another on the upper arm bone (the humerus)—a long, low crest on the upper part that provided attachment for muscles. The hand had a fourth finger that contained no more than three finger bones (phalanges).

The hips were anchored to the spine by three or more vertebrae. The socket where the leg articulated had a hole in the center and an enlarged bony rim around its upper margin. The ball-like part of the thigh bone (the femur) was turned in toward the midline of the animal. The femur had a bump midway along its length (the fourth trochanter), which was also used for muscle attachment. Farther down the leg, the tibia (shin bone), which had a crest (the cnemial crest), was far larger than the calf bone (fibula). The ankle bone (astragalus) had a process that reached up the leg and fitted into a notch on the tibia. The ankle was a simple hinge and dinosaurs walked on long toes.

These key features of both the front and back limbs allowed the legs to swing forward and backward under the animal. This provided a very efficient way of moving, which scientists think may have been one of the reasons that dinosaurs were so successful.

THE HUGE PLANT-EATER *Edmontosaurus had a typical ornithischian pelvis. The backward-pointing pubis allowed enough space for the large intestines that plant-eaters needed to digest their food.*

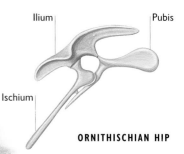

Ilium

Pubis

Ischium

ORNITHISCHIAN HIP

BIRDS' HIPS *look similar to those of bird-hipped dinosaurs, but birds evolved from lizard-hipped dinosaurs, which shared common ancestors with modern crocodiles and alligators.*

THE SAURISCHIANS AND ORNITHISCHIANS

Dinosaurs can be divided into two major groups: the saurischian (or lizard-hipped) dinosaurs and the ornithischian (or bird-hipped) dinosaurs. This division was established in 1887 by the English paleontologist Harry Seeley. Some dinosaurs—the meat-eating theropods (including birds), the long-necked sauropods, and the prosauropods—had a pubic bone (one of the major hip bones) that pointed forward in a lizard-like arrangement, while the others had a pubic bone that pointed toward the rear and ran parallel to another hip bone (the ischium). The latter were called bird-hipped dinosaurs because their hips superficially resembled those of birds.

Some other features, too, are unique to each group. Saurischians had a grasping hand with the thumb offset to the other digits and a second finger that was longer than the others. The neck was long and flexible, curving in an S-shape. These features were modified beyond recognition in some of the more advanced saurischians. In sauropods, for example, the hand developed into an elephant-like foot for bearing the weight of the front of the animal, while in birds the three remaining fingers fused into a complex bone that supported many of the wing feathers.

Ornithischians had only small teeth at the front of the mouth, but these teeth were sometimes lost and replaced by a beak. They also had an extra bone (the predentary) at the front of the lower jaw. This supported the beak. Another ornithischian feature was the development of horns, spikes, plates, frills, and other bone ornaments.

All ornithischians are now extinct, but saurischians survive to this day as birds. As well, all ornithischians were plant-eaters, while saurischians included both herbivores and carnivores.

THE MEAT-EATER *Allosaurus was a saurischian. Its pubis pointed forward between the legs and helped support the leg muscles.*

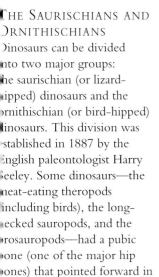

Ilium
supported leg
muscles

Pubis
supported leg
muscles

Ischium
supported tail
muscles

Tibia

Femur

SAURISCHIAN HIP

SKELETONS *and* SKULLS

The enormous diversity of dinosaurs as a group can be seen in the great variety of skeletons that have come to light over more than 200 years.

The dinosaurs were a huge and varied group. This is reflected in their skeletons, which show a variety of forms, ranging from the enormous frames that supported the largest animals ever to walk the Earth to the delicate, elegant structures of the smallest dinosaurs. Despite such a diversity of skeletal forms, many common themes were replayed throughout their history.

SKELETAL DIVERSITY
The secret of the dinosaurs' success lies partly in their design. Their legs were held directly under the body, which allowed them to swing forward and backward and

TRICERATOPS *(right) had a huge skull., with a beak for breaking off plant matter and grinding teeth at the back of its mouth.* Tyrannosaurus *could charge in sudden bursts, but its legs (left) were not designed for long chases.*

meant that dinosaurs avoided the sprawling, ungainly gait that is typical of many other reptiles. A number of groups, such as the theropods, also had hollow bones that provided strength and support while keeping the animals' weight to a minimum.

Sauropods also had weight-reducing adaptations in their skeletons. Despite or, more properly, because of their immense size, their skeletons

had to be as light as possible while still providing the strength needed to support their tremendous weight. The neck vertebrae, for example, contained hollows and cavities with many of the processes reduced to struts. Edward Drinker Cope acknowledged this feature when he named *Camarasaurus* ("chambered lizard") for the hollow, boxlike nature of this dinosaur's neck vertebrae.

There were also parts of the skeleton where structural strength was more important than saving weight. Massive, solid leg and arm bones held up the heavy bodies of

Backbone

Skull

PLANT-EATERS *such as Ouranosaurus (above left) had weak jaw muscles, but they had bands of cheek teeth to grind up their food. Meat-eaters such as Ceratosaurus (above right) had huge jaw muscles and sharp fangs.*

Tail

Hands

Leg bones

Feet

HYPSILOPHODON

HYPSILOPHODON, *an ornithopod from the early Cretaceous, was a lightly built, gazelle-like bipedal dinosaur. It used its long, clawed fingers to grasp plant food or to support its body as it grazed on low-growing plants.*

auropods, ceratopsians, tegosaurs, and ankylosaurs. Veight-bearing legs were eld as straight as possible, mproving their weight-arrying capacity.

Armor, spikes, plates, nd shields made of bone ended to make an animal eavy. It is no surprise that hese features are found in linosaurs that moved on all ours, where the extra veight could be distributed nore evenly.

In small dinosaurs, the mphasis was on flexibility nd agility. Small theropods nd ornithopods had lightly uilt skeletons and a great leal of movement at the keletal joints. They also ended to have very long egs for their size, indicating hat they were fast runners ble to duck and dive away rom larger predators.

KULLS

The heads of dinosaurs were ncased in bone, which is eavier than flesh or muscle. Because of this, the very large eads of some dinosaurs were xtremely heavy.

In the case of ceratopsians, eavy, bony heads were an dvantage because the extra one provided protection

FALSE ALARM

During his dinosaur-hunting days, Jim Jensen, a resident paleon-tologist at Brigham Young University in Utah, found several important sites—such as the Dry Mesa quarry in Colorado—and discovered and named a number of dinosaurs, including the theropods Dystylo-saurus and Torvosaurus.

During his excavations in Colorado during the 1970s, he uncovered two huge "new" sauropods that he named Supersaurus and Ultrasaurus. In both cases, however, these dinosaurs were named from only a few bones and some vertebrae. Although these finds created a stir at the time, it now appears that these were just huge individuals of dinosaurs that were already known to scientists—Diplodocus and Brachiosaurus respectively.

against both attacks from predators and injury during combat with rivals. The mighty weight of a cera-topsian skull was balanced on a short neck and supported by huge muscles.

The heads of sauropods, on the other hand, were perched at the end of long necks.

THE HADROSAUR Corythosaurus (above left) had a crest on its skull and nostrils at the front of its snout. Like all sauropods, Brachiosaurus (above right) had its nasal openings at the top of the head, above the eyes.

These heads had to be big enough to permit the animals to collect sufficient food but small enough not to weigh down the neck. In some sauropod skulls the weight was minimized by expanding holes—or "fenestrae"—in the skull, thus reducing the bone to thin struts and rods.

Theropods generally had large heads, which not only had to be as light as possible but also had to withstand the tremendous forces that were transmitted through the head when the animal bit into its prey or while it held onto another animal in a violent struggle. Theropods' skulls, therefore, also had large holes, but the bony struts that surrounded them were still very solid.

CAMARASAURUS was a large and abundant late-Jurassic sauropod. The enormous nasal openings at the top of its skull may have helped to cool its small brain. This dinosaur walked on all fours. It had massive, pillarlike legs that helped to carry its great weight and deep ribs that supported a large stomach.

Backbone

Skull

Leg bones

Front feet

Tail

CAMARASAURUS

WARM– *or* COLD-BLOODED?

Until quite recently, it was generally accepted that the dinosaurs, like present-day reptiles, were cold-blooded animals. Recent research has raised serious doubts about this assumption.

One of the most lively scientific debates about dinosaurs in recent times has been about whether these animals were, as had long been assumed, cold-blooded creatures, or whether, like mammals and birds, they were warm-blooded. This debate has raised important questions about dinosaur physiology. We may never get a definite answer to this puzzle, for the very reason that, unlike bones, body temperature does not fossilize. However, we can make some inferences about the body temperature of dinosaurs and their capacity to regulate it by looking at the fossil evidence and using our knowledge of living creatures.

Actually, the question is not about whether a dinosaur's blood was warm or cold. The terms "warm-blooded" and "cold-blooded" are commonly used, but they are misleading. On a hot day, for example, a cold-blooded animal such as a crocodile

IN 2000, COMPUTER- *enhanced images of the late-Cretaceous dinosaur Thescelosaurus revealed what looked like a fossilized heart. Some scientists think it has similarities to that of a mammal, lending weight to the theory that dinosaurs were warm blooded. Others think the "heart" is simply a concretion—a deposition of minerals.*

may have a higher blood temperature than a warm-blooded mammal of a similar size. What the debate is really about is this: Were dinosaurs able to maintain a constant body temperature, as birds and mammals do, or did their body temperature, like that of lizards, snakes, and crocodiles, fluctuate in response to the environment?

There are advantages

THE LARGE SAIL on *the back of* Ouranosaurus *may have enabled this big plant-eater to regulate its body temperature.*

and disadvantages in being able to maintain a constant body temperature. The main advantage is that an animal is always ready for action—night or day, hot or cold. This means that it is able to exploit habitats and endure conditions, such as near-freezing nights, that could not be tolerated by animals whose body temperature is very much dependent upon the environment. The main drawback of maintaining a constant body temperature is that it requires a great deal of energy. As a result of this, an animal needs to eat more. A warm-blooded lion, for example, must eat about ten times as much as a similar-sized cold-blooded crocodile.

There are convincing arguments to suggest that dinosaurs displayed a variety of physiologies—that some could be recognized as truly warm-blooded while others were cold-blooded.

THEROPODS

Theropods were the ancestors of the warm-blooded birds and this has suggested to some researchers that they would have been warm-blooded. In addition, recent dinosaur finds in China show that small theropods had "hairy" coats, or even feathers, that would have helped trap heat inside the body. Smaller theropods that weighed less than about 220 pounds (100 kg) could certainly have benefited from maintaining a constant body temperature, as this would have helped to keep them active while hunting. Several of these theropods, such as the dromaeosaurs and the troödontids, had slashing claws that are more typically associated with active warm-blooded creatures rather than with low-energy, cold-blooded animals.

Another argument for warm-blooded dinosaurs cites the small theropods and small ornithopods that have been found at high-latitude sites such as Dinosaur Cove in Victoria, Australia, where Mesozoic winter temperatures were below freezing. Today, such environments are the domain of warm-blooded animals. However, making analogies between the past and the present can be misleading. Remains of other typically cold-blooded Cretaceous animals such as crocodiles and large amphibans have been also found at these once-chilly sites.

EVIDENCE FROM CROCODILES

Recent studies of body temperature in crocodiles are relevant to the question of temperature regulation in larger dinosaurs. Crocodiles lose heat to the environment more slowly as they get larger. In other words, the increasing bulk of the crocodile acts to trap heat within the body. A hypothetical 5-ton (5.1-t) specimen could maintain a constant body temperature just by being large. If this heat-trap system applied to dinosaurs, the largest of them would have needed to get rid of heat absorbed from the environment or generated by moving muscles and digesting food. Long necks and tails, such as those of sauropods, would have helped because they increased the surface area relative to the mass of the animal. Plates, spikes, and sails could also have helped drain heat from the body. This may explain the function of the plates of the stegosaurs or the sails on the backs of *Spinosaurus* and *Ouranosaurus*. Such features would have been useful to large dinosaurs living in warm environments.

DROMICEIOMIMUS *was a small, extremely active predator. It is thought that it may have been warm-blooded.*

SURVIVING IN THE COLD

Husband-and-wife team Tom Rich and Patricia Vickers-Rich migrated from the United States to settle in Victoria, Australia. They are key players in Australian vertebrate paleontology and have made many finds in Mesozoic and Tertiary deposits.

Their most famous site is Dinosaur Cove on the southern coast of the Australian mainland. Here they dug a mine into a sea cliff, following the bed of a Cretaceous stream. Their efforts were rewarded by several dinosaur finds. These included *Leaellynasaura*, a small ornithopod named for their daughter, and *Timimus*, a tiny ornithomimosaur named for their son. In another Cretaceous site, they have found some of Australia's oldest mammal fossils.

Dinosaur Cove has turned out to be the most productive dinosaur site in Australia, and it provides hard evidence that dinosaurs could live in very cold environments. *Leaellynasaura* had huge eyes that would have helped it to see in the extended nights of its high-latitude home. It was too small to migrate to a new area each year so, somehow, it must have survived winters in which temperatures plummeted well below freezing.

SIGNIFICANT FOSSILS WERE DISCOVERED AT THIS LOCALITY, DINOSAUR COVE, IN 1980. FIELD PARTIES COMPOSED PRINCIPALLY OF VOLUNTEERS FROM MONASH UNIVERSITY, THE MUSEUM OF VICTORIA AND EARTHWATCH COLLECTED DINOSAURS AND OTHER VERTEBRATE FOSSILS FROM THREE SITES WITHIN THIS COVE, 1984-1993. MAJOR SUPPORT CAME FROM THE NATIONAL GEOGRAPHIC SOCIETY, ATLAS COPCO, I.C.I., THE DEPARTMENT OF CONSERVATION & NATURAL RESOURCES, AND THE AUSTRALIAN RESEARCH GRANTS COMMITTEE.

THE BRAIN *and* SENSORY SYSTEMS

Recent research has helped dispel many persistent myths about dinosaur brains and intelligence and about how these animals experienced their world.

Like most soft tissue, brains, nerves, and the sensory systems of dinosaurs do not fossilize. But we can learn a lot about what they were like by studying the bones that encased the brains, eyes, and ears as well as the various passages that held nerves.

The brain is surrounded by bones that approximate the size and shape of the living brain. The hole that is left by the brain can be filled with matrix or plaster. This produces an endocast—a copy of the brain space in the skull. One problem with this technique is that it requires pulling the bones apart to get at the endocast, a destructive procedure that could result in irreparable damage to the precious skull. Modern

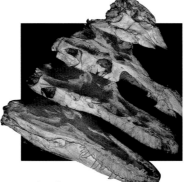

THIS CAT SCAN *of a Tyrannosaurus braincase is in the Field Museum in Chicago, USA.*

technology has helped here in the form of Computer Assisted Tomography (CAT) scans where the skull can be X-rayed in three dimensions and the brain space analyzed on computer.

MISCONCEPTIONS
Ever since Othniel Charles Marsh described the first known endocasts in 1896, it was believed that dinosaurs had relatively small brains for their size. This is, in fact, a misconception. In living animals, brain size does increase with body weight, but to a much smaller degree. The difference in size between a particularly large animal's and a much smaller animal's brain is only slight in relation to the difference in body size.

Taking this into account, dinosaur brains, although small, were proportionally the same size as those of modern reptiles or amphibians. Some small theropod dinosaurs had relative brain sizes comparable to that of living ratite birds such as ostriches and emus. However Stegosaurus had the smallest brain-to-body size ratio of any known terrestrial vertebrate.

Another misconception that characterized popular ideas about dinosaur brains is that some dinosaurs had "helper" brain in their hips. This notion dates back to Marsh's work on *Stegosaurus*. Marsh noticed an enlarged space in the hips that could have accommodated a swelling of the spinal cord. Such a ganglion could have helped relay messages to the rear of the animal or even controlled the posterior parts, freeing up the tiny brain in the head for other cognitive functions. However, this rather fanciful idea no longer holds sway. Scientists now

A MALE PARASAUROLOPHUS

had a huge head crest in which air moved along a complex series of passages. There are several theories about the function that this crest performed. It seems likely, however, that it may have served as an olfactory organ.

STUDYING DINOSAUR INTELLIGENCE

Dale Russell is a Canadian paleontologist now working in the United States. He specializes in theropod dinosaurs and has named several dinosaurs, including *Archaeornithomimus*, *Daspletosaurus* and *Dromiceiomimus*.

Much of his earlier work involved studies of dinosaur brains and endocasts. One of his most controversial ideas is of a hypothetical intelligent dinosaur that he christened the "dinosauroid." Russell reasoned that, because toward the end of the Cretaceous small theropod dinosaurs were developing relatively large brains (for dinosaurs), they may, if they had been able to follow this trend for a few more tens of millions of years, have evolved into an intelligent species that went on to dominate the planet. Only ever intended as a thought experiment, it is indeed food for thought!

believe that the swelling was probably filled with tissues other than nerves.

SENSES

Like the brain, the eyes, ears, and nasal cavities of dinosaurs were surrounded by bones, and a study of these helps us to understand the nature of sensory organs.

Theropods generally had well-developed eyes that included a ring of bone within the eye (the sclerotic ring). As well, the part of the brain that dealt with vision was enlarged. This suggests that these dinosaurs relied on sight as a primary sense for locating prey. Some plant-eaters, such as the ornithopods and pachycephalosaurs seem

to have relied on a keen sense of smell to detect predators at a distance. The small ornithopod *Leaellynasaura* had enormous eyes and optic lobes in the brain that probably helped it see in the extended Antarctic nights. Small theropods probably had a refined sense of balance because the area of the brain that deals with balance is enlarged in these animals.

INTERPRETING FOSSILS

Interpreting fossil structures in bones devoid of flesh requires skilled deductive reasoning. This is particularly the case in structures such as the nasal cavities of ankylosaurs and hadrosaurs. Both developed convoluted pathways for the air passages as they passed

through the skull. The most extreme example of this is *Parasaurolophus*, where the complex air passages extended the full length of a head crest that was over 3 feet (1 m) long. These structures could have been sounding instruments—long tubes that made deep, resonant tones that helped the animals communicate. Another theory holds that the passages were lined with olfactory cells that would have given their owners a very keen sense of smell. Yet another theory maintains that they served to bring warm air into the lungs, or to trap moisture from exhaling air, or even that they helped to keep the brain cool. We may never know which, if any, of these theories are correct, but it could well have been that extended air passages had several functions.

Iguanadon

Rhesus monkey

IGUANODON *was one dinosaur whose brain was particularly small in relation to its body size. The diagrams at left show the relative sizes of an Iguanodon's and a rhesus monkey's brain. (Above) Endocasts of an Iguanodon brain seen from different angles.*

FEEDING *and* DIGESTION

Dinosaurs employed a wide range of strategies,
both to gather or catch their food and then
to digest and process it.

Dinosaur diets can be inferred from a number of lines of evidence. Teeth, claws, and jaws indicate food preference while the occasional fossil with preserved stomach contents provides direct evidence of what a dinosaur was eating. Coprolite (dung) fossils and an understanding of the surrounding flora and fauna enable us to make reasonable assertions about which dinosaurs were eating which types of foodstuffs.

CARNIVORES

Theropods typically had long arms with sharp, curved claws that allowed them to grab their prey and rip at the flesh with rows of slashing teeth. The large Jurassic theropod *Allosaurus* probably hunted animals ten times its size. It may have attacked these huge beasts by ambushing them, slashing at them, then withdrawing until the prey

ALLOSAURUS, *a theropod, had huge jaws and teeth like steak knives.*

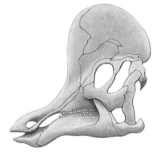

CORYTHOSAURUS *had a horny beak for stripping leaves off plants.*

was weakened by blood loss. *Allosaurus* may also have fed on the young of large sauropods or attacked more modest-sized stegosaurs and camptosaurs. The smaller theropods had flexible skeletons that would have allowed for greater agility.

PROTOCERATOPS *sheared off plant matter with its sharp beak.*

IGUANODON *used grinding teeth to crush plant matter into a pulp.*

ANATOTITAN *was a plant-eater with about 1,000 tiny leaf-shaped teeth.*

They either chased after smaller animals or formed groups to attack larger prey.

The exception among the theropods were the tyrannosaurs, which had puny arms.

SAUROPOD STONES

David Gillette is an American paleontologist whose work has focused mainly on the Jurassic Morrison Formation in New Mexico. One of the specimens he excavated there was the giant skeleton, more than 140 feet (43 m) long, of the late Jurassic sauropod *Seismosaurus*.

During the excavation of *Seismosaurus*, which took eight years, Gillette noted and recorded the exact position of more than 240 gastroliths, most of them the size of apples, that were associated with the specimen. Most of these were collected in an area of the rib cage just in front of where the stomach would have been, indicating the presence of a huge gizzard. Others scattered through the specimen signposted other parts of the animal's digestive tract.

These seem to have been of no use in capturing prey. However, tyrannosaurs had particularly large mouths and the most powerful bites of any known animal, past or present. As well, they were the largest animals in their habitat, so that an individual tyrannosaur could tackle any potential prey.

HERBIVORES

Plants that grew throughout most of the Mesozoic were both poor in nutrients and relatively hard to break down. Plant-eaters employed a number of strategies to deal with these problems, most of which involved processing large quantities of food.

Sauropods stripped and swallowed plant matter largely without processing it in the mouth. While they could thus take in vast amounts of food, they had to break it down to retrieve the scarce nutrients. They appear to have done this in a huge, vatlike pre-stomach, or gizzard, where the incoming food could be

stewed and brewed into a nutrient soup. This process was helped by "gizzard stones," or gastroliths, that were held in the gizzard and helped stir up the brew.

The pachycephalosaurs, ornithopods, and ceratopsians employed a different strategy. They used grinding teeth to break down the food before swallowing it. This process took its toll on the teeth, which quickly wore down. However, a number of times throughout their lives these dinosaurs were able to discard their worn-out teeth and grow new ones. The advanced ornithischians took this technique to its limit, evolving batteries of tightly packed teeth that functioned like a single grinding plate. These

DUNG FOSSILS, *or coprolites, probably from the plant-eater* Titanosaurus, *display remnants of plant matter.*

batteries grew continuously through the animal's life and could contain hundreds of teeth. The teeth at the front of the mouth snipped off the plant material for grinding in the back of the mouth.

Ornithischians lost their front teeth relatively early in their evolution, replacing them with a sharp, birdlike beak. These animals appear to have had cheeks that prevented food from falling out while they chewed. Ridges of bone around the mouth that probably were supports for cheeks have been observed in several of these dinosaurs.

THE HUGE JURASSIC SAUROPOD Apatosaurus *(right) would have fed on such tough plant matter as pine cones and cycads. This food was broken down, and its nutrients extracted, with the help of gastroliths which moved around in the gizzard, and stirred the food into a simmering brew. (Above) These gastroliths were found in the fossilized body of* Caudipteryx.

REPRODUCTION *and the* LIFE CYCLE

The study of dinosaur egg fossils, which dates back to the 1920s, has added greatly to our understanding of dinosaur reproduction and growth patterns.

As with all animals throughout history, dinosaur reproduction relied on mating between the sexes. While it is often very difficult to determine which gender a particular dinosaur skeleton belonged to, there are a number of cases where skeletons of a single species fall into two distinct forms. It is reasonable to assume that these differences were, in some way, associated with courtship, nesting, and the rearing of offspring.

The frills of ceratopsians, for example, are more likely to have played a part in courtship behavior than in defense. The frill of the small ceratopsian *Protoceratops* is, in places, eggshell thin and would have offered little protection against predators.

A MAIASAURA *embryo at an advanced stage of development. The yolk sac, shown here in yellow, provided nourishment for the unhatched juvenile.*

However, roughly half of the hundred or so known *Protoceratops* skulls have a broad neck frill while the others have a less extensive frill. It is possible that the male had the larger frill, and that it may have been brightly colored or used in some other way to impress females or to intimidate rival males. There are several skulls of ceratopsians that show signs of damage from the horns of another ceratopsian. This has been construed by some scientists as direct evidence that fierce rutting took place between bull males that

were vying for the right to copulate with females.

There are two kinds, or morphs, of *Tyrannosaurus*—a heavy form and a lighter, more gracile form. Evidence from the tail bones indicates that the smaller, gracile form is the male. This seems counter to our intuition because, in humans, males tend to be larger. But in many animal species females are larger and this usually confers advantages in egg production or defense of the young.

Among the hadrosaurs there are differences in head crests that also suggest some differences between the sexes

THIS CAMPTOSAURUS *has reached the end of its life cycle, killed either by disease or old age. Small compared to most plant-eaters, it still probably had a life span of at least several decades. The small theropods, Coelurus, which here lurk in the background, would have lived for a much shorter period.*

ROY CHAPMAN ANDREWS *(right), from the American Museum of Natural History, and his assistant, George Olsen, are seen here excavating a nest of about 20 Protoceratops eggs at Bayn Dzak, at the foot of the Flaming Cliffs in the Gobi Desert, Mongolia, in the early 1920s. Both skeletons and eggs of Protoceratops andrewsi, which was named after the famous American paleontologist, were discovered during these early expeditions to Mongolia. Until then, this small, primitive, horned dinosaur had been unknown to science.*

n *Parasaurolophus*, for example, half the known adult specimens had a long crest, while in the rest the crest was much shorter. Perhaps this feature served as a courtship device that allowed the males to boom out a mating call deeper and more striking than the calls the smaller-crested females were capable of.

How Mating Was Achieved

Once mates had been found it was time to copulate. Internal fertilization is a common strategy for terrestrial animals as it prevents damage to the sperm. We can, therefore, reasonably assume that some kind of internal fertilization occurred with dinosaurs and that copulation was necessary. Male dinosaurs almost certainly had penises, because their living relatives, the crocodiles, have penises. Some birds, too, have penises, although most now do not.

THREE CREST SIZES *have been found in fossils of Parasaurolophus. They probably represent adults of different sexes and juveniles with partly formed crests.*

We do not know exactly how dinosaurs copulated. For all dinosaurs, the possession of a prominent tail would have been a significant obstacle to copulation. Some modern male animals with similar tails, such as lizards and crocodiles, have two, sideway-facing "hemipenes" that allow lateral entry into the female. Snakes copulate by wrapping around each other in a spiral, in this way bringing their genital openings together.

Besides tails, there were two other significant barriers to copulation in some dinosaurs. The massive size of the larger dinosaurs suggests that it would have been very difficult for a male to mount a female and that doing so would have placed huge strains on the rump and hind legs of the female. A male-on-top position is particularly

problematic in stegosaurs, where plates and spikes along the back would have presented extra and unavoidable complications for copulation.

Dinosaurs had a significantly different reproductive strategy from modern mammals. In modern mammals with a size range similar to dinosaurs, a few, well-developed offspring are born at a time and they tend to survive reasonably well to adulthood. Dinosaurs, however, appear to have laid lots of eggs during a season and, despite varying degrees of parental care, the survival rate of the young into adulthood seems to have been rather low. Effectively, dinosaurs relied on the quantity of offspring for the perpetuation of a species. In contrast, modern large mammals rely on carefully nurturing a small number young, in order to preserve their kind.

Adult male head

Adult female head

Juvenile head

A CLUTCH *of fossilized Troödon eggs (left). A fossilized embryo of Oviraptor (below left) and skull fragments of a baby dromaeosaur (below right) are part of the collections of New York's American Museum of Natural History.*

NESTS AND BABIES

Most of what we know about dinosaur reproductive behavior has come to light only in the last few decades, when the study of dinosaur nests, nest sites, eggs, and young became reinvigorated. The first dinosaur eggs were discovered in France in 1859, and the first recognized nests were uncovered in Mongolia in the 1920s. It was not until nest sites were uncovered in Montana in the late 1970s, however, that the study of dinosaur reproductive behavior received a significant boost. We now know of more than 200 sites located all over the world that have dinosaur eggs, nests, babies, or the foot-prints of young.

Despite popular myths and misconceptions, dinosaur eggs were not really huge—the largest known egg is about the size of a cantaloupe. They varied in shape from spherical to an elongated ellipsoid and had differing surface textures, including pitting, lumps, bumps, and raised lines.

Dinosaur remains reveal a wide variety of behaviors relating to nesting and the rearing of offspring. Nests have been found in shallow pits that were filled with vegetation, which would have kept the eggs warm as it decomposed. In other cases, eggs seem to have been scattered around with no attempt at building a nest. In some sites, the arrangement of eggs within the nest indicates that the parents had moved the eggs into specific patterns.

Dinosaurs seem to have had favored nesting areas that they revisited year after year. Nests have been found to be isolated, spread out in a haphazard arrangement, or, concentrated in sites where dinosaur rookeries formed, tightly packed together, and separated by distances that are equivalent to the length of the adult animal. In places such as Egg Mountain in Montana, where the famous *Maiasaura* nests were discovered in 1978, it appears that hundreds, possibly even thousands, of dinosaurs congregated into huge dinosaur rookeries during the breeding season.

Some dinosaur parents may have stayed with the nest while the eggs developed, as most birds do today. Such behavior was illustrated very graphically in 1996 when a fossilized adult *Oviraptor* was found still huddled over its fossilized eggs in a posture identical to that of modern brooding emus and ostriches. It also seems likely that other dinosaurs laid eggs and then, as many modern lizards and turtles do, abandoned them. These young would have had to fend for themselves after they hatched. This may have

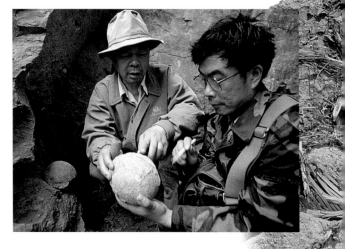

CHINESE PALEONTOLOGISTS
inspect a fossilized dinosaur egg discovered in Hubei province.

een the pattern for the large uropod dinosaurs, where the mall hatchlings could easily ave been trampled underfoot y their gargantuan parents.

EAVING THE NEST

ossils indicate that different pes of dinosaurs hatched om their eggs at different ages of development. auropod hatchlings were elatively advanced in their evelopment and capable f independence. Hadrosaurs, ough, were not particularly ell developed and resilient hen they hatched. Crucial ints in their limbs had not lly formed, and so the tiny atchlings were dependent on eir parents throughout the rst weeks or months of life. some nests, juveniles that ere more developed than eir siblings, and whose teeth owed signs of wear, have so been found. This adds eight to the theory that me dinosaur chicks stayed the nest and were fed by tendant adults.

Dinosaurs do appear to ave matured at quite a nsiderable rate.

For example, a hatchling hadrosaur—perhaps 10 inches (25 cm) long—could grow to over 6 feet (2 m) in a few years and attain an adult length of 26 feet (8 m) in a decade. Dinosaurs appear to have grown rapidly in their earlier years, but their growth rates slowed dramatically at adulthood. Some dinosaurs effectively stopped growing at an adult size, while others may have continued to grow steadily throughout life.

Life spans for dinosaurs are hard to calculate. They may have been as short as four or five years for small ones such as *Troödon*, but as long as 150 years for large sauropods.

Be a good animal,

true to your animal

instincts.

The White Peacock,
D.H. LAWRENCE (1885–1930),
English novelist

EGG MOUNTAIN

John "Jack" Horner is a largely self-taught paleontologist, who works mainly in Montana. His most famous discovery followed a visit with a friend to a fossil shop in the small Montana town of Choteau, where they saw tiny, fossilized bones that they recognized as belonging to baby dinosaurs.

Following directions given by the shop owners, Horner soon found what has become known as "Egg Mountain," the nesting ground of the hadrosaur *Maiasaura*. Although dinosaur nest sites and eggs had been found before, this was the first time that a systematic study of dinosaur nests was possible.

Among the numerous startling and fascinating findings of John Homer's research was the very birdlike nature of a dinosaur rookery and the previously unsuspected degree of dinosaurian parental care.

THIS RECONSTRUCTION *of a Maiasaura nest is modeled on the remarkable "Egg Mountain" site in Montana.*

DINOSAURS *in* MOTION

Dinosaurs moved in many different ways. Some were four-footed giants that ambled along; others were small, agile bipeds capable of spectacular bursts of speed.

One of the keys to the success of the dinosaurs was their posture. Even in the largest quadrupedal dinosaurs, the bulk of their weight was carried by the hind legs. For many dinosaurs, this meant that they could rise up onto their hind legs without too much effort, a stance that would have been very useful, either for defense or to display to members of their own species. In other dinosaurs it meant two modes of carriage: all fours for energy-efficient movement across the landscape; or two legs for fast getaways. Many dinosaurs were entirely bipedal. This meant that their arms and hands were free for grabbing prey or handling food.

The ancestral dinosaurs were all bipedal, and several groups that were quadrupedal evolved this feature independently. The ancestral dinosaurs bequeathed another asset to their descendants: They carried their hind legs directly under the body—held straight vertically and moving backward and forward in the same plane as the body and the direction of travel. Most animals that competed with the dinosaurs had a more sprawling gait—their legs were held out to the sides and they moved by sweeping their legs around in the direction of travel. This

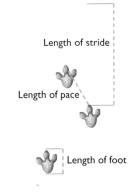

Length of stride

Length of pace

Length of foot

was more cumbersome—and it required more energy—than the streamlined movements of the dinosaurs.

FAST AND SLOW MOVERS

Standing on two long back legs, some dinosaurs, such as the ornithomimids, could sprint at considerable speed. The speed at which a dinosaur could move along can be measured partly by comparing the length of the leg below the knee (the shin) with the length of the leg above the knee (the thigh). The longer the shin, the wider the stride; and the longer the thigh, the more powerful the forward thrust. Ornithomimids and oviraptors had particularly long shins and relatively short thighs—even though their thighs were quite long in

DINOSAUR TRACKWAYS *provide three basic clues to the the speed at which the dinosaurs were moving.*

relation to the animals' overall size. Estimates of just how fast these dinosaurs could move are derived from theoretical calculations that are based on the skeleton and from careful measurements of fossilized trackways. It would appear that fleet-footed theropods and ornithopods could reach speeds of at least 25 miles per hour (40 km/h).

In general, the larger an animal, the more slowly it moves. Large theropods could probably move no faster than 9 miles per hour (15 km/h).

Four-legged dinosaurs were still constrained by the "larger means slower" rule, but the ability to gallop and trot offered gaits that could be sustained for longer periods.

For very large dinosaurs such as the sauropods, speed probably was never an option. Their sheer weight limited them to slow ambling. Their legs were massively built, and the thoracic and lumbar vertebrae were arranged in an arc that supported the weight of the body in a construction that was similar to that of a suspension bridge.

STRUTHIOMIMUS, *with its long, birdlike hindlimbs, similar to the legs of an ostrich (above), was a very swift runner.*

DINOSAUR HERDS

Trackways record how dinosaurs moved. They also supply us with unique information about dinosaur groupings and the structure of herds.

Larger theropods seem to have been solitary creatures, or they moved about only in couples or in small groups. The smaller theropods favored larger groups numbering tens of individuals. In at least one example of fossilized tracks that is located near Winton, in Queensland, Australia, dozens of small theropods gathered with a similar number of small ornithopods in a mixed group, only to be set to flight by the appearance of a lone, large, predatory theropod.

Sauropods appear to have moved in groups of about a dozen individuals of the same species—but of different ages. There is evidence that the younger animals kept to the center of a group, while older animals formed a protective cordon around them.

Larger ornithopods and ceratopsians formed vast herds numbering hundreds, or perhaps thousands. As such large groups of big herbivores would quickly have stripped areas of their plants, they must have survived by migrating annually to seasonal pastures. This theory is supported by dense trackways that show hundreds of animals moving in the same direction and fossils of the same species that have been found in distant locations. In many respects, a migrating herd of ceratopsians or hadrosaurs must have resembled modern migrations of buffalo in North America or wildebeest in Africa.

A PAIR OF SMALL PLANT-EATERS *(right foreground), alarmed by the appearance of two predatory theropods (below), break away from protection offered by a migrating herd of long-necked sauropods as it moves across the North American Jurassic landscape.*

METHODS *of* SURVIVAL

All dinosaurs, both carnivorous and herbivorous, faced challenges to their survival. They evolved a number of strategies to help them find food and escape attack from predators.

Life for dinosaurs, as for all animals, consisted largely of finding enough food to survive while avoiding becoming a meal for another creature. Herbivores evolved complex behavioral strategies and an array of defensive armaments to protect themselves from attacks by predators. Locked into an evolutionary arms race, and often facing keen competition for available prey, predators evolved ever-more deadly weapons that they could bring to bear in attacking and subduing the animals they preyed upon.

SAUROPOD STRATEGIES

For the largest dinosaurs, their sheer size provided an effective defense against most predators. Huge sauropods were probably impregnable against the attacks of smaller predators. But the young sauropods were not protected by size and would have been easy prey. Defense for these animals probably came in the form of social structures, where adults could fend off attacks against their young

by shielding them with their vast bodies.

The tail of an adult sauropod was a weapon that could be wielded like a baseball bat and slammed into an attacker. The slender, more whiplike tails of diplodocids could deliver deadly, stinging blows.

BUILT-IN PROTECTION

The horns of ceratopsians and the tail spikes of stegosaurs could have been brought to bear with devastating effect against predators. These bony structures had a covering sheath of keratin and formed a lethal, piercing point. The spikes that covered ankylosaurs may also have been used as offensive weapons. *Edmontonia*, with its skull protected by plates,

THE HEAD *of* Triceratops *(left) was equipped for both attack and defense. (Above) The sharp, serrated teeth of* Daspletosauru

could have driven its large, sharp, forward-pointing shoulder spikes into an attacker with crippling effect.

An ankylosaur had a club on the end of its tail. This stiffened into a bony mace. Swung from side to side, it became a weapon that would have been most effective in cracking the delicate ankles of theropod predators. Ankylosaurs were also protected by a sheath of bony armor that could have withstood bites and slashes from sharp-toothed and sharp-clawed predators.

Display could also be a useful defensive weapon. The frills of ceratopsians and the plates of stegosaurs may have been capable of flushing with color when the animal was aroused or felt threatened. This display, which also had the effect of making the animal look bigger and more intimidating

EUOPLOCEPHALUS *had studded, bony body armor and a club on its tail.*

FINDS IN THE GOBI DESERT

The Polish paleontologist Zofia Kielan-Jaworowska studied paleontology at the University of Warsaw and later became director of the Institute of Palaeozoology in Warsaw. She headed a series of three joint Polish and Mongolian expeditions to Mongolia between 1963 and 1971.

She and her colleagues found many new sites across the Gobi Desert and made many new finds of various types of dinosaurs, including ornithomimosaurs, pachycephalosaurs, sauropods, and theropods. They also discovered the fossil remains of numerous mammals and other animals.

In 1965, in late Cretaceous rocks of the Nemegt Basin, her team unearthed the terrifying claws and arms of *Deinocheirus* and in 1971 they made one of the most famous of all dinosaur fossil finds: a *Velociraptor* and a *Protoceratops* locked in mortal combat, both apparently killed when a sand dune collapsed on them.

...than it really was, could have persuaded many a would-be predator to abandon its attack.

For many larger ornithopods, safety in numbers was probably their main defense. Herding in tens, hundreds, or even thousands of individuals would have given predators a difficult target to attack. Large herds meant that there were more eyes and ears to seek out out possible attackers, and greater opportunities for alerting others in a herd to an impending attack.

ON THE ATTACK

Predatory dinosaurs needed a suitable armory of weapons with which to press home their assaults. These weapons were probably both behavioral and structural.

Some theropods were probably ambush predators. Waiting unseen beside trails, they were ready to pounce on prey when the opportunity presented itself. Others could have hunted alone and in the open, their size and strength being the decisive factors in any combat.

Pack hunting was an effective tactic for predators smaller than their intended prey. Some dromaeosaurs may have hunted in packs. The fossils of several *Deinonychus* found with a single *Tenontosaurus* could be construed as evidence of cooperative behavior in these hunters. It is also possible that small groups of allosaurs cooperated in attacks on sauropods—some distracting the attention of adults while their accomplices attacked and killed younger individuals.

Theropods were well-armed with cutting and slashing teeth and long, curved claws that could grip or tear at their victims. Some claws, such as the huge hand claws of *Baryonyx* or the thresher claws of *Therizinosaurus*, appear to have grown to extraordinary lengths and probably had very specific functions. Similarly, the slashing toe claws of the dromaeosaurs and the troödontids were highly specialized and perfectly adapted for maiming or killing prey.

THIS DRAMATIC RECONSTRUCTION *shows the small and very agile theropod* Dromaeosaurus *launching an attack with its teeth and sickle-like claws on the largest of the hadrosaurs,* Lambeosaurus.

THE PLANT-EATERS

*For most of the age of dinosaurs, the climate was warm
and moist. Plants grew in abundance, feeding hundreds,
or perhaps thousands of species of dinosaurs.*

Plant-eating dinosaurs came in an extremely wide range of sizes and designs. There were both the ornithischian and saurischian plant-eaters, as well as quadrupedal and bipedal ones. In fact, as far as we know, all the ornithischian dinosaurs were plant-eaters.

THE SAURISCHIA

There are two categories of saurischian plant-eaters—the prosauropods and the sauropods. The earlier prosauropods were medium-to large-sized dinosaurs with long necks and tails, relatively small heads, and large bodies. They were all quadrupedal, although some may have been capable of rocking up onto their hind legs for feeding, defense, or display.

Sauropods probably had a prosauropod ancestor and ranged in size from large to extremely large. Some were the largest animals ever known to have walked the Earth. They are instantly recognizable by their very long necks and tails, large barrel-like bodies, and very small heads.

Both the sauropods and the prosauropods relied for their survival on processing large quantities of low-quality food. They achieved this by rapidly stripping leaves and fronds that were swallowed whole, without chewing, and

were broken down by the process of fermentation in their huge, vatlike stomachs. Gizzard stones, or gastroliths, have been found in the stomachs of many sauropods. These stones were ground together by the muscular action of the stomach and helped to crush the very tough fibers of plant matter.

THE ORNITHISCHIA

While ornithischian dinosaurs represent a great diversity of dinosaur types, all were plant-eaters. Within this group are the shielded thyreophorans, including stegosaurs and ankylosaurs, the ornithopods, including the iguanodontids and the hadrosaurs, and also the marginocephalians, which include the ceratopsians and the pachycephalosaurs.

All thyreophorans had some form of bony armor on their backs. In stegosaurs, this consisted of two rows of bony plates and spikes that were held vertically from the body.

LONG NECKS *enabled sauropods (left) to reach the foliage at the tops of trees. The teeth of* Othnielia *(far left) were completely covered with protective enamel.*

In ankylosaurs, the back was covered in multiple rows of bony lumps that sometimes extended onto the flanks or even onto the belly. Some of these bony lumps, particularly those that were positioned around the edges, could develop into spikes. The armor of stegosaurs and ankylosaurs weighed them down heavily onto their four legs, but some of the earlier thyreophorans, such as *Scutellosaurus*, may have been

ble to get around on two legs or short periods.

Ornithopods take their name (meaning "bird-foot") from the three-toed, birdlike feet of many members of the group. They varied in size from the diminutive *Hetero-ontosaurus* to hadrosaurs that were 30 feet (10 m) or more in length. The group was characterized by animals that had relatively large heads, moderately long necks, and long hind legs. They could travel on all four legs or rise up on two if more speedy or agile movements were required. There is also a trend in this group of dinosaurs to develop bony struts ("ossified endons") along the back, over the rump, and down the ail. These probably helped to hold the tail and the rear of the animal steady, reducing any flexing, and thus helping to control some movements.

The marginocephalians were a group of dinosaurs that featured some form of bony growth around the margin of the head. Pachycephalosaurs ported a series of lumps and

THE FIRST FOSSILS *of Iguanodon to be found were its teeth (right). Their resemblance to those of living iguanas gave the dinosaur its name. Hadrosaurs had a battery of teeth for grinding food (below).*

bumps, while their cousins the ceratopsians evolved a bony frill that, in some later animals, extended well back over the shoulders. Pachycephalosaurs were all bipedal and were readily identified by their thick, bony heads, often ornamented with lumps and spikes of solid bone. They probably used their heads like battering rams against predators or to display for mates.

Ceratopsians were mostly quadrupedal with particularly large heads. The size of the head was further exaggerated by the neck frill and horns and spikes on the face.

Ornithischian plant-eaters dealt with food in different ways from their saurischian relatives. Some, such as the thyreophorans, probably snipped food into tiny pieces in the mouth using small, sharp teeth. Thyreophorans were unable to grind their food like later marginocephalians and ornithopods, which had batteries of teeth that formed grinding plates.

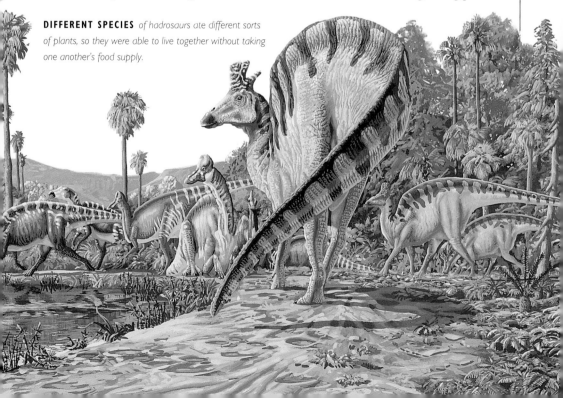

DIFFERENT SPECIES *of hadrosaurs ate different sorts of plants, so they were able to live together without taking one another's food supply.*

THE MEAT-EATERS

Meat-eating dinosaurs ranged dramatically in size. There were some no taller than a chicken and, at the other end of the scale, one that was the largest predator ever to walk the Earth.

The meat-eating dinosaurs are all within one group—the theropods. Some of the earliest known dinosaurs are thought to be theropods, giving them the longest history of any dinosaur group. In fact, because it is now established that birds evolved from theropods and should therefore be considered to be living theropods, this group has a continuous history that stretches over 230 million years.

Theropod fossils tend to be rarer than those of their plant-eating relatives, and they also display a higher diversity of types. Around 40 percent of all valid dinosaur genera recognized by paleontologists are theropods, but most of them are represented by only a single specimen. Because of this, we know less about the interrelationships of theropods than we do of other dinosaur groups, and the way they are organized into groups changes regularly as new material comes to light.

THEROPOD FEATURES

Most theropods were lightly built with large heads. They usually had bladelike teeth that often had serrated edges. Long, slender legs gave them greater speed than most other animals; they were all bipedal. Typically they had long, curved claws that tapered to spiked tips, especially on the hands. They also had hollow bones, a feature that would help birds, their descendants, take to the air and fly.

Another common feature of the theropods was some development of air-pockets or pneumaticity of the skull and vertebrae. They had at least five vertebrae connected to the hip, and an extra joint in the mandible that allowed the jaws to flex sideways to accommodate large pieces of food.

TYRANNOSAURUS *(left and above) had sharp, curved teeth—a typical feature of meat-eating dinosaurs.*

DIFFERENT THEROPODS *had various ways of handling their food.*
❶ Compsognathus, *a coelurosaur, caught and ate prey with its hands.*
❷ Baryonyx *used the huge, hooklike claw on its hand to spear its prey.*
❸ Oviraptor *cracked open eggs with its beak.*

TYPES OF THEROPODS

The theropods can be divided into two basic groups—the ceratosaurs and the tetanurans. The ceratosaurs are known almost exclusively from rocks of the late Triassic and early Jurassic, although some of the theropods from the late Cretaceous of Africa and South America may also be in this group. Typical of the ceratosaurs were dinosaurs such as *Dilophosaurus* and *Coelophysis*. They had four functional fingers on the hand, and clawed toes on the foot.

The tetanurans include all the other theropods. This group of dinosaurs had a maximum of three functional fingers and a foot with three large toes plus a smaller one on the inside of the foot.

COELOPHYSIS *was an agile predator that used its strong, clawed hands to grab small prey, such as the* Planocephalosaurus *that these two* Coelophysis *are chasing up a tree. These and some other meat-eaters also preyed on insects, such as cockroaches and dragonflies, frogs, mammal-like reptiles, and early mammals.*

wounds on the animals that they preyed on.

Recent discoveries, in particular those from China, reveal an abundance of small theropods closely related to birds that firmly establish the link between the two groups. Several of these dinosaurs, such as *Sinosauropteryx* and *Caudipteryx*, have been found preserved with feathers or featherlike structures in place around theropod skeletons. This raises the possibility that such features could have been much more widespread among the theropods, but the vagaries of fossilization have not preserved these features in other known forms.

Theropods were the major carnivores of the day, and they undoubtedly had as much diversity in their habits as do the carnivores of today. The discovery of tens of *Coelophysis* together at Ghost Ranch in New Mexico, and many *Allosaurus* at the Cleveland-Lloyd Quarry in Utah, demonstrates that at least some theropods probably lived in groups of several animals. But the majority of theropod fossils have been isolated finds, which suggests that most theropods lived alone.

Carnosaurs were a group of (mostly) large tetanurans that included dinosaurs such as *Allosaurus* and *Sinoraptor*. This group has changed significant-ly in recent years with many former members being placed in other groups. Originally the carnosaurs were grouped together based solely on their large size, but former members such as *Tyranno-saurus*, the largest of them all, are now no longer thought to be carnosaurs.

Coelurosaurs were mostly Cretaceous tetanurans and included giants such as mighty *Tyrannosaurus* and all the dinosaurs most closely related to them.

More bizarre coelurosaurs included the slashing dromaeosaurs, the ostrichlike ornithomimosaurs, and the strange, crested oviraptors. Ornithomimosaurs and ovi-raptors were virtually tooth-less. This raises the question of what they fed on and how they managed to process their food. Dromaeosaurs had very birdlike skeletons as well as a deadly, retractable killing claw on the second toe that could inflict massive, slashing

THEROPOD DINOSAURS

had serrated teeth (right). Megalosaurus had new teeth ready to move into position to replace those that wore out (left).

CHAPTER FOUR

OUR RELATIONSHIP
with DINOSAURS

Curiosity is one of the permanent and certain characteristics of a vigorous intellect. Every advance into knowledge opens new prospects and produces new incitements to further progress.

The Penny Classics,
SAMUEL JOHNSON (1709–84),
English lexicographer, essayist, poet, and moralist

Dinosaurs *in* Art, Film, *and* Fiction

Modern technology has provided the capacity to show dinosaurs very much as they existed throughout the Mesozoic era.

I t is always a thrill to see dinosaurs mounted in a museum, but museum exhibitions do not give us a real sense of the living, breathing animals as they once were. It is unlikely that we will see cloned dinosaurs in the foreseeable future, so we are forced to use our imagination to bring them to life. A host of media has helped us to do this.

Graphic Arts

Soon after Buckland and Mantell published their discoveries of *Megalosaurus* and *Iguanodon* respectively in the early 1800s, artists began portraying them to a wide audience. Early renderings of *Iguanodon* look like giant iguanas, which was perfectly

MODELS *of King Kong and its pterosaur adversary were created for the classic 1933 movie (above right). (Right) An illustration from Conan Doyle's 1912 novel* The Lost World.

consistent with contemporary scientific opinion. The *Iguanodon* sculptures exhibited in London's Crystal Palace in 1854 were made under the supervision of Richard Owen and, although they look decidedly old-fashioned to modern eyes, they represented at the time the latest in scientific knowledge.

We can literally see the evolution of dinosaur science by watching artists' dinosaur depictions over the years. Most artists have worked with paleontologists to make their representations as accurate as

possible, given the latest scientific data.

In the late 1800s, dinosaurs were generally shown as agile, birdlike creatures, after Thomas Henry Huxley pointed out the similarity between the recently discovered *Archaeopteryx*, the oldest known bird, and other dinosaurs. By the early 1900s, however, the image of dinosaurs as sluggish, cold-blooded animals took over. It was not until the 1970s that energetic dinosaurs once again emerged in graphic depictions.

Dinosaurs in Fiction

Novels that feature dinosaurs date back to the mid- to late 19th century. Most of the early examples featured explorers who stumbled upon prehistoric monsters in

WHAT IS IT ?

HOW MUCH TERROR CAN YOU STAND?

GODZILLA VS. THE THING

IN COLORSCOPE

AN AMERICAN INTERNATIONAL PICTURE · Produced by TOHO CO., Ltd.

IN MOVIES *such as the Godzilla series of the 1950s, actors in costume played dinosaurs and other "monsters."*

DIGITAL REALISM

Modern films take advantage of computer animation technology. Many or all of the dinosaurs in *Jurassic Park* (inset) were completely digital. This made them more realistic than in any previous dinosaur movie. Movements looked more natural, and scenes combining dinosaurs and humans had a more convincing look. The dinosaurs themselves were also updated in line with contemporary scientific knowledge: Their tails were held off the ground and their gaits suggested elevated metabolic rates.

The recent television series from the British Broadcasting Corporation, "Walking with Dinosaurs," incorporates the latest scientific knowledge and represents dinosaurs, and the environment in which they lived, as accurately as is possible. The colors of the dinosaurs, of course, are entirely speculative.

sauropod who graced the world's screens from 1914. At that time, dinosaurs were usually "created" using models that were moved slightly between frame shots.

This was the "stop-action animation" technique that worked so spectacularly with the *King Kong* sensation in 1933. Flat animation (cartoons) has always been popular and reached an artistic height with Disney's *Fantasia* in 1940. Many movies used human actors in costume to represent dinosaurs—a technique made famous by *Godzilla* (1956) and its sequels. Others resorted to putting fake horns or frills on living lizards or alligators and filming them up close.

THE 1940 MOVIE One Million *Years made numerous errors. For example, it brought the age of the dinosaurs much closer to the present and showed dinosaurs and humans existing together.*

remote jungle refuges—as, for example, in Sir Arthur Conan Doyle's *The Lost World* and some of Edgar Rice Burroughs's works. Sometimes—as in the movie version of Jules Verne's *Journey to the Center of the Earth*—the dinosaurs were deep underground. Early novels typically made use of extensive poetic license, often depicting dinosaurs and humans as existing together and also sometimes grossly exaggerating the size of the dinosaurs. But, to do them justice, most of these literary efforts drew on the scientific knowledge available at the time. As scientific concepts of dinosaurs evolved, the popular literature kept pace. Two recent novels by Michael Crighton —*Jurassic Park* and *The Lost World* which bears no relation to Conan Doyle's book)—

depict dinosaurs much as paleontologists of the 1990s peceived them.

DINOSAURS ON SCREEN

For many of us, fictional and graphic representations are not enough. We want to see these fascinating animals in motion. Almost from the beginning of cinema history, dinosaurs featured in movies. One of the first movie cartoon stars was Gertie, a dancing

SOME MODERN DINOSAUR DETECTIVES

A second "golden age" of dinosaur discoveries that began in the 1970s continues unabated at the beginning of the 21st century.

DONG ZHIMING *(above) is a leading Chinese paleontologist. (Left) Philip Currie, at right, and fellow researchers analyze dinosaur finds in the laboratory*

What is often called the first golden age of dinosaur science stretched from the late 1800s to the early 1900s. Although scientists continued to study dinosaurs, research waned somewhat for 40 years after about 1930. In the 1970s, however, there was a great resurgence in interest. This was due in part to John Ostrom's ground-breaking comparisons between birds and small theropods such as *Deinonychus*, as well as new evidence that suggested dinosaurs may have been warm-blooded. The work of Robert Bakker, a student of Ostrom, helped to make popular a "new view" of dinosaurs during the 1970s and 1980s that depicted these ancient creatures, not as sluggish and lizard-like, but as agile, active, and birdlike.

SOUTHERN HEMISPHERE FINDS

Some of the most important discoveries in recent decades were made in

JOHN HORNER *is most famous for his 1978 discovery, in the Montana badlands, of nesting colonies of the hadrosaur Maiasaura.*

Argentina. Here, rocks from the late Triassic—the period when the earliest dinosaurs were living—are exposed. Thanks largely to the work of José Bonaparte and other Argentinians, the existence of the primitive dinosaur *Herrerasaurus* was established. In the 1990s, another Argentinian, Fernando Novas, and the North American Paul Sereno found and described a much more complete *Herrerasaurus* specimen. This filled in many of the gaps in our knowledge of this early meat-eater. Novas's and Sereno's work also yielded *Eoraptor*, an even more primitive dinosaur than *Herrerasaurus*. These discoveries have provided valuable clues to just what the ancestral dinosaur may have looked like.

Other hotbeds of field work in the 1990s were sites in the former Gondwanan continents of South America, Africa, India, and Australia. One particularly successful project was in Madagascar, where parties led by David Krause and Catherine Forster of the State University of New York at Stony Brook, excavated a late Cretaceous fauna, including armored sauropods and some bizarre theropods. These dinosaurs are, paradoxically, more similar to those found in the Cretaceous of South America and India and are related only remotely to Cretaceous dinosaurs from mainland Africa. This suggests that there was a dry-land connection between South America and India that was not joined to Africa.

PAUL SERENO, *of the University of Chicago, is seen here working in the torrid heat of the Moroccan Sahara to unearth the jaw of a* Carcharodonto-saurus.

NORTHERN HEMISPHERE FINDS

In the Northern Hemisphere, paleontologists have been revisiting some of the classic localities that brought fame to earlier researchers. Philip Currie, of the Royal Tyrrell Museum of Paleontology in Alberta, Canada, has continued the tradition begun by Barnum Brown and the Sternberg family. His field work in the badlands of southern Alberta has brought to light new species as well as more complete remains of dinosaurs that had been found by earlier searchers.

Farther south, Jurassic and Cretaceous localities of the western United States continue to yield exciting material. These follow on from famous discoveries during the 1970s and 1980s by John Horner of Montana State University and his colleagues. One of their most celebrated discoveries was a set of duck-billed dinosaur nesting grounds at a place in the Montana badlands that Horner named "Egg Mountain." Horner called the new dinosaur *Maiasaura.*

If finding these fossils is so easy, why didn't anybody do it before? It's a hard one to answer.

Digging Dinosaurs,
JOHN R. HORNER
(b. 1946–), American paleontologist

NEW EMPHASIS

One important difference between the present dinosaur science and that of the previous golden age is the emphasis that paleontologists now place on small fossils. Earlier collectors did look for small dinosaurs, but they were more interested in finding giant skeletons that would make spectacular displays in major museums.

Paleontologists continue to collect large dinosaurs, but they now realize that small ones are just as important for helping us to understand the world of the dinosaurs. Most of the critical

evidence that links birds to their dinosaur ancestry comes from smaller forms. Modern dinosaur scientists are also paying greater attention than their forebears did to the other animals—the mammals, lizards, crocodiles, turtles, and others—that lived alongside the dinosaurs.

These are good times for paleontologists. People who thought the days of great discoveries were over have been proved wrong. All over the world, fossils continue to be found—even at sites that were thought to have given up all their treasures as long as a century ago.

ROBERT BAKKER *is one modern researcher whose work has significantly expanded our knowledge of dinosaur biology. He is shown here with a reconstruction of a* Stegosaurus *skeleton.*

COLLECTING *and* CARING *for* FOSSILS

Fossil-collectors, and the new finds they make, are essential to the health of the now-thriving science of dinosaur paleontology.

The first challenge that confronts any fossil-seeker is to know where to start looking. Not every spot is likely to yield dinosaur, or any other kind of fossils. Paleontologists, therefore, spend a good deal of time in the library, studying maps to find areas with an environment where rocks of the right age might be exposed. They then spend more time writing grant proposals to obtain necessary funds and permission to conduct their search. They also give careful thought to planning their excursion and deciding what materials and equipment—including tools, food, water, and fuel—they will need to take along.

IN THE FIELD

We often describe what paleontologists do as "digging" for dinosaurs. This is not entirely accurate, though some actual digging may well be involved. Once paleontologists have found likely fossil-bearing rocks, they spend most of their time walking round in a stooped, and eventually rather painful, posture with their eyes glued to the ground. They rarely stick their shovels into a random patch of earth and simply start digging. They let natural erosion start the process by exposing bones on hillsides. Most of the time they walk along valleys or washes, looking for fragments of bone that have been weathered from uphill. When bone is found, fragments are traced uphill until the source is located.

Searchers pinpoint the location of any fossil they find on a map. Modern Global Positioning System (GPS) technology has made this task a good deal easier than in past days. Having located their

BETWEEN 1909 AND 1912, *a huge German expedition excavated fossils at Tendaguru. Local workers did the digging and carried the fossils from the site to the nearest seaport (below). (Left) A collection of tools used for uncovering and extracting bones from rock.*

DIGGING TEAM *in Niger (above) carefully cleans the exposed sections of the* ront *and back limbs of a giant sauropod dinosaur. (Above right) Before removing a* rge *and delicate fossil from the site, this team encloses it in a "jacket" of plaster and* acking *and then reinforces the covering with wooden battens.*

ssils, paleontologists must
hen decide how to proceed.
f the bones are small—no
onger than an inch or two—
hey may simply be rolled up
n toilet paper and taken back
o camp; larger fossils will
equire quarrying and
vrapping (a process described
on pages 332-3).

Bringing large fossils out of
he field can be a challenge.
German-led field parties to
Tendaguru, in present-day
Tanzania, before World War I
mployed long convoys of
ocal foot couriers, who
arried the fossils more than
'00 miles (435 km) to the port
of Lindi. Fossils from western
North America were hauled
oy mules in the late 19th and
arly 20th centuries. Today,
ve can use helicopters if funds
permit. If not, we drag the
ossils to nearby trucks.

FOSSILS IN MUSEUMS
When the fossils arrive at a
museum, specially trained staff
emove them from their
urrounding matrix and then
arefully clean them (this
process is described on

pages 334–5). The fossils must
then be stored under special
protective conditions. It is
not a matter of simply putting
them on shelves. Frequent
changes in temperature or
humidity can damage some
specimens, and insects can
destroy specimen labels. Fossils
are kept in closed cabinets,
which in many museums
have sophisticated climate-
control systems.

Fossils belong in museums,
because that is where they are
most readily accessible to
the scientific community.
While most fossils in museums
are never displayed to the
public, they make up the data
set that paleontologists rely
on for their research and for
the advancement of their
knowledge. The fossils that are
on exhibit may well be the
largest or the most attractive
or dramatic, but they may
not, from a scientific point of
view, be the most significant.
The fossils hidden away from
public view often provide the
basic sustenance on which
the science of paleontology
relies for its survival.

ESSENTIAL TOOLS

The first thing that any
fossil-seeker, amateur or
professional, needs to bring
to the field is specialized
knowledge and training.
No one should try to quarry
large vertebrate fossils
without training in the proper
methods, as poor quarrying
can result in the destruction
of critical information. Some
museums and universities
provide training programs for
amateur fossil-hunters.

The next requirement is
an understanding of the
geography and geology of
the region that is being
investigated. A fossil collected
without detailed information
of where it came from will be
of little value.

Yet another essential is a
good supply of patience. For
every exciting moment of a
signficant find, there will
inevitably be long, frustrating
periods of fruitless searching.

Necessary tools include a
rock hammer, a hand lens or
magnifying glass, a camera,
a map, a notebook and
pencil, a set of dental picks or
probes, a shovel (for some
areas), and toilet paper and
plastic bags, for wrapping and
storing what you find.
Perhaps the most essential
single item, however, is a
comfortable, good-quality,
sturdy pair of working boots.

WHERE *to* LOOK *and* WHAT *to* LOOK FOR

A bit of homework, and asking the right people, can make dinosaur hunting that much easier and, hopefully, rewarding.

Most large museums with dinosaur fossils in their collections have on staff one or more vertebrate paleontologists. An important part of their job is to find more specimens for study and display. Where should they—or, indeed, amateur fossil hunters—start to look? We know that only certain types of rocks contain dinosaur fossils, and a little preliminary research will help pinpoint some promising places to start looking.

A SUNSET SCENE *in the Pariah badlands in Utah, USA. Areas such as this can provide rich pickings for fossil-hunters.*

OLD AND NEW SITES

The museum itself is a good starting point. It will have records of where its existing dinosaur fossils came from and may well be willing to share this information with serious enthusiasts. You could try going back to the original site—if one fossil was found there, more will probably be waiting there. Every season erodes the rock a little more, and specimens that were not visible on one trip may come to light on a later one. If the dinosaurs at your museum were collected a long time ago, it's definitely worth a return visit—a good deal of erosion will have occurred in the meantime.

Some rock types, or formations, tend to produce many more fossils than others so if you find out which

LOOKING FOR FOSSILS DOWN UNDER

Australia, like North America, has many of the features that make for good dinosaur hunting—large areas of Mesozoic sedimentary rocks and extensive arid zones. So far, however, only a handful of dinosaur fossils have been found in Australia. Why is this? Part of the answer lies in Australia's small population and the relatively few paleontologists who live there. Probably more important, though, is the fact that during the Ice Ages there were no ice sheets covering Australia— there were no glaciers to produce fresh and rapid erosion of the rock, as there were in the United

States. By contrast, the exposed rocks in Australia have been weathering away relatively slowly for millions of years. We know that there were lots of dinosaurs living in Australia, because there are many good trackways—dinsosaur footprints. Dinosaur hunting, Australian style, can involve much more tracking than digging.

THIS LATE *Cretaceous bone bed in Dinosaur Provincial Park in Alberta, Canada, contains remains of the horned herbivore* Centrosaurus.

The museums that are most successful at finding new specimens are often those that work closely with amateur fossil hunters and local landholders. Many amateur fossil hunters have great enthusiasm for the task and are very skilled. Local landholders know their properties intimately and are more likely than anyone else to find exposed fossils there. Some museums run special programs to help amateur fossil hunters and have also found it worthwhile to spend time showing landholders what to keep an eye out for.

If you think you have found a dinosaur fossil, do not start digging or removing bones. If you have picked up a bone that you think might be a fossil, examine it closely and then put it back exactly where you found it. Look for other pieces that may be lying close by but do not disturb the site unnecessarily. When you have finished searching, take whatever you have found back to the museum for identification. Always note the exact position it was in and ensure that you will be able to find the site when you return.

...ormations produced the existing specimens, you can use a geology map to establish where else you might find these formations. The map will also show places where creeks or roads cut through the rock—these are good places to look.

...N THE FIELD

...ook for sites where the rock is exposed at the surface. Rocky deserts are good fossil-hunting areas. Dry creek beds, cliff faces, road cuttings, and even quarries are also useful places to look.

Often small shards of bone are weathered from a freshly exposed fossil and are moved downslope by wind or water. If you see small pieces lying loose, follow the slope or the creek back to see where they may have come from.

GANTHEAUME POINT, *near the town of Broome, on the north-west coast of Western Australia, is thought to be the site of ancient dinosaur mud baths. Many well-preserved fossils have been found in the region.*

EXCAVATING *in the* FIELD

*A dinosaur dig is like a crime scene—great care is needed
to get every last clue out of the ground.*

When a dinosaur fossil has been found, it needs to be removed from its site as quickly as possible. Even though it may have been lying in the rock for hundreds of millions of years, as soon as it is exposed to the elements, it can begin to erode away more rapidly. However, the removal must be done with great care. Unlike the search, which can be undertaken by a small group, or even a single person, the dig can require a large amount of equipment and a lot of people. Just organizing a dig team can itself be a major task.

FINDING THE WHOLE FOSSIL

Once a part of the fossil has been uncovered, the rest of it needs to be found as soon as possible—whether it is lying in the ground nearby or has been washed halfway down a gully. If the fossil has only just been exposed and has not been moved by rain or wind, then it is likely that the rest of it will be nearby, so the surrounding rock needs to be carefully cleaned away. Gentle brushing and chiseling is usually the best way to do this. In the meantime, someone with sharp eyesight can be set to work combing the surrounding area, or even farther afield, in search of other pieces that may have been dislodged, or washed or blown downhill.

EXCAVATING *a Tyrannosaurus hip bone in South Dakota, USA.*

MAPPING

When you are confident that most of your dinosaur fossil has been found, you can start mapping and labeling the bones. The information gained from the position each bone was found lying in can be as important as recovering the bone itself. Therefore, no bone should be removed until its position has been mapped on a grid, and the bone's orientation and number have been marked.

Usually the site is marked out with string and pegs. Then a 1 square meter

(11 sq. ft) frame supporting a 10-centimeter (4-in) grid is placed in turn over each square meter of the site. A map of the bones lying within each section of the square is drawn onto graph paper and sections of the grid are photographed progressively.

LABELING

In order to create an accurate record of the original find, you need to photograph the bones in the context of the surrounding site before beginning to remove them— a combination of stills and

ALEONTOLOGISTS *work carefully to xcavate a well-preserved dinosaur keleton at Cox's Creek, New South Vales, Australia.*

ideo is best for this. Making n annotated sketch of your ind can also be useful.

The next step is to label he bones. Stick-on labels are 1ot satisfactory, as they are iable to become detached nd get lost. Each bone hould, therefore, be abeled with permanent narker. If you eel you need to onsolidate a fragile bone vith PVA glue before emoving it, you should ipply this before you start abeling, as the glue will isually smudge the ink.

REMOVING FOSSILS

Once you have mapped, abeled, and photographed he fossils, you are ready to emove them. How to do this lepends on both the nature of the fossils and the substrate hey are lying in. If fossils are ving loose in sand or dirt, vou can simply lift them out vith care and then wrap and back them. Very small fossils, uch as bone fragments or eeth, can be wrapped in issue paper and stored for the ime being in small boxes.

Larger bones will need to be wrapped temporarily in cloth or hessian and placed in straw in large crates.

If fossils are embedded in solid rock—or even hard clay—small pieces may be very carefully chiseled out, but you will usually have to remove some of the surrounding rock as well. You can cut the rock around the fossil or you can work existing cracks in the rock to make a series of blocks containing the fossil bones. A wide range of tools is useful for this, depending on the hardness of the rock. Chisels, picks, rock saws, hammers, pneumatic drills, and even humble penknives can be brought into play. Be careful, that an over-enthusiastic blow with a hammer does not send an unwanted crack running through the middle of a bone.

PROTECTING FOSSILS FOR TRANSPORTATION

When the block is ready to come out, you need to protect the fossil on the upper surface—and sometimes the sides of the block as well—before moving it. If the block and fossil are fairly strong, they may only need to be protected by a wrapping of thick, wet newspaper. If, however, the fossil and the block are more fragile, you will have to gradually build up layers of tissue or toilet paper, newspaper, cloth, and then plaster, before it is ready to move. In all, it can be a very painstaking and time-consuming process.

After all that lengthy, delicate work, the moment of taking a mighty blow to separate the block from the rest of the rock can be very satisfying! The block is then lifted, the underside is wrapped—and, if necessary, plastered in the same way as the top—the outside of the block is labeled, and your fossil is ready at last to be transported back to the museum. Once there, it will be prepared for closer study and, perhaps, ultimately, to go on exhibition.

A SCIENTIST *employs a grid to map out the site of a fossil find in Shell, Wyoming, USA.*

BACK *in the* LABORATORY

The long job of preparing a new specimen will require the expertise of some of the museum's most specialized staff.

When a fossil arrives at the laboratory, it is unpacked as soon as possible, while details of the dig are still fresh in people's minds. The bones are then cleaned and washed and, if necessary, they are laid out in the way that they were found in the field (a sandpit can be very useful for heavy blocks). Piecing together a large dinosaur can be like doing a heavy three-dimensional jigsaw puzzle with an unknown number of pieces and no picture to work from!

A TECHNICIAN *in Colorado, USA, uses a powerful magnifying glass as she prepares the fused vertebrae of an* Allosaurus *specimen.*

The specimen must now be conserved and prepared for study and display. There are many types of conservation treatments available for fossils, and each fossil has different conservation requirements. Many bones are treated with glues to strengthen them and most are kept at a constant level of temperature and humidity.

PREPARING THE FOSSIL
Preparing the fossil involves removing any matrix (rock) that is still attached to the bone. Exactly what type of preparation, and how much is undertaken, depends on the

SECTIONING

Many fossils preserve the details of the dinosaur's internal anatomy in fine detail. Fossilized dinosaur bone often contains a great deal of information about the microscopic structure—or the "histology"—of the bone. This can be studied by examining a very thin slice of the bone under a microscope. Dinosaur bone histology has been used to investigate rates of growth and even to examine the question of whether dinosaurs were "warm-blooded."

Sometimes skulls can be sectioned (cut down the middle) to reveal the internal structure of the skull bones, such as the braincase, which is not visible from the outside of the fossil. Sectioning usually involves

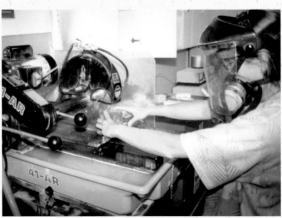

simply cutting the skull in half, but in some cases the fossil has to be finely sliced to reveal the internal detail. This is called serial sectioning. The problem with this process is that it destroys the fossil, so casts and photographs need to be taken throughout. When the preparation is finished, the cast is the only record of the fossil that remains.

Recently, powerful medical scanners, which use X-ray imaging to "slice" the specimen, have been employed in serial sectioning. This has the advantage of revealing the internal detail of the specimen without destroying it, but it does have one important drawback—often the X-ray is unable to distinguish between the rock and the bone.

FRENCH PALEONTOLOGIST

Professor Jean Lautier is seen here in his laboratory in Paris, France, restoring a fossilized dinosaur egg. The preparation and study of dinosaur eggs and embryos have greatly enhanced our understanding of dinosaur reproduction and nurturing behavior.

ature of the fossil and the matrix and what sort of study or display is eventually required.

In most cases this preparation will be either mechanical or chemical. Mechanical preparation involves the use of special drills and chisels to remove the matrix from the bone. With chemical preparation, a weak acid is used to remove the rock. Each method has its advantages and its problems.

Mechanical preparation, if it is not undertaken very carefully, can seriously damage the fossil. A variety of tools—such as small rock saws, chisels, and pneumatic percussion tools—may be used. The advantage of mechanical preparation is that it does not involve the use of chemicals that could eventually harm the specimen.

Acid preparation can be used when the phosphatic bone is enclosed in a carbonate rock, such as limestone—a weak acid will react with the matrix but will not affect the bone. Acid preparation can expose delicate structures that would be damaged if they were subjected to mechanical preparation, but there is always the danger that the acid will penetrate into the specimen and slowly attack it from within.

The preparation of a dinosaur fossil requires a technician with a great deal of skill and patience. He or she must work closely with a paleontologist who has a detailed knowledge of the dinosaur's anatomy. As the bone is slowly

CHINESE PALEONTOLOGIST

Xi Xing carefully brushes and blows sediment from the pubis of a recently discovered therizinosaur, Beipiaosaurus. This dinosaur, at about 7 feet (2.2 m) long, is the longest therizinosaur yet found. This fossil shows evidence that Beipiaosaurus had protofeathers.

revealed, observations are noted and photographs are taken. In order to establish how much rock must be removed, the bone is compared with those of other known dinosaurs.

Preparation can be very time-consuming—a specimen that takes a week to excavate may take years to prepare.

BRINGING *a* NEW DISCOVERY *to* LIFE

The first stage in turning fossil into animal is to slowly and painstakingly reconstruct the dinosaur's anatomy

The skeleton of an animal is made up of its bones, teeth, cartilaginous structures, and skeletal muscles. A dinosaur fossil is usually a record of some part of the animal's skeleton. Because they contain many hard minerals, the bones and teeth of dinosaurs are the structures that most often get fossilized.

A lot can happen to a bone during the millions of years the fossil spends lying in the ground—it may get broken, squashed flat, or crushed. A paleontologist needs to allow for any distortion that may have occurred as a result of one or more of these occurrences. With complex structures such as skulls, this can be quite tricky. Sometimes, powerful computer programs can be used to "uncrush" such misadventures as a badly distorted specimen. In many instances, however, a specimen that is badly crushed or eroded may well prove too difficult to study, or to put on display.

CONSTRUCTING THE SKELETON

A fossil specimen rarely preserves more than a fraction of the 200 or so bones that are present in the vertebrate body. The study or display of the specimen, then, usually involves the reconstructing of the entire skeleton. Scientists therefore try to fill in the missing bones. If, for example, the tail from one specimen is missing, it may still be possible to reconstruct it by making comparisons with the tail of a similar dinosaur that has been found. This process assumes that the restorers have a sound knowledge of anatomy and are familiar with many

EXPERT DRAWINGS *of dinosaur fossils are of great importance in helping scientists reconstruct the appearance of individual dinosaurs.*

different types of dinosaurs. It can work only if specimens of similar dinosaurs have already been found.

Once researchers have reconstructed the bones, they then need to fill in details of ligament and muscle attachments. They can do this by examining the bones for particular clues that indicate at which points ligaments or muscles were attached to them. Using the muscles of living animals as a guide, they can then make a generalized reconstruction of the animal's muscle system.

RECONSTRUCTIONS *of Baryonyx have been made using only some bones (highlighted here) found in a clay pit in south-eastern England.*

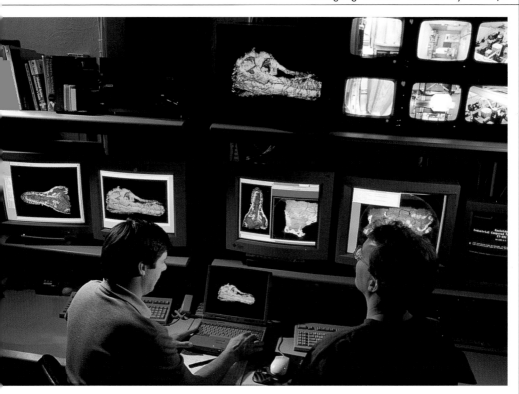

CIENTISTS AT BOEING'S ROCKETDYNE LAB *at Rocket County, California, use ophisticated X-ray techniques to examine a recently discovered Tyrannosaurus skull.*

OUTSIDE AND INSIDE

By this stage of the process, we have a good idea of the size and shape of the dinosaur. The details of the outer covering—the skin, scales, and feathers—are not often preserved in fossils. If a specimen has no fossil record of these features, there is little point in trying to reconstruct them. General reconstructions of dinosaur scales and feathers are based upon those rare fossils that do preserve them, as well as on comparisons with living species.

The internal organs of dinosaurs have only rarely been preserved. Almost all reconstructions of the organ system of dinosaurs are based on comparisons with living animals rather than on direct fossil evidence. However, gut contents are sometimes preserved, and these can provide much valuable information about a dinosaur's last meal—or whether it swallowed grit or stones to help it process its food. There is no fossil evidence that can help us to discover what color dinsoaurs were when they were alive.

GETTING IT WRONG

Educated guesswork often plays an important role in bringing dinosaur fossils to life. However, attempts to reconstruct dinosaurs from limited fossil evidence can lead to false conclusions.

During the 1930s, for example, a pair of huge arms, each with a set of ferocious claws, was uncovered in Mongolia. The dinosaur from which they came was named *Deinocheirus*, or "terrible hand," and for decades there was intense speculation about this mystery dinosaur, which was assumed to be a monster carnivore.

The truth turned out to be otherwise. A series of finds in the late 1980s revealed that the huge arms belonged to an unusual group of theropod dinosaurs—the therizinosaurs. They had long necks, small heads, and teeth that seemed suitable for eating plants. The hips were huge, but the legs and tail were quite short. We now think *Deinocheirus* was a dinosaurian version of the extinct giant ground sloth, which sat on its haunches and used its powerful arms and claws to rip vegetation and pull it toward the mouth.

BARYONYX *reconstructions have been made from the basic skeleton by using information about the muscles, skin, and internal organs of modern reptiles.*

337

LEARNING *from* LIVING CREATURES

Living animals provide us with many valuable leads in our attempts to reconstruct the appearance, anatomy, and behavior of dinosaurs.

The next stage in bringing a dinosaur to life is to reconstruct its behavior and how it lived, using living animals as a model. Because dinosaurs are so long extinct, "bringing them to life" requires some lessons from living animals. Because the entire process of reconstructing a fossil species relies heavily upon a knowledge of the anatomy, behavior, ecology, and evolution of living creatures, a good paleontologist must be a biologist as well as a geologist.

COMING TO CONCLUSIONS

All the characteristics that make up a living animal are influenced both by the features it inherited from its distant ancestors and by the way it lives in its present environment. We can see from living animals that some features vary greatly within one species, while others are surprisingly consistent within a group of related animals. Despite this, making careful and informed comparisons

with living species can allow scientists to reconstruct, with a fair degree of confidence, features that cannot be seen in the fossil.

Though we can observe different scale patterns in living reptiles, species of the same type of reptiles tend to have similar scale patterns. The scale type in dinosaur skin was, therefore, able to be reconstructed by looking at the scale of the living archosaurs—crocodilians and birds. The assumption that dinosaur scales were like those of these living archosaurs has indeed been confirmed by the presence of dinosaur skin in some rare, well-preserved dinosaur fossils.

Because there are plenty of fossilized dinosaur eggs in existence, it may seem reasonable to conclude that all dinosaurs laid eggs. This, however, is based on an absence of evidence to the

THE POWERFUL JAWS *and the teeth of present-day crocodiles are reminiscent of those of their reptilian ancestors, including many carnivorous dinosaurs.*

contrary. Nevertheless, a comparison with living animals shows that all living archosaurs—including birds, alligators, and crocodiles— also lay eggs. This suggests that archosaurs are somehow constrained to laying eggs and does back up the notion that all dinosaurs were egg-layers.

EVIDENCE FROM TEETH

The diet of living animals is strongly related to tooth and jaw structure, and it is reasonable to think, for example, that dinosaurs with teeth like those of modern carnivores tended to eat meat Most reconstructions of dinosaur diets are based on comparisons with the tooth shapes of living animals. The similarity between the teeth of iguanas and those of *Iguanodon*—which inspired that dinosaur's name— indicates that, like the iguana, *Iguanodon* ate plants. By comparing the wear marks on herbivorous dinosaur teeth with those found in living

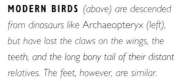

MODERN BIRDS *(above) are descended from dinosaurs like Archaeopteryx (left), but have lost the claws on the wings, the teeth, and the long bony tail of their distant relatives. The feet, however, are similar.*

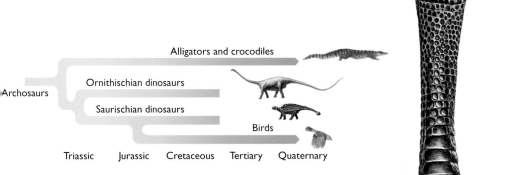

Archosaurs					
	Alligators and crocodiles				
	Ornithischian dinosaurs				
	Saurischian dinosaurs				
			Birds		
Triassic	Jurassic	Cretaceous	Tertiary	Quaternary	

nimals, we can even tell how dinosaurs ate their plant diet. Again, similarities between the teeth of modern Komodo dragons and those of tyrannosaurs suggest that, like Komodo dragons, tyrannosaurs trapped rotting pieces of meat in their teeth and used this rotten meat to inflict infectious bites on prey, although there is no evidence to support this theory.

Teeth, though, are not always a reliable indicator of what an animal eats. Modern bears, for example, have a typical "carnivorous" tooth structure, but many eat large amounts of plant matter.

UNLIKELY COMPARISONS

Sometimes useful comparisons can be made between the most unlikely animals. The fact that dinosaurs laid eggs means that large dinosaurs

BIRDS ARE THE LIVING ANCESTORS *of the dinosaurs that became extinct at the end of the Cretaceous period. Alligators and crocodiles are not directly descended from dinosaurs, but they share a common ancestry through the archosaurs.*

must have laid eggs that were tiny in comparison to their body size. This is because the mechanical properties of eggshell place an upper limit on the size of eggs. No large animal alive today lays such relatively small eggs as dinosaurs did. However, many amphibians, fishes, and even lizards lay eggs that are small compared to their body size, and these animals compensate for the small size of their eggs by laying great numbers—hundreds, or even thousands, of them at one time. It is possible, then, that the reproductive strategy of a *Diplodocus* was more akin to that employed by an insect than to those of modern reptiles.

THE COLOR QUESTION

Comparisons with living creatures can tell us nothing about the colors of dinosaurs. Among living animals, there can be enormous color variation between closely related species, or even between individuals of the same species. Even though there are some general rules of thumb about an animal's coloration, there are so many exceptions that it is impossible to know without direct evidence what an animal's color might have been. All sorts of colors and patterns—including patterns for camouflage, mimicry, threat, or display—can be imagined. In dinosaur reconstruction, the color is often left for the artist to decide. Esthetic appeal rather than scientific rigor is, in this case, the only useful criterion.

DISCOVERIES OF FOSSIL TEETH *from dinosaurs such as Tyrannosaurus (above left) have helped to establish evolutionary links between ancient and modern reptiles. The mud nest (left), which contained Oviraptor eggs, was discovered in 1922. These were the first dinosaur eggs ever discovered.*

IN *the* MUSEUM

Teaching the public about dinosaurs is one of the most important and interesting jobs in the museum.

A visit to a natural history museum can provide the stimulus for an enduring interest in dinosaurs. Every year millions of people go to museums to marvel at the earthly remains of these wonderful animals. There are literally hundreds of dinosaur displays worldwide. Each of them is the end result of a huge amount of work and may involve a very substantial financial outlay.

MOUNTING AN EXHIBITION

Big museums often employ large teams of highly skilled designers and artists whose job it is to put the exhibitions together. The process starts with a paleontologist and a designer deciding on the basic theme of the display. They may, for example, want to demonstrate some aspect of a new theory about a species or highlight a recently acquired specimen. They must decide whether they are going to use mounted skeletons, full-sized "life" reconstructions, robotic dinosaurs, or computer graphics—or perhaps some combination of all of these.

If a skeleton is to be mounted for display, a cast needs to be made of each bone. Fossilized bone is usually too heavy to mount safely in a display, and fossil material that is part of an exhibit is not readily available for further study. Casts are often nearly impossible to tell from the original specimen, and they have the advantage that they can be touched by the visitors. Such hands-on experiences are an important feature of many displays. Making a cast of every bone in a dinosaur specimen, as well as sculpting the missing bones, can take many months Constructing a full-sized model of what the dinosaur looked like in life is often quicker and less expensive. Either way, the job is long and painstaking.

Many recent dinosaur displays use robotics to make the animals move as if they were alive, or use "interactive' computer graphics to add to the effect. Others depict the fossil skeleton as it lay in the ground. This involves re-creating the original dig site. Sometimes a fossil is prepared

A PALEONTOLOGIST *(above) makes casts of dinosaur fossils. (Right) Artist Brian Cooley, in his studio in Calgary, Alberta, Canada, adds feathers to a model of a juvenile* Sinosauropteryx.

LARGE MOUNTED DINOSAUR SKELETONS *dominate the central hall of the Oxford University Museum of Natural History in Oxford, UK.*

in a special laboratory that can be viewed by the public. This means that the fossil is on display almost as soon as it arrives at the museum.

MUSEUM COLLECTIONS

Once a specimen has been displayed to the public, it is sent to its final resting place—as part of the collections of a museum. Though the displays are the most visible part of any museum, the collections are actually more important—they provide a safe keeping place where the fossils can be made available to be studied by paleontologists.

Each specimen is first catalogued, so that it can be located easily, and then stored in whatever way is considered most appropriate for that particular fossil. Usually the collections are kept at a constant temperature and humidity. This lessens the risk of pyrite disease, a condition

that can occur when iron pyrite, a mineral found in many fossils, begins to oxidize. They are also kept reasonably free of dust.

Specimens that represent new species are called "types," and these must be stored with extra care. In many cases, these types will never be allowed to leave the museum. Collections of some very large museums can be so extensive that no one is really sure exactly what they contain. The best place to find a new

It is always the final

thing that one must

research with the most

perseverance.

Letter to Gideon Mantell,
BARON GEORGES CUVIER
(1769–1832), French anatomist

species of dinosaur is sometimes among old bones lying on a museum shelf!

THINKING AGAIN

Some mounted dinosaur skeletons have been in place as long as the museums that house them. However, as ideas about dinosaurs can change over time, older displays can look quite dated. The *Diplodocus* skeleton in the main gallery at London's Natural History Museum has been there for many years. When it was first mounted, scientists believed that dinosaurs used to drag their tails on the ground. The mount, therefore, had its tail snaking along behind it. When it was realized that all dinosaurs held their tails well clear of the ground so that the tail counterbalanced the front half of the body, it was necessary to remount the tail. Visitors can now walk underneath the huge tail and gaze up at a newer, livelier *Diplodocus*.

The creature had teeth knobblier than handles,
suggesting a throat like a hallway and a stomach
like a ballroom arch. It was turned to stone and
embedded in soft rock.

Mr Darwin's Shooter,
ROGER MCDONALD (b. 1941), Australian novelist and poet

CHAPTER FIVE
A GUIDE
to DINOSAURS

USING *the* GUIDE *to* DINOSAURS

This guide gives detailed information about a wide range of dinosaurs, some whose names are very familiar, others that have only recently been discovered.

Fossil finds have provided vital clues about the environments that dinosaurs inhabited, as well as what these creatures looked like, the food they ate, and how they lived. The text in the following pages, supported by lifelike illustrations, presents the most up-to-date facts and figures about almost 80 different species of dinosaur.

The taxonomic data in the panel at the top of a page indicates the group and family to which a dinosaur belonged. This provides a quick reference to how dinosaurs were related to each other.

The genus name of each dinosaur is followed by a guide to how it is pronounced and on which syllables the emphasis should be placed.

Field Notes Panels

■ Meaning of the dinosaur's name

🦖 Approximate maximum size

■ Period in which it lived

■ Where it lived

🏛 Museums around the world where fossil remains or reconstructions of the dinosaur are on display

Ceratopsia/Psittacosauridae

Psittacosaurus
sih-TAK-oh-saw-rus

FIELD NOTES

■ Parrot lizard
🦖 4 feet (1.25 m)
■ Early Cretaceous
■ Mongolia; China; southern Siberia; Thailand
🏛 American Museum of Natural History, New York, USA; Paleontological Museum, Moscow, Russia; Academy of Science, Ulan Baatar, Mongolia; Department of Mineral Resources, Bangkok, Thailand

Psittacosaurus was discovered in Outer Mongolia in 1922, in the early stages of the famous expeditions undertaken by the American Museum of Natural History between 1922 and 1925. Henry Osborn named it for the beaklike appearance of its face. It is known from a number of well-preserved skeletons, which represent about eight different species from Mongolia, southern Siberia, and northern China, as well as from some lower jaw fragments that were discovered in northern Thailand.

Psittacosaurus was one of the earliest dinosaurs to show the typical beaked face of the ceratopsian group. This beak, which was supported by a single median bone—called the "rostral bone"—is the one feature that distinguishes the ceratopsians from all other dinosaur groups.

Psittacosaurus was one of the smallest and most primitive of 418 the ceratopsians. It lacked the

well-developed frill and horns that were typical of more advanced ceratopsians, yet, along with the hard keratinous beak, it had the characteristic skull shape of a ceratopsian. It also featured, in common with later ceratopsians, the high palate and the sharp, slicing teeth with self-sharpening edges that were well suited to nipping off and shredding hard plant matter.

Psittacosaurus's hindlimbs were longer—although only slightly—than its forelimbs, which suggests that it could have moved about in an upright position for short distances. It may have done so to avoid attacks from predators or to forage in low-hanging tree branches.

Some skeletons of Psittacosaurus contain fossils of gastroliths—stomach stones that helped the animal to break down plant matter inside its stomach.

Psittacosaurus lived in the early Cretaceous of Mongolia and other parts of Asia about 90 million years ago. It had relatively long forelimbs and large, grasping hands.

The main text gives a detailed word portrait of each dinosaur, its appearance, and lifestyle.

The illustrated banding at the top of the page is a visual pointer to indicate that the page is part of the Guide to Dinosaurs.

The main illustration provides a vivid recreation, based on the latest scientific research, of how the animal would have looked in life.

Therapoda/Aves

Therapoda/Aves

ceratopsidae

scientific theory. When Charles Darwin published *On the Origin of Species* in 1859, a perceived weakness in his argument was the lack of intermediate animals in the fossil record. If animals and plants have been changing from one form to another through time, as evolution suggests, then at least there should be some fossils of organisms intermediate in structure between different groups.

The first skeleton of *Archaeopteryx* was found just two years after the publication of Darwin's theory and, as predicted, it displayed a mix of bird and dinosaur features. Clearly, evolutionists argued, it was an intermediate form between the two groups.

Since its initial discovery there has been some debate about what kinds of reptiles *Archaeopteryx* is most closely related to. We now recognize that its closest relatives are some theropod dinosaurs, such as the dromaeosaurs and the oviraptors. In fact, the skeleton of *Archaeopteryx* is so theropod-like that one specimen found without feathers was for many years mistakenly identified as the small theropod *Compsognathus*.

As well as the seven complete or partial *Archaeopteryx* skeletons, some isolated feathers have also been found. The superb state of preservation of the delicate, hollow bones and fine feathers was possible only because the fossils occurred in a very fine-grained limestone called lithographic limestone. This was quarried in Bavaria in order to make lithographic printing plates. It was during these quarrying procedures that the specimens of *Archaeopteryx*, as well as thousands of other important fossils, were recovered.

The tail of the Humboldt Museum specimen (above) clearly reveals the very fine lines of the barbs coming off the shaft of the feathers. All seven of the known Archaeopteryx specimens were found preserved in lithographic limestone quarried in Bavaria, Germany (left).

361

oceratops

toh-SAIR-uh-tops

FIELD NOTES

First-horned face
10 feet (3 m)
Late Cretaceous
Mongolia; China; Canada
American Museum of Natural History, New York, USA; Paleontological Museum, Moscow, Russia; Academy of Science, Ulan Baatar, Mongolia

skull showing frill

imal
s of

dant
am
ongolia
ween
these
at
nal that lived

discovered
ratops. These
found, and
ed. Another
atops skeleton
aptor. Whether

or not this find represents an actual act of predation, *Velociraptor*, along with the larger theropods such as *Tarbosaurus*, would almost certainly have been among the main predators on a small plant-eater such as *Protoceratops*.

Thanks to the large number of complete skulls of *Protoceratops* that have been found, scientists have been able to distinguish differences between males and females. In adult males, the frill was more erect and there was a more prominent bump on the snout. This suggests that males used the larger frill, as well as the more protuberant snout bump, as a device to attract females. The bump may also have been used in fights between rival males.

Protoceratops seems to have moved about on all fours. The size and weight of its head and jaws would probably have made a bipedal stance impossible. It would have fed mainly on low-growing plant matter, which it broke off with its beak and then chewed with the many teeth in the back of its mouth.

419

Support illustrations go "behind the scenes" to highlight aspects of a dinosaur's anatomy or skeletal features.

Support photographs on many pages show details of particular features, pictures of researchers who were associated with the discovery of the dinosaur, areas where the dinosaur fossils were found, or exhibits and reconstructions in museums.

Eoraptor

EE-oh-RAP-tuh

Perhaps the most primitive of all known dinosaurs, *Eoraptor* was found in late Triassic deposits—in the harsh badlands of the Ischigualasto Basin in north-western Argentina—in 1993. It was discovered by Paul Sereno, Fernando Novas, and their colleagues in the same set of deposits as *Herrerasaurus*, another relatively primitive dinosaur. *Eoraptor* was discovered almost accidentally—one member of the team was on the verge of discarding a rock before noticing that it contained teeth. A closer examination revealed that this rock contained a complete skull. This led to further examination of the site and the unearthing of a complete skeleton of *Eoraptor*, a hitherto unknown dinosaur almost 230 million years old.

From the evidence of this skeleton, we can be fairly confident that *Eoraptor* was a bipedal predator and a very primitive relative of the theropods. It ran mainly on its hindlimbs but may have walked on all fours from time to time. Although it had five fingers on its hand, the

FIELD NOTES

■ Dawn thief

🦖 3 feet 3 inches (1 m)

■ Late Triassic

■ North-western Argentina

🏛 Not on display

fifth finger was very small. Like other theropods, *Eoraptor* had thin-walled, hollow bones in its arms and legs and stood on feet dominated by the three middle toes. However, unlike in other theropods, the first toe may have helped to support *Eoraptor* when it was walking.

Eoraptor's serrated teeth indicate that it was a meat-eater and the grasping hands on the end of the forelimbs suggest that it was capable of handling prey almost as large as itself. Although we cannot accurately reconstruct this animal's predatory behavior, it seems to have been a very active, fast-moving hunter that preyed upon a range of lizard-sized animals, including some warm-blooded ancestors of today's mammals.

This X-ray photograph shows Eoraptor's skull being held by the hand of Paul Sereno, the paleontologist whose team discovered this dinosaur in Argentina.

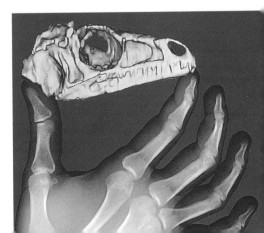

Herrerasaurus

huh-RARE-uh-SAW-rus

N amed after Victorino Herrera, a goat farmer who in 1963 found the skeleton of this dinosaur in the schigualasto Basin in north-western Argentina, *Herrerasaurus* is one of the oldest of known dinosaurs. It was not until 1988, however, when North American Paul Sereno and Argentinian Fernando Novas, and their team of paleontologists, found a more complete skeleton of *Herrerasaurus*, that this dinosaur was finally described.

Sereno's and Novas's description showed that *Herrerasaurus* was a very primitive theropod. As with other theropods, its bones were hollow and thin-walled, its teeth were serrated, and both its upper and lower jaws had a joint that allowed the mouth to open widely while the dinosaur was feeding.

Herrerasaurus's hand had long, sickle-shaped claws and an opposable thumb, which made this hand a formidable weapon for attacking and grabbing prey. Such a hand foreshadowed those of later theropods. However, unlike the hands of other theropods (except that of *Eoraptor*),

FIELD NOTES

■ Herrera's reptile

🦖 6 feet 6 inches (2 m)

■ Late Triassic

■ North-western Argentina

🏛 Instituto Miguel Lillo, Tucumàn, Argentina; Field Museum, Chicago, USA

hindlimb and foot bones

Herrerasaurus's hand had five fingers. The hand differed from *Eoraptor*'s in that the fifth finger was reduced to a single bone (the metacarpal) and was probably covered in tissue. Although the third finger—and not the second as in other theropods— was the longest, all of the first three fingers were very long. Slightly more advanced theropods lost the fifth finger entirely, and in later theropods the fourth finger also disappeared, producing the three-fingered hand we see in today's birds. We can catch a glimpse of the process of evolution by comparing the hands of *Eoraptor*, *Herrerasaurus*, and *Coelophysis* with those of later theropods.

Like *Eoraptor*, *Herrerasaurus* was probably a swift-moving, bipedal predator. As *Herrerasaurus* was about twice the size of *Eoraptor*, it may well have included its smaller contemporary in its prey. Larger predators no doubt hunted both *Herrerasaurus* and *Eoraptor*. These early dinosaurs occupied a small, though significant, niche in the world of 230 million years ago, representing about one-twentieth of all animals alive at that time.

347

Coelophysis

SEE-loe-FIE-sis

long S neck and head in attack positions

FIELD NOTES

■ Hollow form

🦖 10 feet (3 m)

■ Late Triassic

■ North America

🏛 American Museum of Natural History, New York, USA; Carnegie Museum, Pittsburgh, USA; Museum of Northern Arizona, Flagstaff, USA; New Mexico Museum of Natural History, Albuquerque, USA; Smithsonian Institution, Washington DC, USA; Denver Museum of Natural History, Denver, USA

from Ghost Ranch represented adult animals only about 5 feet (1.5 m) long. The remains of some of the smallest specimens were found inside the rib cages of larger *Coelophysis*. This led to a theory that these dinosaurs gave birth to live young. What now seems most likely, however, is that *Coelophysis* was a cannibalistic animal that included members of its own species in its diet.

Most theropod hands had three fingers. The most primitive known theropods, however, had more than three. *Coelophysis* had four fingers on each hand, but the fourth digit was extremely small and may have been invisible in a living animal.

We cannot be certain why so many skeletons turned up in a fairly restricted area at Ghost Ranch. However, geologists think it likely that this region, like tropical regions today, was prone to seasonal wet and dry cycles. It is possible that a whole herd of *Coelophysis* died during a particularly harsh dry season and was buried rapidly during a flood at the beginning of the ensuing wet season.

When Edward Drinker Cope described *Coelophysis* in 1881, his description was based on only a few fragments he found in late Triassic sediments in New Mexico. Thanks, however, to a treasure trove of more than 100 skeletons of various sizes that a team of paleontologists discovered in 1947 at Ghost Ranch in northern New Mexico, *Coelophysis* is now one of the best known of all nonavian dinosaurs. It is also one of the most primitive of known theropods.

Like most other basal theropods, *Coelophysis* was relatively small. Many of the specimens

Plateosaurus

PLAY-tee-oh-SAW-rus

Many skeletons of *Plateosaurus*—which is the best known of the prosauropods—have been found in the south of Germany, as well as in France and Switzerland. A harmless plant-eater with numerous small, pointy teeth, all of uniform size and shape, *Plateosaurus* roamed in herds around the northern part of Laurasia during the late Triassic. It was one of the first of the large dinosaurs.

Plateosaurus had stout limbs that supported the considerable weight of the animal as it walked on all four legs. As with other prosauropods, *Plateosaurus*'s hind legs were stronger than the front ones and were able to take the weight of the creature when it reared up, either to reach higher branches for food, or possibly to defend itself against attack—a particularly large claw on each thumb would have been an effective weapon in such a circumstance. Its long tail would have acted as a counterbalance to the long, thick neck.

FIELD NOTES

◼ Flat lizard

🦖 26 feet (8 m)

◼ Triassic

◼ Western Europe

🏛 American Museum of Natural History, New York, USA; Senckenberg Nature Museum, Frankfurt, Germany; State Museum of Natural History, Stuttgart, Germany

Small ridges of bone around *Plateosaurus*'s mouth supported cheek pouches that could have held a mouthful of leaves while the front teeth went on stripping more leaves from a tree branch. The cheeks also served to prevent food from falling out of the mouth while the animal chewed, breaking the plant matter down into a mush that it could then swallow.

In at least one instance—near the German town of Trossingen—a herd of *Plateosaurus* appear to have been killed in a flash flood. The floodwaters buried the skeletons together in a jumbled mass. From this remarkable deposit paleontologists have been able to reconstruct what a herd of *Plateosaurus* probably looked like. It would have included animals of different ages—from very young to very old—that found safety in numbers as they moved about in search of food.

Paleontologists once thought that prosauropods such as *Plateosaurus* were the ancestors to those later giants of the Jurassic, the sauropods. Now, however, they are recognized as a separate group in their own right.

skull

349

Riojasaurus

ree-OH-juh-SAW-rus

Although *Riojasaurus* was a heavily built animal, with four robust legs and a bulky body, its front legs were particularly short. As a result, its head came close to the ground and the dinosaur could graze on low-growing plants. Thanks to its long, flexible neck, however, *Riojasaurus* could also reach up high into tree branches to gather more varied and enticing food.

Some paleontologists believe that sauropods such as *Riojasaurus* evolved their long necks in order to reach the ever-dwindling supplies of food as the world dried out at the end of the Triassic. As feed plants at ground level became scarce, plant-eaters that could reach up into the trees would have had a distinct advantage—and the further they could reach up, the greater that advantage would be.

FIELD NOTES

■ *La Rioja lizard*

🦕 *33 feet (10 m),*

■ *Late Triassic*

■ *La Rioja, Argentina*

🏛 *San Miguel de Tucumán Museum, Argentina*

Early finds of *Riojasaurus* were headless, and sharp, pointed teeth were often found with the skeletons. This led many to conclude that these dinosaurs were meat-eaters. We now know, however, that they were plant-eaters of elephantine proportions. The pointed teeth probably belonged to meat-eating dinosaurs that fed on the freshly dead carcasses, shedding teeth as they feasted.

Dinosaurs such as *Riojasaurus*, which had a small head at the end of a long neck, needed to minimize the weight of the neck so that they could hold the head high without a great effort. *Riojasaurus* was one of the first long-necked dinosaurs with hollow bones in its neck.

Unlike other prosauropods, *Riojasaurus* and its close relatives were probably not capable of rearing up on their back legs. The sheer weight of these very solid animals kept them firmly anchored on all four legs.

Members of this group, which included *Roccosaurus* and *Vulcanodon* lived as far afield as South America, South Africa, and England. In the late Triassic, there was no Atlantic Ocean to separate the landmasses.

complete skeleton

Ceratosaurus

seh-RAT-oh-SAW-rus

detail showing bony
head and snout

FIELD NOTES

■ Horned lizard

🦖 20 feet (6 m)

■ Late Jurassic

■ North America

🏛 American Museum of Natural History, New York, USA; Dinosaur National Monument, Jensen, Utah, USA; Smithsonian Institution, Washington DC, USA

Ceratosaurus gets its name from the blunt horn at the end of its snout. It is the best known of several therapods that had such a horn. Ceratosaurus also had two other short, thin horns, one over each eye.

We do not know for certain what function these three horns served. They may have worked as social signaling devices, allowing individual Ceratosaurus to recognize each other cross the floodplains on which they lived. They may also have distinguished male and female animals, but as we have only a few specimens of this dinosaur, we do not know if the sexes had differently shaped horns. The horns do not seem large enough to have played a role in defense.

Ceratosaurus is known mainly from the late Jurassic Morrison Formation of the western United States. The Morrison Formation is famous for its incredible diversity of sauropods (including Apatosaurus and Brachiosaurus) as well

as for the more common theropod Allosaurus. Teeth gathered from the Tendaguru Formation of Tanzania, which is roughly the same age as the Morrison, may represent a very large species of Ceratosaurus. This, however, has not yet been firmly established.

Throughout most of the 20th century, paleontologists grouped all large theropod dinosaurs, including Ceratosaurus, under the heading "carnosaurs." Smaller theropods were classed as "coelurosaurs." Beginning in the 1980s, however, scientists began to pay much greater attention to evolutionary relationships when classifying dinosaurs. Scientists now think that Ceratosaurus was only distantly related to most other large theropods, such as Allosaurus and Tyrannosaurus. It was probably more closely related to the smaller-bodied coelophysoids and to the Abelisauridae (including Abelisaurus)—an intriguing group that lived throughout the Southern Hemisphere during the Cretaceous period. Ceratosaurus certainly demonstrates the danger in classifying dinosaurs solely on the basis of size, as large body size evolved numerous times within the theropods.

351

Dilophosaurus

die-LOH-foh-SAW-rus

Fossils of *Dilophosaurus*, one of the earliest of the large theropods, were first found in 1942, in early Jurassic sediments in Arizona. More recently, remains of this animal have also been discovered in China. It was a close relative of *Coelophysis*, and, like this earlier dinosaur, had four fingers on each hand. The fourth finger, however, was very small and probably had no function.

A pair of paper-thin crests ran along the top of *Dilophosaurus*'s snout, projecting behind the eyes. It is these crests that gave the dinosaur its name. Other coelophysoids, such as *Syntarsus*, a contemporary of *Dilophosaurus*, had similar crests, but those of *Dilophosaurus* were larger and more extensive. We do not know what function these crests may have served, but we can tell that they were very delicate structures that had shallow pits and holes which may have served as air sacs. These pits are more apparent in the Chinese specimen, but they are also clearly noticeable in the specimens from Arizona. It is possible that *Dilophosaurus* utilized its crests as a signaling device—to distinguish one species from another. Alternatively, it may have used them as a way of telling males and females apart.

FIELD NOTES

- Two-crested lizard
- 20 feet (6 m)
- Early Jurassic
- Arizona, USA; China
- Museum of Paleontology, University of California, Berkeley, USA; Royal Tyrrell Museum, Alberta, Canada

skull showing crest

Dilophosaurus had long, sharp, pointed teeth. However, it probably did not use its teeth to kill its victims; some scientists have suggested that its jaws were not strong enough to enable it to fed on live prey. It probably used its clawed hands and feet to kill its victims and then fed on their carcasses. It may also have scavenged animals killed by other predators.

In the movie *Jurassic Park*, *Dilophosaurus* is depicted with an extendable frill—rather like that of an Australian frillnecked lizard—and also as spitting poison. However, imagination has ruled the day here for there is no evidence for either of these features. The idea that it spat venom may have resulted from suggestions that, as it seemed unable to attack live animals with its teeth and jaws, it killed them with poison. However, as no living crocodylian or bird is known to use venom in this way, there can be no reason to suppose that *Dilophosaurus* did.

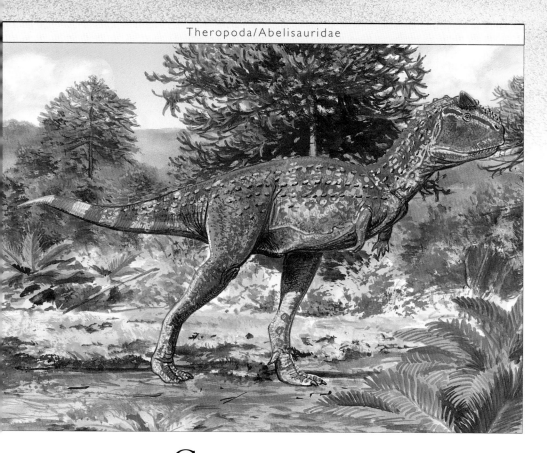

Carnotaurus

KAR-noh-TAW-rus

FIELD NOTES

■ Meat bull

🦖 16 feet (5 m)

■ Early Cretaceous

■ Argentina

🏛 Los Angeles County Museum, USA; Argentine Museum of Natural Sciences, Buenos Aires, Argentina

This bizarre-looking theropod, distinguished by a pair of sharp, stout horns that projected outward above its tiny eye sockets, is known from only a single specimen, discovered by the Argentinian paleontologist José Bonaparte in the Patagonia region of Argentina. The skeleton was almost complete, and there were also some impressions of skin. The whole specimen was protected by a large concretion—a section of very hard rock. These skin impressions, which covered much of the body and part of the skull, had a "pebbly" texture and were described as being reptilelike. However, the scales on the skin did not overlap as they do on some reptiles.

Bonaparte concluded that *Carnotaurus* belonged to a hitherto unknown theropod family—the Abelisauridae. Other specimens of abelisaurids—probable relatives of the Jurassic ceratosaurids—were later discovered in Argentina, India, and Madagascar. This provides us with evidence that these landmasses were connected at some point during the Jurassic or Cretaceous, as no positively identified abelisaurids have been found anywhere else, including mainland Africa.

Like all other abelisaurids, *Carnotaurus* had sharp, serrated teeth that seemed to splay out from the sides, giving the face a rather triangular look when seen from the front. One feature in which *Carnotaurus* resembled the tyrannosaurids was in its forelimbs, which seem ridiculously short for an animal of its size. But the construction of the forelimb was different from that of the tyrannosaurids. In tyrannosaurids, the bones in the lower limb (the radius and the ulna) were shorter than the bone in the upper limb (the humerus), but they were still substantial bones, and the hand had only two functional fingers. In *Carnotaurus*, the radius and ulna were so short that they looked almost like wrist bones rather than lower arm bones, and the hand had four digits.

skull showing lower jaw and teeth

353

Allosaurus

AL-oh-SAW-rus

Abundant remains of *Allosaurus* have been found in the late Jurassic Morrison Formation of the western United States. In many ways this was the quintessential large theropod. It had a deep skull and jaws filled with flattened, serrated teeth. The jaws were capable of bending outward in the middle, thus enlarging the mouth. The head was perched on a slender but strong neck. The dinosaur's forelimbs were heavily muscled and ended in powerful, three-fingered grasping hands with enormous claws. Its hind-limbs were massively constructed to support the animal's weight but were proportioned for rapid

FIELD NOTES

■ Other lizard

🦖 39 feet (12 m)

■ Late Jurassic

■ Western United States

🏛 American Museum of Natural History, New York, USA; Smithsonian Institution, Washington DC, USA; Cleveland Museum of Natural History, USA; Los Angeles County Museum, USA; Denver Museum of Natural History, USA; Utah Museum of Natural History, Salt Lake City, USA; Dinosaur National Monument, Jensen, Utah, USA; University of Wyoming Geological Museum, Laramie, USA; Science Museum of Minnesota, St. Paul, USA

movement. *Allosaurus* stood on only the middle three of its five toes. This formidable predator was probably one of the major threats to any ornithopods, stegosaurs, or sauropods that lived near it. An earlier name for *Allosaurus*—*Antrodemus*, or the "nightmare dragon"—reflects its predatory dominance.

Most specimens of *Allosaurus* are less than 26 feet (8 m) long, but some larger ones, including "Big Al," which is on display at the University of Wyoming, are close to 40 feet (12 m)—and scientists think that Big Al was still immature when it died.

Allosaurus belonged to the allosauroids, a group that peaked in the late Jurassic and early Cretaceous and was found in most parts of the world. This group includes *Giganotosaurus*, *Carcharodontosaurus*, and *Sinraptor*. By the late Cretaceous, however, other large theropods such as the tyrannosaurids and abelisaurids had replaced the allosauroids in most places.

An Allosaurus *and* Camptosaurus *battle in this reconstructed "death scene" from 140 million years ago.*

Eustreptospondylus

yoo-STREP-toh-SPON-dee-lus

One of the larger predators of its time, *Eustreptospondylus* was a powerfully built ceratosaurian that displayed the usual theropod pattern of long, birdlike hindlimbs and quite short arms. The skull was moderately deep—unlike those of more lightly built ceratosaurians such as *Dilophosaurus* and *Coelophysis*—but it lacked the prominent horns of the larger, and later, *Ceratosaurus*. Although not closely related and somewhat smaller, *Eustreptospondylus* was similar in its proportions to the more widely known carnosaur *Allosaurus*.

A number of herbivorous dinosaurs are known from the same habitat, including early kinds of ankylosaurs (*Sarcolestes*), stegosaurs (*Lexovisaurus*), and the sauropods *Cetiosaurus* and *Cetiosauriscus*. *Eustreptospondylus* presumably preyed on plant-eaters smaller than itself, such as the ankylosaurs and stegosaurs, but it may also have attacked the larger cetiosaurs.

Eustreptospondylus is known mostly from a single fragmented, but well-preserved, skull and skeleton that were discovered in the mid-19th century in Oxfordshire, England.

FIELD NOTES

- Well-curved vertebra
- 23 feet (7 m)
- Middle Jurassic
- Oxfordshire, Buckinghamshire, UK
- Oxford University Museum, Oxford, UK

Some bones that normally fuse in adult theropods, such as the postfrontal and postorbital in the skull, and the sacral vertebrae, remain unfused in this individual, so it is thought to have been immature when it died. For many years, this was the best-known of the large carnivorous dinosaurs from the whole of Europe.

Before many complete dinosaur skeletons were known and paleontologists began to realize their sheer diversity, nearly all the remains of large Jurassic carnivores in Europe were assumed to belong to *Megalosaurus*, which was one of the first dinosaurs to be named. It was more than a century—not until 1964—before Dr. Alick Walker recognized inconsistencies with other megalosaur material and the "*Megalosaurus*" skeleton from Oxford was finally given a new name, *Eustreptospondylus*. As well as this skeleton, some limb bones from another site are included in the same species.

skull showing weight-saving holes

355

Megalosaurus

MEG-uh-loh-SAW-rus

Despite its very familiar name and its association with the early scientific study of dinosaurs, we know surprisingly little about *Megalosaurus*. William Buckland's description of *Megalosaurus* in the early 1820s was the first formal description of a nonavian dinosaur. It was based on a collection of fossil fragments—including parts of a leg, a shoulder, a hip, and a jaw—that gave only scant clues to the appearance of the living animal. Since then, remnants of a wide variety of large theropods— including *Tyrannosaurus* and *Allosaurus*—have been mistakenly identified as belonging to *Megalosaurus*, and there are probably still some misidentifications waiting to be corrected.

The available evidence—which relies largely on fossils of the jaws, teeth, and hip bones—suggests that *Megalosaurus* was a massive animal. Estimates of its length

saw-edged teeth

FIELD NOTES

- Great lizard
- 30 feet (9 m)
- Middle Jurassic
- England
- Natural History Museum, London, UK

and height vary, though it probably grew 30 feet (9 m) long, stood up to 10 feet (3 m) high, and weighed about 1 ton (1.02 t). Like other theropods, it was probably a bipedal predator with a grasping, three-fingered hand. However, even this is still speculative, as no remnants of *Megalosaurus*'s forelimbs have yet been found. Huge, inward-pointing footprints found in trackways in southern England, and generally attributed to *Megalosaurus*, suggest that this bulky creature walked, probably slowly and rather clumsily, on two legs. Its powerful hinged jaws and its curved, serrated teeth indicate that it was a strong predator that probably fed on a wide variety of animals, including large sauropods.

Megalosaurus's evolutionary relationships are still something of a mystery to paleontologists. The few analyses that have been done place *Megalosaurus* outside the groups that include the allosaurids and the coelurosaurs and closer to an assemblage that includes the spinosaurids (including *Spinosaurus* and *Baryonyx*). However, even this possible close relationship with spinosaurids has not yet been definitively established.

Ornitholestes

ORN-ith-oh-LESS-tees

FIELD NOTES

- Bird robber
- 6 feet 6 inches (2 m)
- Late Jurassic
- North America
- American Museum of Natural History, New York, USA

In 1900 a group of paleontologists from the American Museum of Natural History discovered the first—and so far the only—remains of the small theropod *Ornitholestes* in the famous Jurassic dinosaur beds at Bone Cabin Quarry in Wyoming in the western United States. Three years later, Henry Fairfield Osborn, who would later become the director of the American Museum of Natural History, described and named the dinosaur. He called it *Ornitholestes* because he speculated that it would probably have been a good bird catcher. This idea was further reinforced some time later when the famed painter of dinosaurs Charles Knight depicted *Ornitholestes* grabbing the earliest known bird, *Archaeopteryx* (which was contemporary with *Ornitholestes* but from a different part of the world), with its hands. There is no evidence to suggest that *Ornitholestes* did catch birds; at the same time, there is no reason to suppose that it did not. The uncertainty is compounded by the fact that Osborn seems to have mistakenly associated a hand from the same site, but from a different species, with the skull and partial skeleton of *Ornitholestes*. This hand had three fingers with sharp, curved claws, which seemed well suited to holding small prey.

The single existing specimen of *Ornitholestes*—consisting of an almost complete skeleton and a complete, but compressed, skull—is on display in New York at the American Museum of Natural History. Some reconstructions of this dinosaur show *Ornitholestes* with a thin horn at the tip of its snout, right above the nose. No horn is evident on the existing specimen, but as the tip of the snout is damaged, it is quite possible that there was a horn there.

skull showing possible horn

Ornitholestes eating a salamander.

Compsognathus

KOMP-sog-NAY-thus

Compsognathus, one of the smallest known nonavian dinosaurs, was about the size of a present-day turkey. Its name refers to the delicacy of its jaw, but its fossils suggest that it was a delicate animal overall. There are two known skeletons of Compsognathus. The first, found in 1859, was from the late Jurassic lithographic limestone of southern Germany. This animal lived alongside Archaeopteryx. It lay on a slab of stone, its legs nearly perfectly preserved and its last meal, a lizard, in its ribcage. The second skeleton was found near Canjuers, in France.

Compsognathus may have had two-fingered hands. While the French specimen had three metacarpal bones (bones in the palm), it is not clear that all three had phalanges (finger bones) attached. Some paleontologists argue that this small, agile predator was—like tyrannosaurids, but unlike any other theropods—effectively two-fingered. However, because the hands

arm and leg skeletal structure

FIELD NOTES

■ Delicate jaw

🦖 6 feet (2 m)

■ Late Jurassic

■ South-western Germany; France

🏛 Bavarian State Museum of Paleontology, Munich, Germany

were not intact, it is possible that the phalanges from the third fingers were either not found or not identified. The hand of the French specimen is too poorly preserved to provide any conclusive evidence. What is certain is that Compsognathus's closest relative, Sinosauropteryx, possessed three-fingered hands.

Compsognathus has long played a central role in studies of bird origins. Because it was found in the same deposits as Archaeopteryx, and was roughly the same size, it provides an easy comparison between a primitive coelurosaur and a primitive bird. During the 19th century, similarities between these two fossils were often cited as evidence of the dinosaur–bird link. Like Sinosauropteryx, Compsognathus may well have had short, fibrous, featherlike structures on its body, although there is no direct evidence of these in the known specimens.

Michael Crichton's novels Jurassic Park and The Lost World gave Compsognathus a venomous bite that allowed groups of these fictional dinosaurs to overwhelm larger prey. It is much more likely, though, that this small animal confined itself to catching small victims and that it used its clawed fingers and toothy jaws to do so.

358

Cryolophosaurus

KRY-oh-loh-foh-SAW-rus

The geologist David Elliott discovered the remains of *Cryolophosaurus*, a moderately large theropod, in 1990. They were high up near the summit of Mount Kirkpatrick in the central Transantarctic Mountains—what would have been, in the early Jurassic, the eastern side of the great southern continent of Gondwana. The remains, which were mixed with those of a prosauropod dinosaur, a pterosaur, and a tritylodont mammal-like reptile, were excavated the following year by Dr. William Hammer. The teeth of two other kinds of theropods that were found in the sediment enclosing the remains suggest that the dead *Cryolophosaurus* had been gnawed by scavengers.

Cryolophosaurus is known from much of the skull and from a partial skeleton. It is particularly significant because it is the only relatively well-preserved theropod that has been found from the eastern part of Gondwana.

FIELD NOTES

■ Frozen-crested lizard

🦖 24 feet (7.5 m)

■ Early Jurassic

■ Central eastern Antarctica

🏛 Not on display

The features that most clearly distinguished *Cryolophosaurus* were the unusual backward-sweeping crests of bone that protruded on the top of the skull above the eyes. Small horns were situated adjacent to these crests. The crests were formed by the lacrimal bone of the skull, which extended along the entire width of the head from between the eyes. As with other crested theropods, such as *Dilophosaurus*, the crests may have been used during courtship displays or as a means of signaling to other members of the species.

Despite displaying a number of primitive theropod features, *Cryolophosaurus* was closely related to the allosauroids of the later Jurassic period. Its serrated, dagger-like teeth were clearly those of a carnivore.

A side-on view of the incomplete, but reasonably well-preserved, skull of Cryolophosaurus *that was discovered in 1990 in Antarctica.*

Archaeopteryx

AH-kee-OP-tuh-rix

FIELD NOTES

■ Ancient feather

🦖 2 feet (60 cm)

■ Late Jurassic

■ Bavaria, Germany

🏛 Humboldt Museum, Berlin, Germany; Natural History Museum, London, UK

Possibly the most important fossil ever found, *Archaeopteryx* combines two rare features. First, five of the seven known specimens are preserved with impressions of the delicate feathers that it had in life. This is remarkable because generally feathers would not be strong enough to withstand the rigors of fossilization. Second, because *Archaeopteryx* displays an unambiguous mix of characters from two linked groups of animals—the birds and the dinosaurs—it is a classic and rare example of an organism on an evolutionary pathway between the two.

Archaeopteryx was a small birdlike dinosaur, about the size of a present-day crow. Its skeleton was very similar to that of some theropod dinosaurs—it had a four-toed foot with the first toe reversed to the other three; a three-fingered hand;

The wing of a bat (top) is made of skin and supported by all five fingers. The wings of Archaeopteryx (center) are made of feathers and arranged similarly to those of a modern pigeon (right).

a long, straight, bony tail; teeth; curved claws on the hands and feet; and a large crest on the upper arm bone.

The most strikingly birdlike feature of *Archaeopteryx* is the feathers. Not only did this dinosaur clearly have feathers, but these were arranged in exactly the same pattern as feathers on the wings of modern birds. Furthermore, they were shaped just like the flight feathers of birds that are capable of powered flight. From this we can probably assume that *Archaeopteryx* was capable of powered flight, but it may have been restricted to short bursts from tree to tree. The areas for attaching the muscles that modern birds need for flight are not very well developed in *Archaeopteryx*. It may well have used both flapping and gliding to move through the air. It probably fed on insects that it found in trees or caught in flight.

Archaeopteryx played a pivotal role in the acceptance of evolution as a mainstream

scientific theory. When Charles Darwin published *On the Origin of Species* in 1859, a perceived weakness in his argument was the lack of intermediate animals in the fossil record. If animals and plants have been changing from one form to another through time, as evolution suggests, then at least there should be some fossils of organisms intermediate in structure between different groups.

The first skeleton of *Archaeopteryx* was found just two years after the publication of Darwin's theory and, as predicted, it displayed a mix of bird and dinosaur features. Clearly, evolutionists argued, it was an intermediate form between the two groups.

Since its initial discovery there has been some debate about what kinds of reptiles *Archaeopteryx* is most closely related to. We now recognize that its closest relatives are some theropod dinosaurs, such as the dromaeosaurs and the oviraptors. In fact, the skeleton of *Archaeopteryx* is so theropod-like that one specimen found without feathers was for many years mistakenly identified as the small theropod *Compsognathus*.

As well as the seven complete or partial *Archaeopteryx* skeletons, some isolated feathers have also been found.

The tail of the Humboldt Museum specimen (above) clearly reveals the very fine lines of the barbs coming off the shaft of the feathers. All seven of the known Archaeopteryx specimens were found preserved in lithographic limestone quarried in Bavaria, Germany (left).

The superb state of preservation of the delicate, hollow bones and fine feathers was possible only because the fossils occurred in a very fine-grained limestone called lithographic limestone. This was quarried in Bavaria in order to make lithographic printing plates. It was during these quarrying procedures that the specimens of *Archaeopteryx*, as well as thousands of other important fossils, were recovered.

Anchisaurus

an-kee-SAW-rus

Anchisaurus was the first dinosaur to be discovered in America. In 1818, a small skeleton of *Anchisaurus* was found in Connecticut sandstone that was being quarried as a building material. At first it was thought to be the remains of a human and it was not until 1885 that it was recognized as a dinosaur. It is one of the many dinosaurs first described by the American paleontologist Othniel Charles Marsh.

Anchisaurus had a particularly small head and, by prosauropod standards, was very small—it was hardly bigger than a present-day sheep. Its body, however, was longer, in terms of its overall size, than those of other prosauropods. Its relatively long neck and tail, strong back leg and weaker front legs, and the defensive banana-shaped claw on its thumb were, however, typical prosauropod features. And, like most of its relatives, *Anchisaurus* could rear up on its back legs when necessary, although it would have spent most of its time walking around on all four legs. It had rounded teeth that were well

FIELD NOTES

■ Near lizard

🦕 8 feet (2.4 m)

■ Early Jurassic

■ Connecticut, Massachusetts, USA

🏛 South African Museum, Cape Town, South Africa

suited to grinding up the plants that it ate.

Anchisaurus lived in New England at a time when the Atlantic Ocean was just beginning to form. This area was a rift valley, similar to the Great Rift Valley in Africa today. The warm, wet climate was favorable to the growth of huge fern forests. These forests would have afforded *Anchisaurus* protection from predators and provided the dinosaur with an abundant supply of food.

Other small prosauropods that were closely related to *Anchisaurus* have been found in Europe and Africa, while fragments from Australia and Asia may also belong to very close relatives.

Anchisaurus
footprints in
Connecticut
sandstone

Massospondylus

MASS-oh-SPON-die-lus

A medium-sized prosauropod, *Massospondylus* had a particularly small head. Its upper jaw jutted out beyond the bottom jaw and its mouth contained a variety of tooth types. According to some researchers, these features indicate that *Massospondylus* was a carnivore. They claim that it used its sharper front teeth to rip flesh from its victims and its flatter rear teeth to chew up this flesh. Most paleontologists, however, argue that *Massospondylus* was a plant-eater—like all its close relatives. The fact that grinding stones have been found from the stomach of *Massospondylus* lends support to this view. It has also been suggested that the lower jaw may have had a horny beak to bring it into line with the protruding upper jaw, but there is no physical evidence for this in the fossils.

Massospondylus was lightly built for a prosauropod, and much of its length was accounted for by its long neck and tail. Its body was similar in size to that of a large dog. The enlarged sickle-like thumb claws seen in

the enlarged thumb claw

other prosauropods were particularly well developed. We do not know exactly how *Massospondylus* used these huge claws. They would no doubt have made formidable weapons when the animal reared up on its hind legs to ward off predators—or perhaps to fight rival member of the species for mates. They may also have been useful in gathering food. The English anatomist and paleontologist Sir Richard Owen first described *Massospondylus* in 1854. He based his description—and named the dinosaur—on the evidence of several large vertebrae. Although the earliest specimens were from southern Africa, in present-day South Africa, Lesotho, and Zimbabwe, it was later found in Arizona in the United States. Such a transatlantic distribution was possible in the early Jurassic, when the continents were joined and dinosaurs could cross what are now wide oceans.

FIELD NOTES

- Massive vertebra
- 16 feet 6 inches (5 m)
- Early Jurassic
- Arizona, USA; South Africa; Zimbabwe; Lesotho
- South African Museum, Cape Town, South Africa; National Museum of Zimbabwe, Harare, Zimbabwe

Brachiosaurus

BRAK-ee-oh-SAW-rus

O ne of the tallest known dinosaurs to walk on all fours, *Brachiosaurus* towered at least 52 feet (16 m) into the forest canopy, where its small head could strip leaves from tree branches. Some finds in the western United States suggest that *Brachiosaurus* may have been able to reach much higher. If that is true, it would have been one of the largest of all dinosaurs.

Unusual among the long-necked sauropod dinosaurs, *Brachiosaurus* had front legs that were much longer than its hind legs and a relatively short tail. The long forearms pushed the shoulders high above the level of the hips, producing the characteristic slope of its back. All of its four legs were straight, columnlike pillars that could support the stupendous weight of the animal.

Compared to the rest of the animal, *Brachiosaurus*'s head was rather small, and its mouth must have been kept busy collecting enough food to keep the creature alive. Some estimates suggest that, if *Brachiosaurus* were warm-blooded, it would have needed 440 lb (200 kg) of food a day; if, however it were

FIELD NOTES

■ Arm lizard

🦕 82 feet (25 m)

■ Late Jurassic to early Cretaceous

■ Colorado, Wyoming, Utah, USA; Portugal; Algeria; Tanzania

🏛 Humboldt Museum, Berlin, Germany; The Field Museum of Natural History, Chicago, USA

skull

cold-blooded, it would have needed much less. Its digestion was aided by grinding stones, or gastroliths, that helped to stir the soupy mixture of food that was constantly brewing in its vatlike foregut.

Its sheer size would have protected an adult *Brachiosaurus* from predators, but juveniles would have been vulnerable to attack. It is likely that this dinosaur formed small herds, where the larger individuals could protect smaller animals from the menace of predators. Specimens of *Brachiosaurus* were recovered by German paleontologists from the rich fossil grounds of Tendaguru in modern-day Tanzania in Africa. One of these specimens is a prized display in the Humboldt Museum in Berlin. An American specimen, collected from Colorado, is the largest mounted dinosaur skeleton in North America. It is on display in the entrance hall of the Field of Natural History Museum in Chicago.

Camarasaurus

KAM-uh-ruh-SAW-rus

skull

When the noted American paleontologist Edward Drinker Cope described *Camarasaurus* in 1877, he was obviously impressed by the hollow, box-like vertebrae in the neck. This feature made the neck much lighter and easier for the animal to carry, and it is this characteristic that gave the animal its name: "Chambered lizard."

Camarasaurus was a stout, compact sauropod with a relatively short neck and short tail. The front legs were slightly shorter than the back legs. The head can be described as a bubble of air encased by thin struts of bone. Huge holes for the nostrils, eye sockets, and other skull cavities made the skull as light as possible but strong enough to withstand the bite forces from the doglike snout.

The teeth were stumpy but strong—much more robust than the peglike teeth of other sauropods—and the jaws had a powerful bite. *Camarasaurus* was probably capable of dealing with a wider variety of tough plants, thereby giving it an advantage in mixed forests.

Camarasaurus is the most common sauropod in North America. A number of complete skeletons have been recovered, as well as numerous partial skeletons and isolated bones. Several specimens can be seen in the rocks of the Dinosaur National Monument in Utah.

As a result of these fossil finds, we now know more about *Camarasaurus* than we know about any other of the sauropod dinosaurs.

FIELD NOTES

- Chambered lizard
- 59 feet (18 m)
- Late Jurassic
- Colorado, Utah, Wyoming, USA; Portugal
- Natural History Museum, London, UK; Peabody Museum of Natural History, New Haven, Connecticut, USA; National Museum of Natural History, Smithsonian Institution, Washington DC, USA; Carnegie Museum of Natural History, Pittsburgh, Pennsylvania, USA

A Camarasaurus *fossil in the Devil's Canyon Science and Learning Center, Fruita, Colorado.*

365

Diplodocus

dip-LOH-doh-kus

It is mainly thanks to the efforts of one man, the American industrialist Andrew Carnegie, that *Diplodocus* is now so well known throughout the world. Carnegie, a wealthy man, had a particular interest in dinosaurs, and in the late 1800s and early 1900s, he contributed liberally to the cause of paleontology. He financed many expeditions and excavations and filled his own museum—the Carnegie Museum of Natural History in Pittsburgh—with fossil skeletons from all over the United States. When his paleontologists discovered a complete skeleton of *Diplodocus*, he was so impressed with its size that he commissioned the making of 11 copies of the entire skeleton, which he gave to major museums around the world.

For many years *Diplodocus* was the longest of all known dinosaurs—it is still longer than any other dinosaur that we know from a complete skeleton. Most of its immense length is accounted for by its very long neck and

FIELD NOTES

■ Double beam

🦖 90 feet (27 m)

■ Late Jurassic

■ Wyoming, Colorado, Utah, USA

🏛 Natural History Museum, London, UK; National Museum of Natural History, Paris, France; Carnegie Museum of Natural History, Pittsburgh, Pennsylvania, USA

One fossil trackway seems to show only the front footprints of Diplodocus. It must have been floating in water and pushing itself along with its front feet.

particularly long tail. It had a small, horselike head, and its peglike teeth were restricted to the front of its mouth. *Diplodocus* used these teeth to strip large quantities of leaves from trees. It then swallowed them whole to await further processing in its huge gut. The last third of its tail was very thin and whiplike. The vertebrae at the end of the tail were reduced to simple rods.

Diplodocus's front legs were shorter than its back ones. This meant that its hips were higher than its shoulders and that its back sloped forward. It is possible that *Diplodocus* could rear up on its hind legs so that the head could reach high into the forest canopy in search of leaves. However, in the opinion of some paleontologists, this dinosaur, given its size and body structure, could not have held this pose for very long. It may well have reared up, but only in order to push over trees so that it could feed on their leaves closer to ground level.

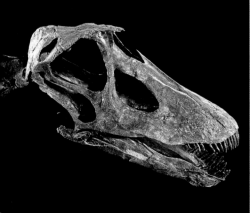

This Diplodocus *skull, recovered from the Morrison Formation in Wyoming, USA, clearly shows the sharp front teeth that this dinosaur used to grasp and shred its diet of leaves and plants.*

Diplodocus's curious name—meaning "double beam"—is derived from the bones on the underside of its tail, known as chevrons. In most other dinosaurs, these are simple V-shaped elements, but in *Diplodocus* they are like side-on Ts, projecting both to the front and back.

Scientists used to think that, like other sauropods, *Diplodocus* was a lumbering beast that dragged its tail along the ground. The 1980s, however, brought a renaissance in our understanding of dinosaurs. It dawned on people that, although there was ample fossil evidence of sauropods walking across ancient landscapes, there were never any impressions of tails on the ground. The only conclusion was that the tail must have been held high. However, how an animal of *Diplodocus*'s weight and dimensions managed this remained a mystery. To hold

aloft a tail that measured almost half its entire body length must have cost *Diplodocus* a huge effort. The answer was in the tail's structure. Examination of *Diplodocus* skeletons revealed that massive tendons ran from the back of the head right to the tip of the tail. This tendon balanced the tail against the weight of the neck and enabled it to be held out straight behind.

This rethinking about *Diplodocus*'s posture was followed by a revision in museum displays. Around the world, copies of the *Diplodocus* skeleton that Andrew Carnegie had given out decades earlier were taken apart and reconstructed in what was now considered to be their authentic pose.

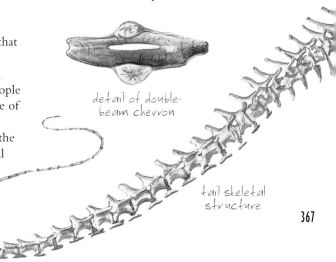

detail of double-beam chevron

tail skeletal structure

367

Barosaurus

BAH-roh-SAW-rus

Visitors to the American Museum of Natural History are greeted by a startling sight. Towering above them is a skeleton of a female *Barosaurus* protecting its infant from the menacing approach of an *Allosaurus*. The reconstruction is, of course, based to some extent on guesswork, but it is a striking depiction of how life might have been 150 million years ago.

Barosaurus is very similar to *Diplodocus*, to which it is closely related. Both were very long animals with relatively compact bodies that supported long necks and tails. Like *Diplodocus*, *Barosaurus* had front legs shorter than the hind ones. As a result, its back sloped gently forward. The neck projected around 30 feet (9 m) in front of the shoulders.

It was once thought that sauropods' long necks allowed them to feed high in tree tops. However, as the neck vertebrae would not have allowed much up-and-down movement, but would have permitted a considerable sweep from side to side, we now think that these dinosaurs fed much closer to the ground on ferns and cycads.

Despite more than a century of searching and the recovery of five partial skeletons, some of them almost complete, the head and the tip of the tail of *Barosaurus* have never been found. The only clues we have about the head are a few bones from the skull collected in Tanzania and comparisons with close relatives such as *Diplodocus*. These indicate that *Barosaurus* had a horselike skull with a long snout and teeth restricted to the very front of the mouth.

The dramatic mother and infant reconstruction of Barosaurus in the American Museum of Natural History in New York.

Mamenchisaurus

mah-MEN-kee-SAW-rus

The longest neck of any animal known to us from any time belonged to *Mamenchisaurus*. It made up half the animal's total length. Reaching perhaps 49 feet (15 m) long, this incredible structure was supported by 19 vertebrae—no other dinosaur had as many neck vertebrae. Because these vertebrae were hollow—and in places the bone was as thin as egg shells—the neck was very light. Long bony struts running between the neck vertebrae would have limited its flexibility, and many reconstructions of *Mamenchisaurus* show it with the neck held straight as a ramrod. Some of these bony struts would have overlapped three or four vertebrae.

Only a few skull fragments have been found of *Mamenchisaurus*. These suggest that it had a relatively short snout with robust, blunt teeth in the front and along the sides of the mouth. The particularly heavy teeth give a clue to its diet. These teeth could have dealt with the coarser, harder parts of plants and would have been especially good for shredding cycads and other fibrous fronds.

Although superficially *Mamenchisaurus* looks similar to North American sauropods such as *Diplodocus* and *Apatosaurus*, we now think that it was part of a group of sauropods unique to Asia. By the late Jurassic, the early Atlantic Ocean had become wide enough to restrict the flow of animals between North America and Europe and, although Europe and Asia were connected by land, there were deserts and mountain ranges that would have restricted the movement of large land animals from east to west.

Mamenchisaurus was described in 1954 by the Chinese paleontologist Chung Chien Young. Young is regarded as the founder of Chinese vertebrate paleontology, and he named many dinosaurs, including *Lufengosaurus* and *Omeisaurus*.

FIELD NOTES

■ Mamen Brook lizard

🦖 82 feet (25 m)

■ Late Jurassic

■ Szechuan, Gansu, Xinjiang, China

🏛 Beijing Natural History Museum, Beijing, China; Museum Victoria, Melbourne, Australia

A long neck allowed Mamenchisaurus to feed from tree tops.

Apatosaurus

uh-PAT-oh-SAW-rus

FIELD NOTES

■ Deceptive lizard

🦖 69 feet (21 m)

■ Late Jurassic

■ Colorado, Utah, Wyoming, Oklahoma, USA; Baja California, Mexico

🏛 American Museum of Natural History, New York, USA; Carnegie Museum of Natural History, Pittsburgh, Pennsylvania, USA; Dinosaur National Monument, Jensen, Utah, USA

Apatosaurus is not as well known as *Brontosaurus*, but they are one and the same animal. *Brontosaurus* was well known because several relatively complete skeletons of gigantic proportions had been found and displayed worldwide. However it was later found that the fossils named *Brontosaurus* were identical to those of *Apatosaurus*, which had been named earlier. Under the rules of nomenclature, an animal can have only one name—the first published one. *Brontosaurus,* therefore, is no more.

Apatosaurus was as long as a tennis court, though still shorter, but more heavily built, than its close relative *Diplodocus*. Proportionally, its neck was shorter than that of

Former reconstructions were wrongly given the skull of Camarasaurus *(top). The correct skull is shown at left.*

Diplodocus, and the body was not as compact, but it still had similar robust, columnlike legs. Its front legs were shorter than its back ones. As was the case with *Diplodocus*, its head had a long snout, and all the teeth were at the front of the mouth. As with other sauropods, we can only puzzle at how such a small head and tiny mouth could have gathered enough food to feed an immense body. Compounding this problem, the teeth could not chew the food. They merely crushed it to extract as much energy as possible. It seems that *Apatosaurus* and its kin spent long periods stripping leaves and other food from plants, which they swallowed whole. These vast quantities of food were held in a vatlike foregut where they stewed up, breaking down to release their nutrients. At least some sauropods swallowed stones that were held in the foregut to help stir and grind the food further.

Despite its huge size, *Apatosaurus* was controlled by a tiny brain no bigger than a cat's. This brain made up just 0.001 percent of the animal's 25-ton (25.5 t) mass. This compares with 2.5 percent in humans.

Scutellosaurus

skoo-TELL-oh-SAW-rus

Scutellosaurus is one of the earliest representatives of the armored dinosaurs (the thyreophorans) that would later include such giants as *Stegosaurus* and *Ankylosaurus*. However, compared to some of its later relatives, *Scutellosaurus* was small and lightly armored. Along its back and extending onto the base of the tail were rows of small bony "shields" embedded in the skin. Some of these shields were flat, while others were pitched, like little roofs. The largest shields formed two rows that ran along the middle of the back.

skin detail

Spread across the back, the shields formed a protective armored layer that would have defended the animal from attacks by such meat-eating dinosaurs as *Dilophosaurus*, with which it shared its early Jurassic world. *Scutellosaurus* would also have been reasonably fleet of foot and therefore able to escape predators by weaving its way through tangled undergrowth.

FIELD NOTES

- Small-shield lizard
- 4 feet 4 inches (1.3 m)
- Early Jurassic
- Arizona, USA
- Museum of Northern Arizona, Flagstaff, Arizona, USA

Scutellosaurus fossils are found in the Kayenta Formation of Arizona. These rocks were deposited by periodic floods that spilled over river banks, but there are also the remains of sand dunes in the area, indicating that *Scutellosaurus* probably lived in an arid or semi-arid environment.

The ancestors of *Scutellosaurus* were bipedal. This feature is reflected in *Scutellosaurus* in its well-developed hind legs. However, the increased weight of the long body resulting from the armored shield would have forced *Scutellosaurus* onto all fours for most of the time. It seems likely that it could still have rocked back onto its hind legs to make a speedy getaway or to reach up and gather the higher plants that it fed on. The long tail, which made up about half its total body length, would have helped it to maintain its balance during such maneuvers.

The teeth of *Scutellosaurus* were leaf-shaped and had serrated edges. These would have been used to snip off leaves, but the lack of wear on the teeth indicates that this dinosaur did not chew its food before swallowing it.

371

Stegosaurus

STEG-oh-SAW-rus

One of the most famous dinosaurs of all, *Stegosaurus* is striking, first of all for its great size. Even more remarkable, though, are the bizarre plates and spikes that stand up, almost vertically like battlements, along each side of its backbone, from the neck right down to the middle of the tail. These plates have fascinated both paleontologists and the general public since the first specimen was described by Othniel Charles Marsh in 1877.

Marsh originally thought that these plates lay flat on the back, forming a kind of roof—hence the animal's name. Later finds showed that the plates stood upright, and that the name, which nevertheless has endured, is a misnomer. There has been ongoing debate about whether the two rows were paired, mirror images of each other, or whether they were staggered and alternating. More recent finds confirm that the plates were staggered.

But what function did these plates serve? They could have been for protection, making it difficult for an attacker to bite into its back. Channels in the plates that held blood vessels suggest that they

FIELD NOTES

■ Roofed lizard

29 feet 6 inches (9 m)

■ Late Jurassic

■ Colorado, Utah, Wyoming, USA

🏛 American Museum of Natural History, New York, USA; Dinosaur National Monument, Jensen, Utah, USA; Senckenberg Nature Museum, Frankfurt, Germany; Denver Museum, Colorado, USA

may have helped to regulate the animal's body temperature. By turning its plates broadside to the sun, *Stegosaurus* could have warmed its blood; by standing with them edge-on to the sun, it could have cooled the blood down. Yet another possibility is that the plates were a display feature. Perhaps, when flushed with blood, they could change color, to impress a potential mate or to scare off a predator. It is possible that the plates in fact performed all of the above functions.

The spikes at the end of the tail—which could be more than 3 feet (1 m) long—would

skeleton clearly showing plates and spikes

have been a very effective weapon. Swinging on the end of the long, flexible tail, they could strike a lethal blow to a potential predator. Most species of *Stegosaurus* had four tail spikes, but one species may have had eight. Unlike the staggered plates, the spikes were arranged in matched pairs.

tip of tail spikes

dorsal plates

lower back plates

The bulk of *Stegosaurus*'s weight was carried by the heavily built hind legs. These were almost twice as long as the front legs. The shorter front legs meant that *Stegosaurus* walked with its shoulders, neck, and head close to the ground.

Stegosaurus had a small head with a long snout. Its teeth were small, but wear that is evident on fossil remains indicates that the animal ground the upper and lower teeth against each other to cut and slice food. All *Stegosaurus*'s teeth were at the rear of its mouth. At the front it had a horny beak that could cut through plants as effectively as a pair of shears. Recent research suggests that *Stegosaurus* had cheek pouches in which it could hold food that was waiting to be chewed.

Not surprisingly, given the interest it has aroused, *Stegosaurus* has generated a number of dinosaur myths. One of them was the "two brain" theory. A prominent cavity in *Stegosaurus*'s hips suggested to some researchers that this "pocket" housed an auxiliary brain that

controlled the rear end of the animal. We now understand that this area housed a bundle of nerves (a ganglion) that acted as a relay center that passed on messages from the brain. It has also been suggested that the animal could move its plates—that it could "wag" them as part of a display to mates or predators. But there are no scars on the skeletons that would mark the places where the huge muscles required to move the plates could have been anchored. Some paleontologists have suggested that *Stegosaurus* could stand up on its hind legs, either to reach higher food or to intimidate rivals and attackers. This now seems unlikely.

As with most dinosaurs, ideas about *Stegosaurus* have been revised in recent decades. We once thought, for example, that it dragged its tail along the ground. Now we think that it held this tail high.

ferns that *Stegosaurus* may have eaten

Fabrosaurus

FAB-roh-SAW-rus

FIELD NOTES

■ Fabre's lizard

3 feet 3 inches (1 m)

■ Early Jurassic

■ Southern Africa

🏛 Not on display

A contemporary of *Heterodontosaurus*, and sharing the same southern African environment in the early Jurassic, *Fabrosaurus* lived on tough plant food, such as ferns and cycads. It was one of the earliest ornithischian (bird-hipped) dinosaurs. Later ornithischians included such diverse forms as the ankylosaurs, ceratopsians, and hadrosaurs. In the much smaller *Fabrosaurus*, however, we can get a glimpse of the sort of animal from which these larger herbivorous dinosaurs evolved.

Fabrosaurus had small front limbs and very long hindlimbs and was therefore well adapted for standing and running on its back legs. Its long tail balanced the body in front of the hips, and the back legs were held vertically under the body and worked like those of a mammal, rather than like the sprawling limbs of most reptiles.

Its small size and light body structure—it had hollow bones and hollow places in the skull—meant that *Fabrosaurus* would probably have been able to flee from a predator at considerable speed.

The hands of *Fabrosaurus* had four larger fingers and a smaller fifth finger. These digits had claws rather than hooves. This dinosaur probably did not often use its front limbs for walking; they would have served mainly for holding foliage while the animal ate.

Compared to those of its later relatives, the small, pointed teeth of *Fabrosaurus* were quite simple in their structure and its jaw action was strictly up and down, allowing it to slice or cut up plant matter. *Fabrosaurus* was not as well adapted for grinding and chewing food as was *Heterodontosaurus* or the later ornithischians.

In the early 1970s, *Fabrosaurus* became widely known as *Lesothosaurus*, after the country where the first fossils were found. Both names are still in use, which is a source of some confusion. However, as *Fabrosaurus* was the first to be used, it should have precedence.

complete skeleton

Dryosaurus

DRY-oh-SAW-rus

Ornithopods of the Jurassic were small to medium-sized herbivorous dinosaurs that relied on their agility and speed, rather than size, armor, or weapons to defend themselves against predators. *Dryosaurus*, was a common and widespread ornithopod of the late Jurassic, and was fairly typical of this group.

The Yale University paleontologist and fossil-hunter Othniel Charles Marsh named *Dryosaurus* in 1894. Thanks to extensive finds of adult, juvenile, and baby specimens, it is one of the best understood of all dinosaurs. It stood, and ran, on its long hind legs, its body counterbalanced by its long tail. The anatomy of *Dryosaurus*'s feet and legs shows that this dinosaur was an adept runner. According to some estimates, it could reach speeds of more than 25 miles per hour (40 km/h)—fast enough to outrun most predators.

The long shin bones in its hindlimbs helped Dryosaurus *to move at considerable speeds when it needed to escape from danger.*

FIELD NOTES

- Oak lizard
- 10–13 feet (3–4 m)
- Late Jurassic
- Europe (England, Romania); Africa (Tanzania); North America (Colorado, Utah, Wyoming)
- Carnegie Museum, Pittsburgh, USA

cycads

Dryosaurus was not only quick across the ground, it was a fast grower, too. Analyses of the bone tissue of baby, juvenile, and adult *Dryosaurus* reveal that it grew continuously. There is no sign that growth slowed down during a cold winter or a harsh dry season as it does, for example, with many present-day reptiles. Many researchers believe that only warm-blooded animals can grow continuously, so the growth pattern of *Dryosaurus* has fueled speculation that dinosaurs, or at least the small ones, were warm-blooded. Whatever the metabolic rate of *Dryosaurus*, its babies did not take long to grow to adult size.

As with many ornithopods, the fast growth rate was facilitated by an efficient battery of cheek teeth, which were thickly enameled and could grind up plant matter almost without pausing. Before grinding up this plant material, *Dryosaurus* cropped it with a sharp, horny beak—it had no teeth at the front of its mouth.

Tyrannosaurus

tie-RAN-oh-SAW-rus

Tyrannosaurus rex exemplifies every image conjured by the word "dinosaur": massive, ferocious-looking, and extinct. It is the only dinosaur that is commonly known by both its generic and specific names. Despite this, fossil evidence for this animal was surprisingly scant until quite recently, and it was only in the 1990s that important gaps in our understanding of Tyrannosaurus were filled in.

Tyrannosaurus was one of the largest of predatory dinosaurs. Some individuals measured as much as 42 feet (12.8 m) long and were up to 13 feet (4 m) tall at the hip, with a skull more than 5 feet (1.5 m) long. By any standards, Tyrannosaurus was a tremendous animal.

This giant was also one of the last of the nonavian dinosaurs. All the Tyrannosaurus skeletons have come from the latest Cretaceous deposits of the United States and Canada, although some researchers regard Tarbosaurus, a large tyrannosaurid from slightly older deposits of Mongolia, to have been a form of Tyrannosaurus.

FIELD NOTES

■ Tyrant lizard

🦖 40 feet (12 m)

■ Late Cretaceous

■ North America (Canada, USA)

🏛 American Museum of Natural History, New York, USA; Carnegie Museum, Pittsburgh, USA; Field Museum, Chicago, USA; University of California Museum of Paleontology, Berkeley, USA; Los Angeles County Museum of Natural History, Los Angeles, USA; Museum of the Rockies, Bozeman, USA; Denver Museum of Natural History, Denver, USA; Tyrrell Museum, Alberta, Canada; Senckenberg Museum, Frankfurt, Germany

Like other tyrannosaurids, Tyrannosaurus had two very short forelimbs and only two functional fingers on each hand. The forelimb of the longest known specimen was hardly any longer than the forearm of an adult human. The front teeth were D-shaped in cross-section, and each cheek bore 12 rather robust teeth, which were shaped more like serrated bananas than the steak-knife shapes seen in most other theropods.

Henry Fairfield Osborn first described Tyrannosaurus in 1905

Parts of a Tyrannosaurus-like skeleton, discovered in the Gobi Desert in Mongolia.

Teeth of Tyrannosaurus.

from fossils that
Barnum Brown
had collected in
Montana. More fossils
that came to light in the
course of the next few years
allowed Osborn to amplify
his interpretation.

Over the years new discoveries were made,
including several more complete specimens.
However, no hand came to light until 1990,
when John Horner, of Montana State University, published an account of a *Tyrannosaurus*
specimen from Montana in which the hand
was preserved. This discovery confirmed the
presence of only two digits—something that
scientists had suspected by analogy with other
tyrannosaurids. Osborn's reconstructions showed
a three-fingered hand—a sensible guess, as all
other theropods known at the time of his
reconstructions had three fingers.

In 1991, a group of commercial fossil-hunters
discovered "Sue" on a ranch in South Dakota.
It is perhaps the largest and most complete
Tyrannosaurus skeleton ever found. A legal battle
over ownership followed this discovery. Finally
the courts awarded the fossil to the rancher, who
in 1997 sold it at auction to the Field Museum
in Chicago. Researchers have high hopes for
Sue and expect it will significantly extend our
knowledge of *Tyrannosaurus*. A high-resolution

computed tomographic (CT)
study of the skull is giving
scientists access to what were
hitherto inaccessible internal
details of this dinosaur's head.

The predatory habits of
Tyrannosaurus are still unclear.
Some people, presuming it was
a slow mover and citing the smallness
of its forelimbs, maintain that it must have
been solely a scavenger. Others, who claim
that it was an active hunter, point to the
strength of this animal's teeth and the evidence
that bite marks found on *Triceratops* bones seem
to have been made by *Tyrannosaurus* teeth.

*In May 2000, nine years after it was discovered, the
reconstructed skeleton of "Sue" finally went on display
at Chicago's Field Museum.*

377

Albertosaurus

al-BERt-oh-SAW-rus

Albertosaurus was a slightly older relative of *Tyranno-saurus* and was very similar in appearance. *Tyrannosaurus* lived between 70 and 65 million years ago; *Albertosaurus* roamed the North American late Cretaceous world between 75 and 70 million years ago. Like *Tyrannosaurus*, *Albertosaurus* was a huge biped with two-fingered hands and thin plates of bone covering some of its skull openings. *Albertosaurus* was smaller and had a narrower skull than *Tyrannosaurus*, and its eyes looked more to the side. In front of its eyes, *Albertosaurus* had a pair of small, blunt horns, which it may have used for sexual display. Perhaps because its body was smaller, *Albertosaurus*'s skeleton was more gracile than that of *Tyrannosaurus*. It was also a faster mover than its more cumbersome successor.

Searches of fossil-bearing beds in south-western Alberta have yielded some amazing discoveries, including a number of nearly complete skeletons of juvenile *Albertosaurus*. While adult *Albertosaurus* had rather stout bones

FIELD NOTES

- Alberta lizard
- 26 feet (8 m)
- Late Cretaceous
- South-western Canada
- Royal Tyrrell Museum, Alberta, Canada; Royal Ontario Museum, Toronto, Canada; American Museum of Natural History, New York, USA; Field Museum, Chicago, USA

Fossil foot from the American Museum of Natural History

tearing chunks of flesh with powerful jaws

in their hindlimbs, the hindlimbs of very young specimens were remarkably slender. In some cases, several *Albertosaurus* skeletons—at different stages of growth—have been found together. On the strength of these finds, some researchers have suggested that these dinosaurs traveled as family groups. However, there is no conclusive evidence that skeletons found together were from animals that actually lived together as a group.

Albertosaurus is the best known of all tyrannosaurids. Recent discoveries include wishbones—a feature it shared with other advanced theropods as well as with birds. The study of many museum specimens of *Albertosaurus* has enabled us to fill in the gaps in our knowledge of *Tyrannosaurus*.

Giganotosaurus

JIG-an-oh-toh-SAW-rus

When the discovery of *Giganotosaurus* was announced to the world in 1995, the news caused a sensation. For almost all of the 20th century, paleontologists had believed *Tyrannosaurus* to have been the largest of all theropods. However, *Giganotosaurus*, from the late Cretaceous of southern Argentina, proved to be at least as large. In their description of *Giganotosaurus*, Argentinian paleontologists Rodolfo Coria and Leonardo Salgado reported a length of 41 feet (12.5 m)—longer than some *Tyrannosaurus* skeletons.

The first *Giganotosaurus* discovery consisted of an incomplete skeleton. Paleontologists could tell that this new dinosaur was an allosauroid—it was obviously closely related to animals like *Allosaurus* and, especially, *Carcharodontosaurus*—but because the material was so incomplete, the estimates of its size were far from conclusive. Since 1995, a number of new discoveries have been made. In one case, several *Giganotosaurus* skeletons were found

FIELD NOTES

■ Giant southern lizard

🦖 43 feet (13 m)

■ Late Cretaceous

■ Patagonia, Argentina

🏛 Academy of Natural Sciences, Philadelphia, USA

close together. This suggests that these animals may have moved around in groups.

In early 2000, a team of Argentinian and Canadian paleontologists announced the discovery of a well-preserved, slightly younger relative of *Giganotosaurus* in Argentina. The newly discovered animal closely resembled *Giganotosaurus* but was larger—it may have been as long as 46 feet (14 m). Early press reports suggested that it was longer than the largest known *Tyrannosaurus*.

Giganotosaurus lived alongside a number of giant sauropods. Some of these had bony plates on their backs, which may have afforded them some protection against attack from above. Only one theropod in the region was large enough to attack them from above—that predator was *Giganotosaurus*.

Size comparison of three theropods, from back to front: Giganotosaurus, Cretaceous; Torvosaurus, Jurassic; Coelophysis, Triassic.

379

Baryonyx

BARE-ee-ON-icks

T he first part of *Baryonyx*—
one of the best known of
British dinosaurs—to be
discovered was a huge claw. In
1983, the amateur fossil-hunter
William Walker happened upon it
in a clay pit in Surrey, in southern
England. A group of paleontologists from the Natural History
Museum in London later visited the site and
uncovered most of the skeleton of *Baryonyx* in
the early Cretaceous deposits.

Baryonyx and its relatives, the spinosaurids,
were very unusual theropods. The claw that led
professional paleontologists to the scene was
from the hand. Although saurischian dinosaurs
ancestrally had enlarged thumb
claws, they were nowhere
near as large as those
on *Baryonyx* and
other spinosaurids.
Baryonyx had very
powerful forelimbs,
so much so that
scientists initially
assumed that it was
capable of walking on all
fours—an idea that has since
380 been discounted. While all

FIELD NOTES

■ Heavy claw

🦕 30 feet (9 m)

■ Early Cretaceous

■ Southern England

🏛 Natural History Museum,
London, UK

theropods had strong, grasping
hands, *Baryonyx*'s hands were
more massive. This suggested
that it made extensive use of
them for grappling with prey.

Some researchers have
suggested that *Baryonyx* was
principally a fish-eater and that
it used its hands to grasp fish and
its long, slender snout to snap prey out of the
water. Living crocodiles that specialize in
catching fish often have similarly slender jaws.
Baryonyx's teeth were less flattened than the
teeth of most theropods and they were very
finely serrated. This feature, coupled with the
thin jaws, has led many scientists to conclude
that *Baryonyx* was not capable of attacking and
bringing down large animals, and so lends
support to the theory of a fish diet.

The fact that *Iguanodon* bones were
found in *Baryonyx*'s ribcage may
suggest that it set its sights on
larger prey. However, there
is no way of knowing
whether *Baryonyx* killed
this *Iguanodon*. It may
simply have happened
upon, and scavenged, an
Iguanodon corpse.

*This huge fossil claw of the carnivorous
dinosaur Baryonyx was discovered in
a Surrey clay pit in 1983.*

Suchomimus

soo-koh-MY-mus

skull showing elongated jaw

Suchomimus was one of the largest known spinosaurid dinosaurs. It was discovered in Niger by a party led by Paul Sereno from the University of Chicago and was first described in 1998. Shortly before that, Dale Russell and Philippe Taquet announced the discovery of a very similar dinosaur from another part of Niger, but the fossils that were described by Sereno were much more complete and allowed for a more detailed reconstruction.

Like other spinosaurids, *Suchomimus* had a low and slender snout, much the same as that of a modern crocodile—hence this animal's name. *Suchomimus* and other spinosaurids had a secondary palate. The nasal passages stretched all the way to the back of the mouth cavity, as they do in living mammals and crocodiles, and did not open within the mouth, as they do in many living reptiles and most dinosaurs. This was possible because the nasal openings were set back from the tip of the snout. We do not know why these animals evolved these features, but the secondary palate may have strengthened the narrow snout or even allowed *Suchomimus* and its relatives to keep the tip of the snout submerged while they hunted for fishes.

Like *Baryonyx*, *Suchomimus* had pointed teeth with very fine serrations. Also like *Baryonyx*, it had massively built forelimbs and a large sickle-like claw on each thumb. The nature of the teeth, together with its slender, gracile snout, suggests that *Suchomimus* may have been unable to catch large prey and so fed largely on fishes—possibly either picking them up with its muzzle or grasping the slippery creatures with its bladelike claws.

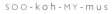

This reconstruction of Suchomimus was for some time at the National Geographic Center in Washington DC, USA.

Spinosaurus

SPY-noh-SAW-rus

FIELD NOTES

■ Spiny lizard

🦖 33 feet (10 m))

■ Late Cretaceous

■ North Africa (Egypt, Niger)

🏛 Not on display

At the beginning of the 20th century, the German paleontologist Ernst Freiherr Stromer von Reichenbach, of the University of Munich, began a series of expeditions to Egypt, where he discovered, in the western Sahara, the remains of several formerly unknown late Cretaceous dinosaurs. The most significant of these finds was *Spinosaurus*. It was so named because of the tall spines on its vertebrae. Stromer collected some fragmentary remains of *Spinosaurus* in 1912 and described the dinosaur in 1914.

Unfortunately, the 20th century has been unkind to this dinosaur. Stromer's specimen of *Spinosaurus*, as well as those of several other Egyptian dinosaurs he described, were destroyed in bombing raids during World War II, and much of the important information concerning specific localities was lost during both the world wars. Fortunately for science, however, Stromer

internals of the sail

published an extensive and meticulously detailed description of the material he collected.

In many ways, *Spinosaurus* resembled a number of other theropods, such as *Allosaurus*. Unlike other spinosaurids, however, it had neural spines on its vertebrae. What set *Spinosaurus* apart was the great size of these spines, which rose more than 5 feet (1.5 m) high and formed a "sail" over the back, much like that of the Permian mammal relative *Dimetrodon*. We now suspect that these spines were connected by skin, but we have no clear idea of how the sail functioned. It could have helped *Spinosaurus* to radiate or absorb heat and thus regulate its body temperature. It may also have served as a social signaling device or as a means of sexual display.

Like other spinosaurids, *Spinosaurus* had a long, slender snout. Its teeth, which in many ways resembled those of present-day crocodiles, were unlike those of most theropods. They were conical and straight, rather than curved, and the serrations were very fine.

Gallimimus

GAL-ee-MY-mus

FIELD NOTES

■ Chicken mimic

🦕 10 feet (3 m)

■ Late Cretaceous

■ Mongolia

🏛 Paleontological Museum, Mongolian Academy of Sciences, Ulan Baatar, Mongolia

Gallimimus was one of the largest and best known of the ornithomimid, or "bird mimic," dinosaurs. It was one of the important discoveries made by joint Polish–Mongolian expeditions to Mongolia during the 1960s, and skeletons from several stages of this dinosaur's growth have been collected. The largest were animals 10 feet (3 m) long. More than two-thirds of this length, however, is accounted for by the neck and tail.

As with other ornithomimids, *Gallimimus*'s skull was relatively small and its jaws were toothless. Its limbs and neck were very long and slender, and the bones of the palm—the metacarpals—were particularly long. Even the metacarpal for the thumb was much longer than in most theropods, where the thumb is usually markedly shorter than the other digits.

We think that *Gallimimus*, and the other ornithomimids, were capable of great bursts of speed—they were certainly depicted as fast-moving animals in the film *Jurassic Park. Galli-mimus*'s arms had considerable freedom of movement, although they do not seem to have been able to reach very high. To compensate for this, its long neck could probably have stretched down, allowing *Gallimimus* to bring food items from its hands up to its mouth.

This dinosaur probably fed on small animals—including, perhaps, insects—and also possibly on plant matter. Its hands, which were more suited to digging than grasping, may also have scooped up the eggs of other dinosaurs from the soil and then cracked them open with the broad beak at the tip of its long snout.

Mongolian ornithomimids such as *Gallimimus* are typically found along with large tyrannosaurid theropods and duckbills, but not with the horned ceratopsians. North American ornithomimids, on the other hand, are more commonly found with diverse and abundant ceratopsians. This suggests that Asian and North American members of this group lived under different conditions. However, just what these differences were we have yet to discover.

long beak and neck

Struthiomimus

STROO-thee-oh-MY-mus

Picture a plucked ostrich with a long tail stretching stiffly out behind and a pair of human-sized arms with hands with three claws attached to them, and you have a mental image of *Struthiomimus*. This long-necked, long-legged theropod is, along with the Mongolian *Gallimimus*, the most well known member of the ornithomimid, or "bird mimic," dinosaurs.

Struthiomimus was roughly the same size as a modern ostrich and could probably reach a similar top speed of about 50 miles per hour (80 km/h) on flat, open ground. With its small and very lightly built skull, toothless beak, and very large eyes, it was strikingly similar to today's flightless birds. The three large, clawed, forward-facing toes on each of its feet were typical of theropod feet, but they were also very birdlike. Ornithomimids lacked true feathers and may have had naked

skin. However, some juvenile specimens display a partial covering of downlike filaments similar to those discovered on other birdlike dinosaurs.

The lightly built head and toothless beak imply that *Struthiomimus* could not have killed or eaten large animals, but it would certainly have been able to pursue and swallow small reptiles and large insects. With the long, hooklike claws on its hands it could either have dug small animal prey out of shallow burrows or pulled succulent leaves and primitive fruits down from low trees. By stretching its neck, it could have reached reasonably high into tree branches. Gastroliths (gizzard stones) that have been found at the front of the rib cage of *Struthiomimus* skeletons indicate that plant material was an important component of its diet. This unusual theropod was, therefore, either omnivorous or entirely herbivorous.

First described in 1902, *Struthiomimus* was long known only from a single complete skeleton and several partial skeletons. A number of complete skeletons have recently come to light.

skeleton

Oviraptor

oh-vee-RAP-tuh

FIELD NOTES

■ Egg robber

🦖 10 feet (3 m)

■ Late Cretaceous

■ Mongolia

🏛 American Museum of Natural History, New York, USA; Academy of Science, Ulan Baatar, Mongolia

O*viraptor* was a strange-looking animal, especially for a theropod. It had a short snout, toothless jaws, and a rounded mass of thin bone over its nose, rather resembling a chicken's comb. *Oviraptor* had slender limbs and, like its closest relatives, was probably fast on its feet. Though *Oviraptor* is known only from the late Cretaceous of Mongolia, other *Oviraptor*-like animals are known from the Cretaceous of other parts of Asia and western North America.

This dinosaur was discovered during the 1920s American expeditions to Mongolia. Most of the specimens were found near nests of dinosaur eggs. Because the eggs were thought to belong to *Protoceratops*—a small, common ceratopsian in that region—it was assumed that *Oviraptor* was stealing the eggs. The eggs, however, lacked embryos. When, in the 1990s,

Two species of Oviraptor: *O.* philoceratops *(above) and O.* mongoliensis *(right). Dinosaur crests were very diverse and changed constantly during the animal's lifetime.*

American teams returned to Mongolia, they found more of the same kinds of eggs, including some that contained the delicate skeletons of embryos—but they were embryos of *Oviraptor*, not of *Protoceratops*. Soon after that, more amazing fossils came to light. They were of *Oviraptor* skeletons sitting on nests, with their forelimbs wrapped around the eggs. These were probably skeletons of parents incubating and protecting their own eggs. *Oviraptor*, it would seem, was named for a crime that it did not commit.

Oviraptor was one of the most birdlike of the nonavian dinosaurs. Its ribcage in particular displayed several features that are typical of birds, including a set of processes on each rib that would have kept the ribcage rigid.

Recently a relative of *Oviraptor* was found with a pygostyle—a set of fused vertebrae that would later help support the tail feathers of birds.

385

Troödon

TROO-oh-don

FIELD NOTES

■ Wounding tooth

🦖 10 feet (3 m)

■ Late Cretaceous

■ North-western North America

🏛 Museum of the Rockies, Bozeman, USA

The first fossil of *Troödon* was a single leaf-shaped tooth discovered in 1854 in the Judith River Formation in Alberta, Canada. On the basis of this tooth, Joseph Leidy described and named the animal in 1856. However, Leidy considered *Troödon* to be a lizard and not a dinosaur. Later discoveries of teeth, from the late Cretaceous of Montana, confirmed *Troödon* to be a dinosaur. For some time this dinosaur was thought to be a carnivorous ornithopod—its teeth resembled those of some ornithopods—but eventually it was confirmed to be a small birdlike theropod.

serrated-edged tooth

Thanks to the discovery of a number of sometimes fragmentary skulls and skeletons, we now know that *Troödon* had a long snout. However, instead of the row of long, curved teeth that were typical of most theropods, *Troödon* had a large number of relatively small teeth. Each side of the lower jaw may have had as many as 35 teeth, all of them with large serrations. No other theropod is known to have had so many teeth. The teeth varied in shape, depending on their location in the jaw.

Troödon is famous for the great size of its brain cavity. *Troödon* and other troödontids may have had the largest brains, relative to body size, of any nonavian theropods. This has led many scientists to conclude that *Troödon* and its close relatives were more intelligent than other dinosaurs. Such a belief is based on the observation that in living animals there is a rough correlation between relative brain size and degrees of intelligence. However, as intelligence leaves no trace in the fossil record, this must remain a matter of speculation. *Troödon*'s very large eye sockets have also led some researchers to believe that it may have been a nocturnal animal.

Recent studies suggest that the troödontids were among the closest extinct relatives of birds. They may also have been very closely related to the dromaeosaurids, such as *Deinonychus* and *Velociraptor*. The claw on *Troödon*'s second toe was longer than those on its other toes, but *Troödon* lacked the long "killer" sickle that characterized the dromaeosaurids.

Velociraptor

vel-OSS-ee-RAP-tor

*V*elociraptor is the night-marish villain of the movie *Jurassic Park*. Swift, birdlike and intelligent—as presented on film, it embodies all the dynamic qualities that, until quite recently, dinosaurs were thought to lack.

Although in life *Velociraptor* was most likely a swift-running predator, the real animal—from the late Cretaceous of Mongolia—differs in several significant ways from its cinematic namesake. For one thing, the skull was narrower than was depicted on screen. In fact, the heads of the movie "raptors" more closely resemble that of *Deinonychus*. The tail, too, was different.

Velociraptor was a dromaeosaurid, and dromaeosaurid tails were broomhandle-stiff, not the flexible structures that were seen in the movie. Most important of all is the question of their size. The *Velociraptor* of the late Cretaceous was barely longer than 3 feet (1 m); in the movie, however, it was shown to be the size of a large adult human—and it looked all the more ferocious as a result. It is interesting to note that while *Jurassic Park* was still being filmed, the remains of *Utahraptor*—a previously unknown dromaeosaurid, which was about the same size as those "faked" for the movie, were found in Wyoming.

As with other dromaeosaurids, *Velociraptor* probably used its hooked talon to kill its prey. One celebrated *Velociraptor* skeleton, found in Mongolia in 1971, seems to confirm this theory. *Velociraptor* was entangled with a *Protoceratops* skeleton, the *Velociraptor* foot claw embedded in the *Protoceratop*'s rib cage. A sand dune must have collapsed on the two animals as they were grappling with each other, smothering both and preserving this dramatic scene of predation and disaster for millions of years.

In May 1997 a replica of Velociraptor, as it appeared in the movie Jurassic Park, went on display as part of a special exhibition at the American Museum of Natural History in New York, USA.

387

Deinonychus

die-NON-ee-kus

lthough it was not the first of the dromaeosaurs to be discovered, *Deinonychus*, which was one of the largest of them, was the first to be fully described. After it was described, the dromaeosaurids, which are now improperly known as "raptors," became recognized as some of the most chillingly efficient predators that have ever lived.

Deinonychus was an agile bipedal theropod with large, partly forward-facing eyes, a relatively large brain, and a long, narrow snout lined with recurved, serrated, bladelike teeth. *Deinonychus* was an intelligent, very well-equipped predator that used the three long-clawed fingers on each of its large hands to snatch small prey or to inflict terrible wounds on large animals. It may also have employed its claws as grappling hooks to clamber up on the bodies of larger dinosaurs that it hunted and attacked in packs.

FIELD NOTES

- Terrible claw
- 10 feet (3 m)
- Early Cretaceous
- Montana, Wyoming, Oklahoma, USA
- 🏛 Peabody Museum of Natural History, New Haven, USA

Deinonychus walked, ran, and jumped mainly on the outer (third and fourth) toes of each foot. These toes had long, sharp claws. The first toe was also clawed but this claw was quite short. The claw on the second toe was, by contrast, an extra-large, curved slashing weapon up to 5 inches (13 cm) long that was able to swivel through 180 degrees. *Deinonychus* usually held this claw back off the ground in order to keep the point sharp, loaded, and "cocked" ready to go in for the kill.

Deinonychus's foot was equipped with three sharply clawed toes (right). The "terrible claw" on the second toe of each foot (above) was a highly flexible weapon.

388

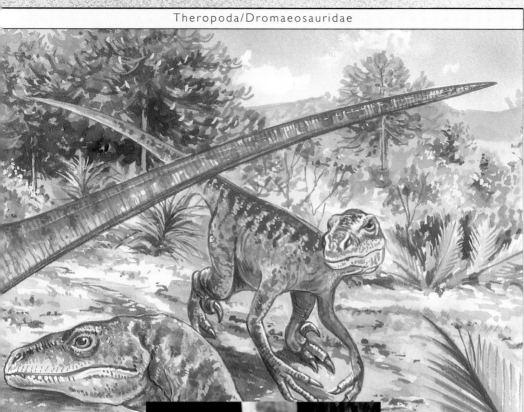

As in many other dinosaurs, the tail of *Deinonychus* was stiffened for about three-quarters of its length by bundles of overlapping bony rods, which, however, were flexible at the base. This stiffening allowed the tail to be controlled by a few large muscles that connected to the hips and hindlimbs. It helped *Deinonychus* to make rapid lunges or to change direction suddenly when running— *Deinonychus* may even have been able to turn around in mid-air while leaping to catch prey. It also prevented the tail from flexing from side to side in time with the limb movements while the animal was running, thus preventing energy from "leaking away" into the tail and helping the dinosaur to run faster and more efficiently.

Grant Meyer and Professor John Ostrom of Yale University first discovered remains of *Deinonychus* in southern Montana in 1964. Excavation at this site produced remarkable finds—nearly complete skeletons of four *Deinonychus*, together with a skeleton 20 feet (6 m) long of the *Iguanodon*-like ornithopod *Tenontosaurus*. When Ostrom described and named *Deinonychus* in 1969, he suggested that *Tenontosaurus* was its preferred quarry and that

This model of Deinonychus shows its predatory features.

this association of predators and prey was evidence for pack hunting behavior in *Deinonychus*. Certainly a single *Deinonychus* would not have been capable of killing a herbivore as large as *Tenontosaurus*, though the death of four *Deinonychyus* in the attack could hardly be considered typical.

If, as seems probable, *Deinonychus* did live in packs and hunted much larger dinosaurs, it must have been similar in behavior and ecology to present-day wolves, hunting dogs, and hyenas. This implies that *Deinonychus* was not only an acrobatic predator with an armory of deadly weapons, but also an endurance athlete—and one that existed, probably, as part of a caring, cooperative social group. Territories near the migration routes or breeding sites of large herbivores could have supported large packs of 20 or more *Deinonychus*, dominated by a few breeding individuals. Non-breeding adults would have defended the territory from rival groups of *Deinonychus* and other carnivores, and they would also have helped to feed the young of the dominant breeding animals.

389

Dromaeosaurus

droh-MAY-oh-SAW-rus

FIELD NOTES

■ Running lizard

🦖 6 feet (1.8 m)

■ Late Cretaceous

■ Alberta, Canada

🏛 Royal Tyrrell Museum, Alberta, Canada

Although until recently *Dromaeosaurus* was known almost exclusively from a skull and some fragmentary bones found by Barnum Brown in 1914, in the Judith River Formation in Alberta, Canada, it has given its name to a family of dinosaurs—the dromaeosaurids. Similar in most ways to its better understood cousins *Deinonychus* and *Velociraptor*, *Dromaeosaurus* was a small, birdlike theropod with a claw that resembled a switchblade on the second toe of each foot. Even though new evidence of *Dromaeosaurus* has come to light in recent times, the scarceness of its fossil remains suggests that it may have been a rare theropod.

One feature common to all dromaeosaurids was the extreme stiffness of their tails. The tails of most theropods were stiffened, at least for part of their length. This relative inflexibility was caused by the lengthening of the attachment processes (bony rods known as zygapophyses) on the vertebrae. In the dromaeosaurids, however, these rods became greatly elongated, each of them extending over several vertebrae and effectively bracing them together.

As a result of this, the thin tails of the dromaeosaurids became completely inflexible. The stiff tail would have helped *Dromaeosaurus* in pursuing prey by acting as an effective counterbalance behind the hip.

The world of *Dromaeosaurus* was filled with giant ceratopsians, duckbills, pachycephalosaurs, ankylosaurs, and tyrannosaurids such as *Alberto-saurus*. An individual *Dromaeosaurus* would probably have been regarded as no more than a minor nuisance by most of these, but it would have been a source of terror to smaller dinosaurs and other vertebrates in its territory. Hunting in groups, however, may well have given *Dromaeo-saurus* the capacity to target and bring down much larger prey.

The Dromaeosaurus skeleton at the Royal Tyrrell Museum in Drumheller, Alberta, Canada.

Avimimus

AY-vee-MY-mus

FIELD NOTES

■ Bird mimic

🦖 5 feet (1.5 m)

■ Late Cretaceous

■ Mongolia

🏛 Not on display

As its name clearly suggests *Avimimus* was a very birdlike dinosaur. It was a lightly built, long-legged animal that may have made its living by chasing after small reptiles and mammals. *Avimimus*'s diet is still a subject of debate; some scientists believe that it probably fed mainly on insects. It was capable of swift speeds, which would have both enhanced its efficiency as a predator and helped it to avoid falling prey to larger meat-eating dinosaurs.

Avimimus was a strange-looking dinosaur. It had a long neck and a short head with a tooth-less mouth. It had a large braincase, which suggests that its brain, too, was relatively large. In place of teeth it had a powerful beak, similar to that of a present-day cockatoo. The bones of its wrist were fused together as they are in birds and the three long fingers could be held tucked under the body. In fact, *Avimimus* could fold its whole arm against its body in a similar fashion to the way a bird folds its wing. Its long legs ended in three toes, with a smaller fourth toe nestled on the inside of the foot. All the toes and fingers were tipped with sharp, curved claws. Unlike

a bird, however, *Avimimus* had a long, bony tail and its pelvis resembled those that are seen in other theropods.

It is possible that *Avimimus* had feathers of some kind, but the deposits in which it has been discovered are too coarse for such features to have been preserved. However, a rough ridge on the forearm of *Avimimus*—similar to the one on *Caudipteryx*, which supported a half-wing—may well have served to anchor feathers. However, even if *Avimimus* did have feathers, it seems unlikely that it would have been capable of flight.

We have known about *Avimimus* for only a relatively short time. Russian expeditions into Mongolia in the late 1970s and early 1980s were the first to discover fossils of it, and it was described and named only as recently as 1981. Since then, Chinese paleontologists have unearthed other fossils, but remains of *Avimimus* are still very rare. Only three partial skeletons—and no complete skeletons—have so far been discovered.

head and beak

391

Sinosauropteryx

SIGH-no-saw-ROP-ter-ix

Sinosauropteryx caused a sensation when it was revealed to the world in 1996. Here was a clear and perfectly preserved skeleton of a small theropod dinosaur, but covering most of the body were impressions of an enigmatic fuzz, a coat of fine filaments up to 1½ inches (4 cm) long.

Skin impressions found for some dinosaurs reveal that they had scales. But the growing recognition that birds evolved from dinosaurs raised the possibility that some dinosaurs had feathers, or at least some kind of protofeather-like body covering that later evolved into the feathers of present-day birds. However, feathers are relatively soft and rarely fossilized.

A juvenile Sinosauropteryx shows "protofeathers," an epidermal feature that evolved before true feathers, rising from behind the head and on the neck and back.

FIELD NOTES

- Chinese lizard feather
- 3 feet (1 m)
- Earliest Cretaceous
- Liaoning, China
- Not on display

It is likely that several birdlike dinosaurs may have had feathers or similar structures, but, as they were not preserved, we know nothing about them.

Then *Sinosauropteryx* was found in the fabulous Liaoning deposits in China. Here was the right kind of dinosaur (a small, advanced theropod) with much of its back, rump, and tail covered in a fine, filamentous fuzz that appeared to be a furlike coat made up of thousands of short, single strands. While lacking the complex structure of a feather, it was a more intricate body covering than simple reptilian scales.

The fuzzy coat seemed to form a downy layer that would have been perfect for trapping body heat and keeping the animal warm. This observation lends more weight to the ongoing debate that some dinosaurs were warm-blooded. It is also possible that the fuzz was used when displaying to attract mates.

In one of the specimens, located right where the gut would have been in life, was the remains of its last meal, a small, unidentified mammal—providing proof that this little ancestor of the birds ate the ancestors of modern mammals. One of the other specimens revealed unlaid eggs in the oviducts.

Sinornithosaurus

SIE-nor-nith-oh-SAW-rus

T he small predatory dinosaur *Sinornithosaurus* was
a dromaeosaurid—one of a
group of agile bipedal runners with
large eyes, relatively large brains,
and long, narrow snouts equipped
with steak-knife teeth. The three
fingers on each hand and the four
toes of each foot had long, curved, wickedly
sharp claws for hooking into prey, with the
second toe claw being extra large. As in many
other dinosaurs, especially fast-running kinds,
the tail was stiffened by overlapping bony rods.

While much smaller than its famous relatives
Deinonychus and *Velociraptor*, *Sinornithosaurus*
would have been an equally effective predator
on a small scale. It may have been a solitary
hunter of large insects, lizards, primitive birds,
and small mammals, but it is also possible that
groups of *Sinornithosaurus* cooperated to hunt
and bring down small
plant-eating dinosaurs
and other prey bigger
than themselves.

The only known
skeleton of *Sinornitho-
saurus* was described
in 1999 and is missing
most of the vertebral

FIELD NOTES

■ Chinese bird lizard

🦖 3 feet 6 inches (1.1 m)

■ Early Cretaceous

■ Liaoning, China

🏛 Not on display

column and rib cage, but the
skull, shoulders, hips, and limb
bones are well preserved. Many
details of the skeleton are similar
to those of the primitive bird
Archaeopteryx, providing evidence
that dromaeosaurids were the
dinosaurs most closely related to
birds. The forelimbs are about four-fifths as long
as the hindlimbs, and the shoulder sockets face to
the side, allowing a wide range of movement, as
in *Archaeopteryx*. Although unable to fly, *Sinornithosaurus* might have been able to "flap" its arms
and snatch small flying prey out of the air.

Another birdlike feature of *Sinornithosaurus* is
a dense covering of downlike filaments over most
of its body. Many other dinosaurs may have had
these protofeathers, but only under exceptional
geological conditions are they preserved during
fossilization. Similar structures are found in four
other kinds of small
theropods from the
same locality in Liao-
ning province, China.

Sinornithosaurus *has several
birdlike features, including
a furcula, or wishbone, which
all birds possess.*

393

Mononykus

mon-oh-NIE-kus

Most small theropods had long forelimbs and long, grasping hands. *Mononykus* and its closest relatives—its fellow alvarezsaurids—are conspicuous exceptions to this rule. *Mononykus* had very gracile hindlimbs, but its forelimbs were extremely short and its hand was effectively reduced to a single digit—the stout, clawed thumb for which the animal is named. An almost imperceptible second digit is no more than a nubbin.

Mononykus was one of the prizes collected in joint Mongolian–American expeditions to Mongolia undertaken in the mid-1990s. Other alvarezsaurids are known from the Cretaceous of North and South America. It is also possible that members of this family occurred worldwide.

Mononykus's forelimbs were too short to be able to reach its face, but they were powerfully built—the construction of the elbows suggests the existence of large extension muscles.

FIELD NOTES

- One claw
- 3 feet (1 m)
- Late Cretaceous
- Mongolia
- American Museum of Natural History, New York, USA

structure of arm and hand

In some ways they resemble the forelimbs of digging mammals such as moles. What would a small theropod with graceful legs and a slender body have done with such arms? Might *Mononykus* have been a digging animal that used its strong, though very short, arms to rip open termite mounds? Perhaps it was, but the rest of the skeleton is absolutely unlike that of any known burrowing animal.

The scientists that discovered *Mononykus* originally thought they had discovered a very primitive bird. It had small teeth and a bony tail, but the breastbone had a small keel and the fibula did not reach to the ankle—features found in birds more advanced that *Archaeopteryx*. However, it is clear that *Mononykus* was incapable of flight. Some recent analyses suggest that *Mononykus* was a very close relative of birds. Others classify it as being closely related to the ornithomimids, such as *Gallimimus*. Although it seems likely that *Mononykus* will remain classified as a theropod, its distinctly birdlike features are undeniable. In fact, a recently discovered alvarezsaurid from Mongolia preserves thin fibers that scientists think may be primitive feathers around parts of its body.

Caudipteryx

kaw-DIP-tuh-rix

FIELD NOTES

■ Tail feather

🦖 3 feet (1 m)

■ Early Cretaceous

■ Liaoning, China

🏛 Not on display

The discovery of the bizarre theropod *Caudipteryx* in 1998 was an exciting event for the science of paleontology. Scientists had long realized that if birds evolved from dinosaurs, somewhere along the line there ought to be a dinosaur with half a wing—a limb that was more than a simple dinosaur arm but not developed into a fully functional wing. *Caudipteryx* was just such an animal. Here was a long-legged, gracile theropod dinosaur with well-developed but short arms—and impressions of small feathered wings trailing behind its forearms.

How *Caudipteryx* used these "wings" is a puzzle. They were too small to have been used for flight. Perhaps they helped the animal catch insects, or they may have combined with the tuft of feathers on the tail to make a stunning sexual display. Whatever their function, we can now be certain that an animal with half a wing once existed.

The exquisite state of preservation of *Caudipteryx* and other fossils from the Liaoning deposits reveals a wealth of detail. Not only were there long feathers on *Caudipteryx*'s arms and tail, but shorter downy feathers covered most of the body. The head was small and rounded. Long, sharp teeth were restricted to the very front of the mouth and projected more forward than downward. Perhaps they were part of an early horny beak. In the gizzard region there was a collection of tiny pebbles, or gastroliths, that the animal swallowed to help it grind up food—yet another birdlike feature. *Caudipteryx* had a well-developed wishbone, a feature seen only in birds and the theropods.

Caudipteryx's long legs suggest that it was a speedy runner that probably made a living chasing after insects or other small animals.

Feathers extending from the arms of Caudipteryx can be seen clearly in this fossil. Above the feathers, gastroliths are visible. These were small stones that helped to grind up the food that the animal ingested.

Segnosaurus

SEG-noh-SAW-rus

FIELD NOTES

■ Slow lizard

🦕 19 feet 6 inches (6 m)

■ Late Cretaceous

■ Mongolia

🏛 Academy of Science,
Ulan Baator, Mongolia

Few dinosaurs have caused as much speculation and debate among paleontologists as *Segnosaurus*. It has taken a long time to work out exactly what kind of dinosaur it was. *Segnosaurus* had a highly unusual collection of features that resembled bits of many other dinosaurs and dinosaur groups, combined with some uncommon characteristics only found in *Segnosaurus* and its close relatives, the segnosaurs.

The front of the snout of *Segnosaurus* was toothless and may have supported a beak, as in some ornithischian dinosaurs. *Segnosaurus* also had a hip arrangement similar to that of the ornithischians. The current consensus is that *Segnosaurus* and its close relatives *Erlikosaurus*, *Nanshiungosaurus,* and *Enigmosaurus* form a strange group of theropod dinosaurs. Features they share include a three-fingered hand; a four-toed foot; toes and fingers with curved claws; and a high, narrow skull. Curiously, the jaw curved downward and had rows of small pointed teeth along each side. This feature is also seen in the other segnosaurs.

Exactly what use this strange combination of features was to *Segnosaurus* is widely debated. It has been suggested that it was a plant-eater descended from a meat-eating ancestor or, perhaps, a specialist termite hunter that used its huge claws to rip open termite nests. Alernatively, it may have been a specialist fish-hunting dinosaur, hooking fish out of the water with its claws.

Segnosaurus is a relatively new dinosaur, described in 1979, and known only from fragments and isolated bones. This makes it difficult to understand what it was really like.

Mongolia and China have produced many unusual theropods, such as *Segnosaurus*, from late Cretaceous deposits. These groups are not found anywhere else, indicating that what is now central Asia was isolated from the rest of the world by mountains and seas for most of the later Mesozoic era.

fossil remains of fish that may have been food for Segnosaurus

Saltasaurus

SALT-uh-SAW-rus

FIELD NOTES

■ Salta lizard

🦖 39 feet (12 m)

■ Late Cretaceous

■ Salta, Rionegro, Argentia; Palmitas, Uruguay

🏛 Argentine Museum of Natural Sciences, Buenos Aires, Argentina

When *Saltasaurus* was described in 1980, it was quite a surprise for a number of reasons.

First, *Saltasaurus* was the first sauropod to be found with dermal armor. Previous fragments of armor had been found in the area and were thought to belong to an otherwise unknown ankylosaur. The armor comprised bony studs that interconnected to form a shield over the back of the animal. These varied from pea-sized to the size of a adult human's fist. Although the larger lumps tended to be aligned into rows, the shield did not exhibit any formal pattern.

The second surprise is that *Saltasaurus* comes from rock laid down almost at the very end of the age of the dinosaurs. Sauropods dominated the late

eating from tree tops

skin detail

Jurassic but were scarce for most of the Cretaceous. Strangely, *Saltasaurus* and its kin, the titanosaurids, seem to have been making a reappearance just as the age of the dinosaurs was drawing to a close.

By sauropod standards, *Saltasaurus* was quite small. It was also quite stocky with relatively short, stumpy legs. The tail was long and ended in a whiplike lash similar to that of *Diplodocus*. The bones of the tail interlocked, thus stiffening the whole structure and possibly providing support for the animal when it reared up on its hind legs.

Several specimens of *Saltasaurus* have been found, representing three species. Most of the skeleton is known except for the greater part of the skull and many of the foot bones.

Saltasaurus was one of the dinosaurs named by the famous Argentinean paleontologist José Bonaparte. Bonaparte has described many dinosaurs from Argentina, including the strange horned theropod *Carnotaurus*.

397

Edmontonia

ed-mon-TOH-nee-ah

FIELD NOTES

▪ of Edmonton

🦕 23 feet (7 m)

▪ Late Cretaceous

▪ Alberta, Canada; Montana, Texas, USA

🏛 The Royal Tyrrell Museum of Paleontology, Drumheller, Alberta, Canada

Edmontonia was one of the largest nodosaurids, one of the two main groups of the armored ankylosaurs. Nodosaurids characteristically had a boxlike head and bony armor covering the neck, back, and upper surfaces of the tail. This armor consisted of three types of bony elements embedded in the skin. The largest were pronounced spikes, on the shoulders and forming two rows running along the sides of the animal. Shieldlike scutes of varying sizes were arranged in several rows, running lengthwise from the back of the neck to the tip of the tail. In between the scutes and spikes were thousands of small, pea-sized ossicles. Together the spikes, scutes, and ossicles formed an impenetrable shield against the attacks of predators. Even the head had a set of interlocking bony plates over the upper surfaces to protect the brain, eyes, and nose.

The huge spikes on the shoulders gave Edmontonia an offensive weapon. By tucking its bony head below them, Edmontonia could drive these spikes forward into an attacker with potentially lethal effect.

detail of head with reinforced plates

As with most nodosaurids, Edmontonia's belly was unprotected by armor and would have been vulnerable to attack if the animal were flipped over. To prevent this from happening, Edmontonia was very low-slung with relatively short, stumpy legs spread wide by broad hips and shoulder girdles. Edmontonia was built rather like a huge coffee table! Edmontonia's boxy head had a cropping beak at the front of the mouth and rows of small, serrated, triangular teeth in the cheeks. Wear on these cheek teeth indicates that Edmontonia snipped its food into tiny pieces before swallowing it.

Edmontonia was one of the last of the nodosaurid dinosaurs, appearing late in the age of dinosaurs. Other nodosaurids are known from around the world in older rocks dating back to the latest Jurassic.

Minmi

MIN-mee

The most complete and best known dinosaur from Australia, *Minmi* was also the first armored dinosaur found in the Southern Hemisphere.

While it is clearly one of the armored ankylosaurian dinosaurs, it is not clear whether *Minmi* is a nodosaurid, an ankylosaurid, or a representative of a new, third group. Like other ankylosaurs, *Minmi* had a back covered by rows of bony shields and nubbins. Unlike most other ankylosaurs, however, this armor extended onto the flanks and belly and even onto the upper parts of all four legs. The tail had two rows of large, bladed spikes occurring in pairs for most of its length.

Similar to other ankylosaurs, *Minmi* was a broad but squat animal with four short legs. The hips were very wide and formed a bony raft across the rump. The head was generally flattened and quite broad at the back, narrowing to a thin snout. The front of the snout had a horny beak for snipping off leaves. The leaves were then

FIELD NOTES

- Named after Minmi Crossing, where it was first found
- 8 feet (2.5 m)
- Early Cretaceous
- Queensland, Australia
- The Queensland Museum, Brisbane, Australia

sliced into small pieces by rows of small teeth along the sides of the mouth.

Minmi was first described from a set of three vertebrae found in southern Queensland in the 1960s. In 1990 an almost complete skeleton was found near Hughenden in central Queensland. The prized skeleton is in an extremely hard limestone that is slowly being dissolved in weak acid. It will take some years before the fossil's secrets are revealed.

Australia in the early Cretaceous was still connected to Antartica and was much farther south than it is today, with only its northernmost parts outside what is now the Antarctic Circle. The fact that Australian dinosaurs such as *Minmi* are so different from dinosaurs occurring elsewhere in the world at that time indicates that the emerging continent had only very limited access for land animals.

This skeleton of Minmi was found in Queensland, Australia, in 1990.

Euoplocephalus

yoo-oh-ploh-SEF-uh-lus

Built like an armored tank, *Euoplocephalus* ambled through the late Cretaceous landscape, well equipped to withstand attack from any other dinosaur. Low slung and broad, the back of *Euoplocephalus* bore rows of bony shields with some taller spikes over the shoulders and at the base of the tail. There were also spikes on the dinosaur's cheeks and behind each eye, protecting the head.

The most lethal weapon in *Euoplocephalus*'s armory was the double-headed club at the end of the long, stiffened tail. The base of the tail was quite flexible, but the last third was welded into a stiff rod by long struts growing out of each vertebra. The tail club could be swung most effectively from side to side, swiping at the feet of an attacking predator. If it connected with full force, it could shatter the ankle bones of the attacker, a wound that could later prove fatal.

Euoplocephalus had a compact, rounded head. Like other ankylosaurids, but unlike nodosaurids, it had

> **FIELD NOTES**
>
> ■ Well-armored head
>
> 🦖 23 feet (7 m)
>
> ■ Late Cretaceous
>
> ■ Alberta, Canada; Montana, USA
>
> 🏛 National Museum of Natural Sciences, Ottawa, Canada

a complex and convoluted nasal passage in the skull, but the function that this served is not clear. Perhaps the extra length given by the twists and loops allowed air to be warmed while the animal was breathing in, or perhaps this passage collected moisture from air being exhaled. The passage may also have been lined with sensors that gave *Euoplocephalus* an enhanced sense of smell for detecting food, predators, or potential mates.

The mouth had a broad beak at the front and a wide palate lined with small teeth. This arrangement suggests that *Euoplocephalus* was not particularly selective about what it ate and would consume almost any plant material that it could reach.

Around 40 specimens of *Euoplocephalus* have been found. All were isolated finds, which suggests that these animals were loners rather than pack or herd animals. Packs and herds provided plant-eaters with a defense against predators but, perhaps because it was so heavily armored, *Euoplocephalus* had no need to rely on group behavior for protection.

A Euoplocephalus skull

Ankylosaurus

an-KEE-loh-SAW-rus

The last and largest of all the armored dinosaurs, *Ankylosaurus* was found in some of the very youngest beds that contain dinosaur fossils. With its massive tail club and a suit of armor, a solitary *Ankylosaurus* would have had nothing to fear from most predators.

Ankylosaurus gives its name to the group to which it belongs (the ankylosaurs) and takes its name from the bony nature of its skeleton. "Ankylosed" means "stiffened with bone"—and this is a fair description. The head was covered with an extra layer of bony plates and spikes, the back and tail were covered by interlocking bony shields, and the vertebrae at the end of the tail were welded together by bone.

The heavy, bony tail club was wielded like a wrecking ball and could do serious damage to any attacking predator. Despite the weight of the tail club and its position at the end of a long, heavy tail, the club was carried clear of the ground. Trackways made by *Ankylosaurus* and its kin show no signs of a tail dragging behind.

Like its close relative *Euoplocephalus*, *Ankylosaurus* had a complex systems of loops and twists in its nasal passages. These may have been

FIELD NOTES

- Stiff lizard
- 33 feet (10 m)
- Late Cretaceous
- Montana, Wyoming, USA; Alberta, Canada
- Provincial Museum of Alberta, Edmonton, Canada; American Museum of Natural History, New York, USA

for warming air, reclaiming water from expiring air, or for enhancing the sense of smell. It is also possible that they were used as a resonating chamber, helping the creature to make loud mating or distress calls.

Ankylosaurus was one of the many dinosaurs found and named by the famous paleontologist Barnum Brown. In 1910, Brown found a particular specimen that is now on display in the American Museum of Natural History in New York. As the story goes, he didn't have time to dig the specimen out himself, so he paid some local ranchers to do the job for him. When he returned a year later, the ranchers had excavated nearly 1,180 cubic yards (900 m³) of solid sandstone, mostly by hand but also using a little dynamite. Despite this stupendous effort, only a partial specimen was recovered.

tail club

Hypsilophodon

HIP-sill-OFF-oh-don

FIELD NOTES

■ High-ridged tooth

🦖 7 feet (2.1 m)

■ Early Cretaceous

■ Isle of Wight, England

🏛 Natural History Museum, London, UK

One of the most famous of small dinosaurs, *Hypsilophodon* was also one of the earliest to be studied. It was discovered in 1849, in the same Wealden rocks in southern England that had yielded fossils of the ornithopod *Iguanodon* 20 years earlier. Indeed, at first *Hypsilophodon* was thought to have been a juvenile *Iguanodon*. In 1869, the English zoologist Thomas Henry Huxley recognized that it was a different animal and named it after the strong ridges that were visible on its teeth. Huxley realized that this small animal would have been agile and would have moved principally on its hind legs. This was a suprising view, considering that at the time most scientists considered dinosaurs to be ponderous creatures that moved about on all fours.

Early reconstructions of *Hypsilophodon*'s foot mistakenly showed it to have a reversed hallux (first toe). Such a reversal is common in animals that live in trees, as it allows them to grip branches while they perch. As a result, early

skull

reconstructions of a complete *Hypsilophodon* showed it perched up in branches, rather like an ancestral tree kangaroo.

Eventually the foot was reconstructed correctly and *Hypsilophodon* was brought to ground as a fast-running ornithopod, similar in many respects to the Jurassic *Dryosaurus*. Like *Dryosaurus*, *Hypsilophodon* had long hind legs that were well suited for running at high speed. *Hypsilophodon*'s tail, like *Dryosaurus*'s, was long and was held stiffly off the ground to counterbalance the weight of its body.

Hypsilophodon's teeth and jaws were well adapted for grinding the tough plant matter on which it fed. It had a fleshy cheek, where food could be stored before it was chewed, and a horny beak that cropped food as it entered the mouth. Unlike *Dryosaurus,* and most other ornithopods, *Hypsilophodon* still retained some front teeth in the upper jaw. In this respect, *Hypsilophodon* was probably more primitive than *Dryosaurus*, even though it lived 300 million years after the more advanced ornithopod had become extinct.

Leaellynasaura

lay-ELL-lye-nuh-SAW-ruh

Since 1978, hundreds of dinosaur bones have been collected from early Cretaceous rocks at a site known as Dinosaur Cove in Victoria, Australia. There are very few complete skeletons in these rocks—the bones are from many different animals and they have been jumbled together—but studies have shown that most of the bones belonged to small dinosaurs that were closely related to *Hypsilophodon*. The first of these new "hypsilophodontids" to be named by science was *Leaellynasaura*.

The material that has so far been found relating to *Leaellynasaura* is incomplete, but it does indicate that this was a small dinosaur, even in comparison with other hypsilophodontids.

FIELD NOTES

- Leaellyn's lizard
- 3 feet (1 m)
- Earliest Cretaceous
- Victoria, Australia
- Museum Victoria, Melbourne, Australia

The first *Leaellynasaura* bones are from an animal that would have weighed no more than about 2 pounds (0.9 k) and was almost certainly a juvenile. One specimen preserves an internal cast of the braincase. It shows that the optic lobes (the parts of the brain that process visual information from the eyes) were very large compared with those of other dinosaurs. As with other hypsilophodontids, the bone tissues show that *Leaellynasaura* grew continuously and quickly. Seasonal variations in temperature did not slow down its growth rates, and this has led some scientists to speculate that this dinosaur may have been warm-blooded.

During the early Cretaceous, Victoria was well within the Antarctic polar circle. This means that *Leaellynasaura* was living, and apparently thriving, at latitudes that no reptile lives at today. The fact that even juveniles had enlarged optic lobes suggests that this dinosaur had large eyes that helped it to see its way through the long, dark polar winters.

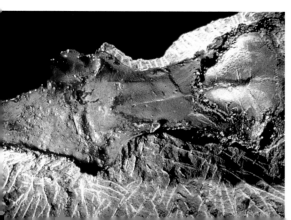

This fossilized Leaellynasaura skull, from Dinosaur Cove in Victoria, Australia, is still partly encased in rock.

403

Tenontosaurus

ten-ON-toh-SAW-rus

FIELD NOTES

■ Tendon lizard

26 feet (8 m))

■ Early Cretaceous

■ Montana, Wyoming, USA

🏛 Peabody Museum of Natural History, New Haven, USA; Academy of Natural Sciences, Philadelphia, USA

Most ornithopod dinosaurs have strong tendons running along their backbone in the hip region. On *Tenontosaurus* these tendons were so well developed that they inspired the dinosaur's name. These thick tendons were ossified (strengthened with bone) and were arranged in bundles that ran parallel to the length of the spine. As a result, the spine of this dinosaur, from the lower back to the upper tail, would have been very stiff. This would have helped the animal to support the weight of its body across its hips; the torso was held stiffly in front of the hips and was balanced by the tail, which stretched out horizontally behind. Because the spinal column was almost parallel to the ground, the tail, which was very thick and bulky, would have been held high. This is confirmed by trackways of ornithopods which show no signs of marks made by tails dragging along the ground.

Tenontosaurus fed on plant matter, which it broke off with its horny beak and then chewed with its teeth, all of which were at the back of its mouth.

Tenontosaurus being attacked by five Deinonychus

The small, swift-moving *Deinonychus* was *Tenontosaurus*'s main enemy. The teeth of this predator have been found along with *Tenontosaurus* skeletons. Some scientists therefore believe that *Deinonychus* hunted the larger animal in packs, but there is no real evidence to support this. In spite of what would seem to be the advantages of having clawed feet and a huge tail, *Tenontosaurus* would have been easy catch for packs of sharp-fanged *Deinonychus*.

There is still debate about the proper classification of this dinosaur—some maintain it was an advanced hypsilophodontid while others argue that it was an early iguanodontid. *Tenontosaurus* does appear to have been a transitory form between the smaller ornithopods, such as *Dryosaurus*, which arose in the Jurassic, and the larger ornithopods, such as *Iguanodon*, which arose in the Cretaceous.

Ouranosaurus

oo-RAN-oh-SAW-rus

This early Cretaceous orni-thopod from west Africa is one of the most puzzling dinosaurs ever discovered, and paleontologists are still trying to work out what it looked like. This is surprising, because *Ouranosaurus* is known from an almost complete skeleton—which was discovered in 1966—and its closest known relative, *Iguanodon*, is one of the best understood dinosaurs of all.

The problem lies with the backbone. The neural spines—the bones that projected upward from the main part of the vertebrae and which usually supported important sets of the back muscles and tendons—were simply huge in *Ouranosaurus*. Imagine an animal with a chest the size of a modern racehorse's, with a set of spines more than 27 inches (0.7 m) tall along the length of its back. What function could these spines have served?

Some scientists believe that *Ouranosaurus* sported a huge sail-like structure on its back. "Sail-backed" animals are known from the Permian period,

FIELD NOTES
- Brave lizard
- 23 feet (7 m)
- Early Cretaceous
- Niger
- National Museum of Niger, Naimey, Niger; Civic Museum of Natural History, Venice, Italy

260 million years ago, and it is thought that these "sails" helped them to regulate their body temperature. In some recon-structions, then, *Ouranosaurus* is shown as an unremarkable, medium-sized ornithopod, except for its long sail.

Others disagree with the "sail" theory. They point out that in the hot, dry climate in which it lived, *Ouranosaurus* would not have needed a sail to get warm. Overheating would have been more of a problem, and a sail would have been of no use in getting rid of heat. Plus, the spines of *Ouranosaurus* bear little resemblance to those of the Permian sail-backs. They look more like the spines that form the withers in modern mammals such as bison. Some scientists therefore reconstruct *Ouranosaurus* as an unusual ornithopod with a huge humped back—a kind of dinosaurian version of a camel or buffalo.

skeleton showing bones that supported the hump on the back

405

Iguanodon

ig-WAHN-oh-don

I n a way *Iguanodon* could be called a "founding father" of dinosaurs—not in the sense that it is ancestral to all other dinosaurs, but in terms of our scientific understanding of dinosaurs. In 1825, *Iguanodon* became the second dinosaur to be named by science, and it was one of the three animals around which the British paleontologist Sir Richard Owen constructed the scientific concept of "Dinosauria" in 1842. Ever since, studies and reconstructions of *Iguanodon* have played an important role in advancing our knowledge of dinosaurs in general.

Iguanodon was widespread in the early Cretaceous—species have been described from Europe, North America, and Mongolia. The first fossils of this dinosaur to be found came from the Wealden rocks of southern England—rocks that were formed in an extensive series of shallow lakes and estuaries. The very first fossils were only teeth, which looked much like the teeth of living iguanas—hence the name. As more bones came to light, researchers reconstructed this dinosaur as a large quadrupedal herbivore—

FIELD NOTES

■ Iguana tooth

🦕 33 feet (10 m)

■ Late Jurassic

■ Western USA; Western Europe; Romania; Mongolia

🏛 Royal National Institute of Natural Sciences, Brussels, Belgium

hand showing thumb spike

a sort of reptilian rhinoceros— and, in what turned out to be one of the most celebrated mistakes in the history of paleontology, a large bony spike that had been found with other parts of the skeleton was placed on the end of the nose. This early reconstruction helped to reinforce the perception of dinosaurs as lumbering animals—a perception we now know to be inaccurate.

It took one of the most remarkable fossil finds of all time to shake this stereotype. In 1878, workers in a coal mine in southern Belgium unearthed a large bone full of what they thought to be gold. The "gold" turned out to be "fool's gold" (pyrite), but the possibility of riches inspired further digging and led to the discovery of dinosaur skeletons. After three years, the complete skeletons of 31 *Iguanodon* had been recovered—at the time, they were the best preserved dinosaur fossils

that had ever been found. Study of these specimens showed that, far from being a heavy, lumbering quadruped, *Iguanodon* was relatively light for its great length and could move on its back legs. These skeletons also put the nose spike where it belonged. In fact, *Iguanodon* had two spikes—one on each thumb.

For almost a century after that, *Iguanodon*, and other large ornithopods, such as the hadrosaurids, were reconstructed rather like colossal kangaroos, standing on their hind legs with the head held high and the tail stretching out along the ground. It was not until the 1970s that new studies revealed that *Iguanodon* had strong front legs and that the central three fingers ended in hooves. This implied that *Iguanodon* spent some time on all fours, and probably ran on its hind legs when it needed to move quickly. As in other ornithopods, its spine was supported by large, ossified tendons around the hips; unlike in other ornithopods, however, the tendon bundles were arranged diagonally in a trellis pattern, rather than parallel to each other.

The jaws and teeth of *Iguanodon* made it an efficient plant-eater.

A reconstructed Iguandon *skeleton, based on an original in the Royal National Institute of Natural Sciences in Brussels, Belgium.*

A formidable battery of closely packed cheek teeth were well suited to grinding up tough plant matter—the upper surface of each tooth was broad and ridged. The jaw bones that held the teeth moved upward and outward in the skull as the animal chewed, thus allowing the grinding surfaces to move against each other and thereby contributing to the efficiency of the chewing action. The same arrangement has been observed in a number of other ornithopods, but in *Iguanodon* it appears to have been particularly well developed.

The roughened bulge halfway down this Iguanodon *hip bone shows where it broke and healed slightly out of alignment.*

407

Edmontosaurus

ed-MONT-oh-SAW-rus

The hadrosaurids, or duck-billed dinosaurs, were a family of large ornithopods, which are informally named after the wide, flattened front part of their mouths. This was covered in a horny, toothless beak and looked like the bill of a monstrous duck. *Edmontosaurus* would have used this beak to bite off plant matter, which it chewed with the many tightly packed teeth—there may have been up to a thousand—that lined both of its jaws. As teeth wore out, they were replaced with new ones.

Edmontosaurus was one of the last hadrosaurids, and also one of the largest. In fact, it was, along with *Tyrannosaurus* and *Triceratops*, one of the last surviving dinosaurs, living right to the end of the Cretaceous. To help it cope with its huge body weight—a large *Edmontosaurus* may have weighed up to 5 tons (5.1 t)—it had

FIELD NOTES

- Edmonton lizard
- 42 feet (13 m)
- Late Cretaceous
- Alberta, Canada
- Peabody Museum of Natural History, New Haven, USA; Smithsonian Institution, Washington DC, USA; Royal Ontario Museum, Toronto, Canada

The strong jaws of Edmontosaurus contained tightly packed rows of tiny, leaf-shaped teeth that were ideal for grinding.

strong front legs and hooves on its "hands." As well, its spine was supported by huge bony tendons, which criss-crossed all the way down. *Edmontosaurus* probably spent most of its time on all fours, rising up on its back legs only when it needed to run.

Spectacular finds of *Edmontosaurus* from Alberta, Canada, have preserved impressions of the skin around parts of the body, including the "hand." It was one of these "mummified" fossils that led to early reconstructions of hadrosaurids as mainly aquatic animals. The skin of *Edmontosaurus*'s hand shows a structure between the fingers that looks like the webbed foot of a duck. It was realized only later that what looked like webbing was really the remains of padding behind the hooves. Many present-day hoofed animals have similar padding, which helps to bear the animals' weight. Modern reconstructions of *Edmontosaurus* and other hadrosaurids show them as fully terrestrial animals.

408

Maiasaura

MY-uh-SAW-rah

O rnithopod nest sites have provided scientists with excellent opportunities to see how dinosaurs were born and grew up. It seems that hypsilophodontid babies could walk as soon as they were hatched, and they may have left the nest soon after. Hadrosaurids had a rather different reproductive strategy. No animal shows that better than *Maiasaura*.

In fact, the first fossils ever found of *Maiasaura* were a huge nesting colony, about 75 million years old. It was discovered in the badlands of Montana in 1978 by John Horner and Robert Makela. This colony contained eggs (many of them still intact), babies, and adults; even the arrangement of the eggs in the nest could be

FIELD NOTES

■ Good mother lizard

🦖 30 feet (9 m)

■ Late Cretaceous

■ Montana, USA

🏛 Museum of the Rockies, Bozeman, USA

protecting the nest

seen. Careful study of the site led to some interesting insights into the nurturing habits of *Maiasaura*. Many of the baby *Maiasaura* were clearly too large to be newly hatched but were evidently still living in the nest. Like the leg bones of some species of modern birds, the bones in the legs of the baby *Maiasaura* were not fully formed. Despite this, their teeth showed signs of wear. The logical conclusion was that the babies were being fed in the nest. This seeming demonstration of parental care inspired the name of this dinosaur, which was bestowed on it by its discoverers in 1979.

It appears that young *Maiasaura* grew quickly. To some researchers, this suggests that they were warm-blooded. The nests that Horner and Makela found also throw light on the social organization of these hadrosaurs. The number and proximity of the nests indicate that females nested in large groups. Some scientists believe that *Maiasaura* were strongly social animals that lived in herds of many thousands.

The reconstructed skeleton of a juvenile Maiasaura. *As these animals grew, their heads became flatter and wider.*

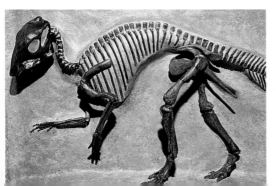

409

Corythosaurus

koh-RITH-oh-SAW-rus

The best known of the crested duckbill dinosaurs (lambeosaurine hadrosaurs), which lived beside the ancient inland sea of western North America, *Corythosaurus* walked on all four limbs. It had flattened, blunt claws on its four-fingered hands but, as with other ornithopods, most of its body weight was supported by the large three-toed hindlimbs and balanced by the large tail. Criss-crossing ossified tendons stiffened the tail all the way from the hips, preventing the tail from swinging from side to side when the dinosaur ran. The spine was strongly flexed, or "hunched," at the shoulders, suggesting that *Corythosaurus* fed on low-growing plants—probably on the flowering plants that had evolved earlier in the Cretaceous—but that it could also raise its head above shoulder level to check for danger and to communicate with other members of the herd.

Like other duckbills and some other late Cretaceous plant-eating dinosaurs, *Corythosaurus* had huge numbers of teeth crammed together

skull showing crest

into "batteries" forming a single grinding surface on each side of the upper and lower jaws. This allowed the dinosaur to process large amounts of food at once. The hadrosaurines had broad, "ducklike" snouts to cut a wide swathe through the herb layer, while lambeosaurines such as *Corythosaurus* had narrower snouts and presumably fed more selectively.

The most distinctive feature of the lambeosaurines was the hollow bony crest on top of the head. The size and shape of these crests varied greatly. As a result, different skeletons of *Corythosaurus* have been identified as belonging to at least seven different species. However, comparison of more than 20 skulls has shown that the crest changes as it grows and differs between the sexes. Only a single species is, therefore, now recognized. The large-crested individuals are thought to be the adult males. They probably used the crest in behavioral displays to attract mates and to intimidate other males. The skin covering the crest may have been brightly colored or patterned, and the hollow within the bone, which was connected to the airway, may have been used to produce distinctive honking calls.

FIELD NOTES

- Corinthian-crested lizard
- 33 feet (10 m)
- Late Cretaceous
- Alberta, Canada; Montana, USA
- American Museum of Natural History, New York, USA; Royal Ontario Museum, Toronto, Canada

Lambeosaurus

LAM-bee-oh-SAW-rus

One of the largest of the crested duckbill dinosaurs (lambeosaurine hadrosaurs), *Lambeosaurus* lived in the same area and at the same time as several other members of this group of low-browsing herbivores. It seems, in fact, that several species of *Lambeosaurus* lived at the same time. They were distinguished by different-shaped bony crests on the tops of their heads, in much the same way that different kinds of modern deer and antelope have different-shaped antlers or horns. *Lambeosaurus lambei* had a hatchet-shaped crest projecting slightly forward from the top of its skull and a solid spur farther back on the head, whereas *L. magnicristatus* had a single-piece crest more like that of *Corythosaurus*. As in other lambeosaurines, the hollow crest

FIELD NOTES

■ Lambe's lizard

🦖 49 feet (15 m)

■ Late Cretaceous

■ Alberta, Canada; Montana, USA; Baja California, Mexico

🏛 Royal Tyrrell Museum, Alberta, Canada

would have formed a resonating chamber for its calls, amplifying them and making a distinctive sound in each species. The shape and patterning of the crest would also have helped individuals to recognize each other in the herd.

Nearly 20 skulls and skeletons of *Lambeosaurus* have been described. One fossil deposit, a "bonebed" containing hundreds of jumbled up skeletons buried by floods, includes specimens of *Lambeosaurus* along with *Corythosaurus*, *Prosaurolophus*, *Gryposaurus*, and *Parasaurolophus*, which suggests that these duckbills shared the same habitat and may even have migrated in huge mixed herds.

Some *Lambeosaurus* fossils display detailed impressions of the skin, showing that the skin of the body had a "pebbly" texture and that a weblike sheath of skin joined the fingers. When they were first described, these "webbed hands" were thought to prove the now-outmoded idea that duckbills were aquatic. The "web" actually enclosed a fleshy pad on the palm like that on a camel's foot.

Barnum Brown built a boat to reach the rich fossil sites along the Red Deer River, in Alberta, Canada..

411

Saurolophus

SAW-roh-LOW-fus

The most distinctive feature of *Saurolophus*—the one that gives this dinosaur its name—was the sharp, pointed ridge of bone that projected from the top of its head. This large hadrosaur is now known from several well-preserved, complete skeletons. The first species to be discovered, *Saurolophus osborni*, was named by Barnum Brown in 1921. It was based on a complete skeleton and additional skull material collected from the Horseshoe Canyon Formation of southern Alberta, Canada. A second species, *S. angustirostris*, was named in 1952 by the Russian paleontologist A. Rozhdestvensky. This species, which was the larger of the two, and which also had a larger crest, is one of the most common dinosaurs to be found in the latest Cretaceous beds of the Gobi Desert in Mongolia.

Some specimens of *Saurolophus* are so well preserved that they show skin impressions. From these we can tell that *Saurolophus* had leathery, fine-scaled skin. Except for some minor

Saurolophus may have inflated the skin that covered its crest in order to make sounds or as a form of courtship display.

FIELD NOTES

■ Ridged lizard

🦕 42 feet (13 m)

■ Late Cretaceous

■ Alberta, Canada; Mongolia

🏛 American Museum of Natural History, New York, USA; Paleontological Institute, Moscow, Russia

differences in the overall size and in the shape and height of the crest, the two species of *Saurolophus* are almost identical. This strongly suggests that by the end of the Cretaceous this dinosaur had a widespread distribution across the Northern Hemisphere.

The pointed ridge on *Saurolophus*'s head may have been covered by fleshy nostrils or nostril flaps. *Saurolophus* may have used its bony skull structure to send honking-like sound signals to other members of its species, perhaps, as a form of courtship display. It is possible that colored skin covered the crest and stretched between it and the back of the animal's head; *Saurolophus* may have been able to inflate this skin covering by breathing through a hole in the front of the crest.

Saurolophus had large numbers of closely packed teeth that were well suited to chewing the hard plant material, such as ferns and conifers, that constituted its diet.

Parasaurolophus

PAR-uh-SAW-roh-LOH-fus

FIELD NOTES

■ *Side-ridged lizard*

🦖 *35 feet (10.5 m)*

■ *Late Cretaceous*

■ *Montana, New Mexico, USA; Alberta, Canada*

🏛 *Royal Ontario Museum, Toronto, Canada; Los Angeles County Museum, USA*

With its snout bones drawn up into a giant snorkel-like structure, *Parasaurolophus* was one of the most bizarre of all the hadrosaurs. It lacked a hole in its apex, and because of this it is clear that this bony structure was not used as a breathing apparatus while the animal was swimming or feeding underwater. It seems more likely that it helped *Parasaurolophus* produce noises for signaling to mates or, if it was colored, for courtship displays. We know from the specimens that have been discovered that soft tissues adorned the bony crest.

The first skeleton of *Parasaurolophus* was collected in 1921 by Levi Sternberg in the region of southern Alberta, Canada, that is now the Dinosaur Provincial Park. This early find is still the most complete specimen to have been discovered. Three species of *Parasaurolophus* are recognized

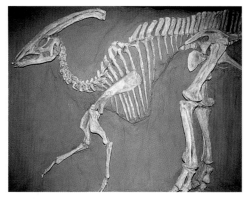

A cast of the almost complete skeleton of Parasaurolophus *that Levi Sternberg found in 1921.*

from their skulls. *P. cyrtocrystatus* had a short crest; on the other two species—*P. walkeri* and *P. tubicen*—the crests were much longer. The internal structure of the crest, which, unlike the crest of *Saurolophus*, had a hollow area that connected with the nostrils and the back of the throat, was more complex in *P. tubicen* than in other *Parasaurolophus* species.

Like all hadrosaurs, *Parasaurolophus* was a plant-eater. It had many closely compacted teeth, each of which had a central ridge. The teeth formed a strong dental battery that made it easier to chew tough vegetable matter

The principal dangers this dinosaur faced were from the larger predators such as *Albertosaurus*. *Parasaurolophus* probably sought protection from its enemies by living in large herds, in the same way that herbivores that inhabit the African plains do today.

413

Muttaburrasaurus

MUT-uh-BUH-ruh-SAW-rus

A large ornithopod that stood about 16 feet (5 m) high, *Muttaburrasaurus* is known from about 60 percent of its skeleton. A Mr. David Langdon found the skeleton in 1963 on Muttaburra Station in northern Queensland—hence this dinosaur's name. A second well-preserved skull, slightly older than the original specimen, was discovered on another property in north central Queensland. As well, a number of isolated bones and teeth of *Muttaburrasaurus* came to light on the Lightning Ridge opal field in northern New South Wales.

Muttaburrasaurus probably walked on all fours for most of the time. But it could also stand up on its hindlimbs to reach high into tree branches. Its most distinctive feature was a well-developed bump on the snout (called a "nasal bulla"),

FIELD NOTES

■ Lizard from Muttaburra

🦕 33 feet (10 m)

■ Early Cretaceous

■ Northern Queensland, New South Wales, Australia

🏛 Queensland Museum, Brisbane, Australia; Western Australian Museum, Perth, Australia

which it is thought may have housed an acoustic organ for calling to other dinosaurs.

Muttaburrasaurus had large areas of jaw muscle attachments, which greatly enhanced its chewing ability. This feature, in conjunction with teeth that were suited to shearing rather than to grinding food, has led some to believe that *Muttaburrasaurus* may have eaten meat from time to time.

Early reconstructions of the *Muttaburrasaurus* were modeled after *Iguanodon*, with a thumb spike. Scientists now believe this dinosaur was not closely related to the iguanodontids, but that it belonged to a family of its own. It may have been a large relative of the hypsilophodontid dinosaurs, such as *Atlascopcosaurus*. These dinosaurs inhabited the polar forests of Victoria and New South Wales in the early Cretaceous.

A skeleton of Muttaburrasaurus *on display in the Queensland Museum, Australia.*

Carcharodontosaurus

kuh-KAR-oh-dont-oh-SAW-rus

T he very name of this dinosaur conjures powerful
images of how it may have
dispatched its prey—*Carcharodon*
is the generic name for the widely
feared ocean predator, the great
white shark. Like other theropods,
Carcharodontosaurus had teeth that
were serrated along the front and back.
However, *Carcharodontosaurus*'s teeth were
triangular and did not curve back as much
as those of most theropods. To Ernst Freiherr
Stromer von Reichenbach, the German paleontologist who first described this dinosaur in
the 1930s, these teeth seemed peculiarly
sharklike. This observed similarity led to the
naming of the dinosaur.

FIELD NOTES
- White-shark-toothed lizard
- 43 feet (13 m)
- Late Cretaceous
- Argentina
- Not on display

sample of teeth

The remains on which Stromer had based
his description came from the late Cretaceous
of Egypt but they were far from complete. Although more fossils—including some claws and
teeth that French paleontologists found in the
Sahara in the 1970s—came to light elsewhere in
north Africa, all that could definitely be deduced
from them was that *Carcharodontosaurus* was a
huge creature. Eventually, during the 1990s,
Dr. Paul Sereno from the University of Chicago
discovered a skull of *Carcharodontosaurus* in
Morocco. When restored, this skull measured

about 6 feet (2 m) long—as large as that of
Tyrannosaurus. However, the cavity that contained the brain of *Carcharodontosaurus* was
much smaller.

Carcharodontosaurus was obviously a close
relative of *Giganotosaurus* from South America.
Both of these dinosaurs had deep, domed snouts
and teeth that were smaller and more numerous
than those of *Tyrannosaurus*. It is possible that
these two contemporaneous, but geographically
separated, dinosaurs shared a common ancestor
that lived at a time when South America and
Africa were still parts of the same landmass. When
this landmass broke apart, different lineages could
have developed. Like *Giganotosaurus*, *Carcharodontosaurus* may have preyed on large sauropods. 415

Pachycephalosaurus

PAK-ee-kef-AH-loh-SAW-rus

Incomplete dinosaur skulls featuring centrally thickened domes have been known from North America since the early years of the 20th century, but the nature of the group of dinosaurs to which these skulls belonged continued to be a mystery to paleontologists until 1940. In that year the first well-preserved complete skull—belonging to *Pachycephalosaurus*, the largest member of the group—was found in Montana. This skull had thick, spiky nodules of bone around the rim of the smoothly domed head and smaller protruding horns on the snout. *Pachycephalosaurus* is known only from its skull. No other fossils of this dinosaur have so far come to light.

Studies of the anatomy of *Pachycephalosaurus* skulls, and those of close relatives such as *Stygimoloch* and *Prenocephale*, indicate that these dinosaurs probably used their skulls in vigorous head-butting competitions during their

FIELD NOTES

- Thick-headed lizard
- 26 feet (8 m)
- Late Cretaceous
- Wyoming, South Dakota, Montana, USA
- American Museum of Natural History, New York, USA

A huge dome of bone protected the brain of Pachycephalosaurus from powerful impacts, deflecting shock waves to the animal's backbone.

charging attack

courtship battles, in much the same way that modern sheep and goats do. Alternatively, they may have engaged in head-to-head or head-to-flank pushing battles. The central part of the head consisted of very thick bone that would have acted like a helmet, protecting the dinosaur's small brain by carrying any shock waves away from the area of impact, down the sides of the head, to the backbone. The numerous ossified ligaments that strengthened the backbone would then have dissipated the effects of the shock.

The skull, which was almost 2 feet (60 cm) long, was nearly 8 inches (20 cm) thick at the central part the dome.

Pachycephalosaurus had triangular teeth with coarse serrations along the edges for shredding tough plant matter.

416

Stygimoloch

STY-gee-MOH-lok

FIELD NOTES

■ River of Hell devil

🦖 20 feet (6 m)

■ Late Cretaceous

■ Wyoming, Montana, USA

🏛 Not on display

With well-developed horns and spikes protruding from the base of its domed skull and from its snout, *Stygimoloch*—its name refers to the Hell Creek site in Montana, where it was found—was more elaborately ornamented than most other pachycephalosaurs. What we know about this relatively elusive plant-eating dinosaur has been gleaned from only about five skull fragments and parts of the body skeleton. Like its larger cousin *Pachycephalosaurus*, with which it shared the late Cretaceous North American landscape, *Stygimoloch* walked upright and probably had small forelimbs and a long, stiff tail. Males may have used the horns at the base of the skull for locking heads with opponents in head-pushing contests for winning mates. The horns, which were not very strong, may, on the other hand, have been purely ornamental and employed only for courtship displays.

Because fossil remains of *Stygimoloch* are so scarce, our understanding of this dinosaur is still very limited. Those parts of the skull that scientists have so far been able to study show that holes present in the rear of the skull roofs of many pachycephalosaurs—known as the "temporal fenestrae"—had closed up in *Stygimoloch*. This indicates that *Stygimoloch*'s skull was more robust and suggests that this dinosaur, along with *Pachycephalosaurus*, was one of the more advanced of the pachycephalosaurs.

Stygimoloch lived in a lowland habitat, where the principal predators would have been large theropods such as *Tyrannosaurus*, *Albertosaurus*, and *Aublysodon*. As well as being on the lookout for these, *Stygimoloch* would also have needed to be wary of a much smaller, though agile and rapacious, predator that probably hunted in large packs—*Dromaeosaurus*.

skull of Stygimoloch showing horns surrounding the domed skull and on the snout

417

Psittacosaurus

sih-TAK-oh-saw-rus

Psittacosaurus was discovered in Outer Mongolia in 1922, in the early stages of the famous expeditions undertaken by the American Museum of Natural History between 1922 and 1925. Henry Osborn named it for the beaklike appearance of its face. It is known from a number of well-preserved skeletons, which represent about eight different species from Mongolia, southern Siberia, and northern China, as well as from some lower jaw fragments that were discovered in northern Thailand.

Psittacosaurus was one of the earliest dinosaurs to show the typical beaked face of the ceratopsian group. This beak, which was supported by a single median bone—called the "rostral bone"—is the one feature that distinguishes the ceratopsians from all other dinosaur groups.

Psittacosaurus was one of the smallest and most primitive of the ceratopsians. It lacked the

FIELD NOTES

■ Parrot lizard

🦕 4 feet (1.25 m)

■ Early Cretaceous

■ Mongolia; China; southern Siberia; Thailand

🏛 American Museum of Natural History, New York, USA; Paleontological Museum, Moscow, Russia; Academy of Science, Ulan Baatar, Mongolia; Department of Mineral Resources, Bangkok, Thailand

Psittacosaurus *lived in the early Cretaceous of Mongolia and other parts of Asia about 90 million years ago. It had relatively long forelimbs and large, grasping hands.*

well-developed frill and horns that were typical of more advanced ceratopsians, yet, along with the hard keratinous beak, it had the characteristic skull shape of a ceratopsian. It also featured, in common with later ceratopsians, the high palate and the sharp, slicing teeth with self-sharpening edges that were well suited to nipping off and shredding hard plant matter.

Psittacosaurus's hindlimbs were longer—although only slightly—than its forelimbs, which suggests that it could have moved about in an upright position for short distances. It may have done so to avoid attacks from predators or to forage in low-hanging tree branches.

Some skeletons of *Psittacosaurus* contain fossils of gastroliths— stomach stones that helped the animal to break down plant matter inside its stomach.

Protoceratops

PROH-toh-SAIR-uh-tops

One of the earliest of the neoceratopsian dinosaurs, *Protoceratops* had a well-developed frill that extended back from the face and over the neck. However, it lacked the horns of the more advanced members of the group, although some species featured a small bump on the snout that may have supported a keratinous horn, similar to that of a modern rhinoceros.

Protoceratops was a very common animal in the late Cretaceous lowland habitats of Mongolia. Fossilized remains of this dinosaur were among the most abundant fossils found on the American Museum of Natural History expeditions to Mongolia that Roy Chapman Andrews led between 1922 and 1925. The abundance of these fossils has led scientists to believe that *Protoceratops* was a highly social animal that lived in herds.

The American expeditions also discovered eggs and nests belonging to *Protoceratops*. These were the first dinosaur nests ever found, and the discovery was widely publicized. Another famous find was that of a *Protoceratops* skeleton interlocked with that of a *Velociraptor*. Whether

FIELD NOTES

■ First-horned face

🦖 10 feet (3 m)

■ Late Cretaceous

▦ Mongolia; China; Canada

🏛 American Museum of Natural History, New York, USA; Paleontological Museum, Moscow, Russia; Academy of Science, Ulan Baatar, Mongolia

skull showing frill

or not this find represents an actual act of predation, *Velociraptor*, along with the larger theropods such as *Tarbosaurus*, would almost certainly have been among the main predators on a small plant-eater such as *Protoceratops*.

Thanks to the large number of complete skulls of *Protoceratops* that have been found, scientists have been able to distinguish differences between males and females. In adult males, the frill was more erect and there was a more prominent bump on the snout. This suggests that males used the larger frill, as well as the more protuberant snout bump, as a device to attract females. The bump may also have been used in fights between rival males.

Protoceratops seems to have moved about on all fours. The size and weight of its head and jaws would probably have made a bipedal stance impossible. It would have fed mainly on low-growing plant matter, which it broke off with its beak and then chewed with the many teeth in the back of its mouth.

419

Centrosaurus

SENT-roh-saw-rus

Centrosaurus was one of the most abundant of the large browsing ceratopsians at the end of the Cretaceous. Because its fossil bones have been discovered concentrated in a thick layer, scientists have theorized that tens of thousands of animals, roaming in large herds, were killed in a flood. The layer of bones, which is widespread throughout the rich dinosaur deposits of Alberta, Canada, is now known as the *Centrosaurus* bone bed.

This dinosaur had a well-developed frill that was made lighter by large holes (known as "fenestrae"). In life the frill and the holes would have been covered with skin. Small tongues of bone hung downward from the top of the frill, and there was a large curved horn near the front of the snout. *Centrosaurus* was first described in 1876 by Edward Drinker Cope and given the name *Monoclonius*, meaning "single horn." However, as the name and the description were based only on the partial skull of a juvenile, many scientists doubt the validity of the name. The dinosaur was renamed *Centrosaurus apertus* by Lawrence Lambe in 1904. Several other species were subsequently named, but these are now recognized as variations (possibly male–female differences) within a single species. Many complete *Centrosaurus* skeletons have recently been unearthed, including those of juveniles at different stages of development. Some skin impressions have also been found.

Centrosaurus, which moved on all fours, had powerful front limbs that would have enhanced tha animal's speed and agility. A ball-and-socket joint in the neck would also have been useful in defense. It allowed *Centrosaurus* to turn its head swiftly and bring its sharp horn into play against large predators, such as *Tyrannosaurus*, that attacked from the rear.

Reconstructed skeleton of Albertosaurus standing over
Centrosaurus at the Royal Tyrrell Museum, Alberta, Canada.

Styracosaurus

sty-RACK-oh-SAW-rus

FIELD NOTES

- Spiked lizard
- 18 feet (5.5 m)
- Late Cretaceous
- Alberta, Canada; Montana, USA
- American Museum of Natural History, New York, USA

A moderately large ceratopsian, *Styracosaurus* is known from several skeletons and skulls. In most respects these skulls were similar to those of its closest relative, *Centrosaurus*. They were characterized by an extensive bony frill with two large openings, or fenestrae, situated symmetrically on either side of the frill. As with *Centrosaurus*, these openings would have significantly reduced the weight of the frill. Again like *Centrosaurus*, *Styracosaurus* had a large pointed horn on its snout and a pair of small horns above the eyes. In *Styracosaurus*, however, the snout horn was straight, rather than curved, and the frill was fringed with numerous smaller, sharp, projecting horns.

Of the two dinosaurs, then, *Styracosarus* seems to have been better equipped for defense. However, there is some doubt about the effectiveness of the horns on the frill. As they extended back over the neck, they certainly would have afforded some protection against predators and would have looked formidably threatening when viewed from the front, but as they stuck out to the side, they would have been difficult to employ as stabbing weapons. It is possible that the elaborate horned frill, which would have been covered with skin, served more as an accoutrement for courtship display than as a weapon of defense. There is no doubt, however, that *Styracoaurus* would have used its deadly snout horn to defend itself, or even to make pre-emptive strikes, against potential predators such as *Tyrannosaurus*.

Styracosaurus was one of the first horned dinosaurs to be discovered. Lawrence Lambe found the first skull along the exposures of the Belly River in Alberta, Canada, and in 1913 he formally named the dinosaur *Styracosaurus albertensis*. In 1930, Charles Gilmore named a second species *S. ovatus*. Today, however, scientists generally regard them as being male–female variants of the same species.

horned skull of Styracosaurus

Triceratops

try-SAIR-uh-TOPS

Triceratops is one of the best known of all dinosaurs and was the largest of the ceratopsians. Its massive head bore a short frill of solid bone along with the three large horns for which it is named—one above each eye and a smaller one on the snout. Traces of blood vessels found in the frill and horn have suggested to some paleontologists that the frill may have served as a means of regulating the animal's body temperature. As with other ceratopsians, the frill would have been covered with skin and may also have been used during courtship display.

Triceratops, which moved on all fours, had a heavy, robust body—this was necessary to support the weight of its head—and a short tail. Its solidly built forelimbs were shorter than the hindlimbs and do not seem to have been made for fast movement.

Fragmentary remains of large horned dinosaurs had been found in North America since 1855, but it was not until 1889 that John Bell Hatcher, who was searching the area around

FIELD NOTES

■ Three-horned head

🦖 30 feet (9 m)

■ Late Cretaceous

■ Alberta, Saskatchewan, Canada; Colorado, Montana, South Dakota, Wyoming, USA

🏛 American Museum of Natural History, New York, USA; Smithsonian Institution, Washington DC, USA; National Museum of Natural Sciences, Ottawa, Canada; National Museum of Natural History, Paris, France; Senckenberg Nature Museum, Frankfurt, Germany; Birmingham Museum, UK; Natural History Museum, London, UK; Hunterian Museum, Glasgow, UK; Royal Scottish Museum, Edinburgh, UK

Niobrara County, Wyoming, happened upon the first complete skull. Othniel Charles Marsh studied the discovery and in 1899 bestowed upon it the evocative name Triceratops horridus. Over the next three years, Hatcher collected about 30 neoceratopsian skulls, most of them identified as belonging to Triceratops. Barnum Brown is also credited with collecting many Triceratops skulls between 10 and 20 years later.

Some 16 different species were eventually named, about half of them by Marsh. Many of these species identifications were based on isolated horns and variable features of the skull. However, recent research by Dr. Catherine Forster, from the State University of New York at Stony Brook, has reduced the number of Triceratops species to just two—T. prorsus, which had straight horns above the eyes and a well-developed nose horn; and Marsh's original T. horridus, which was considerably larger but had a much smaller nose horn and slightly curved eye horns.

Triceratops's lifestyle was probably quite similar to that of that lumbering present-day herbivore, the rhinoceros. Its many rows of closely packed grinding teeth suggest that it was a feeder on a range of coarse vegetation, such as conifers, ferns, and cycads, as well as on some of the flowering plants that first appeared in the late Cretaceous. It cropped this plant matter with its long, powerful, pointed, horny beak. Its jaw mechanism was adapted primarily for cut-ting. Large jaw muscles attached from the lower jaw up onto the frill and powered the shearing action of the jaws.

different stances while moving

Triceratops was one of the last known dinosaurs. Isolated horn cores belonging to this dinosaur show that, along with its main predator, *Tryannosaurus*, it persisted right to the end of the Cretaceous. *Triceratops* may have charged at potential predators such as *Tyrannosaurus*, stabbing them with its three horns and using its thick, bony frill to protect its vulnerable neck. The great abundance of *Triceratops* fossils from the latest part of the Cretaceous provides convincing evidence of this dinosaur's ability to survive despite the numerous predatory theropods that shared its territory.

This skeleton of Triceratops horridus *shows its formidable armory of three horns and a bony neck plate.*

423

Chasmosaurus

KAZ-moh-SAW-rus

FIELD NOTES

- Chasm lizard
- 17 feet (5 m)
- Late Cretaceous
- Texas, USA; Alberta, Canada
- Royal Ontario Museum, Toronto, Canada

One of the earliest of the longer frilled dinosaurs, *Chasmosaurus* was a moderate-sized neoceratopsian. It had two short, upwardly curved horns above its eyes and a smaller horn on its snout. At the back of its long, narrow skull was a huge bony frill that stretched back over the animal's neck and shoulders. Within the frill were two enormous openings, or fenestrae, which made *Chasmosaurus*'s frill much lighter than that of any of its relatives. The bony part of the frill, which had right-angled upper corners with small ornamental horns, consisted of little more than a framework for the openings. This spectacular feature, covered with skin, was almost certainly a device for courtship display.

Lawrence Lambe, working with the Sternberg family on the Red Deer River in Alberta, Canada, discovered *Chasmosaurus*. He named it in 1914 after the chasm in which he found it. This dinosaur is now known from several skulls and skeletons. From the skeletons we can observe that the vertebral column above the pelvis was reinforced by many ossified ligaments. The pelvis itself was fortified by eight fused vertebrae. These helped dissipate the shocks that this large animal generated when it moved quickly.

Early studies made on skulls from Alberta and the northern United States suggested that they belonged to several different species. Today, however, most paleontologists consider that the variations reflect male-female differences within the same species—*C. canadensis*. Another species, *C. mariscalensis*, from Texas, is known from pieces of the skull and isolated bones which together make up an almost complete skeleton. *C. mariscalensis* differed from its northern counterpart mainly by having larger, more backward-curving horns.

stags challenging for dominance

Torosaurus

TAW-roh-SAW-rus

FIELD NOTES

■ Bull lizard

🦎 25 feet (7.5 m)

■ Late Cretaceous

■ Wyoming, South Dakota, Colorado, Utah, USA; Saskatchewan, Canada

🏛 Peabody Museum of Natural History, New Haven, USA; Academy of Natural Sciences, Philadelphia, USA

Torosaurus skull

human skull

Torosaurus, one of the most advanced of the long-shielded neoceratopsians, had a gigantic head that measured up to more than 8 feet (2.5 m) long. This means that its skull was longer than that of any other land animal that has ever lived. Torosaurus's neck frill, too, was enormous and made up about one-half the total skull length. The frill had two large, symmetrical openings that reduced its weight. Torosaurus had two prominent horns above its eyes and a very small horn on its snout. All three horns pointed forward.

In terms of length, Torosaurus was not much smaller than its contemporary, and close relative, Triceratops, but because of its more slender build, it probably weighed considerably less. The fact that relatively few specimens of Torosaurus have come to light suggests that this dinosaur was much less abundant than Triceratops.

John Bell Hatcher discovered a skull of Torosaurus in Niobrara County in Wyoming in 1889. He sent the specimen to Charles Othniel Marsh, who in 1891 named it Torosaurus latus, in recognition of the bull-like size of its skull and its large eye horns. This skull has been in the possession of the Peabody Museum in New Haven, Connecticut, ever since.

Partial remains of another four Torosaurus skulls have been found and have resulted in the naming of several species. However, differences between them have since been attributed to male–female variations.

Like other neoceratopsians, Torosaurus was a plant-eater that sheared off tough plant matter with a sharp beak powered by its strong shearing jaws. It then ground this food with the many rows of teeth in the back of its mouth.

An interesting study of a Torosaurus frill, undertaken in the 1930s by Dr. R. Moodie, showed irregular holes in the bony surface that may have been caused by cancers.

Huge fossil bone from Argentinosaurus

RECENT DINOSAUR DISCOVERIES

Although the rule of the dinosaurs ended 65 million years ago, the discovery of hitherto unknown types of dinosaurs continues. Furthermore, understanding of what dinosaurs were like is subject to constant scrutiny and review.

Perhaps the most astounding series of dinosaur finds in recent years are those from the early Cretaceous Liaoning locality in China. Liaoning had already yielded several important dinosaurs such as *Sinornithosaurus*, *Beipiaosaurus*, *Sinosauropteryx* and *Caudipteryx* that clearly demonstrate the link between dinosaurs and birds. Now more fossils have emerged to fill in the details of this evolutionary transition.

A rabbit-sized dinosaur so far only known by its catalog number NGMC 91 clearly preserves several "half feathers," structures attached to the skin that are half way between single hair-like filaments and the branching structures we recognize as true feathers. These tufts of fur

Beipiaosaurus

closely resemble down feathers still seen on birds today. The skeleton of NGMC 91 is clearly that of a small dromaeosaur which raises the possibility that other dromaeosaurs such as *Velociraptor* and *Deinonychus* may also have had similar "proto-feathers." This conclusion is supported by the discovery of a new specimen of *Sinornithosaurus*, also from Liaoning, that also has proto-feathers surrounding its body, and a feathered therizinosauris, *Beipiaosaurus*, demonstrates that feathers were widespread among advanced theropod dinosaurs.

Microraptor, also from Liaoning, provides another important piece in the bird-to-dinosaur puzzle. The arguments against the theory are that dinosaurs were too large to be the ancestors of birds and that the likely bird ancestor ought to live in trees—no tree-climbing dinosaurs had been found.

Deinonychus

Microraptor answers both these issues being a dromaeosaur about the size of a crow and having claws and hind limbs very similar to tree-climbing birds.

New finds push back our knowledge of when some dinosaurs groups first appeared. A turkey-sized animal found in Brazil may be the world's oldest dinosaur. This pointy-headed bipedal dinosaur is known from a couple of skulls and other partial skeletons. It was found in rocks between 235 and 240 million years old, making this unnamed dinosaur significantly older than the *Argentinean Eoraptor*, the 228 million year old fossil that previously held the title of world's oldest dinosaur.

Late Triassic rocks of Thailand have yielded the world's oldest sauropod. *Isanosaurus* is only known from some vertebrae, ribs, and parts of the front legs, but it appears to be a very primitive sauropod about 20 feet (6.5 m) long. *Paralititan* from the late Cretaceous of Egypt is a much larger sauropod that may have measured 72 to 90 feet (24–30 m) long and weighed 60 to 70 tons (61.5–71.5 t). This makes it one of the largest terrestrial animals of all time but currently it is only known from a single arm bone and fragments of the shoulder blades and vertebrae. Meanwhile, new material from South America of the gigantuan sauropod *Argentinosaurus* have confirmed that, at more than 70 tons (71.5 t), it was the heaviest-known terrestrial animal of all time.

A bizarre sauropod from older deposits in north Africa has paleontologists scratching their heads. At over 54 feet (18 m) long, *Jobaria* does not comfortably fit into any known sauropod group and probably belongs to a uniquely African group of sauropods. It has a relatively short neck and spoon-like teeth. Several skeletons of *Jobaria* were found at the one site suggesting that this late Jurassic dinosaur lived in groups.

Other investigations into dinosaurs have changed the way we think about them. One analysis has shown that paleontologists probably have been putting the nostrils in the wrong place! By comparing where the fleshy nostril sits on the face relative to the hole in the skull underneath it for several types of living animal, it has been shown that the nostril is at the front of the underlying hole in the skull. Dinosaurs, however, have been reconstructed with the nostrils further back and toward the top of the boney hole.

Two specimens of toothless ornithomimids reveal that they had soft nets of material lining their mouths that could have been used to strain food from mud. The diet of ornithomimids has never been fully understood but the finding of two different ornithomimids (one *Ornithomimus* and one *Gallimimus*) with similar soup-straining structures in their mouths suggests that they probably fed in a manner similar to flamingos.

Another remarkably preserved dinosaur, this time from Italy, has preserved skin and muscles as well as impressions of the intestines and some other internal organs. *Scipionyx* is a small theropod, barely the size of a chicken, and it is thought to be a juvenile.

And, while we have known about a variety of dinosaur remains including their bones, skin, muscles, feathers, dung, tracks and eggs, 2001 marked the finding of another, previously unrecorded type of dinosaur fossil. Spain has produced the world's first dinosaur vomit. More technically, it is likely to be a pellet, similar to those produced by owls, that is a regurgitate of the indigestible parts of their meals. This vomit, which is Cretaceous in age, preserves the remains of four small birds mixed together and slightly digested. It is not known for sure which dinosaur the pellet comes from but several small theropods known from the area are the most likely culprits.

Gallimimus

Scipionyx

CHAPTER SIX

A GUIDE *to* DINOSAUR
SITES *and* MUSEUMS

But there is one single moment that is never quite
duplicated ... when the first specimen is secured.

Galápagos, World's End,
CHARLES WILLIAM BEEBE (1877–1962), American scientist

USING *the* GUIDE *to* DINOSAUR SITES *and* MUSEUMS

Dinosaur fossils are often found in remote locations that few can visit.

Fortunately there are numerous museum collections open to public view.

The following pages feature a selection of the world's most famous dinosaur fossil sites as well as museums that house and display important collections of dinosaur fossils. Many of the museums promote the science of paleontology and are a good source for finding out more about the history of dinosaur finds and ongoing research programs.

The illustrated banding at the top of the page is a visual pointer to indicate that the page is about a site or a museum.

Dinosaur Sites and Museums

Color plates show a detail of the landscape of a site and a particular find related to that site, or the façade of a museum, and an interior display area.

Field Notes Panels

✳ Location of the site

■ Period to which a dinosaur fossil site belongs

🐾 Names of the dinosaurs discovered at the site or on display in the museum

🏛 Names of the main museums that display dinosaur fossils from the site featured

Dinosaur National Monument

Utah, United States of America

The United States National Parks Service established Dinosaur National Monument on October 4, 1915. Its establishment was the result of a decree by President Woodrow Wilson, which was designed to protect this extra-ordinary late Jurassic site from the depredations of unscrupulous fossil-hunters. This decree was prompted by an unsuccessful attempt on the part of the Carnegie Museum of Natural History in Pittsburgh, Pennsylvania, to file a claim to the site, which is located just north of the Jensen, and close to the border between Utah and Colorado.

The site was discovered in 1909 when Earl Douglas of the Carnegie Museum noticed the skeleton of a large sauropod eroding out of an exposed sandstone ledge on the banks of the Green River. Scientists from the Carnegie Museum soon began excavation work, and a seemingly endless succession of fossils was brought to light. So many bones were found at the site that field work continued without interruption until 1923. The final outcome of these excavations was that approximately 350 tons (357 t) of fossil bones were shipped back to the Carnegie Museum for preparation and study. The specimens contained the most complete skeleton of the sauropod *Apatosaurus* ever found (this was the very specimen that was found by Douglas in 1909). Charles Whitney

The entrance to Utah's Dinosaur National Monument.

Gilmore, of the Smithsonian Institution, worked on this skeleton for many years, finally publishing a detailed monograph describing *Apatosaurus* in 1936.

The lengthy excavations also uncovered nearly complete skeletons of *Allosaurus*, *Campto-saurus*, *Dryosaurus*, and *Stegosaurus*, all of which eventually became mounted displays at the Carnegie Museum. After the museum's expeditions had finished at the site, work continued over the next two decades, first by parties from the Smithsonian, under the auspices of Gilmore, and then by teams from the University of Utah.

The Dinosaur National Monument we see today is an exposed wall of sandstone that has

436

The text describes the features of a site and how it was discovered. In the case of the museum, it details the history of the institution, its importance to the study of paleontology, and the key people involved in its development.

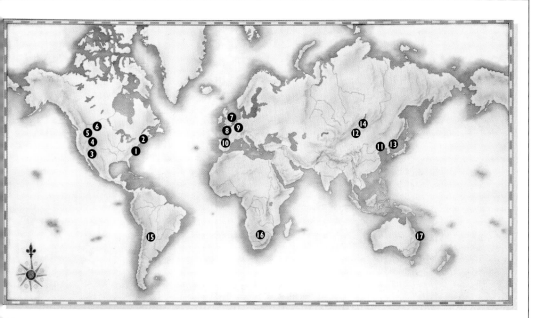

SITES AND MUSEUMS

1. Smithsonian Institution, Washington DC, USA

2. American Museum of Natural History, New York, USA

3. Dinosaur National Monument, Utah, USA

4. Hell Creek, Montana, USA

5. Dinosaur Trackways of the Western United States, USA

6. Dinosaur Provincial Park, Alberta, Canada

7. Natural History Museum, London, UK

8. Musée National d'Histoire Naturelle, Paris, France

9. Holzmaden and Solnhofen, Germany

10. Las Hoyas, Spain

11. Institute of Vertebrate Paleontology and Paleoanthropology, Beijing, China

12. Zigong Dinosaur Park, Szechuan, China

13. Liaoning, China

14. Flaming Cliffs, Mongolia

15. Valley of the Moon, Argentina

16. Karroo Basin, South Africa

17. Lark Quarry, Queensland, Australia

Dinosaur National Monument

FIELD NOTES

South-western United States

■ *Late Jurassic*

Allosaurus, large sauropods, Stegosaurus, Camptosaurus

🏛 *University of Utah, USA; Cleveland Museum of Natural History, USA; replica skeletons (e.g. Diplodocus, Allosaurus) in many of the world's major museums*

■ *Open to visitors as a national park*

...lly excavated to reveal ...dinosaur bones. They ...repared in high relief ...naturally within the ...the Morrison ...his wall is within the ...r Center. Opened ...nter completely ...all and protects it. ...s a partial skeleton ...amarasaurus, along ...nes of several ...such as *Apato-* ..., *Allosaurus*, and *Dryosaurus*. ...ell preserved for their age, ...n 155 and 148 million years. ...ferent genera of dinosaurs have ...he site. This means that it ...diverse late Jurassic dinosaur ...n the world.

...ormation is exposed through- ...length of the United States. ...ps indicate a dry desert en- ...around Utah the sequence ...saurs there once inhabited ...re, lowland alluvial plain.

...stands in front of Dinosaur Visitor Center.

The richness of the fossil finds suggests that the dinosaurs were probably swept away and drowned by large, meandering rivers during floods. At the bends where the river currents slowed down, the carcasses would have been dumped, gradually forming a mass burial site. Later on, the bones of the decaying carcasses would have been scattered by scavenging predators or moved around by the action of the water, resulting in the random jumble of different dinosaur remains, some par- tially articulated, that are exposed for visitors to the site to see today.

437

Smithsonian Institution

Washington DC, United States of America

The Smithsonian Institution was established in 1846 from a private bequest by James Smithson. Today its National Museum of Natural History contains almost 50 million fossil specimens, held in 450 separate collections. Its dinosaur collection, started at the beginning of the 20th century with specimens assembled under the auspices of Charles Othniel Marsh, includes more than 1,500 specimens. There are examples of late Jurassic dinosaurs such as *Allosaurus, Stegosaurus, Ceratosaurus,* and *Diplodocus,* collected from the Morrison Formation in Wyoming and from various sites in Colorado. Also, the collection features many skulls of *Triceratops* found by the famous dinosaur hunter John Bell Hatcher from the late Cretaceous deposits of Lance Creek, Wyoming.

Under the direction of Charles Whitney Gilmore, late Cretaceous dinosaurs were systematically collected from New Mexico and Montana. Gilmore's early finds from the Two Medicines Formation in northern Montana included the horned dinosaur *Brachyceratops* as well as bone beds that contained juvenile hadrosaurids and many other kinds of vertebrates.

Other dinosaurs collected under Charles Whitney Gilmore include the only titanosaurid sauropod that is known from North America (*Alamosaurus,* from New Mexico) and a range of interesting specimens that reveal pathological abnormalities in dinosaur bones.

Gilmore was one of the most productive of the early 20th-century dinosaur scientists. His work describing the nearly complete skeleton of *Apatosaurus,* first located by Earl Douglas in 1909, was critical to the forming of the Dinosaur National Monument in Utah. The Smithsonian Institution worked the sites in this area during the 1920s and 1930s, extracting many fine dinosaur specimens.

This reconstruction of Stegosaurus is a popular exhibit in the Smithsonian Institution.

A lifelike reconstruction in the Smithsonian of the giant pterosaur Quetzalcoatlus with its wings spread in flight.

By 1940 the Institution had become home to one of the largest collection of dinosaurs in the world. Gilmore wrote a summary paper—published in 1941 in the museum's proceedings—detailing the history and development of the Smithsonian's remarkable vertebrate paleontology collection.

The Smithsonian's collection of dinosaur type specimens contains over 40 named species. Many of the earlier ones, though, have since been dropped as valid species names or recognized as belonging to other known species. *Dystrophaeus viaemalae*, the first type dinosaur of the Institution was collected by John Strong Newberry in 1859 and named by Edward Drinker Cope in 1877. However, these fossils are now thought to belong to *Camarasaurus*, whose name takes priority.

Some of the museum's most important specimens are the skeletons of *Alamosaurus sanjuanensis*, *Stegosaurus stenops*, *Brachyceratops montanus*, *Edmontia rugosidens*, *Pachycephalosaurus wyomingensis*, *Camptosaurus brownei*, *Ceratosaurus nasicornis*, *Edmontosaurus annectens*, *Styracosaurus ovatus*, and *Thescelosaurus neglectus*.

The permanent exhibitions of the Smithsonian's Natural History Museum include several mounted dinosaur skeletons containing more then 50 percent original material. Among these exhibits are *Albertosaurus*, *Allosaurus*, *Camarasaurus*, *Diplodocus*, *Ceratosaurus*, *Corythosaurus*, *Edmontosaurus*, *Stegosaurus*, and *Triceratops*.

As well, there are mounted casts of the skeletons of a baby *Maiasaura* and the small South African dinosaur *Heterodontosaurus*. Other interesting material on display includes the skull of *Centrosaurus* and a cast of a *Tyrannosaurus* skull from the collections of the American Museum of Natural History.

Today, the Smithsonian's Department of Paleobiology is a major research body for all aspects of paleontology—marine microfossils, marine mollusks, fossil whales, and plant evolution, as well as dinosaurs. Further detailed information about the work of the staff, the collections, and the research programs being held can be found on the Smithsonian's web site.

FIELD NOTES

🦅 Superb displays of late Cretaceous theropods, hadrosaurs, and neoceratopsians, and late Jurassic dinosaurs from the Morrison Formation in Wyoming

433

American Museum of Natural History

New York, United States of America

The American Museum of Natural History (AMNH), in New York City, was first incorporated in 1869. Now the largest private museum in the world, AMNH houses a huge collection of dinosaur specimens, including the largest collection of real dinosaur material anywhere in the world. More importantly, it is a major research center for work on dinosaur systematics and evolution.

The AMNH began conducting field trips in 1897 with the early expeditions concentrating on the rich dinosaur localities found around Como Bluff, Wyoming. The team of eminent paleontologists included Henry Fairfield Osborn, Barnum Brown, William Matthew, Walter Granger, Jacob Wortman, and Albert Thomson. They made important finds of the sauropods *Diplodocus* and *Apatosaurus* (which was formerly known as *Brontosaurus*), and of the theropods *Allosaurus* and *Ornitholestes*. In 1898, the AMNH expeditions discovered the famous Bone Cabin site in Wyoming, where more than 50 partial dinosaur skeletons were collected. They included the remains of *Camarasaurus*, *Camptosaurus*,

FIELD NOTES

🐾 A wide range of dinosaur exhibits, both saurischian and ornithischian.

Spectacular skeletons include Tyrannosaurus, Diplodocus, Triceratops, and Euoplocephalus

Dryosaurus, and *Stegosaurus*. As well as these, they found new fossils of the species that they had unearthed earlier at Como Bluff.

In 1902, Barnum Brown, an eccentric character who often wore elaborate fur coats in the field, led an AMNH expedition to the Hell Creek region of Montana where he discovered the first *Tyrannosaurus rex* specimen. Later at this site—in 1908—he found an almost complete *Tyrannosaurus*, the mounted skeleton of which has been on display at the AMNH for more than 50 years. Between 1910 and 1915 Brown scoured the Red Deer River region of Alberta, Canada, using a custom-built wide barge that could cruise on the river and allow him access to remote sites. From these expeditions, he brought back substantially complete skeletons of the hadrosaurs *Corythosaurus* and *Saurolophus*. In the 1930s, he returned to the Jurassic deposits of Wyoming and collected many other dinosaur specimens for the AMNH.

Between 1922 and 1925, AMNH teams, under the leadership of the adventurer-scientist Roy Chapman Andrews and including Walter

434

Jacob Wortman, Walter Granger, and Peter Kaiser unearthing Apatosaurus from the Bone Cabin Quarry site in Wyoming.

Granger and Henry Osborn, ventured much farther afield to explore the rugged Gobi Desert of Mongolia. These now famous expeditions were originally undertaken in order to uncover fossil evidence of early humans; instead, they brought back a fine collection of late Cretaceous dinosaurs, including the first discovery of a complete nest of dinosaur eggs—belonging to *Protoceratops*. The Flaming Cliffs region was found to be particularly productive. Here, the AMNH field parties collected specimens of *Velociraptor*, *Protoceratops*, *Oviraptor*, *Pinacosaurus*, and *Saurornithoides*.

During the 1990s, teams from the AMNH made regular visits to these sites in the Gobi Desert, where they worked with paleontologists from the Mongolian Academy of Sciences. These recent expeditions have resulted in many new and extraordinary dinosaur, bird, and mammal discoveries, including specimens of the theropod *Oviraptor* brooding over a nest of its eggs. Remarkably, some of these eggs have yielded well-preserved embryonic dinosaur skeletons.

The AMNH's new Halls of Saursichian and Ornithischian Dinosaurs, which were completed in the mid-1990s, display more than 100 dinosaur specimens. About 85 percent of these—including the famous skeletons of *Tyrannosaurus*, *Apatosaurus*, *Triceratops*, and *Euoplocephalus*—consist entirely of original material. The collections of the AMNH form the basis of its highly successful research programs and include many thousands of important dinosaur fossils, large quantities of which were collected years ago and are still awaiting preparation and classification.

In recent years, the AMNH has produced a series of guide books that illustrate and give details of all the important specimens on display. It has also produced a number of large-format illustrated books about the history and development of the museum's vast collections.

435

Dinosaur National Monument

Utah, United States of America

The United States National Parks Service established Dinosaur National Monument on October 4, 1915. Its establishment was the result of a decree by President Woodrow Wilson, which was designed to protect this extraordinary late Jurassic site from the depredations of unscrupulous fossil-hunters. This decree was prompted by an unsuccessful attempt on the part of the Carnegie Museum of Natural History in Pittsburgh, Pennsylvania, to file a claim to the site, which is located just north of the Jensen, and close to the border between Utah and Colorado.

The site was discovered in 1909 when Earl Douglas of the Carnegie Museum noticed the skeleton of a large sauropod eroding out of an exposed sandstone ledge on the banks of the Green River. Scientists from the Carnegie Museum soon began excavation work, and a seemingly endless succession of fossils was brought to light. So many bones were found at the site that field work continued without interruption until 1923. The final outcome of these excavations was that approximately 350 tons (357 t) of fossil bones were shipped back to the Carnegie Museum for preparation and study. The specimens contained the most complete skeleton of the sauropod *Apatosaurus* ever found (this was the very specimen that was found by Douglas in 1909). Charles Whitney

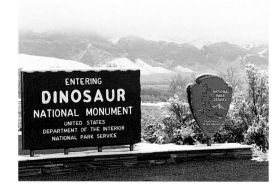

The entrance to Utah's Dinosaur National Monument.

Gilmore, of the Smithsonian Institution, worked on this skeleton for many years, finally publishing a detailed monograph describing *Apatosaurus* in 1936.

The lengthy excavations also uncovered nearly complete skeletons of *Allosaurus, Camptosaurus, Dryosaurus,* and *Stegosaurus,* all of which eventually became mounted displays at the Carnegie Museum. After the museum's expeditions had finished at the site, work continued over the next two decades, first by parties from the Smithsonian, under the auspices of Gilmore, and then by teams from the University of Utah.

The Dinosaur National Monument we see today is an exposed wall of sandstone that has

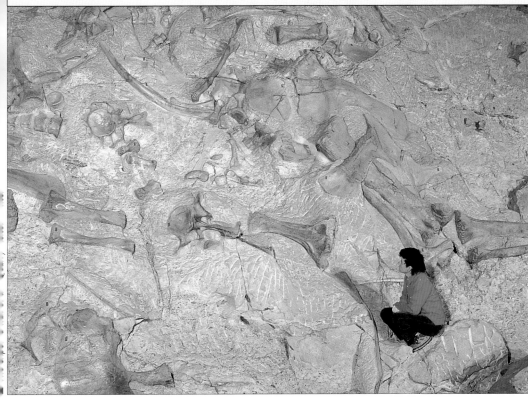

been carefully excavated to reveal some 1,500 dinosaur bones. They have been prepared in high relief as they occur naturally within the sandstones of the Morrison Formation. This wall is within the Quarry Visitor Center. Opened in 1958, the center completely encloses the wall and protects it. The wall shows a partial skeleton of a juvenile *Camarasaurus*, along with isolated bones of several other dinosaurs, such as *Apato-saurus*, *Diplodocus*, *Allosaurus*, and *Dryosaurus*. The bones are well preserved for their age, estimated between 155 and 148 million years.

To date, 10 different genera of dinosaurs have been found from the site. This means that it stands as the most diverse late Jurassic dinosaur locality anywhere in the world.

The Morrison Formation is exposed through-out the north–south length of the United States. In the south, outcrops indicate a dry desert en-vironment, whereas around Utah the sequence suggests that the dinosaurs there once inhabited an area that was a large, lowland alluvial plain.

FIELD NOTES

✶ South-western United States

■ Late Jurassic

🦅 Allosaurus, large sauropods, Stegosaurus, Camptosaurus

🏛 University of Utah, USA; Cleveland Museum of Natural History, USA; replica skeletons (e.g. Diplodocus, Allosaurus) in many of the world's major museums

■ Open to visitors as a national park

The richness of the fossil finds suggests that the dinosaurs were probably swept away and drowned by large, meandering rivers during floods. At the bends where the river currents slowed down, the carcasses would have been dumped, gradually forming a mass burial site. Later on, the bones of the decaying carcasses would have been scattered by scavenging predators or moved around by the action of the water, resulting in the random jumble of different dinosaur remains, some par-tially articulated, that are exposed for visitors to the site to see today.

A reconstructed Stegosaurus *stands in front of Dinosaur National Monument's Quarry Visitor Center.*

437

Hell Creek

Montana, United States of America

The exposures at Hell Creek represent a sequence of late Cretaceous river deposits that have been dated to between 70 and 65 million years ago (the late Maastrichtian stage)—the very last years of the age of dinosaurs. In 1902 Barnum Brown from the American Museum of Natural History (AMNH) first began searching the Hell Creek area for dinosaurs. He named the sedimentary rocks exposed there as the Hell Creek Beds, and today the 450-foot (137 m) thick succession of sandstones, siltstones, and mudstones are known formally as the Hell Creek Formation. These outcrops are protected within Hell Creek State Park, situated north of Jordan, Montana. In 1902, Brown discovered the first, and largely incomplete, *Tyrannosaurus* skeleton at Hell Creek and in 1908 he found an almost complete one, as well as the first skull of *Triceratops* from the region.

Part of the Hell Creek Formation in Montana.

In the years since then, the Hell Creek Formation has been searched by many field parties and has produced a great number of splendid dinosaur fossils, including, among others, *Torosaurus*, *Edmontosaurus*, *Stygimoloch*, *Pachycephalosaurus*, *Stegoceras*, *Albertosaurus*, *Aublysodon*, *Ornithomimus*, *Troödon*, and *Ankylosaurus*. The pachycephalosaur *Stygimoloch* was actually named for the Hell Creek site, its name

A collector at work in the Hell Creek Formation, where many species of fossil plants and animals have been found.

The skeleton of *Thescelosaurus*, found in the Hell Creek Formation

The distinctive domed skull of Stygimoloch.

meaning literally "river of Hell devil." Although many species of dinosaur are present here, very few are found in any degree of articulation. Most of the dinosaurs of Hell Creek are smaller animals, which suggests the area may have been fairly densely forested. As well as dinosaurs, the Hell Creek Formation has yielded the remains of several different kinds of tortoises, giant monitor lizards, and tree-dwelling multi-tuberculate mammals.

The Hell Creek region is also of scientific significance because the upper few yards of its sedimentary rocks possibly date into the Paleocene (the earliest stage of the Cenozoic era). High concentrations of the rare trace element iridium (an element found in abundance in meteorites) have been found in a layer here. This has been suggested as evidence for a giant meteorite impact at the end of the Cretaceous, an event that may have been the main cause of the extinction of the dinosaurs. The controversial occurrences of dinosaur remains within Paleocene deposits at Hell Creek has led some paleontologists to suggest that dinosaurs could have survived the meteorite

FIELD NOTES

North-western United States

Late Cretaceous

Triceratops, Tyrannosaurus, hadrosaurs, pachycephalosaurs

Denver Museum, Colorado, USA; Carnegie Museum, Pittsburgh, USA; Smithsonian Institution, Washington DC, USA; American Museum of Natural History, New York, USA

Hell Creek State Park is open to visitors

impact and lived on for a short while in the early part of the Paleocene. Others, however, interpret these occurrences as being nothing more than the re-siting of Cretaceous remains into Paleocene layers as a consequence of the erosion of the Cretaceous deposits.

The Hell Creek exposures have produced more than 190 species of fossil plants, and the microflora (based on pollen and spore species) suggests that up to 300 different species of plants grew in the floodplain and surrounding mountain settings. In the dry, subtropical conditions that prevailed there, the landscape would have been dominated by flowering plants.

Many of the Hell Creek dinosaurs went into the collection of the Denver Museum of Natural History, and displays there feature skeletons of *Tyrannosaurus* and *Edmontosaurus*, the latter showing fossilized evidence of a wound that may have been inflicted by the former.

439

Dinosaur Trackways of the Western United States

United States of America

Dinosaur trackways are relatively common fossils and are found in nearly all parts of the world. They date back to most parts of the Mesozoic era. Dinosaur footprints were first described as long ago as 1858 by the English clergyman and paleontologist the Reverend Edward Hitchcock. Hitchcock allocated names to the different kinds of dinosaur tracks he identified, and some of these, such as the large Triassic theropod tracks called *Eubrontes*, are still widely used today.

The best preserved dinosaur footprints are those that were formed when animals walked along a flat, wet, sandy area, such as a coastal plain or large river mouth delta. The feet left impressions in the wet sandstone which baked hard in the sun, later becoming buried by fine-grained, wind-blown, or water-borne sediments. The layer containing the footprints would have turned to hard, sedimentary rock once it had been buried by the deposition of minerals between the sediment grains. At a later time, the uplift of the Earth's crust and erosion would have once again exposed the footprint-bearing layer at the surface.

Trackways can tell us a great deal about dinosaur behavior—such as how the animals walked or ran, at what speeds they traveled, and the nature of dinosaur herd behavior. In some instances, they provide insights into the nature of dinosaur predatory habits.

The western United States has a large number of significant trackway sites, ranging from the late Triassic through to the late Cretaceous. Most of these occur in river, lake, shoreline, and desert dunefield settings.

Triassic dinosaur trackways occur in the Chinle Formation of New Mexico, Arizona, and Colorado. They comprise mainly the footprints of small coelurosaurs such as *Coelophysis*, and were left in riverside sediments. Late Triassic or early Jurassic dinosaur trackways occur in southern Utah from the Warner Valley south of Zion National Park and near Tuba

A large early Jurassic theropod footprint in the Kayenta Formation, near Tuba City, Arizona.

City, Arizona. In the Moenave and Kayenta formations in this region, there are well-preserved, three-toed prints of theropods that have been given the names *Grallator, Kayentopus,* and *Eubrontes. Grallator* tracks may have represented a small dinosaur similar to *Coelophysis; Eubrontes* may have been a large plateo-saurid prosauropod; *Kayentopus* appears to have been a medium-sized theropod—it may have been *Dilophosaurus,* fossils of which occur in the same rock layers. The top layers of the Entrada Sandstone, which out-crops prominently in the Arches National Park, northern Arizona, is rich in dinosaur trackways. The late Jurassic Morrison Formation has some layers that contain many trackways. Perhaps the most celebrated is the Purgatoire Valley, south-eastern Colorado, where the tracks are preserved in rocks that were once an ancient shoreline. The trackways representing some 1,300 prints, from around 100 dinosaurs—principally theropods and sauropods, but including some rarer ornithopods—are recorded.

FIELD NOTES

✷ Central western United States; western Canada

■ Late Triassic to late Cretaceous

🐾 Many kinds of sauropods, theropods, ornithopods, and thyreophoran trackways

🏛 On-site trackways at Dinosaur Valley State Park, Texas, USA and Picketwire Canyonlands, Colorado, USA; Texas Memorial Museum, Austin, USA; American Museum of Natural History, New York, USA; Royal Tyrrell Museum, Alberta, Canada

■ Many sites open to visitors; others on private land require permission

The early Cretaceous Dakota Group of Colorado shows layers with a high density of footprints, which results in a trampled effect on the sedimentary layers. In the Laramie Formation of the Denver region, one set of layers of "trampled" rock made by ornithopod dinosaurs can be traced for tens of miles. Tracks of neoceratopsians and medium to small theropods are also recorded here.

The early Cretaceous Paluxy River trackways are exposed near Glen Rose in Texas (Glen Rose Formation). Large theropod tracks here were possibly made by *Acrocanthosaurus;* the largest sauropod tracks could have been made by *Pleurocoelus.* These trackways are famous for the insights they give into sauropod herd behavior. They show that the largest sauropods walked on the outside of the herd with the smaller juveniles positioned safely in the center of the group. Other trackways preserved here show possible attack trails made by large, predatory theropods closing in on sauropods.

441

Dinosaur Hall in the Royal Tyrrell Museum

Dinosaur Provincial Park

Alberta, Canada

FIELD NOTES

✦ South-western Canada

■ Late Cretaceous

🦤 Many dinosaur types, including ceratopsian and hadrosaur species; Albertosaurus, Tyrannosaurus

🏛 Royal Tyrrell Museum, Drumheller (on-site), and many museums worldwide

■ Open to visitors as a national park

The extensive outcrops of the late Cretaceous Judith River Group—which dates back to between about 77 and 73 million years ago—along the Red Deer River near central southern Alberta, have yielded a greater number of complete dinosaur specimens than any other site on Earth. In 1955, an area of 28 square miles (73 km²) of this land was officially established as Dinosaur Provincial Park, and in 1979 the region was designated as a World Heritage Site by UNESCO for its exceptional preservation, diversity, and the abundance of dinosaurs and related fauna. The deep gullies and river outcrops of the park were formed by erosion caused from glacial meltwaters retreating from the last ice age—between about 14,000 and 12,000 years ago—exposing a section 400 feet (125 m) thick of late Cretaceous sandstones, mudstones, and siltstones that are collectively called the Dinosaur Park Formation.

The Dinosaur Park Formation represents an estuary-river setting. Large numbers of dinosaur skeletons may have got caught up here when floating carcasses became entangled in accumulations of logs (log jams) at river bends. Massive flood events may have killed thousands of dinosaurs at one time, as can be seen in the *Centrosaurus* bone bed.

The history of Dinosaur Provincial Park dates back to 1909, when a rancher, John Wagner, reported to New York's American Museum of Natural History (AMNH) that he thought he had dinosaur bones on his property. In the next year or so, Barnum Brown started to search the area. Brown soon realized that the dinosaur-bearing rocks were best exposed along the banks of the Red Deer River. He therefore built a wide raft with a tent over the top of it so that his field crew could sail down the river, stopping to search at each new exposure. At the end of each field season, as the cold weather closed in on them, the fossil-hunters hauled the raft onto the banks and stored their finds until the next season.

By 1912 the boundaries of the park were established around the exposures. Brown's early finds included complete skeletons of *Gorgosaurus*, *Corythosaurus*, *Prosaurolophus*, *Centrosaurus*, and *Struthiomimus*. Collector Charles Sternberg and his family also worked the sites within the park.

An eroded rock formation in Dinosaur Provincial Park

The Royal Tyrrell Museum (left), one of the world's most important paleontological museums, is situated within Dinosaur Provincial Park.. The skull (above) of the horned dinosaur Pachyrhinosaurus is part of the museum's collection.

They found skeletons of *Albertosaurus* and *Chasmosaurus* with delicate skin impressions, as well as beautifully preserved skulls of *Centrosaurus* and *Styracosaurus*.

Field work has continued in the park over the succeeding years, and has yielded as many as 250 articulated dinosaur skeletons that represent some 36 different dinosaur species, including *Struthiomimus*, *Anchiceratops*, *Lambeosaurus*, *Dromaeosaurus*, *Troödon*, *Gravitholus*, *Gryposaurus*, *Brachylophosaurus*, *Edmontia*, *Euoplocephalus*, and *Panoplosaurus*. Approximately 300 different fossil species of animals and plants have been recorded for the Dinosaur Park Formation. This includes

84 species of fishes, frogs, salamanders, turtles, lizards, crocodiles, pterosaurs, birds, and mammals, as well as many species of fossil plants.

The Royal Tyrrell Museum of Paleontology established a permanent field station within the park in 1987. This provides a base for ongoing field studies for the collection of new dinosaur remains, and also functions as a center where visitors to the park can view displays and find information about the discoveries that were made there. The exhibits include the skeletons of the horned *Centrosaurus* and the large predator *Daspletosaurus*. Today, the dinosaurs that have been collected from the park can be viewed and studied in more than 30 institutions all around the world.

Natural History Museum

London, United Kingdom

For the past two centuries London's Natural History Museum has housed the first dinosaur fossils ever found and described. As well, it has built up an enormous collection of fossils from around the world. The British Museum first opened in 1753 in the part of London known as Bloomsbury. There, it displayed a wide range of natural and historical curiosities. The museum's first significant collections of fossils and geological specimens were made up of both purchases and donations from the private collections of a number of eminent "gentlemen" naturalists of the time. Among the donors were William Smith—often referred to as the "father of geology"—and Gideon Mantell, who discovered remains of *Iguanodon*. All the specimens that Charles Darwin collected on his voyage on the *Beagle* came to reside in the museum.

The museum moved location in 1845, but by 1856 the collections were so large that another building was required. Specimens from the far corners of the British Empire came rolling in; among them were vast numbers of foreign fossils collected by the British Geological Survey. The current impressive building that stands in South

FIELD NOTES

🦆 A huge range of important specimens from all around the world. Prominent among them are Euoplocephalus, Diplodocus, Triceratops, Iguanodon, Baryonyx, Hypsilophodon, Brachiosaurus, Archaeopteryx, and Scelidosaurus.

Kensington was completed in 1881. One of the activists behind the push for the new museum, and a contributor toward its design, was the famous anatomist Sir Richard Owen. It was Owen who in 1842 coined the term "Dinosauria," after he undertook a thorough revision of all the British dinosaur remains that were known at the time. Owen's revision was based principally on far from complete specimens of *Megalosaurus*, *Hylaeosaurus*, and *Iguanodon*.

In 1963, the Natural History Section of the museum separated from the British Museum (whose collections are now predominantly historical and archaeological). It became known officially as the Natural History Museum. In 1986, its collections were increased when those belonging to the former Geological Museum, situated nearby, were incorporated into them.

Today the Natural History Museum holds some 9 million specimens, including approximately 30,000 specimens of fossil reptiles and amphibians. The museum is renowned as a center for research in all aspects of paleontology, including the study of dinosaurs. Among its most prominent dinosaur specialists over the past three

decades have been Dr. Alan Charig and Dr. Angela Milner.

The dinosaur collections of the Natural History Museum contain many important specimens such as *Megalosaurus*, *Baryonyx*, *Cetiosauriscus*, *Hylaeosaurus*, *Hypsilophodon*, *Dacentrurus*, *Rhabdodon* (=*Mochlodon*), *Polacanthus*, *Euoplocephalus*, *Thecodontosaurus*, and *Brachiosaurus*. The London specimen of *Archaeopteryx*, perhaps one of the most famous fossils of its time, and one of only seven known specimens, was acquired by the museum in 1861 for what was then considered a princely sum—£700 ($1,070). Sir Richard Owen's study of this specimen was a seminal work on the origin of birds, even though nowadays *Archaeopteryx* is generally regarded as the first bird by definition, even though it is more dinosaurian by design.

Another of the museum's most famous dinosaurs is the small, armored *Scelidosaurus* which Sir Richard Owen described from a nearly complete skeleton found in Dorset, in the south of England, in 1863. In the 1960s, technicians at the Natural History Museum developed the very valuable technique of preparing fossil bones out of limestone rock by using weak solutions of acid. By this means, *Scelidosaurus* has now been

This specimen is a jumble of Iguanodon bones known as the "Maidstone Slate." It was developed in 1834 by the eminent naturalist Gideon Mantell..

carefully prepared to more clearly display many details of its anatomy.

The Natural History Museum also contains type specimens of many very poorly known dinosaurs, such as the opalized bones of *Rapator*, *Walgettosuchus*, and *Fulgurotherium* from Australia. In addition there are numerous other named dinosaurs in the collections whose validity is under question, such as the type specimen of the theropod *Aristosuchus*, from the Wealden of England, and *Proceratosaurus* from the Jurassic of southern England.

The dinosaur display at the Natural History Museum was updated in 1991 in order to show dinosaurs in the light of their reconstructed biology and behavior. Visitors walking into the main entrance hall of the museum find themselves in the presence of impressive mounted skeletons of *Diplodocus* and *Triceratops*.

445

Musée National d'Histoire Naturelle

Paris, France

The Institut de Paléontologie, part of France's Musée National d'Histoire Naturelle, is situated in the beautiful setting of the Jardin des Plantes in Paris. The museum houses the large comparative anatomy collection of the great French anatomist Baron Georges Cuvier (1769–1832) together with a great number of important fossil specimens from around the world. It has many dinosaur specimens, especially from France, Africa, and parts of South-East Asia.

Triassic dinosaurs in the institute include French material of the prosauropod *Plateosaurus* (from Saint Lothan), an undescribed prosauropod from Alzon, and Moroccan specimens of *Azendohsaurus*. From 1955 to 1959, expeditions to Lesotho, in southern Africa, under the leadership of Dr. L. Ginsberg and Drs. F. and P. Ellenberger, collected specimens of the large prosauropod *Euskelosaurus* and a lower jaw of the ornithischian *Fabrosaurus* from Maphutseng.

Jurassic dinosaurs in the institute include several local species. The theropod *Poekilopleuron bucklandii* is now known only from casts, as the original bones, first described in 1838,

were destroyed in World War II. The theropod *Piveteausaurus* is known from a braincase found at Calvados in Normandy and a partial sauropod skeleton, *Bothriospondylus*, came from Damparis.

Baron Cuvier described the bones of a reptile from Honfleur, which he thought was a large crocodile but which was later identified as a theropod dinosaur and named as *Streptospondylus cuvieri*. The most complete Jurassic dinosaur known from France is a small skeleton of the little theropod *Compsognathus corallestris* from the area around Canjuers.

The institute contains some large Jurassic sauropod bones from Africa and Madagascar. In 1940–1941, Dr. A. de Lapparent collected *Cetiosaurus* from El Mers, Morocco, and in 1962, Dr. L. Ginsberg collected *Lapparentosaurus* and *Bothriospondylus* from Kamoro, Madagascar.

Cretaceous dinosaurs are generally poorly known, some by only a few, isolated bones. The institute's collections include the theropod *Genusaurus* from Bevons, a hadrosaur jaw bone from Saint Martory, and from the latest Cretaceous deposits of Fox Amphoux, specimens that were collected in 1939 by

FIELD NOTES

Iguanodon, Allosaurus, Diplodocus, Tyrannosaurus, Tarbosaurus

Professor Philippe Taquet is a former director of the museum.

Dr. de Lapparent. These include part of a nodosaurid as well as titanosaur sauropod bones, hypsilophodont bones, and some theropod teeth and bones. Unfortunately, the start of World War II put a stop to de Lapparent's productive dinosaur excavations at this site. Dinosaur eggs from the late Cretaceous were also collected from Bouches de Rhône, in southern France.

The institute has a good representation of Cretaceous dinosaurs from Africa. In 1950, Dr. Lavocat first collected bones and teeth of the giant theropod *Carcharodontosaurus* from Kem-Kem in Morocco. In 1995, an almost complete *Carcharodontosaurus* skull was found by Dr. Paul Sereno's team from the University of Chicago. Lavocat also found bones of the sauropod *Rebbachisaurus* from Morocco, and Dr. Philippe Taquet led major field expeditions into the Niger Republic, Africa, between 1966 and 1972 and discovered the nearly complete skeleton of the hump-backed iguanodontid *Ouranosaurus*. The institute holds only a cast of this dinosaur; the original specimen resides in the National Museum of Niger. Other finds from these expeditions held in Paris include a femur of the dryosaurid *Valdosaurus* and bones of the spined theropod *Spinosaurus*.

The first dinosaurs collected from the rich Cretaceous sites of Madagascar are part of the institute's collection. These include bones of the sauropod *Titanosaurus madagascarensis*, and a peculiar piece of a domed skull that was originally identified as belonging to a pachycephalosaur. In 1998, a complete skull of this dinosaur, by the name of *Majungatholus*, was discovered by Dr. Scott Sampson and his team. As a result of this find it is now known to be an abelisaurid theropod similar to *Carnotaurus*.

In recent years Professor Taquet has led several expeditions into Laos and Cambodia to sites first worked in the 1940s by the French geologist J. Hoffet. New specimens of sauropods, hadrosaurs, and theropods have been collected but they await detailed study.

The institute also has a skeleton of *Edmontosaurus*, and a skull of *Triceratops*, specimens that were purchased in 1911 from the Canadian fossil-hunter Charles Sternberg.

447

Holzmaden and Solnhofen

Germany

These late Jurassic sites are famous for the fine state of preservation of their vertebrate fossils. These include *Archaeopteryx,* the rare feathered dinosaur from the Solnhofen deposits, and the complete body fossils at Holzmaden of ichthyosaurs and other marine reptiles.

Holzmaden has yielded the world's best fossils of marine reptiles, especially plesiosaurs and ichthyosaurs. Ichthyosaur fossils showing the outline of the entire animal, including its dorsal fins, have been preserved there. Some fossils, astonishingly, show young inside adult females and there is even a remarkable fossil of an ichthyosaur giving birth. Such fossils occur when mud slides or freak storm events bury the animals without warning. To date, no dinosaurs have been found at Holzmaden, but its fauna includes at least four different types of ichthyosaur, a pliosaur, a plesiosaur, and two species of teleosaurid crocodilians.

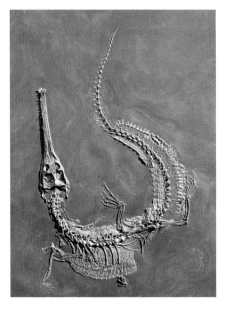

This beautifully preserved Jurassic crocodilian, Steneosaurus, *was found at Holzmaden.*

The Solnhofen deposits are of finely layered lithographic limestones, which outcrop in an east–west belt north of Munich and south of Nuremberg. The main sites are around the towns of Solnhofen, Eichstätt, and Kelheim. They have produced an extremely diverse and well-preserved fossil assemblage of some 360 species of invertebrates, vertebrates, and plants, which inhabited the shallow waters of a lagoon. The bed of this lagoon could not support life, so that animals and plants that fell to the bottom were not scavenged or disrupted but became buried intact.

The vertebrate fauna of Solnhofen includes 54 species of fossil fishes, 28 kinds of reptiles (mostly pterosaurs, but also some ichthyosaurs, plesiosaurs, and crocodilians), and two dinosaurs. These are the complete skeleton of the little coelurosaur *Compsognathus* and the

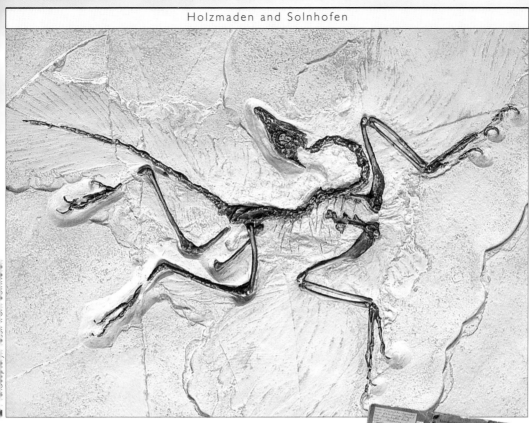

feathered dinosaur *Archaeopteryx*, now known from about eight specimens in total.

In 1855 the first *Archaeopteryx* discovery—of a partial skeleton without feathers—went largely unnoticed. A feather was found in 1860, which alerted anatomists that an early bird might have existed in the Jurassic. In 1861, a complete skeleton with feathers was found and was purchased by the British Museum of Natural History. This was the subject of Sir Richard Owen's monograph on the anatomy of the first bird. The next specimen was not found until 1877. The most recent finds of *Archaeopteryx* specimens, between 1951 and 1996, have shown the existence of two species—*A. lithographica* and *A. bavarica*. The little dinosaur *Compsognathus* is so similar in its skeletal form to *Archaeopteryx* that one of the first *Archaeopteryx* specimens was for many years mislabeled as a *Compsognathus*, mainly because it lacked feathers.

Solnhofen has also produced many superb pterosaur fossils including *Rhamphorhynchus*, *Scaphognathus*, *Pterodactylus*, *Anurognathus*, *Ctenochasma*, *Gnathosaurus*, and *Germanodactylus*.

FIELD NOTES

✵ Central Europe (Germany)

■ Late Jurassic

🌱 Solnhofen: Archaeopteryx, Compsognathus; Holzmaden: ichthyosaurs, plesiosaurs

🏛 Jura Museum, Eichstätt, Germany; museums in Munich and Berlin; Natural History Museum, London, UK; Holzmaden ichthyosaurs in many museums worldwide

■ Natural exposures can be visited in some areas. Some private sites not accessible to visitors

Pterosaur fossil from the Solnhofen deposits.

Some specimens show exquisite preservation of the delicate wing membranes of these flying reptiles as well as outlines of the tail rudders. Other vertebrate fossils from Solnhofen deposits include rare but very well-preserved ichthyosaurs and crocodilians. Many kinds of fishes and invertebrates were present in the lagoon, and these were what probably lured pterosaurs and small dinosaurs to the water in the first place.

In 1994, a superb book showing the extraordinary riches of the fossil fauna and flora of the Solnhofen sites was published by Dr. Karl Frickhinger.

449

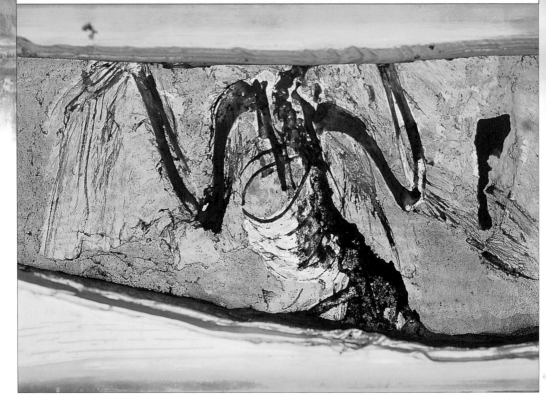

Las Hoyas

Spain

The Las Hoyas site in Spain, in the Iberian Mountain Ranges of Cuenca Province, is an ancient lake deposit which has produced some of the world's best preserved fossil birds and rare dinosaurs, as well as a wealth of fossil plants, fishes, amphibians, reptiles, insects, and crustaceans.

The site was discovered in the late 1980s, and the first publication detailing its fossil fauna was released in 1988. The deposit lies within the Calizas de la Huerguina Formation and is dated at the Barremian stage of the early Cretaceous (approximately 117–114 million years old). The fossils are preserved in two kinds of environmental settings—one a lake deposit, the other river sediments marginal to the lake. The detrital river sediments of the formation have yielded less complete remains but nonetheless they make a contribution to our understanding of the entire original fauna and flora of the region. The lake deposits are made up of very fine-grained limestones. This means that carcasses that sank to the bottom of the lake would have been buried quickly, with their organs intact. This kind of preservation shows the feathers on the birds and the outlines of

soft tissue on the other organisms—such as skin impressions for the reptiles, and outlines of horny sheaths over the claw bones of the foot. Furthermore, any bony fossils found in such limestone layers can be prepared out in three-dimensional form using weak acid solutions. Several of the best of the bird specimens, as well as the dinosaur *Pelecanimimus*, were prepared in this manner after first being embedded in a sheet of epoxy resin.

Las Hoyas has yielded thousands of beautifully preserved complete fossil birds. These belong in three genera: *Concornis*, *Iberomesornis*, and *Eoalulavis*. *Iberomesornis* is the most primitive of the three (with regard to its hindlimb and pelvic structure), as it shares certain features with the primitive avian theropod *Archaeopteryx* from the late Jurassic of Germany. Both *Eoalulavis* and *Concornis* belong to the enantiornithine group.

Dr. José Sanz, who is currently in charge of excavations at Las Hoyas, examines the fossil of a hatchling bird.

University students search for fossils at Las Hoyas

A fossilized head (above) and feet (below) of Pelecanimimus, found at Las Hoyas.

These were true flying birds, but they fit in right at the base of the radiation of modern birds. *Eoalulavis* is of particular importance in that the alula is present in its wrist. This bone is necessary for controlled, low-speed flight maneuvers, and crucial for more efficient take-offs and landings.

Only three dinosaurs have been found in the Las Hoyas deposits. Some isolated bones of the ornithopod *Iguanodon* and an as yet undescribed sauropod have come from the detrital river sediments, and a remarkably well-preserved partial skeleton of a primitive ornithomimosaur, *Pelecanimimus*, has come from the fine-grained lake sediments. *Pelecanimimus*, which was about 6–8 feet (2–2.5 m) in length, shows the impressions of skin and integumentary fibers as well as a keratinous sheath over the foot claws. The skull is very primitive in retaining a high number of teeth (about 220 in all). This has led to the theory that ornithomimosaurs did not lose their teeth but gradually incorporated many smaller ones into the edges of the beak. The beak was too thin and delicate for slicing and probably would have been used for filter feeding.

Las Hoyas, like Liaoning in China, is one of the world's most important fossil sites for understanding the transition from dinosaurs to birds. Current excavations at the site, which are under the direction of paleontologist Dr. José Sanz, are expected to bring to light new, well-preserved dinosaur remains and more exquisite fossil birds.

This crocodile fossil, found at Las Hoyas in 1993, dates back to the early Cretaceous.

Institute of Vertebrate Paleontology and Paleoanthropology

Beijing, China

In 1929 at Zoukoudian Cave near Beijing, a Chinese scientist, Pei Wen-Zhong, discovered an extraordinary fossil skull of a primitive human. This specimen would become world famous as "Peking man," and the discovery provided Chinese authorities with the impetus to start investigating the science of vertebrate paleontology.

The Cenozoic Research Laboratory of the Geological Survey of China thus began to collect vertebrate fossils and in 1957 a separate institution, the Institute of Vertebrate Paleontology, was established. In 1960, its name was changed to the Institute of Vertebrate Paleontology and Paleoanthropology (IVPP), and its scope was widened to include research on human evolution.

The founding director of the IVPP, Professor Yang Zhongjian (1897–1979), became better known in the Western world as Professor C. C. Young. During

FIELD NOTES

♥ Chinese dinosaurs, including Lufengosaurus, Monolophosaurus, Psittacosaurus, Protoceratops, Tuojiangosaurus

the 1950s, Professor Young undertook fieldwork at the Cretaceous dinosaur localities of Shandong Province, where he discovered remains of the unusual hadrosaurid *Tsintaosaurus* as well as skeletons of psittacosaurids. Young also studied the giant sauropod *Mamenchisaurus*, an almost complete skeleton of which was collected in Szechuan in 1957. Between 1963 and 1966, Dr. (now Professor) Dong Zhiming began exploring the Jungaar and Turpan basins of northern China. Here he discovered a fauna that included the dinosaurs *Monolophosaurus*, *Tienshanosaurus*, *Bellusaurus*, *Psittacosaurus*, *Wuerhosaurus*, *Jaxartosaurus*, and *Kelmayisaurus*. Throughout the 1970s and 1980s, teams from the IVPP, often working

In 1993 the IVPP moved into this modern building in Beijing.

452

in conjunction with local scientific authorities from the various provinces of China, made many exciting dinosaur discoveries.

Professor Dong has probably discovered and named more dinosaurs than any other 20th-century paleontologist. Perhaps one of his most important discoveries was the Dashanpu Dinosaur Quarry near Zigong in Szechuan Province. Today, an impressive museum has been built above the site to house many of its important specimens as well as to show the excavations in progress. More than 8,000 fossil bones, including many complete dinosaur skeletons, have been excavated or exposed from the site.

During the late 1980s and early 1990s, joint expeditions of the IVPP and the Royal Tyrrell Museum, Canada, explored the remote regions of northern China and inner Mongolia and discovered numerous new dinosaurs and other vertebrates. Many of the specimens that they found, such as the theropod *Sinraptor*, are now in the IVPP collections.

The IVPP conducts research on all aspects of vertebrate paleontology and paleoanthropology and curates a huge collection of fossil specimens. Each year its field parties scour the far corners of China in their search for fossils. The IVPP is divided into three departments—paleoichthyology and paleoherpetology (fishes, amphibians,

Professor Dong Zhiming, one of China's most celebrated paleontologists, is a prolific discoverer of new dinosaurs.

reptiles, and dinosaurs), paleomammalogy (fossil mammals), and paleoanthropology (human fossils). In the early 1990s, the IVPP had a full-time staff of 230 people. Results of the IVPP's research work are published through its three scientific journals as well as through major international scientific journals. The IVPP holds over 200,000 specimens of fossil vertebrates. These include most of the type or reference specimens for many Chinese dinosaurs.

In 1993 the IVPP moved into a new, larger building which has a three-story public area for fossil displays. In the last few years, the IVPP has collected a number of extraordinary remains of feathered Chinese dinosaurs and primitive birds from the early Cretaceous Liaoning sites in northern China.

453

Zigong Dinosaur Park

Szechuan, China

The Zigong Dinosaur Park, in central Szechuan Province, near Dashanpu, Zigong, opened in 1987. It was erected over the top of a rich site that contained many dinosaur skeletons alongside other fossil vertebrates. The fossils occur in gray-green sandstones and mudstones of the middle Jurassic Shaximiao Formation, an ancient river setting. Dinosaurs and other animals probably drowned in flood events and their bodies would have accumulated at river bends where the current slowed down. In this respect the Dashanpu site is the Chinese equivalent of the rich bone bed at Dinosaur National Monument in Utah.

The Zigong Dinosaur Museum was the first museum dedicated solely to dinosaurs to open in Asia. Today it features the most impressive display of Chinese dinosaur skeletons in any one place, with an excavation of real bones exposed for public viewing in the museum's bedrock. Fossils were first found near Dashanpu in 1972 by geologists from the Szechuan Bureau of Geology and Mineral Resources—they came

The Dinosaur Museum in Dashanpu, in Szechuan Province, was opened in the spring of 1987.

upon a dinosaur bone sticking out of a roadside cliff. The site was first excavated in 1977 and produced a large sauropod skeleton. It was named by Professor Dong Zhiming and his colleagues as *Shunosaurus*. On December 17, 1979, Professor Dong and Zhou Shiwu discovered many more dinosaur remains, exposed in situ in the Dashanpu region. Excavations at the site from 1979 to 1981 produced further skeletons of *Shunosaurus*, as well as the theropod *Gasosaurus*, a beautifully preserved stegosaur *Huayangosaurus,* and a new sauropod named *Dataousaurus.* Further excavations the following year by He Xinlu of the Chen-Du College of Geology uncovered skeletons of small ornithopods at the site, together with a large, new sauropod, *Omeisaurus.*

In 1984, while the museum was being built, almost 5,400 square feet (500 m²) of bedrock had to be cleared. This resulted in more fossil discoveries, such as a skull of a late-surviving

The center of the museum's main hall

Local villagers watch the activities of a group of scientists working on dinosaur fossils in the Zigong Dinosaur Park.

skeletons. These include the sauropods *Omeiosaurus* and *Shunosaurus*, the stegosaur *Huayangosaurus*, the theropod *Gasosaurus*, and the small ornithopod *Xioasaurus*. The most spectacular part of the display is the exposed bedrock in the center of the main hall, which shows a large number of dinosaur and other vertebrate bones just as they were found.

Geological investigations at Dashanpu have shown that the site has enormous potential for more discoveries. Today the excavated area covers some 31,000 square feet (2,800 sq m) but the bone bed continues for an estimated 215,000 square feet (20,000 sq m). To date, over 8,000 bones of dinosaurs and other vertebrates have been excavated from the site. Research on the Dashanpu fossils is ongoing—excavations are revealing more bones every year.

labyrinthodont amphibian, *Sinobrachyops*, and the skull of a mammal-like reptile, *Bienotheroides*. Remains of freshwater fossil fishes, turtles, crocodiles, a plesiosaur, and a pterosaur have also been excavated from the site. The pterosaur, *Angustinaripterus*, was a close relative of *Rhamphorhynchus* from Germany. The total number of vertebrates collected from the Dashanpu Quarry is now 23 species, eight of which are dinosaurs.

The museum's basement is used for fossil storage and fossil preparation and there are two floors of displays. Displayed in the main hall are 10 almost complete, mounted dinosaur

FIELD NOTES

✺ Central China (Szechuan)

■ Late Jurassic

🌷 Large sauropods and theropods (e.g. Shunosaurus, Omeiosaurus, Yangchuanosaurus)

🏛 Zigong Dinosaur Museum, Dashanpu (on site)

▪ Open to visitors

455

Liaoning

China

Quarries near Sihetun in the province of Liaoning, northern China, have recently become famous, due to their remarkable preservation of primitive birds and small dinosaurs, with feathers and integumentary coats preserved. The animals drowned in a lake and sank to the muddy bottom, where they were rapidly buried by nearby volcanic ash falls without any disruption of their remains. Today their fossils occur in fine-grained, layered siltstones, which can be split with chisels to reveal the specimens. The site is of uncertain age, some estimates placing it as latest Jurassic, but recent work supports an early Cretaceous date (around 140–120 million years ago). The bird fossils are especially significant in being the first record in geological time of birds after the famous late Jurassic *Archaeopteryx* specimens from Germany.

The discovery of the little dinosaur *Sinosauropteryx* in 1996 caused a sensation because it was the first dinosaur to be found showing an integumentary coat of what appeared to be fiberlike feathers. Further analysis has shown that these are primitive feathers, but they lack the complex bifurcations seen in the feathers of flying birds. Other soft-tissue preservation in the dinosaurs of this site show the remains of gut contents, eggs inside oviducts, and impressions of soft organs, such as the eye capsule.

Paleontologists from the Institute of Vertebrate Paleontology and Paleoanthropology in Beijing excavate layers of sedimentary rock at Jianshangou in Liaoning Province.

To date, several kinds of theropod dinosaurs have been excavated from Liaoning. All show feathers or fibrous coats over parts of the body. *Sinosauropteryx*, the most primitive of these theropods, is a small coelurosaur that is similar to *Compsognathus*. *Sinornithosaurus*, a primitive dromaeosaurid, and *Beipiaosaurus*, a therizinosaur, also have simple fibrous feather coats, similar to that seen in *Sinosauropteryx*. Two small dinosaurs, however, are extraordinary in that they have longer feathers with bifurcating broad

areas, as evident in typical bird feathers. These are *Caudipteryx* and *Protoarchaeopteryx*. Both dinosaurs have longer arms and shorter legs than the other dinosaurs of Liaoning, and clearly represent a more advanced step toward the evolution of birds. They still lack arms large enough for them to be functional flying wings, but their overall general appearance does resemble that of birds more than it does dinosaurs.

Many thousands of very beautifully preserved primitive birds are known from the Liaoning site, the most primitive species being *Concornis* and *Confuciusornis*. Both of these are toothed birds, slightly more advanced in their skeleton than *Archaeopteryx*. If *Archaeopteryx* is considered to be a feathered dinosaur, then they probably represent the first true birds.

No site on Earth has done more to reveal the many stages of evolution from agile, running dinosaurs to flying birds than Liaoning. A large on-site museum has recently been built to oversee further excavations, house the collections,

FIELD NOTES

✳ Northern China

◼ Early Cretaceous

🌱 Feathered dinosaurs (e.g. Sinosauropteryx, Sinornithosaurus), Psittacosaurus; birds

🏛 On-site museum; IVPP, Beijing, China

◼ On-site museum open to visitors

and display the most impressive specimens for vistors. It will also serve as an important research facility for scientists. Since the first feathered dinosaur was discovered there, scientists from the Institute of Vertebrate Paleontology and Paleoanthropology in Beijing have been working closely with paleontologists from Canada, the United States, and European countries to study the new discoveries that continue to come out of this rich and exciting site.

Li Yinfang, the farmer who in 1996 discovered the first fossil specimen of Sinosauropteryx.

457

Flaming Cliffs

Mongolia

This renowned site in the remote pre-Altaic Mongolia was discovered in 1922 by the famous Central Asiatic Expedition into the Gobi Desert, led by Dr. Roy Chapman Andrews of the American Museum of Natural History (AMNH). The expedition became lost and stopped to ask directions from a local Mongolian settlement. While Andrews went to talk to the locals, the expedition photographer, J.B. Schackelford, wandered off toward some nearby red rocks to take photos. Within minutes he was standing on a huge cliff, at the base of

which he started to find fossil bones. He quickly alerted his colleagues, and by the end of that day they had found the first ever dinosaur nest and a skull of *Protoceratops*. The expedition had little time to explore. However, when they returned in 1923, the researchers found a complete nest of eggs they thought were those of *Protoceratops*, but are now known to be those of *Oviraptor*, and skeletons of articulated dinosaurs, including the theropods *Velociraptor*, *Sinornithoides*, and *Oviraptor*, the ankylosaur *Pinacosaurus*, and abundant remains of the neoceratopsian *Protoceratops*.

The expedition gave the name Flaming Cliffs to the uppermost part of a 6-mile (10 km) escarpment of late Cretaceous sandstones known as Bayn Dzak. The rocks outcropping there belong to the Djadokhta Formation and are composed in the main of poorly cemented dune and alluvial plain sandstones dated at Campanian stage (around 87–72 million years old). Bayn Dzak is now the designated type section for the geology of the Djadokhta Formation.

In 1948 a Russian expedition was made to Flaming Cliffs, and between 1963 and 1971 Polish–Mongolian teams, led by Professor Zofia Kielan-Jaworowska visited the site a number of

Members of the 1922 American expedition to the Gobi Desert on a cliff top in the badlands at Urtyn Obo.

Members of the American and Mongolian field crews search for dinosaur fossils in the Gobi Desert in 1991.

times. In 1965 one of the Polish–Mongolian expeditions, comprising some 23 participants, discovered a nest of juvenile *Pinacosaurus* skeletons and more dinosaur eggs at the site.

The expeditions that followed over the next few years concentrated on searching for small vertebrate fauna at Bayn Dzak. They discovered many species of lizards, crocodiles, and small mammals. Other discoveries in the Djadokhta Formation included articulated skeletons of *Protoceratops* in upright positions, suggesting that they were buried suddenly in sandslides.

Perhaps their most famous find from the region was made in 1971 at a site called Toogreeg, 50 miles (30 km) from Bayn Dzak. This was two complete, interlocked dinosaur skeletons, the arms of the *Velociraptor* gripping the skull of the *Protoceratops*, suggesting they were fighting when suddenly buried by a freak sandstorm.

Since 1990, expeditions led by Dr. Mike Norell with Dr. Mark Norell of the AMNH, have again explored the Djadokhta Formation outcrops and made many finds from new localities such as Ukhaa Tolgod, which was dis-

FIELD NOTES

- ☼ Gobi Desert, Mongolia
- ■ Late Cretaceous
- 🦃 Large and small theropods (e.g. Tarbosaurus, Jenghizkhan, Velociraptor, Therizinosaurus), sauropods, hadrosaurs, neoceratopsians
- 🏛 IVPP, Beijing, China, Academy of Science, Ulan Baatar, Mongolia; American Museum of Natural History, New York, USA;
- ■ Access very difficult

covered in 1993. These finds include the first articulated skeletons of oviraptorids brooding over their nests of eggs, some of which contain embryonic dinosaur skeletons. The site's geology suggests that when these dinosaurs lived it was a hot, arid environment with irregular rainfall. The site seems to have preserved animals like snapshots in time as huge sand and dust storms buried them rapidly, without warning. Ukhaa Tolgod is, according to Dr. Mark Norell, the richest Cretaceous site yet found in Asia, possibly the world, for its abundance of well-preserved vertebrate

459

Atacama Desert, Valley of the Moon

Valley of the Moon

Argentina

T he Valley of the Moon
(Valle de la Luna) is a
region in the north-west
of Argentina in the Province of
La Rioja, where there is a thick
succession of middle to late
Triassic sedimentary rock outcrops. The Valley of the Moon
and the region that surrounds it
are famous for their Triassic
vertebrate localities. These contain the oldest
well-preserved dinosaur fossils anywhere in the
world as well as a range of other more primitive
archosaurian reptiles that show evolutionary
links to the first dinosaurs.

The earliest dinosaurs come from the famous
Ischigualasto Formation. This formation is a
succession of sandstones, mudstones, and siltstones that have weathered to form the strange,
alien-looking landscape of deeply eroded gullies
and steep cliffs for which the valley is named.
The fossils of the Ischigualasto Formation come
from outcrops in the foothills of the Andes, and
are dated within the Triassic period as belonging
to the Carnian stage, between approximately
226 and 220 million years ago.

Dinosaurs from the region are very sparse,
and intensive fieldwork was required to find the
few specimens that have been discovered there.

FIELD NOTES

✴ Southern South America

◼ Late Triassic

🦖 Herrerasaurus, Staurikosaurus,
Eoraptor, other archosaurians

🏛 Buenos Aires Natural History
Museum, Argentina

◼ Remote location, but accessible

The first dinosaurs from the
region were discovered by
Dr. Osvaldo Reig between
1959 and 1961. In 1960 he
found the bones of the basal
saurischians *Herrerasaurus* and
Ischisaurus and he formally
described them in 1963. Soon
after that, the first primitive
ornithischian dinosaur—based
on some jaw fragments, a few leg bones, and
some vertebrae—was discovered here. It was
described by Dr. R. Casamquela in 1967 as
Pisanosaurus mertii.

During the 1988 field season, a combined
team of paleontologists from both North and
South America made many discoveries in the
Valley of the Moon and its surrounding sites.
More complete material of the basal dinosaur
Herrerasaurus was uncovered, and these new
finds have made *Herrerasaurus* one of the most
fully described dinosaurs from the region. At
15 feet (4.5 m) long, it was the largest predatory
dinosaur known from the late Triassic.

As well as *Herrerasaurus*, the team discovered
an almost complete skeleton of a new, very
primitive little carnivorous dinosaur. Dr. Paul
Sereno and his colleagues named it *Eoraptor
lunensis*. *Eoraptor* was only about 3 feet (1 m)

Los Flamencos National Reserve, Valley of the Moon

Dr. Osvaldo Reig, who first discovered dinosaurs in the Ischigualasto Formation.

long and its skull displayed almost all the basic traits of a dinosaur. It is still a controversial fossil: Some scientists believe *Eoraptor* to be the oldest true dinosaur, whereas others think it may be too primitive to be considered a dinosaur. The debate hinges on the arbitrary criteria that are used to define the dinosaur group.

The Valley of the Moon has produced other interesting animals in addition to its dinosaurs. *Sillosuchus*, a predatory archosaur, was discovered in the region in 1979 by paleontologists from the National University of San Juan. Remains of a juvenile rhynchosaur, *Scaphonyx*, were also discovered inside the ribs of one *Herrerasaurus* specimen, providing valuable direct evidence of the diet of some of these early dinosaurs.

Underlying the Ischigualasto Formation is the Los Chanares Formation, which has yielded

the skeletons of advanced archosaurs that are considered to be immediately ancestral to the first dinosaurs. These beasts—*Lagosuchus*, *Lagerpeton*, and *Pseudolagosuchus*—lived between about 230 and 225 million years ago. They were the first reptiles to develop upright running postures.

Most of the dinosaurs and archosaurians found from the Valley of the Moon are housed in the collections of the Buenos Aires Natural History Museum.

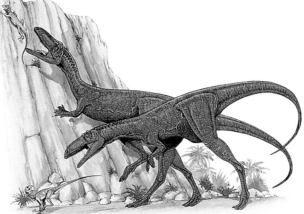

Herrerasaurus was named after a goat farmer, Victorino Herrera, who discovered the first skeleton of this dinosaur in 1963.

461

Part of the Karroo Basin landscape

Karroo Basin

South Africa

The Karroo Basin covers almost two-thirds of the surface area of South Africa. It is a thick sequence of sedimentary rocks laid down by large river systems, ranging in age from the middle Permian through to the early Jurassic (about 190 million years ago). The Karroo rocks are subdivided into a number of sequences, of which the Beaufort Group (middle Permian–middle Triassic) has yielded most of the important specimens of amphibians, reptiles, and mammal-like reptiles. The Stormberg Group (late Triassic–early Jurassic) is situated above the Beaufort Group and contains examples of the oldest dinosaurs in southern Africa.

The Beaufort Group has been subdivided into a number of biostratigraphic zones based on the fossil assemblages they contain. The significance of the Karroo Basin sequence is that its 50-million-year fossil record is largely unbroken, so that the evolutionary patterns of the different animal groups can be followed through time.

About 240 million years ago, in the middle Permian, South Africa's first terrestrial reptiles evolved. Some were gigantic meat-eaters, some were large plant-eaters, and

others were small, active predators. The fossilized skeletons of these animals are often found complete and undisturbed in Karroo sediments, and it is possible that many died after becoming trapped in the soft mud in which their bones were preserved. The synapsids, or mammal-like reptiles, were the dominant animals of the early Karroo. The first mammals evolved from these early in the late Triassic. Among the most spectacular of the Karroo reptile finds were the dinocephalians. Some of these large animals, such as *Anteosaurus*, were meat-eaters; others, such as *Moschops*, were herbivores.

The many layers of sedimentary rocks in the Karroo Basin have each yielded distinct faunas (thus enabling geologists to correlate the rock sequences across the African continent), and serve as a basis for correlations right across parts of Gondwana. Such zones are based on the most common animals that have been uncovered in each layer and they are named accordingly—for example, *Cynognathus* zone or the *Lystrosaurus* zone. Since the

Andrew Geddes Bain, the Scottish engineer who found the first fossil reptiles in the Karroo.

first fossil reptile find in 1838 by Andrew Geddes Bain, several of these Triassic reptile fossils from the Karroo Basin have turned up in other Gondwana regions. *Lystrosaurus*, for example, is now known also from India, China, and Antarctica.

Rocks of the Karroo zones are exposed in several classic localities throughout South Africa. The *Tapinocephalus* zone, the earliest part of the Karroo succession, is exposed in the area lying south of Beaufort West. The *Endothiodon*, *Cistecephalus*, and *Dicyodon* zones have outcrops throughout the Beaufort West district. Fossils of the *Lystrosaurus* zone, which mark the base of the Triassic Period, are found near Middelburg (Cape), Bethulie, Bergville, Bloemfontein, and Harrismith. The classic *Cynognathus* zone localities are Burghersdorp and Aliwal North, while the red beds of the Molteno and Elliot formations surround the Drakensberg Mountains and can be seen in the Herschel, Matatiele, and Fouriesburg districts.

FIELD NOTES

South Africa

■ Middle Permian–early Jurassic

Massospondylus, Euskeleosaurus, Syntarsus

South African Museum, Cape Town; Bernard Price Institute, Witwatersrand University, Johannesberg, South Africa; various other South African museums

■ Most sites on private land; accessible only with owners' permission

The most notable sites for dinosaur and reptile fossils in the Karroo Basin are in the early Jurassic Elliott Formation and Bushveld Sandstone. Here, well-preserved remains of a number of early dinosaurs, such as the prosauropods *Melanorosaurus*, *Massospondylus*, and *Euskelosaurus*, have been found, together with the basal ornithischians *Heterodontosaurus* and *Fabrosaurus*, the small ceratosaur *Syntarsus*, and the large, predatory archosaurian reptiles such as *Euparkeria* and *Chasmatosaurus*. Theropod footprints have also been found in the Molteno Formation of the Karroo Basin

The Karroo Basin shows the most detailed record of the transition of life on land across the Permian–Triassic boundary, which, like the later Cretaceous–Tertiary boundary, was one of the Earth's major global extinction events.

An example of theropod footprints found in the Molteno Formation of the Karroo Basin.

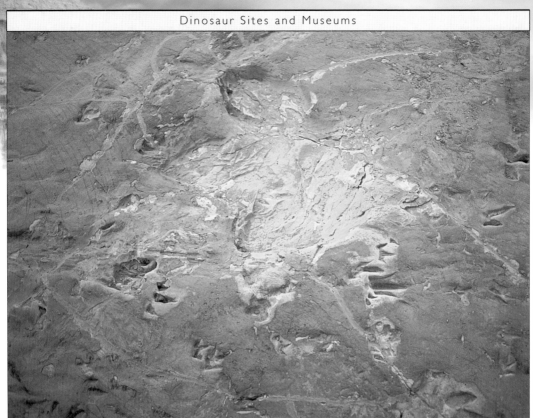

Lark Quarry

Queensland, Australia

Lark Quarry, near Winton, Queensland, in north-eastern Australia, is one of the best preserved dinosaur trackway localities in the world. The site documents the activities of three different species of dinosaurs. The footprints are preserved in a fine-grained sandstone which is known as the Winton Formation and is dated at between about 95 and 90 million years old. More than 3,300 footprints, representing some 150 individual dinosaurs, tell the story of what took place in about 10 seconds of time. The footprints are now on public display and protected by an enclosure at Lark Quarry on the road outside of Winton.

A herd of small, grazing plant-eaters (which have been given the footprint type name *Wintonopus*) and a large number of small, predatory coelurosaurs (footprint type name *Skartopus*) were disturbed by a large carnivorous dinosaur (footprint type

name *Tyrannosauropus*), which is thought to have cornered them against some rocky bluffs. The smaller dinosaurs had no choice but to run out past the meat-eater, their tracks indicating that they sprinted at top speed—about 12 miles per hour (20 km/h) judging by the length of their strides—to get around their enemy. The dinosaur footprints were studied by Drs. Tony Thulborn and Mary Wade, who published their results in 1984 in the *Memoirs* of the Queensland Museum.

At the Lark Quarry site, there are more than 1,000 well-preserved footprints that represent *Wintonopus*. These prints are recognizable by their asymmetry, rounded toes and lack of a heel impression. Thulborn and Wade suggested that the animal that made these

The sandstone of the Winton Formation has preserved thousands of dinosaur footprints.

464

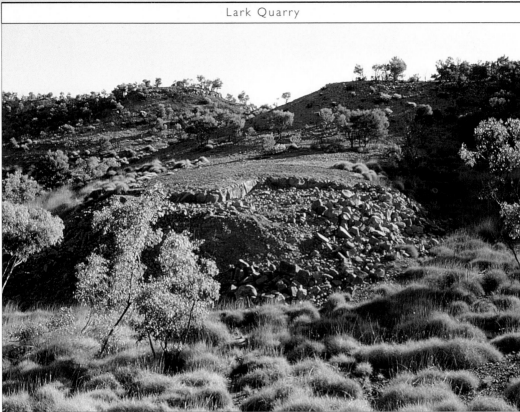

Landscape near Winton, Queensland

prints was a medium-sized ornithopod. Of 57 tracks analyzed, only one appeared to have been made by an animal larger than 3 feet (1 m) high at the hip; in fact, 81 percent of them seemed to be less than 20 inches (50 cm) high at the hip. The animals moved at a fast, running gait at about 7–12 miles per hour (12–20 km/h). The tracks show no evidence that the animals were slowing down.

Skartopus has left sharp, three-toed prints, which are almost symmetrical and range in length from a little over 1 inch (2.9 cm) to 2¼ inches (5.7 cm). The animal that made these tracks was probably a small coelurosaur (in the size range between "bantams and half-grown emus," according to Thulborn and Wade), and was moving at a mean speed of 8 miles per hour (13 km/h). A measured sample of 34 of the tracks concluded that the animals represented a range of normal size variation, and that they had a maximum hip height of about 8½ inches (22 cm). The fact that the *Skartopus* tracks are

One of the 11 footprints of Tyrannosauropus *that have been preserved at Lark Quarry.*

running in the direction opposite to those of the large carnivore suggests that there was a herd of these animals trying to escape the predator.

Tyrannosauropus's trackway is represented by 11 footprints, some of which show evidence of a sharp, pointed claw on the end of each toe. The prints have a mean length of 20½ inches (52 cm), suggesting the predator was 30–33 feet (9–10 m) long. Unlike those of *Megalosauropus*, the largest of which are of similar length, the *Tyrannosauropus* prints are broader and deeper, suggestive of a heavier animal—probably similar to *Tyrannosaurus*. The stride of the large predator ranged from 9 to 12 feet (2.8-3.7 m) and it moved at about 3–5 miles per hour (5–8 km/h)—a walking gait. It seems to have taken a slightly weaving course, with a tendency to slow down, as the first four strides are longer and deeper than the next four.

FIELD NOTES

☀ North-eastern Australia

■ Early late Cretaceous

♥ Superb trackways of Skartopus, Tyrannosauropus, and Wintonopus

🏛 On-site display

■ Accessible to visitors

465

The height of heaven, the breadth of earth, the abyss, and wisdom—who can search them out?

Apochrypha,
ECCLESIASTICUS 1:3

INDEX *and* GLOSSARY

INDEX *and* GLOSSARY

In this combined index and glossary, **bold** page numbers indicate the main reference and *italic* page numbers indicate illustrations and photographs.

CONTRIBUTORS

ROCKS AND FOSSILS

Arthur B. Busbey III, B.S. and M.A. Geology, and Ph.D. Anatomy, is an Associate Professor of Geology at Texas Christian University, Austin, USA. He has published papers on fossil reptiles, especially crocodilians, and on satellite remote sensing and geographic information systems.

Robert R. Coenraads, BA (Hons) Geology and Geophysics, M.Sc. Geophysics, Ph.D. Geology, works as a geological consultant, specializing in gemstone, gold, and base metal exploration. He lives in Australia and designs and leads geological-archeological field trips in the Americas and the Pacific region.

David Roots, B.Sc.(Hons) Geology, Ph.D. Marine Geophysics, is a research consultant at Macquarie University, Sydney, Australia. He specializes in structural geology, marine geophysics, and plate tectonic motor modeling. He leads groups on tours during which he explains the geological basis for various features of the scenery.

Paul Willis, Ph.D., has been associated with several important fossil excavations. He enjoys communicating science to popular audiences, and has toured Australian elementary schools with a life-size inflatable *Tyrannosaurus rex* as his lecture companion. He is currently a science reporter with the Australian Broadcasting Corporation.

DINOSAURS

Michael K. Brett-Surman, Ph.D., is the museum specialist for dinosaurs at the National Museum of Natural History, Smithsonian Institution, Washington DC, and an adjunct associate professor at George Washington University. He is the author/editor of two award-winning books on dinosaurs and a reviewer/consultant for scientific and popular book publishers. He resides in Virginia.

Christopher A. Brochu obtained his B.S. in geology at the University of Iowa and his Ph.D. in vertebrate paleontology at the University of Texas. He was formerly a research scientist at the Field Museum in Chicago, working on a full description of *Tyrannosaurus rex* based on "Sue," the most complete skeleton of this species thus found. His overall research focuses on developing phylogenetic answers for historical questions, especially with crocodiles and dinosaurs. He is an assistant professor of geoscience at the University of Iowa, U.S.A.

Colin McHenry is the managing curator of the Age of Fishes Museum in Canowindra, New South Wales, Australia.

John Long, Ph.D., is Curator of Vertebrate Paleontology at the Western Australian Museum. His research has focused on the early evolution of fishes and Mesozoic reptiles. He has published more than 100 scientific papers, over 60 popular articles, and is the author of four books.

John D. Scanlon, Ph.D., lives in Townsville, north Queensland. John is a research associate of the Australian Museum, Sydney, and has also worked at Monash University, Melbourne, the University of Queensland, Brisbane, and the Friedrich-Wilhelms Universität, Bonn, Germany. He works mainly on Australian snakes, including the systematics and behavior of living species as well as fossils.

CAPTIONS

Page 3: Dinosaur Quarry, Dinosaur National Monument, Utah, USA

Pages 4–5: Buildings carved into rock at Petra, Jordan

Pages 6–7: Sedimentary rock layers with dinosaur fossil, San Francisco, California, USA

Pages 8–9: Valley of the Moon, Los Flamencos National Reserve, Atacama Desert, Chile

Pages 10–11: Diplodocus bones, Dinosaur Quarry, Dinosaur National Monument, Utah, USA

Pages 12–13: Precipitated limestone flows at Mammoth Hot Springs, Yellowstone National Park, Wyoming, USA

Pages 12–13: Columnar basalt formations at Giant's Causeway, Northern Ireland, UK

Pages 28–29: 25-million-year-old plugs from a hot-spot volcano in the Glasshouse Mountains, Queensland, Australia

Pages 58–59: Buda limestone formation, Big Bend National Park, Texas, USA

Pages 84–85: Agatized dinosaur bone from the Morrison Formation, Colorado

Pages 110–11: A graptolite fossil from the lower Ordovician, Mount Hunneberg, Sweden

Pages 124–25: The opening to Leviathan Cave, a giant limestone cave in Nevada, USA

Page 132–3: A polished slab of rhodochrosite

Page 132 (inset top): Salt formations at Scammon's Lagoon, Baja, Mexico

Page 132 (inset bottom): Detail of obsidian

Pages 172–3: Eroded limestone spires, Bryce Canyon, Utah, USA.

Page 183 (inset top): Eruption of Kimanura, Virunga National Park, Zaire

Pages 190–1: Fossil site at Riversleigh, far north Queensland, Australia

Pages 194–5: Kauri pine fossil from New South Wales, Australia

Page 195 (inset top): Coral fossil

Page 195 (inset bottom): Ammonite fossil, *Placenticeras* species, from Morocco

Pages 226–227: Dinosaur footprints from Lower Jurassic, La Sal Mountains, Utah, USA

Page 227 (inset top): Insect preserved in amber

Page 227 (inset bottom): Cell structure in fossilized dinosaur bone

Pages 252–253: Detail of *Sinornithosaurus* head, showing large teeth and filaments rising from head

Pages 254–255: Agatized dinosaur bone from Morrison Formation, Jurassic, Colorado, USA

Pages 270–271: Oxalis-Hoh Rainforest, Olympic National Park, Washington, USA

Pages 298–299: Mesosaurus fossil, Irati Formation, Brazil, South America

Pages 322–323: Still from a film by Oliver Leclerc, courtesy of Le Cinema Fantastique

Pages 342–343: Apatosaurus trackways, Purgatory Site, Morrison Formation, Jurassic, Colorado, USA

Pages 428–429: "Capitol Reef" landscape with mesa, badlands, and approaching storm, South Utah, USA

Pages 272–273: Fossilized wood in Petrified Forest National Park, Arizona, USA.

PICTURE CREDITS

1 John Cancalosi/Aus. 2 Ben Osbourne/OSF. 3c PCP. 4–5 Nicola
Sherriff/RGS. 6–7 Ken Lucas/California Academy of Science/
PEP. 8–9 Jaime Plaza Van Roon/Aus. 10–11 John Cancalosi/BCL.
11–12 Jeff Foott/TSA. 14–15 Tom Till/Aus. 16tl NHM; c Reg
Morrison; b Jocelyn Burt/BCL. 17tl Rich Buzzelli/TSA; tr and b
NHM. 18tl Bob Buduwal, Peter Cook Collection/Australian
Institute of Aboriginal and Torres Strait Islander Studies; tr Kristinn
Ben/Mats Wibe Lund/Icelandic Photo; cr Geolinea; b MEPL. 19t
Sinclair Stammers/SPL/TPL; cl Geolinea; cr John Cancalosi/Aus.
20tl MEPL; tr Krafft/Aus; b Hulton Deutsch/TPL. 21t François
Gohier/Aus; c MEPL/Explorer/Aus; b Bettman/APL. 22t MEPL;
bl Geoff Doré/BCL; br Explorer–Archives/Aus. 23tl Paul Harris/
RGS; tr MEPL; b Reg Morrison. 24 Jay M. Pasachoff/VU. 23 Reg
Morrison. 26tl and background Geolinea; tr and b John Reader/
SPL/TPL. 27t Tashi Tenzing; c Jane Burton/BCL; b NHM. 28–29
Reg Morrison. 30l Reg Morrison; r George J Wilder/VU. 31tl
Granger; tc Alain Compost/BCL; tr Image Library, SLNSW,
Sydney; bl Peter Ryan/SPL/TPL; br NASA/GSFC/TSA. 32tl
Dennis Harding/Aus; tr Scott Berner/VU; b Robin Smith/TPL.
33c Albert J Copley/VU; bc Gary Lewis/TPL; br Fritz Prenzel/
BCL. 34 Dieter and Mary Plage/Aus. 35t Keith Gunnar/BCL; c
David Parker SPL/TPL. 36t NASA/Tsado/TSA; b David Foster/
VU. 37tl Ferrero/Labat/Aus; tr Mats Wibe Lund/ IPPS; cl Bruce
Davidson/OSF. 38t NASA/ Tsado/TSA; tc Science
VU/WHOI, D. Foster/VU. 39tl Ferrero/Labat/Aus; l Bruce
Davidson/OSF; r Mats Wibe Lund/IPPS. 40 Restec, Japan/SPL/
TPL; 41t David Matherly/VU; b David Bertsch/VU. 42tl David
Hardy/SPL/TPL; c Werner Stoy/BCL; bl Mats Wibe Lund/Bragi
Gudmunds/IPPS; br David Roots. 43tl Dieter and Mary Plage/
BCL; tr Jay M. Pasachoff/VU; c Mats Wibe Lund/Gardar Pálsson;
b Glenn Oliver/VU. 44t MEPL; c Austral; b AAP. 45tl AAP; tr
stf/str/AAP; c AAP; b NHM. 46t Jane Burton/BCL; bl Tony
Waltham/Trent University; br Reg Morrison. 47t Tony Waltham/
Trent University; bc Jens Rydell/BCL; br Museum of Victoria,
Mineralogy. 48tl AJ Copley/VU; tc David B. Fleetham/TSA; tr
Kevin Schafer/TSA; b Fritz Prenzel/BCL. 49t and c M Krafft/Aus;
br Brian P. Foss/VU. 50tr Gary Milburn/TSA; cl A. J. Copley/VU;
cr TSA; b Rod Planck/TSA. 51t Jules Cowan/ BCL; c Oliver Benn/
TPL. 52t NHM; c Jean-Paul Ferrero/Aus; b Reg Morrison/Aus.
53t Hans Reinhard/BCL; c Jane Burton/BCL; b Reg Morrison.
54t Andrew Syred/TPL; c Jeff Foott Productions/BCL. 55t Colin
Monteath/Aus; c Peter Knowles/PL; b Jules Cowan/BCL. 56t
John Fennell/BCL; c Nigel Hicks/TPL; b John C. Cunningham/
VU. 57tl John Shaw/BCL; tr APL; cr Keith Gunnarr/BCL; b
Konrad Wothe/BCL. 58–59 Robert P. Carr/BCL. 60tl Scott
Camazine/OSF; tr David Nunuk/SPL/TPL; b MEPL. 61t Image
Library, SLNSW; c David B Fleetham/TSA; bl Norman Tomalin/
BCL; br TPL. 62tl, tr and br NHM; c RRC; bl AM. 63tl Herve
Berthoule/Aus; tr and br AM; c NHM; b Roberto de Gugliemo/
SPL/TPL. 64t AM; c RRC; b Robin Smith/TPL. 65t J. M. la
Roque/Aus; b RRC. 66tl RRC; cr Rich Buzzelli/TSA; b Tom
Till/Aus. 67t Paul Thompson/TPL; bl John R. Jones/RGS; br AM.
68t NHM; b Werner Stoy/BCL. 69 Manfred Gottschalk/TSA.
70tl RRC; tc Vaughan Fleming/SPL/TPL; tr AM; b Roberto de
Gugliemo/SPL/TPL. 71 AM. 72tl Vaughan Fleming/SPL/TPL; cr
and b AM. 73t, cr, bl AM; cl and br NHM. 74t NHM; b AM. 75t,
c, bl, br AM; bc RRC. 76tl Harold Taylor/OSF/TPL; tr LM Labat/

Aus; bl AM; br Marvin E. Newman/Image Bank. 77t Image
Library, SLNSW; cl AA&A; cr Roberto de Gugliemo/SPL. 78tl
Museum of the American Indian, Heye Foundation, New York/
Werner; cr, b John Cancalosi/Aus. 79t Reg Morrison; c AM; b
NHM. 80 Hulton Deutsch/TPL. 81t Arnulf Husmo/Tony Stone/
TPL; c Arthus Bertrand/Explorer/Aus; b Hiroshi Higuchi/TPL.
82tl Schimmel Collection, New York/Werner; tr, bl NHM. 83tl
RRC; tr Atlantide/BCL; b TPL. 84–85 Francois Gohier/Aus. 86t
Brett Gregory/Aus; c Haupt/Naturmuseum Senckenberg,
Frankfurt A.M., Germany; bl Sinclair Stammers/SPL/TPL; br Reg
Morrison. 87 NHM. 88t MEPL; c SPL/TPL; b Muso Episcopal,
Vich/BAL. 93t Downe House, Downe, Kent/BAL; c (illustration
by C. R. Darwin)/RGS; b MEPL. 90t SPL/TPL; b NHM. 91l John
Cancalosi/Aus; r Kevin Scafer/TSA. 92l NHM; c Robert Noonan/
TPL; r Reg Morrison. 93 Keith Gunnar/BCL. 94t Jim Frazier/
Mary White; c John Cancalosi/Aus; b David M Dennis/TSA. 95t
Theodore Clutter/TPL; c Francois Gohier/Aus; b Kjell B. Sandved/
TPL. 96c Peter Murray; bl D. Parer and E. Parer–Cook/Aus. 97t
Sinclair Stammers/SPL/TPL; cl and cr MEPL; b NHM. 98tl John
Green/Entomology Division, CSIRO; b A. Roslin/Explorer/
MEPL/Aus. 98–99 Reg Morrison/Aus. 99tl Kev Deacon/Aus; tr
David M. Dennis/TSA; b Tom McHugh/TPL. 100t Gunther
Bishop and John Cleasby/Macquarie University, Sydney; c Reg
Morrison; b Jens Rydell/BCL. 101tl Reg Morrison/Aus; tr
Norman Tomalin/BCL; b Reg Morrison. 102l NHM; r David M.
Dennis/TSA. 103t John Cancalosi/Aus; c Neil McAllister/BCL; bl
John Cancalosi/Aus; bc and br Bologna University. 104 Jim Frazier/
Mary White. 105t Jean-Paul Ferrero/Aus; c Martin Land/SPL/
TPL. 106t John Fennell/BCL; b Breck P. Kent/AA/ES. 107t Jura
Museum; c John Fennell/BCL; b Kevin Schafer and Martha Hill/
TSA. 108tl Kathie Atkinson; tr NHM; b John Cancalosi/BCL.
113t Alfred Pasieka/SPL/TPL; b Jens Rydell/BCL. 110–111 Jens
Rydell/BCL. 112t NHM; c MEPL/Aus; b MEPL. 112–113 Ken
Lucas/PEP. 113t Aus; b NHM. 114b Victoria Keble-Williams/
RGS. 114–115 MW Gillam/Aus. 115t Jaime Plaza Van Roone/
Aus; c Stephen Krasemann/NHPA; b Robert Kristofik/Image
Bank. 116t Jim Frazier/Mary White; bc Jane Burton/BCL; br Paul
Harris/RGS. 117t MEPL/Explorer/Aus; c Michael McKinnon/
PEP; b AM. 118t and b AM; c Ross Arnett . 119t and c Kathie
Atkinson; c Carl Bento/AM. 120t Carl Bento/AM; c Ross Arnett;
b Elido Turco/Geolinea. 121tl Kathie Atkinson; tc Geolinea; c
Geolinea; b Carl Bento/AM. 122t Bologna University; c Haupt/
Naturmuseum Senckenberg, Frankfurt a.M., Germany; b Michael
Archer. 123tl Kathie Atkinson; tr Haupt/Naturmuseum Sencken-
berg, Frankfurt a.M., Germany; b Kathie Atkinson. 124–125 Tom
Till/Aus. 126–127 John Cancalosi/Aus. 127ti Randy Morse/TSA;
bi Tony Waltham/Trent University. 130–131 Rich Buzzelli/TSA.
131ti Bruce Davidson/OSF; bi John Cancalosi/Aus. 132t Don
Duckson/VU; c Doug Sokell/VU; bl RRC; br Steve Elmor/TSA.
141t John Bertsch/VU; c Albert J. Copley/VU; b Werner. 134t
Doug Sokell/VU; c Albert J. Copley/VU; b Jean–Paul Ferrero/
Aus. 143t Doug Sokell/Aus; c A. J. Copley/VU; c Kevin Schafer/
VU. 136t Reg Morrison; c NHM; b Doug Sokell/TSA. 145t Jeff
Foott Productions/BCL; c Jules Cowan/BCL; b Tony Waltham/
Trent University. 138t and b Jules Cowan/BCL; c Tony Waltham/
Trent University. 139t Paul Harris/RGS; c NHM; b MPL Fogden/
BCL. 140t Reg Morrison; c Martin G. Miller/VU; cr and b J. M.
Labat/Musée des Antiquites Nationales/Aus. 141t Francois Gohier/
Aus; c Reg Morrison; b Jane Burton/BCL. 142t Atlantide SDF/
BCL; c Jean–Paul Ferrero/Aus; b BAL/TPL. 143t Ian Paterson/
TPL; c NHM; b Reg Morrison. 144t M Nimmo/FLPA; c NHM;
b Albert J Copley/VU; b NHM. 153t Jean–Paul Ferrero/Aus; c A. J. Copley/
VU; b NHM. 146t and b NHM; c Sinclair Stammers/SPL/TPL.
147t, c NHM; b Museum of Victoria, Mineralogy. 148 NHM.
149t, cl, b Jim Frazier/MW; cr Vaughan Fleming/SPL/TPL. 150t, c
NHM; b Allen B. Smith/TSA. 151t Jim Frazier/MW; c Roberto
de Gugliemo/SPL/TPL; b Michel Viard/BCL. 152t Museum of
Victoria, Mineralogy; c Jim Frazier/ MW; b Jim Frazier/MW. 153t
and br Jim Frazier/MW; c NHM; bl Roberto de Gugliemo/SPL/
TPL. 154t Tony Waltham, Trent University; c GeoScience Picture
Library; bl NHM; br Private Collection/WFA. 155t, c, br Jim
Frazier/MW; bl Adrian Davies/BCL. 156t Brian M England; c
GeoScience Picture Library; bl Jim Frazier/MW; br NHM. 157t
NHM; c Jim Frazier/MW; b AJ Copley/VU. 158t Brian England;
c, bl Museum of Victoria, Mineralogy; cr Jim Frazier/MW. 159t M.
Nimmo/FLPA; c Tony Waltham, Trent University; b Clive Collins.
160t Martin Land/SPL/TPL; c, b Jim Frazier/MW. 169t, c Jim
Frazier/MW; b AM. 162t John Cancalosi/Aus; c Jim Frazier/MW;
b Museum of Victoria, Mineralogy. 163t, c RRC; b NHM.
164t NHM; c John Cancalosi/TSA; b NHM/Werner. 165t Bob
McKeever/TSA; c Tony Waltham/Trent University; b Clive
Collins; b NHM/Werner. 166t NHM; c Brian Parker/TSA; b Allen
B. Smith/TSA. 167t NHM; c, b Jim Frazier/MW. 168t Museum of
Victoria, Mineralogy; c Brian Parker/TSA; b Johnathon T. Wright/

ILLUSTRATION CREDITS